DOES CHRISTIANITY CAUSE WAR?

Does Christianity Cause War?

DAVID MARTIN

CLARENDON PRESS · OXFORD
1997

Oxford University Press, Great Clarendon Street, Oxford OX2 6DP
Oxford New York
Athens Auckland Bangkok Bogota Bombay
Buenos Aires Calcutta Cape Town Dar es Salaam
Delhi Florence Hong Kong Istanbul Karachi
Kuala Lumpur Madras Madrid Melbourne
Mexico City Nairobi Paris Singapore
Taipei Tokyo Toronto Warsaw
and associated companies in
Berlin Ibadan

Oxford is a trade mark of Oxford University Press

Published in the United States by
Oxford University Press Inc., New York

British Library Cataloguing in Publication Data
Data available

Library of Congress Cataloging in Publication Data
Data available

ISBN 0–19–829267–8

1 3 5 7 9 10 8 6 4 2

Typeset by Best-set Typesetter Ltd., Hong Kong
Printed in Great Britain
on acid-free paper by
Biddles Ltd, Guildford and King's Lynn

To
Stella Miriam Martin

PREFACE

THIS book is made up of eight lectures given under the auspices of the Sarum Lectureship in the University of Oxford during Hilary term, January to March 1995. I am very grateful to the electors for inviting me to give these lectures and thereby inciting me to write what otherwise I would have postponed indefinitely.

The original germ of the idea was formulated in one of the two opening lectures for the Centenary of the Scandinavian Peace Bureau in Helsinki in September 1991 (and subsequently printed in *Crucible*, January–March 1995). However, it did not include discussion of Richard Dawkins until I encountered his views in the media.

One of the gains for me in giving this series was that I found myself reviewing and re-integrating work done since I first published my work on *Pacifism* in 1965 and, round about the same time, raised the problematic of secularization. In the event, I was able to make connections between my interest in the structural aspects of secularization and my interests in Christian imagery and liturgy. I was also able to bring to bear a long-standing interest in Anglo-American religion and complementary interests in religion in Latin America and in Eastern Europe. I was even able to infiltrate some modest materials reflecting occasional incursions into the social history of music. Undoubtedly the most difficult among these various attempts at connection was that between structures and 'signs'. Part III is concerned with 'signs' and is stylistically quite distinct. The rest of the book is written from outside in a standard academic manner but in Part III, and especially in Chapter 6, I deal with imagery in its own terms. I do not believe there is any other way. Images are understood in their use.

As ever, this book was heard by my wife during the two months in which I wrote it and, as ever, it benefited greatly from her criticism and support.

DAVID MARTIN
Easter 1995

CONTENTS

PART I

The Problem and the Approach

1

Can We Blame Religion or Human Nature?

I would like to answer a question that people actually ask. Even in secular Britain most people believe in God in some sense and about four in ten of any survey sample would even accept the description 'religious'. Yet they have their doubts about religion. Of course, they acknowledge it can be a good thing. Religion teaches you to be responsible, to respect what is another's, and to act as a good neighbour. It recommends reconciliation and forgiveness. And obviously there are hundreds of agencies of Christian concern, such as hospices, orphanages, soup kitchens, shelters for the homeless, aid programmes, and networks for mutual support. Many ordinary people might well accept Professor Christie Davies's recent rehabilitation of a discernible relation in British society over the last century and a half between rates of crime and degrees of religious involvement.[1]

On the other hand, much of what you hear on the news suggests that religion can be rather dangerous. It

---

[1] Christie Davies, 'Crime and the rise and decline of the relational society', in Jonathan Burnside and Nicola Baker (eds.) *Relational Justice* (Winchester, 1994), 31–41.

seems believers not only die for it but kill for it. So people are in two minds. The evidence is they want religion in schools because it teaches you to love your neighbour. But it also seems that somehow, somewhere else, in Newry or in Armagh, or in Sarajevo and Bihac, or in the Gaza strip, religion causes mayhem. A letter to the *Independent* put the point succinctly: Why teach our children Christian values when their effects are so visible across the Irish Sea?

It has to be confessed that few people really know much about Ulster or Bosnia or the Middle East. Most of us, reading the sports pages or the gossip columns, live in a picture-book world of television and hear words which identify rival groups as Catholics and Protestants, or as Catholic Croats, Orthodox Serbs, and Bosnian Muslims, or as Orthodox Jews, fundamentalist Jews, and fundamentalist Muslims. We view Jewish settlers enlarging their enclaves on the West Bank or Hindus burning down a mosque. A Presbyterian minister (or a Catholic aspirant to the priesthood) walks into an abortion clinic in the USA and opens fire. And all that kind of thing links with an older strain of scepticism going back to Tom Paine and beyond, accusing religion of being the source of dogmatism, fanaticism, prejudice, ignorance, repression, and persecution. According to this view religion, especially State religion, is more part of the problem than part of the cure. Or, as Lucretius famously put it, *Tantum religio potuit suadere malorum*—religion can incite us to so much evil.

I said I wanted to discuss a question which is actually asked. I have to say that I hardly ever run into a query about God, whereas I do encounter puzzlement over Ulster and Bosnia. Some religious intellectuals, like those in the 'Sea of Faith' group, appear to think the difficulty is God and to believe religion would gain a new lease of life provided it were relieved of His incredible presence. Such a suggestion could only come from people who believe intellectual élites are the advance party of the future rather than the fifth wheel of history. I recently surveyed the evidence, superficial though it is, for Europe as a whole, and it points in a quite contrary direction, except maybe in Estonia or in what was East Germany. In those countries the religious substratum, already weakened by secularization and Nazism, was almost erased by ferocious communist propaganda. The evidence overall suggests that the effective argument against God or faith is not how far we are context-bound by our discourse or any such esoteric matter. The effective argument is either a one-line and passionate plaint about undeserved suffering or it is what I call 'the argument from Bosnia'. How is it, as Dean Swift said, that we have just enough religion to hate one another but not enough to love one another? That is a question people really ask, though I would not care to guess how long they would stay for an answer. In so far as they themselves have an answer, they would probably say that is just the way of human nature. It is part of folk wisdom that humans will bend the best ideals to the most malign purposes. Or could it be—and this is the alternative view—that religion is *the* singular virus which more than anything else undermines the red corpuscles of reason and persuades us to evil courses: too many offspring, burning books in Bradford, patriarchy, fundamentalist insurgency in Algeria, sexual repression? These then are the two simple answers.

As a sociologist I am bound to find all such popular explanations badly flawed. Yet to those who offer them they appear blindingly obvious. Just look around you. Face the brute facts. Either humans are generically brutish or religion makes them brutal. People are dying in Sarajevo, or Jerusalem, or wherever. Use your eyes. But, of course, it is the object of sociology, indeed of any serious knowledge, to question the obvious. Things are usually more complicated than they seem and the obvious is often the false. We can surely assume that the role of religion in human society is one of the most complicated ever to perplex the human intelligence.

I can now raise the deceptively simple question. Is religion, more particularly Christianity, more trouble than it is worth? Oddly enough, I have never raised the question before, and still feel uneasy in doing so. My sense is that, when it comes to religion, people actually prefer to live by unconsidered tags which, in other contexts, they would dismiss as intolerably naïve and riddled with category mistakes. Perhaps the democratization of opinion on religious matters in Protestant and in post-Protestant society leads us to think it is enough simply to display an attitude. But it isn't. This is in part an empirical question, which depends no doubt on your angle, your focus, your categories, but none the less remains empirical because particular assertions rest on evidence and admit falsification. Under what *particular* circumstances does the proximity of Catholics and Protestants lead to conflict, *given that mostly it doesn't*? The rubric for answering that question properly is immensely long. It is a key part of the broad question of the role of religion in human society. Nearly one in three of our fellow humans live in the Christian constituency. For better, then, or for worse? Or perhaps we need to reformulate the question.

The Argument from Bosnia

It is now time to put 'the argument from Bosnia' in a relatively sophisticated version. This is the standard view that religion is to blame. My conversational partner for this purpose is not the average person in the pub, but one of the contemporary arbiters of acceptable opinion, say a television producer or a journalist on one of the broadsheet newspapers. Elicit such a person's background assumptions and they might quite often go like this. Religion . . . is a special kind of tunnel vision which gives rise to intolerance, fanaticism, persecution, and indoctrination, and is based on exploded beliefs. Indoctrination imprints views on the psyche beyond rational scrutiny or empirical revision. The great historical religions, especially perhaps the monotheistic ones claiming descent from Abraham, would—if they could—secure conformity among the faithful (as the Pope has attempted to do over female ordination), establish censorship in society, and wage war against the infidel. If believers today appear not to be so inclined, at least in the West, that is because we have entered an advanced age of progress in which all reasonable people are semi-secularized. If they were really religious that is how they would behave. Perhaps we can even measure their religiosity by the extent to which they are illiberal and censorious. A fundamentalist is a truly religious person and a fundamentalist may be defined by his aggressive intolerance and militancy. That is how we use the word.

After all, go back into history and you will see what the Church of England and the Puritans did when they had the opportunity; look at the more backward countries where Catholicism ruled the roost until the day before yesterday; and look at those genuinely benighted parts of the world today where Islam dominates the State and civil society. Of course, Quakers and Unitarians are fairly reasonable and harmless, but that only makes the point. They believe in next to nothing and are numerically insignificant.

Our producer or journalist might expand these views somewhat. Religion rigidifies social attitudes, refrigerating the genial currents of natural vitality. It distorts sexuality with repressions, and papers over the cracks in the psyche with stereotypical responses. Religion is power operated by a hermaphroditic priesthood on the basis of superstition and posthumous threats, and chronically resistant to universal, revisable, testable truth. Religion expropriates hope, turning illusory hopes against real ones, and holding them up for adoration in alienated form as liturgical enactment or as icon or as tantalizing myth, for ever unearthed and unearthly. Thus the energies properly devoted to a political agenda of structural reform are confiscated and transported to realms of soulfulness and misplaced yearning. At bottom, it may well all be an emanation of the primitive fear of death and inability to face uncertainty. It therefore represents the ultimate cowardice of our vulnerable condition. In sum, religion is a deadly psychological evasion and a social suction, policing boundaries, demonizing the other, subserving the malign powers of hierarchy and primal cohesion. Above all, it idolizes alienated power through the collusive ceremonies of Church and State as they jointly seek to dominate the human and the humane. *Ecrasez l'infame!*

If you want to uncover religion in its naked madness and riotous irrationality you need only study the cults and sects. Waco and the People's Temple tell it as it really is. The fresh-faced and neatly suited youngsters preaching at your door are both the perpetrators and the victims of psychic cramps and social deprivations. Those who are converted to such faiths live out lives of stunted conformity and eschatological resentment in utilitarian sheds built on dreary estates. As for the exploiters who washed their brains and worked on their desperate hopes or needs, it would be a public service to unmask them.

The Counter-Argument from the Way Things Are

So much for the strong version of the explanation which holds religion itself to be responsible. It is, I suspect, the last refuge of the Whig interpretation of history. Now I want to contrast it with the other explanation based on human nature. Perhaps my conversational partner here should not be a television producer, but a teacher of classics or a world historian, taking the long view of the tally of human folly and the corruption of our highest ideals. It is not at all required that such people be Christians. They are quite often those who hold original sin to be the only really plausible bit of theology. They are rather like Winston Churchill: outside buttresses of the Church rather than pillars of piety. The point for them is to secure a just estimate of likelihoods by achieving a realistic level of expectation. The rejection of religion in our time stems from the sentimentality of education after Rousseau. Of course, we all know true believers did terrible things in the name of religion, but today people do things no less terrible in the name of political utopias or simply in order to acquire wealth and power. We are a murderous breed made in the image of Cain and our motives are overweening. You have only to look at Castro's Cuba, or Ceausescu's Romania, or Hoxha's Albania, or Hitler's Germany.

This secular variant of original sin stresses the ubiquity of corruption in a fallen world. The corruption of reason and of the party of humanity is just as likely as a corruption of the religion of love. All hubristic projects nourish their own deadly deterioration once they are part of history and social process.

Quite *how* you articulate that particular point about social process doesn't matter all that much. Maybe social process constantly distorts the pristine flexibility of our original nature or—turning it around—maybe our fractiousness and lust for dominion constantly distort the dynamic of social process. Either way, draconian powers have to be held in reserve for worst-case scenarios, at least some of which are bound to come about. Even on a best-case scenario the protection of the weak will always require severe constraint of the strong and vigorous measures to curb the corruptions of power to which we are all of us subject. That is why order and degree are the prerequisites of even a modestly amiable sociability.

It follows that the just ruler must always be ready to stamp out the forest fire of chaos if he is to protect the common weal. Social life is not, and never can be, made on the model of an academic seminar where anyone can go on communicating suggestions and nothing has to be decided and organized. The question is, for all who have responsibility for real projects: what is to be done? No doubt authority is responsible for limitless crimes against humanity, but authority is at the same time the ineluctable basis of all peace and justice. And again, who can deny that the promotion of legitimacy may rigidify the structures of power and obscure the possibility of alternatives? But without legitimacy and its buttress in the sacred, everything is questioned all the time and we are placed for ever on the defensive with no settled social space. Without habits of deference to rules and authorities you decline towards the war of all against all. Do not imagine that amity and sociability flow naturally from our amiable adjustment each to the other. On the contrary, any order, any stable and civil interaction, is a recondite and precarious achievement, hardly won and easily dissipated. This, no doubt, is where religion plays its role, sustaining—in Salman Rushdie's words—the great codes of civilization, and raising a sacred umbrella over the spawning multitudes of our chaotic world.

From this viewpoint, most of the ills misattributed specifically to religion should be subsumed into the generic dynamism of our precarious sociability and the flawed condition of our humanity. When it comes to shaping such recalcitrant clay as ourselves in the mould of modest civility there needs to be a firm imprint on the psyche, habituation, rituals, respect, settled hierarchies, authorized and authoritative myths able to frame origin and purpose, to suggest vocabularies of motive, and to generate arts and sciences. Society requires legitimate disciplines, agreements over priorities, shared and prestigious codes of conduct and communication and expectation, markers of the boundaries between inner and outer, between other and own, intimate and public, kin and stranger, civil and uncivil. Religion is implicated in all this, both with regard to its advantages and, no doubt, with regard to its costs. There is no advantage acquired without cost. The sacred texts of religion, together with the ancient classics, help safeguard perennial wisdom from fashion and arbitrary decree, just as the icons and images of faith preside over our most necessary and most primal solidarities.

So, then, the frail children of dust should expect little in the way of perfection. Armed with proper realism, they should aim only to achieve a compassionate viability. Trim the ship of state and be watchful. At least you will not pave the path to hell by constructing systems so perfect nobody will ever need to be virtuous. Let us hope at best for some access of guilt in the mighty, some sentiment of shared culpability in our judges, some limits to the corruption of power, even a point of transcendent reference—God if you will—from which to qualify and criticize the unrestricted legitimacy of the secular order. God knows it is not ultimate, and its sanctities are for the interim. Such a reference point helps sustain rituals of reversal within the accepted corpus of tradition. And after all, within the tiny range of options actually open to us, there is only one option worse than being incorporated in the great metropolitan civilizations and that is being left to stagnate, remaindered at the unconsidered and barbarous marches of the civilized world. You are right to be shocked by the Inquisition but you are not right to blame Galilee and the religion of love. Equally, you are right to be shocked by the Stasi and the Securitate, but you cannot blame the Enlightenment. It is the way of the world.

A More Particular Fall

So much for the general image which attributes the malignant aspects of social process to our human nature or to our social condition as such. It has some virtues, but its defect is precisely its generality. It does not discriminate adequately between the kinds and degrees of corruption, nor does it offer specific explanations. It fails to provide explanations of those particular circumstances which generate particular ills and particular conflicts. So it is not really theoretical and remains at the level of a broad perspective. However, it is rather surprisingly linked to a contemporary theological view which postulates a particular circumstance facilitating the Fall of the Church, and that is the establishment of Christianity by Constantine. This plays the role of a supplementary Fall. In other words, all the corruptions already referred to—power, wealth, hierarchy, violence—have indeed been experienced by Christianity, but for a specific reason and at a particular time. In the fourth century Christianity was led into the temptation of establishment and *therefore* faith lost its pristine power and its prophetic voice. It will regain these only through the abandonment of its relationship to power and by identification with what St Paul called 'the offscourings of the earth'.

Now, this view has one or two genuine observations incidentally locked inside its overall ideology, but if it identifies spiritual power with marginality then it harbours a dire illusion. There are different spiritual costs and different opportunities associated with varying distances from or proximity to the seats of power. It is, of course, true that disestablishment *can* be associated with certain gains, notably the competitive edge fostered by pluralism. And it is obviously a good policy to separate the tendrils of faith from their social frames once these frames are in danger of collapse. There is a good argument for disestablishment and it includes the assertion that it is going to happen anyway. But that is quite different from postulating a Paradise Lost by establishment and a Paradise Regained by the separation of Church from State.

Contextualization and Naming the Real Difficulties

The kind of views just canvassed, whether promoted in a standard secularist form or cast in terms of theology, lack either sociological method or sociological analysis. The sociological insight which they may contain is incidental or it is very general. That is hardly surprising because most of the time such views are used as rhetorics of praise and blame. You encounter versions of them every day in the media, and the participants generally aim to tot up moral and political points in rival columns. Even the most serious discussions on radio, let alone television, commit fundamental category mistakes or make short-cut inferences every two or three sentences. If possible, I want to stand back from the business of totting up points, and to suggest some of the difficulties of this kind of debate from the viewpoint of the human sciences, more especially sociology.

These difficulties mainly arise for the following reasons: an enormous amount depends on how you delimit and define your categories; it is very difficult to make useful general statements about whole categories of human activity, like religion or politics; in every concrete situation there are a large number of different elements and it is notoriously easy to mistake correlation for causation. Comparison is of the essence but how do you ensure you compare like with like? There is a further difficulty which has to do with the problem of mediation, meaning the successive fluid elements through which the generators of action, if indeed there *are* such generators, must pass. So complex is this last issue and so closely bound in with many of the others that it requires some further elucidation.

Consider the conflict in Bosnia, since after all I have called this issue 'the argument from Bosnia'. For the purposes of identification, we use shorthands, and in this particular conflict we refer to two ethnic categories, Serb and Croat, and one religious category, Bosnian Muslim, though, in fact, there are Bosnian Serbs and Croats allied to the Bosnian Muslims as well as Bosnian Serbs and even Bosnian Muslims who are the inveterate enemies of this alliance. To some extent these media shorthands reflect the usage of the combatants, but they can be seriously misleading as guides to the elements effectively at play in the conflict. If media accounts were framed in terms of Catholic, Orthodox, and Muslim, we would be inclined to identify those elements as religious and talk about a religious war; if, however, they were framed in terms of Serb, Croat, and Bosnian, we would identify the whole thing as a struggle between secular nationalisms.

Clearly, the problem arises, as do so many comparable problems, from the collapse of an overriding repressive power, in this case the disintegration of the communist South Slav state. Where populations are fairly homogeneous and securely on one side of the great divides of Byzantium and Rome, East and West, Ottoman and Austro-Hungarian, as in Slovenia, there is no problem. But where boundaries have been drawn arbitrarily for geopolitical or colonial or economic purposes, and where there are mixed populations with majorities and minorities on either side of the great divides, and where these are large enough for each to threaten the other, as well as capable of being used as pawns and proxies by outside political players, then the consequences we see today are virtually unavoidable. Each group will mobilize the traditional markers of its own identity, and in this context ethnicity and religion will mediate each other. Serbian Orthodox identification was growing even before the current clashes, but Bosnian Muslim identification is also growing with every extension of the conflict. Sarajevo, which was once a cosmopolitan city like Beirut, is now being ghettoized like Belfast. In parenthesis, it would do no harm to remember that the rival leaderships in Serbia and Croatia and the middle-ranking strata in Bosnia consist of *apparatchiks* who have transferred themselves from loyalty to the proletariat to loyalty to the ethnic group. Their piety is their survival.

Now it is difficult to decide the extent to which the increasing mobilization of the markers of identity (which are religio-ethnic) is a consequence of the conflict, or how far the conflict arises precisely because such markers of identity happen to be present. In addition, we have also to consider the role of mythic histories retrospectively amplified by the work of nationalist poets and intellectuals.

The precise details hardly matter since the point here is the fuzziness of the elements to be identified and the contorted spirals of historical causation. In one important sense the conflict arises because markers of identity, religious or ethnic or more likely some fused and

mediated mixture, are bound to be mobilized and reinforced in the particular sets of circumstances just
outlined.

The point is that all of us entertain such markers,
since they are deeply implicated in knowing who we are,
where we came from, and where we belong, culturally
and territorially. We are all of us involved in mythic
histories, reaching back in our own English case to
Shakespeare's historical plays and beyond and—as
Linda Colley has suggested—reassembled for Protestant Britain as a whole in the eighteenth century.[2] For
much of the time such markers, whatever their nature,
are primary sources of solidarity. Indeed, in certain contexts we esteem them beneficent and regard any erasure
of difference as a diminution in the richness of human
kinds and the diversity of cultures. But we cannot have
it every which way. If markers of difference are to be
cherished then we have to accept that in circumstances
which can be specified, in Bosnia or Lebanon or Armenia or wherever, they will be mobilized and accentuated
in such a way as to dehumanize 'the other'. If we
prefer them to be held in check by the British, Austro-
Hungarian, Ottoman, or Russian empires we should say
so. There might even have been some case to make out
along these lines, though I am not inclined to make it.
The point is that we all shift our positions to keep our
ideological charge sheets clean. We trim according to
circumstances and so evade the costs attending every

[2] Linda Colley, *Britons: Forging the Nation 1707–1837* (New Haven and London, 1992). See also John Wolffe, *God and Greater
Britain* (London, 1994).

position. It is so much easier to float above a situation, keeping our positions in reserve, and every now and then swoop down to deploy a rhetoric of praise and blame based on the saving clause which begins 'if only'.

So what am I suggesting? I am first of all making a point about mediation, where one element, (say) religion, mediates the element of ethnicity and vice versa, and where the markers of identity, whatever they are, provide in *special definable* circumstances the preconditions of conflict and are in turn mobilized and reinforced by that conflict. Among those special definable circumstances is the collapse of empires, which sets in train a turn to historic markers as the basis of a political community and as a criterion of its physical borders. Each community seeks the maximum extension of such borders, in accordance with a historic memory of expropiations, expulsions, and migrations. And there is always a plausible case to hand. Even the IRA has one. In the end it comes to this, that if you want to exorcize conflict then erase history and eliminate difference. But be well assured that any such policy will be the occasion of the most ferocious conflict. As for selecting a generic actor, say religion as *the* cause of *the* trouble, it makes virtually no sense whatever, beyond the simple observation that whatever brings people together will also separate them, and will under definable circumstances foster enmity rather than amity.

It is a point to which I shall return, but for the sake of completeness I should also make it here. I know of no evidence to show that the absence of a religious factor in the contention of rival identities and incompatible claims leads to a diminution in the degree of enmity and ferocity. Rwanda is a case in point: criteria of difference can even to some extent be invented. In Swiftian terms, all you need is the difference between Big-endians and Little-endians. The warring peoples of Central Asia can engage in ethnic cleansing and remove foreign bodies from what they consider their cultural, economic, and territorial patrimony without the slightest intervention of serious religious difference. All this means that the selection of religion as the source of evil needs itself to be analysed as a cultural trope residually derived from the massive conflict in European culture, especially Latin European culture, over the role of religion during the past two centuries. The ideologies of secular establishment have promoted the idea so successfully that Christians have internalized it and asked forgiveness for it when, in terms of a serious contribution to a debate, it is a vast over-simplification. In this matter Christians might spare their breath to cool their porridge.

2

Dawkins's Viewpoint; Social Differentiation

MY argument so far is that the only way to approach the question of the social consequences of Christianity, specifically the vexed issue of religion and war, is by examining conflicts in different social contexts to find out whether any contribution is made by religion and to ascertain the nature of that contribution. From a sociological viewpoint, the role (and nature) of religion varies according to the kind of society in which it is present, and its relationship to warfare will likewise vary. That is why statements to the effect that 'religion causes war' are not likely to be taken very seriously by sociologists. Any understanding of the relationship between these two phenomena has to work its way through studies of contexts and has to typify *kinds* of contexts. That is why I offer here an account of social differentiation, because differentiation specifies types of connection between religion and peace and war according to context. I should add that the theory of social differentiation is a component in the general theory of secularization on which I have worked on and off since 1964.[1]

---

[1] David Martin, *A General Theory of Secularization* (Oxford, 1978).

In this endeavour I use the views of a zoologist, Richard Dawkins, as a focus and a foil. I need therefore to give an account of Dawkins. It so happens the matter is very short and very simple: Dawkins believes that religion causes wars by generating certainty. That is virtually all that needs to be said, and what I need to do is to indicate why assertions of this kind could not meet with much favour among sociologists.

How, then, would a sociologist deal with such a statement? Initially, one would have to place a query against the notion of 'certainty', especially if intellectual certainty is intended. Such a notion only makes sense at a late stage in the development of some religions when they have acquired an intellectual formulation; and it is very difficult to determine what role 'certainty' might play in the ensemble of other kinds of commitment, such as faith and trust (even ingrained habit and identification with a way of life).

Of course, it is true that in the course of history, myriads of men and women have given themselves to and for causes, which may include faith or tribe or both together. Such dedication is often an aspect of identification, which need have no militant edge at all but can acquire it under certain circumstances. Thus one can point to situations where religion is so woven into the way of life of a society that the members of that society treat it as natural and inevitable. But when that society encounters another which is simultaneously 'other' and potentially threatening then all the resources of identity may well be mobilized. In such a situation religion acts as a marker of difference among others, and the role of a specifically religious certainty is likely to be slight. Much more relevant would be a lack of response to the possibility of difference and choice, and that lack inheres in a particular stage of social organization.

In one way, however, the statement is irrefutable because there certainly have been wars where religion played a role. In another way it is indefensible since there certainly have been wars where religion has played no role whatever. Conflicts occur for all kinds of reasons, and hardly ever for just a single reason. So when we hear Richard Dawkins say, as he did in a radio interview, that 'religion causes wars' we must assume he means it is a *major* factor in an *unacceptably large* number of conflicts. One inserts the adverb 'unacceptably' because there is no doubt that Dawkins's empirical proposition includes an adverse moral judgement. Not merely does Dawkins regard religious beliefs as childish mistakes which we should learn to grow out of. He contends that what is scientifically wrong is at the same time morally evil. So clear a moral judgement may seem surprising from the author of *The Selfish Gene*, since in that book he indicated a degree of programming for survival that might seem to make free will and therefore moral judgement otiose.[2] After all, in Kantian terms an 'ought' has to imply a 'can'. But in that matter, Dawkins can be left either to fellow zoologists who may wish to falsify his premiss or to moral philosophers who

[2] Richard Dawkins, *The Selfish Gene* (Oxford, 1989). It might be useful to provide an example of the kind of public polemic engaged in by Dawkins, especially as its level of understanding is all of a piece with other comment frequently made in the media. This example is

may wish to undermine the status of his moral conclusion.

Strictly speaking, the rest of Dawkins's views are irrelevant. The intellectualism underlying his emphasis on certainty can be inferred and criticized, but it is not significant for the critique I offer here. Likewise it is not at all significant that Dawkins considers that religion spreads like a virus. It so happens he holds that whole populations are infected and 'come down' with religion as people once came down with plague. This notion looks like a metaphorical transfer from the field of epidemiology to that of sociology, and in my view would attract virtually no support whatever from sociologists. Happily its status and its plausibility are alike irrelevant.

taken from his conversation with Sue Lawley on 'Desert Island Discs' in spring 1995.

S.L.: It is not surprising really that theologians see you as Public Enemy No. 1 when you have put God on a par with Father Christmas and the tooth fairy. But you don't draw those analogies lightly, do you?

R.D.: No, I think it is a very serious analogy. I think that Father Christmas and the tooth fairy are childhood props. They are aids to children to understand (—though they don't provide very much understanding in that case—) and I think that God is very much like that, except that people don't give up God when they should; when they become old enough to give up God they persist.

S.L.: But is it more than that? Do you see God not as an irrelevance like the tooth fairy, but as positively harmful?

R.D.: Certainly it can be positively harmful in various ways, obviously in causing wars, which has happened often enough in history, causing *fatwas*, causing people to do ill to one another because they are so convinced that they know what is right. Because they feel it from inside—they've been told from within themselves what is right—anything goes—you can kill people because you know that they're wrong. That is certainly evil.

I try to take Dawkins's view about religion, certainty, and war in a common-sense meaning and, apart from some methodological comments below, which are I admit rough reading, I provide what I hope is a commonsensical and popular response. Of course, such a response is bound to be more roundabout than the proposition it rebuts and attempts to confute. One would not be able to fit this kind of response into a television interview: you have to grasp methods, problems, premises, and theoretical frame, and that takes time and effort. Sociological arguments have to be conducted *in extenso*. They *are* complicated.

Nevertheless, my response needs to be popular rather than technical since this is a typical case of a view gaining credence because the person who advances it has a scientific expertise of a certain kind which is treated as transferable outside his own subject. In any case, the proposition he advances is embedded in an Enlightenment narrative which is very widely disseminated and tends to be accepted uncritically. Here, then, we have a natural scientist pointing to the coincidence of two phenomena, postulating a connection, specifying a mechanism, and—above all—pronouncing authoritatively. What he proposes chimes plausibly with an established popular superstition, that is, an empirical belief held beyond or above the evidence. The trouble is that ideas are not necessarily influential by reason of actual scientific content but because they chime with an established narrative and are authoritatively promulgated under the auspices of a scientific magisterium.

One can certainly assume that this kind of view

attracts widespread support, even among people otherwise given to critical scrutiny of whatever is put before them. The view is so much part of accepted everyday assumptions that even people in possession of the evidence do not bother to subject it to critical pressure. A recent television series on 'The Crusades' assembled a great deal of material to show how complex, varied, and often non-religious were the motives animating the crusaders, only to revert in the final seconds to a conclusion based on the inherent character of religion. Were 'Dawkins's theory' merely the maverick private sentiments of a zoologist they would hardly merit the diversion of intellectual resources for a rebuttal. The point is their surface plausibility as a trope in an established narrative.

Social Scientific Objections

If social scientific objections to this kind of generalized proposition were to be set out they would probably be ranged under the following heads: (a) the extraordinary variety of reasons for war at any time, including the so-called wars of religion; (b) the relative unimportance of religious 'certainty' among such reasons; (c) the fact that integration is an inherent element in the constitution of society and sociologically implies both internal and external conflict; and (d) the problem of defining religion so as to hold the specified 'religious' variable constant over time and to avoid slipping into definitional circles whereby religion is identified with any principle of integration, thus rendering the proposition true by definitional fiat. (There would be further problems about the nature of cause, but there is no call to stockpile weaponry beyond what will do the job.)

With regard to the variety of reasons for war, it is imperative to underline the range of possible reasons and the number at play in almost any conflict you care to name. To provide a complete exposition of this complexity would require a statement of geopolitical dynamics in general, and this is no place for that.

The important point is that one can generally assume *raison d'état* to be a crucial principle, based on the pursuit of collective self-interest with respect to alliances, balances of power, and so on. Cardinal Richelieu, who is generally regarded as a major source in the formulation of that principle, made alliances primarily in accordance with the interests of France, not religious affinity. Similarly, Christian societies have allied themselves with Muslim powers from the seventh century to the twentieth in terms of perceived self-interest and convenient balances and alliances. This is not to say that mobilization, including mobilization on a basis of *raison d'état*, may not make a primary appeal to religious difference and, indeed, take off from it. Philip of Spain entertained precisely such reasons in sending out his Armada to subdue England. And the reverse may also be true, so that the Doge of Venice masked *raison d'état* behind religious reasons prior to sacking Byzantium in 1204. The point to recognize is the systematic presence of *raison d'état* as a structure of reasons and motives in relation to a calculus of international advantage. No society is exempt and, if it were, would soon cease to represent its non-existent category. It would have gone down the chute of history.

Beyond such considerations, it is also important that the initial and overt *casus belli*, for example, the keys of the holy places in the Crimean War, is not necessarily of much importance in the fundamental causation of conflict, except that certain symbolic markers of difference are always 'available' between major civilizational blocs. In that sense, of course, symbolic markers *do* matter, because they are keys to a civilization's identity. The problem is that the role of symbolic markers of identity often leads to combatants 'naming' themselves in these symbolic terms, and offering their identity cards as reasons for their mutual antagonism. They may well name each other and abuse each other in terms of rival identities, for example, 'the unspeakable Hun'. But the First World War did not *come about* because of the unspeakable Hunnishness of the Germans.

In the contemporary situation one notes that Serbs name their opponents as 'Muslims' and media commentators follow suit. But the 'reasons' for the war—as already indicated—are partly lodged in such matters as the dynamics of survival in the ex-communist government of Serbia, and beyond such matters in circumstances which are no longer present and active 'reasons' at all, such as the geopolitical considerations which lay behind the creation of the South Slav ('Yugoslav') state after the First World War. If you will you can 'blame' the Allies and their fear of Germany for assembling Yugoslavia in that particular way, and then you can 'blame' Germany for disposing of enough hegemonic potential to make Allied fears at least plausible and understandable. 'Blame' wriggles back and back in such a way that statements attributing 'blame' to specific *kinds* of facts, for example, religion, have virtually no explanatory value whatever. It should be obvious that geopolitical blame is a vast can of variegated worms.

With regard to the second objection, the specification of 'certainty' as the operative mechanism is highly problematic. In so far as religious elements are from time to time involved in wars, the role of 'certainty' is not likely to be all that crucial. For example, there was an important religious element in the American War of Independence in that 'established' Churches, especially the Anglican Church, tended to support the London government, and the descendants of dissenters, especially Scots-Irish Presbyterians, tended to support the patriots. In a way, as Jonathan Clark has persuasively argued, this Civil War in the North Atlantic community was a re-run of the English Civil War of 1642–8.[3] But the variety of other causes was immense and the religious component, such as it was, had virtually nothing to do with certainty. Patriot and loyalist generals did not enter into battle for the Thirty-Nine Articles or for the Shorter Catechism, or on account of dogmatism. The involvement of religion was primarily as a marker, though, of course, a distinctive marker with distinctive cultural meanings.

The same would be true of any small contemporary nation whose members cited religion among the reasons

---

[3] Jonathan Clark, *The Language of Liberty* (Cambridge, 1993).

for their resistance to absorption into some wider entity. If Basques resist incorporation into Spain (and if a small minority do so violently) their actions relate to history, to identity and territory. Their Catholic religion is fused in their collective way of life. So long as a certain kind of local integration is securely in place they can imagine no alternative, and to consider an alternative would be to contemplate the evacuation of their social and especially their familial being. Religion is simply implicated in a cultural resistance. The question of 'certainty' does not arise. That is how they *are*: Catholic and Basque.

With regard to the third objection, all principles of integration imply internal and external conflict once one assumes a right to socialize, that is, educate the next generation in cultural norms and so maintain difference over time. If, of course, this basic premiss concerning continuity over time and recognizability over generations is not understood, then the logic of difference is itself opaque. Continuity and difference mutually imply each other. But once admit difference—and after all, difference will emerge whether or not you admit it— then conflict of some sort under circumstances a . . . n *must* follow. Religion is part of that socio-logic of difference. Given that groups exhibit a social imperative to survive (or else don't survive), and given that they will exploit the advantages of their geopolitical niche to maximize that survival, then in so far as religion is associated with the socio-logic of difference, then under certain circumstances conflict is bound to come about. Of course, 'in so far' in that sentence is very important, otherwise the association of religion with conflict becomes a useless definitional tautology.

That leads on to problems in the fourth group, that is, extremely complex matters to do with the 'essentially contested' definition of religion and the danger of arguing in a definitional circle, thereby chasing one's own conceptual tail. What Dawkins would do with this problem is irrelevant. Anyone who can publicly commit himself without embarrassment to 'religion causes war' is not likely to be worried about what he might mean by religion, let alone by 'cause' or by 'war'. And at one level, there is indeed a sort of common-sense point of reference for assertions about religion which might save Dawkins and myself from simply talking past each other and enable us to argue before a common court of appeal.

Nevertheless, my otherwise 'popular' argument has to include this point about the 'essentially contested' nature of the concept of religion. If the concept of religion hangs together it does so on a basis of 'family resemblance' and overlapping circles, not by possession of a clear core and demarcated perimeter. Unfortunately, the situation is further complicated by the way sociologists use functionalist definitions to discuss what functions religion subserves in social integration, and *also* deploy substantial definitions based on specific religious content in order to deal with the variation in religious beliefs and practices. I happen to believe it is important to note the kind of interesting consequences which follow from relating religion to integration in a functionalist mode, because that links up with points made above about the socio-logic of integration being also a socio-logic of conflict. But I also hold that once the functionalist definition is adopted, one is arguing in a definitional circle to the effect that social integration *is* religion and vice versa. So it is important that in this context I am arguing for empirical propositions, framed '*in so far*' as a *given* religion with a particular content may be to this or that extent implicated in social integration. The 'in so far' is contingent, and the reference to a 'given' religion takes care of and acknowledges the variety of kinds of religious beliefs *and* their varieties of institutional expression.

This stance leans more in the direction of Max Weber than that of Emile Durkheim. It is precisely because I acknowledge the variety of understandings of 'the world' present in different religions that I mainly refer to Christianity. Christianity presumably counts as a religion from the viewpoint of Dawkins, and so my discussion of it counts logically as an attempted rebuttal of his views on religion 'in general'. I take it he is not engaging in an opaque and coded attack on Islam. But from my standpoint differences make a difference. My own conceptual procedure is to treat Christianity as a specific repertoire of linked motifs, internally articulated in a distinctive manner, and giving rise to characteristic extrapolations, but rendered recognizable by some sort of reference back to the New Testament and 'primitive tradition'.

At the same time, I treat the sacred as a conceptually and empirically distinct category, overlapping religion and Christianity but certainly not coextensive with them. For Christians the sacred is minimally located in the birth, proclamation, death, and resurrection of Jesus Christ, in how that re-presents the Presence of God, and is ritually re-enacted. But the sacred also obeys an independent dynamic whereby it is attracted to the religious collective itself (which in this case means the Church), and to the collective 'presence' of society as such. Thus, *in so far as* a religion is socially established, the sacred will provide a 'comprehensive cover', half-fusing the core of Christian faith with the sacrality of the Church and with the *majestas* of the Polis. The whole of my argument shows how these elements are once more disentangled in the process of differentiation. It also indicates a certain *limited* usefulness attaching to the functionalist approach in that different concatenations of these elements may occur at different times in relation to the nation and to secular ideology, and even to the organization of political parties. *In short, the functionalist argument indicates how the sacred may migrate to successive principles of collective integration, separately or in collusion*, as when (say) communist ideology fuses in part with a secular nationalism.

The problem embedded here will become specially evident in my discussion of Christian semiotics in relation to mass slaughter in world wars. A nation under threat summons the sacred to its aid, including its Christian tradition, with its specific and distinct locus for the holy in the death of Christ. The partial fusion of nation, Church, and Christian faith which then takes place is eloquently witnessed in thousands of war memorials.

Indeed, there is even a variant of Christianity that takes its stand precisely at this point of fusion, but only at the price of making an irony available to those not taking that stand. Charles Péguy, for example, as quoted in Geoffrey Hill's 'The Mystery of the Charity of Charles Péguy', pronounces a beatitude on those who 'die for the *terre charnelle*'.[4]

But note that Péguy at any rate is not to be eliminated from the moral accountancy of Christianity as in this respect not Christian. That is the definitional exit used by all who shuffle off reality in favour of purity. I simply note qua sociologist that this particular fusion of the New Jerusalem and the secular city, of Church and Nation, occurs under specifiable circumstances, and I believe one is allowed to measure the conceptual distance between Péguy's beatitude and the beatitudes put forward by Jesus Christ in the Sermon on the Mount. By the same token, I take Sir Henry Newbolt, writing in the heyday of British imperialism, to be a Christian. At the same time, I think it highly significant that what he worships as sacred is embedded in the body of empire, and that as differentiation proceeds such a notion of the sacred becomes less and less easy to promote within the body of the Christian Church. The half-fusions and significant separations of different forms of the collective sacred, and their connection with or separation from the holy in primitive Christianity, are precisely the data to be understood. And they *are* complicated. It is not surprising that primitive Christianity

---

[4] Geoffrey Hill, *Collected Poems* (London, 1985), p. 188.

---

[34]

was regarded as 'atheism'. Perhaps it is also worth noting that it is precisely such tensions as these which have led some theologians, such as Cantwell Smith, to argue that Christianity is not a religion, and others, such as J. G. Davies, to deny the presence of 'the holy' (as understood by Otto) in the New Testament. Not all religions give rise to such tensions, which is why it is important sociologically fully to acknowledge the differences between religions.

Social Differentiation

Though Dawkins's theory about religion and war presumably applies to religion as such, the data which might lie behind it are probably located in the relatively recent past of ten or so centuries covered by the theory of social differentiation. At any rate, the key issues can be covered within that ambit. There is not much to be gained by talking about the consequences of religion before it has become a distinctive and distinguishable feature of social structure, has acquired organizational backbone, and has articulated a *doxa* by which to determine who constitutes the faithful and who do not. That means we shall not, for example, be looking at the religion of the Hopi of north-eastern Arizona, noting their peaceability and observing that they do not cause mayhem among those of their neighbours who fail to celebrate the winter solstice or do not properly perform the snake dance.

Social differentiation is a subsection of the general theory of secularization. Because it traces the changing role of religion according to structural developments it enables one to focus on the specific effects of religiosity in so far as these are progressively distinguishable from the general dynamics of the social whole. It is probably best characterized as an empirical theory, indicating what happens in so far as certain conditions are fulfilled, rather than as a theory of evolutionary progressions. In setting it out here, there is no need to specify the underlying mechanisms operative within the increasing division of labour, but only to indicate the broad outline of change. A theory of this kind is, of course, contrasted with the largely descriptive Enlightenment narrative whereby the priests of established superstition cling manipulatively to power and prestige until the intellectual martyrs of secularity secure a free open space and systematically draw the teeth of error. Matters are certainly more complicated than *that*.

In a relatively undifferentiated society such as that of the European Middle Ages, religion was intimately embedded in the body of society, and theology provided the modality of discourse. The Church was implicated in the structure of power, since ecclesiastical élites overlapped the landed and warrior élites and were to a large extent recruited from the same nurseries. It follows that religion will adjust itself to the characteristic mores, character structure, priorities, and power drives of the groups which have adopted it. Notoriously, conversion is a two-way process, especially for a religion like Christianity, which exalts meekness and blesses peacemakers and so lacks appeal to warriors. Thus the moral perspective of the primitive faith must be tuned to the social institutions of family honour and the feud. The general character of Christianity's adjustment to the institutional requirements of the Roman Empire, the feudal system, the early urban civilization of western Europe is well known, but unhappily it is not properly conceptualized from the point of view of the issue currently under discussion.

It therefore needs to be stated with some clarity. When religions are subsumed into the structure of fully functioning social systems, in particular, their structures of internal power and their drives to external power, they themselves receive and exhibit the stigmata of power. They become rooted in territory, they accumulate wealth, and they reflect the assumptions of the key strata as well as becoming admixed with the general culture of other strata. Analytically, two processes occur, though in actual practice these are fused in one. Religions adjust to the general social dynamics of survival in an intensely competitive world. In their relationships with each other societies are quasi-Darwinian. And religions also adjust to the particular dynamics of a given *type* of society, as, for example, feudalism. This is not in any way to say that religions are mere reproductions of social systems and their properties, or that they are reflections of given types of society (or to imply that types are in practice not riven with contradictions). It is to say that where societies exhibit a relatively low level of differentiation and where religion provides the modality of integration, the consequence must be a vigorous and comprehensive adjustment to 'system properties'. It follows that a religion like Christianity, not created in the crucible of a functioning social system, will undergo more extensive adaptations than religions actually created out of that adjustment. The admixtures of Christian symbolism with particular social institutions will always be extremely instructive, for example, in the construction of the ideal character of a warrior class. Presumably Chaucer's 'verray parfit gentil knight' is an example of such an ideal specification. Presumably some of the complexities of the codes of chivalry are illustrated in a work such as C. S. Lewis's *The Allegory of Love*.[5] The details of such adjustments between faiths and system properties are not of major concern here. What is required is some sense *both* of the integrity of the code carried forward 'on the books' by a salvation religion such as Christianity *and* of the system properties to which it must relate, and alongside which it will evolve over time. The conversion of Clovis I (AD 466–511), the Merovingian founder of the Frankish kingdom, offers a characteristic individual example. Clovis did not repudiate his previous values after his long-delayed conversion to Catholicism and responded to the story of the crucifixion by saying, 'Would I had been there with my Franks.' Moreover, Gregory of Tours in his account of Clovis has no qualms about attributing his success in battle to his conversion to Catholicism. Religions are not disembodied notions but codes which penetrate into and are shaped by system properties and by given social systems. If that is not accepted as a starting-point then we conduct a Cook's tour of history

[5] C. S. Lewis, *The Allegory of Love* (Oxford, 1936).

from our study window, awarding moral marks from our own vantage point, irrespective of context. (Curiously enough, this tendency to award moral marks is not entirely unconnected with our religious roots.)

If the description above represents the general character of the relationship between religion and relatively undifferentiated societies, then social differentiation represents a loosening of that relationship, in particular with the increasing division of labour and separation of social spheres. The Church relinquishes or is forced to relinquish or gradually loses its relationship to the State, though that may be preceded by an interim period when it virtually becomes a department of State. The spheres of education, administration, justice, the care of the sick and needy, social control, and so on are gradually hived off in distinctive spheres which are run by their own professionals according to their own specific expertise. As differentiation increases so religious participation in the basic processes of power, social control, violence, and warfare diminishes, though a generalized association with 'the nation' has consequences to be canvassed later.

There are plenty of examples of the kinds of process involved from quite recent history. There was a period when the Established Church was quite closely integrated with the structures of power in the English countryside. It was perfectly 'natural' for a clergyman, as a guardian of morals, to be also a Justice of the Peace, and so an agent of an overt form of social control. Clergymen now are not often Justices of the Peace. The role of 'binding up the broken-hearted' and 'setting at liberty the captive' is nowadays less easily combined with executing judgement on the evil-doer and sending some evil-doers to jail. Diverse multifunctional roles of this kind were reconcilable in certain kinds of integrated power structure, but as these disintegrate they become difficult to harmonize. Indeed, clergymen are no longer viewed as appropriate bearers of social control. They, too, have their sphere and are not expected to double both as confessor and as judge.

The example is itself an interesting one because as a clergyman (minister or priest) becomes increasingly defined in terms of his sacred role and his specific religious character and expertise, he becomes distanced from the agencies of violence, whether these are canalized through the forcefulness of law or through the 'forces' of national aggression and defence.

The subsumption of spheres in an undifferentiated society does imply that in earlier times we are dealing with certain kinds of 'secular practice', notably in relation to warfare and money, power and wealth, which are everywhere and always resistant to moralization. What differentiation does, then, is to introduce a redistribution of secular and sacred space. Morally resistant social activities once carried on inside sacred space and under its umbrella appear in secular space outside that umbrella. In undifferentiated societies, councils of war were held and people carried on commercial activity even during the celebration of the Mass. In a differentiated society, however, sacred space is set aside for distinctively religious activities, while the autonomous secular dynamic of money and power occupies an entirely different sector.

And just as there is a 'secular' sector actually inside the sacred space of an undifferentiated society, so there is a sacred carry-over into secular sectors of a differentiated society. Thus the redistribution of the sacred in the course of transition from undifferentiated to differentiated societies is very complicated, and made more so because in a differentiated society the sacred acquires a life of its own outside both the ecclesiastical and the religious. The sacred may lodge itself in new structures of power, cohesion, identity, and legitimacy, particularly in relation to land and nation. The sacred can be attracted to the idea of land and nation without any reference to any specific Church or to any Church whatsoever. In the United States Church and State, Church and land are thoroughly differentiated but that does not inhibit a sacred aura from becoming attached to the United States, its people, its flag, and its territories. Wales has no established Church but the RAF was unable to establish a bombing run on the Lleyn Peninsula on account of its sacred character. Political parties can attract elements of the sacred into their orbit, as well as reproducing patterns of behaviour supposed to inhere in religious bodies, such as rituals, creeds, dogmas, texts, coronations, priesthoods, gurus, charisma, exemplars, witch-hunts, exorcisms, and appeals to the original covenant. Marxist societies, putative heirs to the Enlightenment, have reproduced virtually every characteristic once thought to be the special property of religion.

And, for that matter, defences of the integrity of the human body can acquire a sacred aura once located in the sphere of religion. Modern cults of purity with regard to the body, food, and the environment take over where the older Puritanisms leave off. Indeed, sometimes they are the same Puritanisms given new life by being put under new management and renamed.

So, while Christianity, at least as embodied in the Church, sheds many roles and functions, the aura of the sacred migrates quite freely, sometimes attracting Christian motifs into its gravitational field, especially in relation to the nation. All such redistributions and attractions suggest that what we impute specifically to any undifferentiated category of religion or to a specific historical religion should more properly be seen as a feature of *every* deployment of the sacred in the creation and maintenance of social integration.

The conclusion must be then that religion in modern (and post-modern) society is separated off in a distinctive sphere, as well as undergoing various changes following the erosion of all kinds of authority and most kinds of settled local and communal activity. Differentiation allows the sacred to attract some Christian motifs into the secular transcendence of the nation and allows the Christian Church to distance itself from motifs of secular nationalism. What was once a confluence of the sacred diverges into distinct though interconnected channels. This suggests that statements about *the* consequences of religion would at least need specification with regard to the developmental stage to which they are intended to refer. Just as they are extremely doubtful in relation to societies in which religion has no specific institutional location, so they are extremely doubtful in societies in which the institutional location of religion is highly specific. If they have any plausibility at all it is in relation to a particular phase, when religion is embodied in a distinct institution but nevertheless provides a covering note for the identity and integration of the whole society.

Once religion has acquired institutional autonomy separate from the dynamics of the whole society, its consequences ought to be able to be isolated and capable of being monitored. If religion 'as such' is responsible in any serious way for war then those subject to religious socialization ought to display a more militant proclivity than others. Unfortunately, however, this is a type of enquiry where the notion of a purely religious effect is highly problematic and where intruding factors, or factors which are mixed or fused, are particularly difficult to deal with. One might perhaps ask certain questions that *seem* to bear on the issue but without any secure hope that one has isolated the effect of 'religion as such'. The point is that one is trying to isolate religion as a practice with a psychic interior from its historic role as a marker of identity.

What questions, then, might be interesting? One might ask whether Gerald Adams with his IRA colleagues and their mirror images in the loyalist paramilitaries are specially marked out by personal piety and prolonged prayer. One might ask whether the Catholic and Protestant clergy in Ulster are notably more prone to warlike behaviour than those for whom the words 'Catholic' and 'Protestant' are merely markers of identity. One might examine the comments of the Roman Catholic Cardinal Archbishop of Armagh and the Anglican Archbishop of Armagh for evidence of exceptionally high vituperative content. But then one would run into the problem of the Revd Dr Ian Paisley, whose prominence is political and whose political prominence is dependent on voicing the feelings of people and a land—and of a section of the Ulster working class. In other words, Paisley illustrates the logic of a relatively undifferentiated condition while happening to lead a small and distinctive denomination.[6]

Another line of questioning might focus on the pronouncements made by functionally specific ecclesiastical bodies (for example, the World Council of Churches) to see how far they contain exhortations either to secular nationalist conflict or to the kind of antagonism towards other religious bodies which might lead to overt conflict or war. I have not attempted explicitly to carry out such an examination but, from some prolonged acquaintance with this type of material, I am reasonably certain the evidence points in the direction of adamant peaceableness. Again, one might examine core members and marginal members of religious bodies to see how far the additional impact of extensive religious socialization heightened antagonism towards all kinds of out-group. Again, without having carried out such a study, my judgement is that the net result of

[6] Steve Bruce, *God Save Ulster* (Oxford, 1986).

such studies as we have does not show any excess of militant zeal for war or ethnocentrism among the more pious and committed. One may, perhaps, even ask why such a conclusion would be counter-intuitive whereas the generalized statement about religion and war is much less counter-intuitive. Could it be that the one relates to a specific religious effect and the other relates to generalized identities where religion acts as a marker? Are we in a confused manner already making that distinction?

Here one probably needs to insert some caveats about the relation of differentiation to time, since although some relatively undifferentiated societies do share a calendar date with differentiated societies, they do not share social time. During the last century many societies went through a period of *intégriste* Catholicism in which religion and identity were temporarily reassembled, and in the present century such reassemblages can be observed in parts of the Islamic and Hindu worlds. Something further needs to be said about these, since in such societies the sacred and the religious run very closely together and the religious marker seems to run dangerously close to the definition of full national citizenship. Another way of putting it is perhaps to suggest that what in ex-Christendom constituted a succession or progression from religious integration to the secular transcendence of the nation (with in some cases a period of overlap and reinforcement between the two) is now present in many societies in what used to be called the Third World.

Two 'Worst Case' Scenarios

Here, for the sake of conspicuous fairness, it might be instructive to take worst cases rather than typical ones. Supposing, for example, we take two cases: *intégriste* Catholicism in France and Islamic agitation in Algeria. In subsequent chapters I shall look at other 'worse case' instances, notably Serbia.

So far as French Catholic *intégrisme* is concerned, it seems that French society split in two, with each half integrated around a different principle. One half was integrated by secular nationalism and the other half around nationalist Catholicism. It was even possible for a kind of nationalist Catholicism to develop in the form of Action Française (and especially Charles Maurras) which retained the structure of prejudice but threw overboard the New Testament. (This is the exact reverse of some contemporary forms of ultra-orthodox Judaism, which hold to the defining documents of the faith and throw overboard the nation of Israel).

It seems to me that this kind of reaction formation might be described as 'impacted integration', especially in the period of maximum tension between 1870 and 1905. In Catholic generals like Pétain and De Gaulle, France appeared as a metaphysical mistress of her children, and could be invoked in quasi-religious terms as an ultimate. However, this potent overlap had virtually no implication for militancy between religions. Its militancy was directed solely towards the nation, though that could, of course, be reinforced by certain kinds of piety, such as the devotion to Jeanne d'Arc and the pilgrimage to the Black Virgin of Rocamadour. However, once the crisis period for French nationhood passed, this point of overlap rapidly lost its potency and appeal. The French Church to a large extent ceased to be supported on grounds of French identity and in turn ceased to support the remaining *intégriste* sectors in French society. When M. Le Pen tried to reassemble these *intégriste* elements around a racialist programme, the French Church proved singularly uncooperative, for example, by refusing him access to Rheims Cathedral.[7]

The situation in Algeria is, of course, closely bound up with the previous colonization by France. Indeed, it is interesting that, while France is just about able to absorb some two to three million Algerians, a newly independent Algeria was not able to cope with about a million *colons*. The pluralistic capacities of the nation state are quite limited, particularly, of course, where there is a large cultural gap between rival ethnic groups and where one of them is an imperial intruder which once dominated the other.

But, in any case, in Algeria the FLN retained a notable imprint of French culture. This means that the current war between the Islamic groups and the government is comprised of several strands. One strand is Islamic traditionalism faced by the impact of the modern (and Western) world. Another is a militant revolutionary strand once carried by Marxism but now translated in Koranic terms. This is where the religious

[7] José Casanova, *Public Religion in the Modern World* (Chicago, 1994).

component is to be identified, but it runs in tandem with several other strands, among them acute economic misery and the refusal of the government to accept the results of democratic elections. This is, in turn, associated with a polarization between a Francophone middle class, including Westernized women, who support the government, and the masses of the 'damned of the earth', who want to complete the Algerian revolution and set up a government of militant Islamic nationalism. Just how many are included in the militant Islamic groups is difficult to estimate, but one can certainly say that for them the cause of the nation and Islam become interfused. They kill French Catholic priests and mutilate or murder Westernized women and civil servants, as embodying foreign presences in the body politic of the nation. Similar processes are at work in Iran and Pakistan.

The point of the Algerian example is to provide a case where an ex-colony experiences very strong pressures towards a nationalist and cultural integration, in this case carried by Islam. But you have only to read (say) the propaganda of the Latvian Homeland Front to see that in such situations the pressures and strategies all have a family resemblance. The underlying point is that these strategies and pressures can occur without religion being involved at all. The Khmer Rouge behaved in an identical manner. In China over the whole period from 1948 to the mid-eighties there were massive agitations simultaneously defending the purity of the State and of 'the revolution'. Religion did not enter into it, unless, of course, as indicated earlier, one defines such pressures and agitations as 'religious'. And in that case one's position is validated by definitional fiat.

PART II

Mapping Transitions

3

First Example: Romania

Elements in a Comparison

SO far the argument has dealt with the structural conditions affecting the relation of religion to warfare, and with the changes in that relation following the transition from the organic implication of religion in society to a situation where Churches are voluntary associations. Now that transition has to be mapped, preferably in case studies which provide a contrast between advanced differentiation and slight (or inhibited) differentiation, hence the selection of England and Romania. The frame of the comparison comprises the relations of majority religions with power and with ethnic minority and voluntary faiths, and the way these relations play into the dialectic of 'centre' and 'periphery'.[1]

Societies can be placed along a continuum according to various criteria, not only the degree of differentiation but partially associated criteria like the speed of change, or whether change is generated internally or from outside, or the degree to which voluntarism and/or individualism have found expression in religion. France, for

---

[1] 'Centre' and 'periphery' are not used as evaluative notions but in the senses used by Edward Shils, by theorists of 'internal colonialism', and such historians as Linda Colley and Hugh Kearney.

example, is a highly differentiated society and one where change was mostly generated internally. But voluntarism in the specifically religious sphere was suppressed for a whole century following 1685, and it never recovered.

At one end of these continua one would place the USA and at the other a country like Serbia. In the USA the voluntary principle represents the historic norm over centuries. Secular nationalism remoulds divine Providence into Manifest Destiny and, though flag and altar remain juxtaposed in the various churches, the national icons are projected high above any institutional contamination. In Serbia, by contrast, the Church and the State, along with religious and national identity, are closely allied, and any expansion of voluntary faiths is accounted a loss of Serbian identity, particularly under war conditions. This is so even though dechristianization has been quite extensive and committed participation restricted to a minority. If, then, the USA and Serbia are located as contrasting cases at the extremes, England and Romania offer almost equally dramatic contrasts, with England only one step along from the USA and Romania only one step along from Serbia.

In the Romanian case one step along from Serbia makes a considerable difference, and one which provides supporting evidence for the contentions of this book. If Romania is treated as including the north-west territory now within its present borders, then during the immediate Post-Reformation period it saw a remarkable and early instalment of pluralism. This was not classical voluntarism on the Anglo-American model but a legally ratified acceptance of four religious groups, Catholic, Lutheran, Calvinist, and Unitarian, each to a large extent rooted in an ethnic constituency. A fifth religious group, Orthodoxy, though not legally accepted, was tolerated in practice as the faith of ethnic Romanians.

However, for very complicated historical reasons, including the shifting borders of Ottoman or Austro-Hungarian control, the modern emergence of Romania in the nineteenth century came about in an atmosphere of romantic and linguistic nationalism. Nationalists regarded the Romanian Orthodox Church as one major carrier of the national identity of the Romanian ethnic majority. As in Greece, the Resurrection also carried the resonance of national renaissance. As for classical religious voluntarism, that did not appear till the late nineteenth century, and it expanded most easily in those north-western areas where ethno-religious pluralism already existed, that is, in Transylvania and the Banat.

How far might the Romanian situation allow a linkage between religious and political pluralism? So far as political pluralism is concerned, its development was severely inhibited from the thirties to the eighties, first by periods of semi-Fascist authoritarianism and then by Marxist totalitarianism. Indeed, in the earlier period, the National Christian Party was part of a strong current of anti-Semitism. Inevitably, regimes of both right and left stitched the Orthodox Church in to the state apparatus. Nothing emerged to parallel the Christian Socialism of Slovenia.

Two points are relevant to present concerns. One is that over the period from the early seventies till today there has been a staggered and partial relationship between the potential for political pluralism and the two kinds of religious pluralism—the historic but static ethno-religious identities, especially among Hungarians, and the rapidly expanding voluntary denominations, notably the Baptists and the Pentecostals. The other point relates to the manner in which the generic symbolic repertoire of Christianity floats free of particular institutional attachments and of any ties these may have to political regimes. The argument which follows tries to illustrate a relationship between the 'degrees of freedom' which become available at particular junctures with the advent of both kinds of pluralism and the availability of this symbolic repertoire. The most dramatic juncture was, of course, the massive disturbances of December 1989, which began in the mixed ethnic areas of the north-west 'periphery' before spreading to the 'centre', and were sparked off by the protests of a Hungarian Reformed pastor, the Revd Lazlo Tokes.

In England, by comparison, there has been a staggered and partial relationship between religious and political pluralism, and between voluntaristic religious dissent and political dissidence, for more than four centuries. If we extend the discussion to the whole territory which became the United Kingdom we have a complex relation between ethno-religion and voluntarism, not only on one periphery as in Romania but in four: Scotland, Wales, Ulster, and Catholic Ireland. Each of these has in different ways and at different times counterbalanced the hierarchical powers of the English 'centre' and also nourished relatively egalitarian cultures. Indeed, in the case of the religious cultures of Scotland and Ulster, they combined with English voluntarism to help create the nascent culture of what became the United States. So, since about 1600, there has been a complex interplay of establishment and dissidence at work in the English 'centre', while along the northern and western peripheries (including North America!) there has been a complex interplay between ethnoreligious pluralism and classical voluntarism.

As both the Romanian and English cases illustrate, ethno-religion is itself an ambiguous phenomenon in the promotion of full pluralism because it can aim to constitute a new centre and so in turn marginalize rivals in its own heartlands. By its very nature the voluntaristic tradition lacks this particular ambiguity but, nevertheless, it has an ambiguity of its own. On the one hand it creates and implies social models based on variety by unhooking religion from state, territory, residence, and ethnicity. And it promotes participation within the group and a peaceable temper. But voluntary religion also needs to promote its own survival by erecting strong borders against 'the world' and by an emphasis on social orderliness and non-violent obedience which in troubled times is both pragmatic and principled. Thus, from St Paul's cautionary remarks about respect for 'the powers that be' in Romans 13 to the firm loyalism of much of Hanoverian English dissent and of early nineteenth-century Methodism, there is a tradition of political quiescence moving in harness with the revolutionary implications both of merely existing and of the kind of internal organization adopted.

The point about voluntary bodies is worth restating. The peaceable temper inculcated by denominations such as Methodism and Pentecostalism includes in its scope personal conduct, attitudes towards war, and attitudes towards the civil power—whatever the nature of that civil power. At the same time, the very existence of such voluntary bodies mediating between the mass of the people and the State has radical implications and these are extended by the further implications of organizational experiments in self-governance, lay initiative, popular preaching and participation, and—sometimes—local autonomy. Naturally, a leadership remains in place which may well ensure cohesion by administering a strict discipline, but these leaders are not intimately bound in with social control in the wider society. Whereas in Catholic societies there were routes through the Church to a universally recognized eminence, in the voluntary denominations people achieve mobility and social approval first in the body of the faithful, especially through the pastorate, and then later—perhaps in future generations—they may translate religious achievement into secular advancement. All these radical potentials depend on and assume a peaceable temper. That this is so might be incidentally illustrated from the black Churches of the USA. Luther King's Baptist church abuts an institute for the study and practice of non-violence. And one notes that the manse where he was brought up illustrates very well the personal advancement the family achieved through the pastorate. Precisely the same patterns appear visible in today's Romania.

The final theme to be explored is secular nationalism. In this respect Romania is a standard instance. Mention has already been made of the positive relation of nationalism to the majority Church, and also of the free-floating symbolic repertoire of Christianity. These same elements can also be illustrated from English (and British) material. Secular nationalism in England has included the idea of a Protestant nation and that involves a positive relation between nationalism and the majority Church of England. At the same time, the symbolic repertoire of Christianity has been a constant resource, sometimes by way of legitimating power but also of protest. The national hymn 'Jerusalem' is simultaneously a celebration of 'Albion' and an idealistic aspiration to a better society. Christian symbols can defend the pomp of power and be woven into themes of protest and autonomy. They can go with the flag or against it.

In the course of the following chapter it will be shown how in recent decades the Anglican Church has itself deployed Christian sign language to express a tension between Christian priorities and the imperatives of state policy. For that matter, the clergy of other Churches have tended to adopt similar positions. This partial coalescence of the free-floating symbolic repertoire with ecclesiastical and clerical criticisms is one sign that England is a more differentiated society than Romania, and one where all denominations approximate voluntary status. Indeed, there are even occasions where the ambiguity of the symbolic repertoire leads to a contrast between clerical reservations about State policy or about nationalism and a continuing popular attachment to civil religion and to a nationalistic faith. At the beginning and end of the Falklands War the religious ceremonies in the naval city of Portsmouth were to a significant extent lay occasions. The ambiguity of Christianity can emerge in all kinds of ways.

There are, then, a small group of themes to be explored in relation to two very different and contrasting national histories. There is the theme of ethno-religious minorities and there is the theme of voluntarism, and the two themes have to be woven together, particularly as they relate to the dialectic of centre and periphery. Both themes are part of the disengagement of religion from the 'system properties' of organic society where religion is hooked into territory, residence, and state. However, both themes are ambiguous. Ethno-religious minorities are ambiguous because while they split up the larger organic entity they can aim to assemble an organic entity of their own. Voluntary religion is ambiguous because its revolutionary potential is held back within strong institutional borders and kept at a reduced level of threat by the principle of obedience.

The third theme is the free-floating symbolic repertoire of Christianity, which is also ambiguous, because it can be deployed both for legitimation and for protest, for the flag or against it. All symbols are, of course, ambiguous in this way, but as the argument is pursued further in Part III it will emphasize the special ambiguity of Christianity whereby pristine faith appropriates

'Zion' and literally dislocates it and creates a 'Jerusalem which is above', the capital of another peaceable country inhabited by 'all nations and tribes and tongues'. Underneath the free-floating symbols there lies the deep structure of a given religion over which is laid the mosaic of fundamental signs centred around the Christian cross.

Romania in the Context of Communism
in the Eastern Bloc

Romania, then, provides an instance of religious and political homogeneity in the early stages of breakdown. That in part derives from the fact that it has been for decades part of the Eastern bloc, as well as from its place among the many nations in Eastern Europe which have emerged over the past century and a half from foreign rule. Some account has to be given, therefore, of the general conditions which have obtained until recently in the Eastern bloc and of the special role of religion in the revolutions of 1989–90.

Eastern Europe has been, over the past two or three centuries, an area of nascent nationalism struggling against multinational empires, in particular the Turkish, the Austro-Hungarian, and the Russian. In the struggle for autonomy a major role has been played by language and by ethno-religion. These two in harness have been the major carriers of national identity. However, most Eastern European countries have also had periods of totalitarian rule, often Fascist, sometimes clerico-Fascist, interspersed with periods of parliamentary monarchy and conservative authoritarianism. They have also had several decades of communist rule following the Russian victory over Nazi Germany and conquest of Eastern Europe. Whereas under Fascist regimes there has been intermittent tension between Churches and the State, but also cooperation, under communist regimes there has been outright conflict and prolonged oppression of believers. But both kinds of totalitarianism, Communist and Fascist, have endeavoured to control and/or infiltrate the majority Church of the people and ensure its docile acceptance of State policy. Indeed, in communist Romania from the late 1940s on both Church and State were in ambivalent alliance.

The main focus here is on communism and the postwar period that came to an end in 1989–90. Communism is an 'organic society' organized along military lines, and in communist practice nationalism and communism are welded together so far as may be possible. Both communist and Christian universalism are subject to the particularistic pull of nationalism, and how that bears on their relation in a given country depends on how far religion and communism are associated with alien domination or alternatively regarded as vehicles of national culture and autonomy. Thus the relationship between ruling communist parties and Churches has varied according to the relationship to the nation donated by history to one side or the other. In Poland post-1945 the donation of history favoured the Roman Catholic Church; in Czechoslovakia (or more strictly in Czech lands) the donation of history defined Catholicism as alien. In Romania both communism and the majority Church defined themselves nationalistically and they cooperated.

Such varying balances of power in relation to the nationalism of ethnic majorities affected the way communist governments treated minority faiths. On the whole, majority Churches enjoyed better relations with communist governments than did the minority ethnoreligions, if only because the latter could be carriers of forces making for national disintegration. As for voluntary denominations, they were often viewed as Anglo-American incursions, though also valued as creating a solid citizenry, disciplined and teetotal, and not likely to be rooted in dissident ethnic groups.

If one were to sum up the Eastern European situation in relation to Church and State, one might say that the Church was a subjected, restricted, and subsumed agency of the State. If it was sometimes given support, for example, by the renovation of buildings or the payment of priests and pastors, that was part of the thrust to total control. One reason both for the support and the control was the service that Churches could render in the sphere of international relations, in particular by involving themselves in 'peace conferences'. Much of this was a matter of cynical manipulation, though there were Christians, such as the Czech Protestant theologian, Josef Hromadka, who sincerely sought peace through such meetings. Church representatives were allowed out of the country to promote peace and to block criticism of their situation by Western Christians.

Believers were not only involved in peace as part of the foreign policy of communist states. They were also capable of protest against the militarization of whole societies which was such a conspicuous feature of communist regimes. In Hungary, for example, though the official Church had been decapitated and bent to State policy, an underground Church came into being with strong pacifist overtones. The same pacifist tendency was embraced in East Germany, not only by underground groups but even by socially visible representatives of the Lutheran Church. Indeed, in the later stages of communist rule in East Germany many Christians adopted green positions as well as pacifist ones, sometimes in a framework of liberation theology.

This variety in the relationships between the State and religion was reflected in the variety of roles played by religion in the events of 1989–90. But however that role was played, the changes of that time were astonishingly peaceful given their scale and their character. Clearly the role of Polish Catholicism was crucial. In Poland the Church was the mainstay of national consciousness and the success of its resistance increasingly acted as an example to other nations, particularly after the election of a Polish Pope. In Hungary, though there was a serious religious revival dating from the mid-1970s, the Church did not present a leading edge in the eventual toppling of communism. In East Germany the Lutheran Church was a major conduit for social change and created significant free space even though it was numerically very weak. In the Balkans and in the Caucasus there was a very strong link between religion and national identity, and this led to conflict where sizeable populations were on the wrong side of frontiers.

Some special theoretical interest attaches to what happened in the vast territory of the Ukraine. There was a strong link between (mainly) Catholic religion and national identity in the western part of the country which expressed itself in the protest movement known as 'Rukh'. But in the eastern Ukraine the population was partly Russian or Russified. Indeed, the Ukraine taken as a whole can be characterized as a semi-plural society. There are different ethnic and religious balances in different areas and there are various ethnic and ethno-religious niches, including a reviving Jewish community, as well as extensive penetration of both historic and recent voluntary religious bodies. Happily in the event these groups, though rivals with incompatible claims to buildings, managed to coexist with no more than localized clashes.

A further analytic point arising from the Ukranian example is that in the past local cultures might be large or small, semi-autonomous or externally controlled, at ease with their immediate neighbours or not. It is particularly important that past relationships in south-eastern Europe were by no means always antagonistic. In Albania, for example, Christians and Muslims shared festivals. Their contemporary potential for conflict arises as multi-ethnic empires collapse and as borders are questioned. And borders are questioned in part because the geopolitical and administrative, not to say economic, reasons for locating these borders have been

by no means coextensive with ethnic and cultural criteria. The location of economic resources is a particularly
important criterion when it comes to drawing borders,
as Chechenya illustrates only too well.

In most of the movements spreading from Prague to
Tbilisi and from Tallinn to Sofia the peaceable mobilization of religious symbols was particularly marked in the
early stages. To give but one example from a rather
unlikely location, the first baptism in the mainly Catholic area of northern Albania became a mass gathering.
In a country where all religion had been forbidden any
religious act was political, and at one stage protest was
expressed simply by dragging up church bells buried for
decades and hanging them on trees. Thus throughout
Eastern Europe the early resonance of protest and
change was carried by bells or by recitations of the
Lord's Prayer or—as in Vilnius—by the re-erection of
crosses. And similarly where protest encountered violent reprisals, as it did in Romania, the population
responded with candles, carpets of flowers, crosses, processions. The later stages of protest were more overtly
political and pragmatic, but the inital resonance of
change could be carried by the generalized reference of
the religious sign.

The Romanian Nation and the Orthodox Church

The Romanian Orthodox Church is the majority
Church in Romania as a whole, and is adhered to in
particular by most ethnic Romanians. This means, given
the distribution of ethnic groups, that the southern and

eastern 'heartlands' of Romania are relatively homogeneous. Turkish oppression of the Romanians ensured that they were as Orthodox in their loyalty as the Irish were Catholic. The currents of romantic nationalism swept alongside the rock of the Church but at no point threatened to carry it away. The poetry of Eminescu, and the literary revival and establishment of the language, ran together with Orthodox spirituality. As in all the nationalisms of this period, this amalgam was to some extent constructed as well as projected back on to an idealized organic past. When an independent Romania first emerged in the 1860s and 1870s the Orthodox Church was naturally linked to the State, and it also penetrated deep into the interstices of everyday life. Its rites were part of the frame of existence. Nobody expected it to take up an independent political stance but everybody accepted it as a focus of the national spirit.

That remained the case throughout the whole time of independence, and indeed, as already indicated, during the communist period Romania remained remarkable for the way the Church retained its position. No doubt this had something to do with the fact that Romania saw itself as a Latin island in a Slav ocean and insisted on independence from its neighbours, above all from Russia. At any rate, though the Church was tightly controlled, indoctrinated, and infiltrated, it retained a great deal of its historic influence in the hearts of ordinary Romanians. Access to the traditional repertoire of sign and symbol was never lost as it was in parts of Russia and (for example) Estonia.

As already mentioned above, the initial break in religious homogeneity came in the immediate Post-Reformation period in the north-west with the recognition of Hungarian Catholics and Reformed, of Unitarians, and of German Lutherans, and with the semi-toleration of Romanian Orthodoxy among ethnic Romanians. This type of pluralism was therefore ethnically based, and the novelty lay in the degree of tolerance extended within a given territory. Church and State were not identical. Naturally the borders of the State were continually shifting, not only with the slow retreat of the Ottomans but with the variable territorial reach of Hungary and of Austro-Hungary. Today, in the areas north and west of the Carpathians, there are often three names for cities, one German, one Hungarian, one Romanian. The situation is further confused by the fact that the Hungarians, who are something over 50 per cent Reformed, are not only concentrated along the border with Hungary but also have major areas of settlement deep within the Romanian national territory.

This background is necessary to understand the partial link between ethno-religous pluralism and voluntarism and the openings towards political pluralism in 1989–90. This partial link was particularly visible in Transylvania and the Banat, that is, in the north-western 'periphery', rather than in the central heartlands of the south and east. But, first, there should be some analysis of the emergence of voluntarism and of its link with ethno-religious pluralism.

The Emergence of Voluntarism

The emergence of voluntary religion in any society is a major event, however insignificant the beginnings, because it presages the fragmentation of the dominant majority faith and may also signal in the symbolic and cultural realm the advent of political pluralism and of a rich culture of intermediate organizations between State and individual. Voluntary religion arrived in what is present-day Romania through the activities of German Baptists in the late nineteenth century. From that time on the growth of Baptists tended to be greatest in the north-west, in Transylvania, that is, in the 'periphery' already most influenced by ethno-religious pluralism, ethnic variety, and Central European culture. The Baptists were followed in the course of the twentieth century by Pentecostals who made some impact in Moldavia in the north-west as well as in Transylvania. At the present time in the 1990s, Pentecostals are probably twice as numerous as Baptists, so that there is an overall voluntary sector of about 2 or 3 per cent with a lively network of international contacts extending from Albania to the Ukraine, not to mention Britain and the United States. What the visitor to Transylvania observes is an area of rich ethnic and religious variety, which includes Roman and Uniate Catholics, Hungarian Reformed, Romanian Orthodox, German Lutherans, a small remnant of a once flourishing Jewish community, Baptists and Pentecostals, and other smaller groups.

A traveller through the countryside also notices in particular the appearance of small Baptist chapels in village after village, and to the present writer this represents an echo of the similar chapels now to be observed in tens of thousands of villages from Lower California to the south-eastern coast of Brazil. In other words, it is as well to remember that this particular wave of change, breaking up the historic unities of religious culture and creating autonomous subcultures, now involves hundreds of millions of people worldwide.

Inevitably there is tension in this area because pluralism opens the gate to tension. Broadly this is of two kinds. There is, first, ethnic tension which can flow to some extent along the channel of ethno-religion. It is associated in particular with the Hungarian minority of two million, which in certain areas constitutes a local majority. The tension is expressed through a Hungarian 'Federal' Party seeking local ethnic autonomy, and also through some Hungarian religious leaders, among whom the best known is the Reformed pastor (now bishop) Lazlo Tokes, the pastor whose defence of freedom of religion and human rights (as well as of Hungarian culture) sparked off the events of 1989. The other tension arises because the culture of the Romanian majority and the strong tie of ethnicity and religion among Hungarians both resist the fragmentation represented by voluntary religion. Baptists and Pentecostals are often described as 'not any longer' Romanian, and are perceived as different precisely because they cross ethnic boundaries.

Here one needs parenthetically to notice the existence of a form of voluntarism which has developed inside the Romanian Orthodox Church. The Lord's Army is an organization of several hundred thousand people. It was founded in the 1920s, and was regarded with some ambivalence by the hierarchy, partly because it could develop as an alternative power base and partly because it offers scope to the laity and opposes ceremonial formalism. During the communist regime its leaders were imprisoned, sometimes with the connivance of Church leaders. Not all voluntarism exists outside the Church in overt opposition; the Lord's Army is a conspicuous instance of that, with an odd resemblance to the revivalism of Scandinavia.

In the context of voluntarism in general we encounter key processes of human integration, which require some modest exposition, above all the resolute marking of boundaries through criteria of difference. Any development, such as differentiation and fragmentation, which crosses borders of historic identity, above all the primordial territorial or land-based identity anchoring the ethno-religious tie, sets up a reactive tension. People man the borders to prevent crossings and defend the integrity of their personal identity and of their collective, historic culture. Moreover, they become increasingly militant when the signs and symbols displayed in the public forum are not their own. For example, Hungarians in the border town of Oradea press for public signs written in Hungarian as a recognition of their presence. Or again, Uniate Catholic culture was suppressed in this same area by the communist regime as a salient of 'the West' (with the result that since 1989 the

Uniates have made some conversions). Or again, the presence in Oradea of a large Baptist church holding some 3,000, even though away from the centre of the town of Oradea, is seen as a symbolic challenge to the majority culture (or cultures).

In short, people desperately want to feel 'this is ours' and represents 'us', and deeply resent alien salients because these carry the message that *they* are aliens in their 'own' land. It is precisely the same tension that even in Anglo-American culture tries to prevent mosques being built in the *centre* of Bradford or temples erected in key areas of North Dallas. Buildings can be viewed as declarations of cultural war; and in actual war, as can be seen from the former Yugoslavia, they are burned down. However, nobody need suppose that the razing of Catholic churches in Krajina from 1991 to 1995 had anything whatever to do with a disagreement over the *filioque* clause in the Creed or something labelled by Richard Dawkins as religious 'certainty'. It is about the historic integrity of culture in a place, and occurs in relation to perceived and actual threat, moving in accelerating spirals of mutual repulsion and self-fulfilling prophecy.

Happily, so far, at least in Transylvania (and the Banat), the spirals of tension resulting from ethno-religious pluralism and from the rapid expansion of voluntarism have not been activated to a dangerous degree, though one never knows when opportunist politicians might try to mobilize them, or echoes from elsewhere across the Serbian border give them increased salience.

The sociological conclusion is clear enough and highly relevant to any understanding of the supposed relation of religion to violence. It is that those changes which initiate pluralism, whether based on ethnic variety or on voluntarism, activate the fundamental processes of cultural defence of which *in other contexts we approve*. In Wales or Scotland, or among Muslim minorities, or in the Andes, or on the Burmese border we approve of these measures for the defence of history and land and cultural integrity, but they are the same processes which, *under given conditions*, result in massive conflict. And since that is the case we have to note that in a huge number of instances, perhaps the vast majority, the passage of change encounters such a build-up of countervailing pressures that change is aborted or its proponents come to mirror its opponents. In Romania the build-up of countervailing pressures is fairly high but probably not fatal. In the Anglo-American cultures, here chosen as a contrast, the 'given conditions' were uniquely favourable to pluralism and voluntarism, but even so the turbulence of change lasted for centuries and the build-up of countervailing forces has occurred time and again, for example, among American 'nativists' in the nineteenth century or in the anti-Chinese agitation in Britain at the beginning of the twentieth century. It is endemic.

But to return to Romania and the general problem of loosening the ties of solidarity and authority, it is interesting that the most militant and entrenched resistance to change was provided by an ideology—Marxism—claiming to be the ultimate heir of Enlightenment and claiming to replace and subvert precisely the endemic processes just identified in the process of arriving at an undifferentiated 'pure' humanity. So, it is now necessary to describe the operation of that Enlightenment ideology as it became the vehicle of oppressive power and totalitarian national integration up to 1989. If it should seem unfair to identify Romanian communism in general and the Ceausescus in particular as 'enlightened', it has to be emphasized yet again that if the Christian label adheres to certain conspicuous historical malefactors then the same applies to the label of the Enlightenment. The issue is not some easy moral accountancy, *but understanding the social processes in which both Christian religion and enlightened ideology are involved.* Blame is easy and social science complicated.

Organicist Reaction: Nationalistic Communism

Communism, like Roman Catholicism, is only officially internationalist. In practice it is nationalistic and if the nation happens to be large, like Russia or China, communism is a useful tool of imperialism against sub-nationalisms. Indeed, in the period of maximum Soviet power communism did succeed in partially suppressing non-Russian nationalisms. In the case of Ceausescu (and Tito, for that matter) communism united itself to a local nationalism as a defence against Russian communist imperialism, and in so doing set out to crush its *own* local ethnic and religious pluralism. Ceausescu's plan to uproot many thousand villages had the additional merit in his eyes of destroying Hungarian culture.

The effectiveness of communism in promoting organicist reactions against pluralism is actually improved by its progressive credentials. Thus, movements for change in Transylvania could be condemned as Hungarian revanchism and the bourgeois variety of nationalism. Religion could be suppressed, more especially non-Romanian religion, on the ground that it was an outdated social formation, based on pre-scientific superstition and on class contradictions and likely to divert people from their true and proper loyalty. (Ceausescu would have appreciated at least some of Dawkins's arguments. Arguments which in one context are deployed in the cause of liberality can in another context be used to justify persecution.)

The most severe persecution of religion in Romania fell on the ethno-religions concentrated in the northwest, and on the voluntary denominations. Interestingly enough, it was in the north-west during the 1970's that an intense spirituality associated with Pastor Tson emerged, which proved capable of resisting the persecution and attracting a strong core of believers.

The Ceausescu regime has often been described and its character requires no elaboration here. But mention was earlier made of the role of buildings, public spaces—and names—as crucial indicators of organic integrity and concentrated social power. The Ceausescu regime very well understood and exploited the role played by monuments in public space. Over twenty years it demonstrated the geography of power in a truly Napoleonic programme of building designed to symbolize ideological dominance in collusion with (enforced) national unity. Thus, in Bucharest, large parts of the city, including many historic churches, were torn down to create a triumphal way culminating in a palace larger than any other outside Peking. Facing the palace is a semicircle of apartments rivalling the piazza in front of St Peter's, Rome, and these were to be occupied solely by members of the Securitate.

In other cities special hotels were built, reserved for the reception of royal progresses. In Timisoara, for example, Ceausescu even planned to construct a building across the central square in order to block out the view of the cathedral because it offended his sense of untrammelled power. He felt about this building just as Stalin felt about the (now rebuilt) cathedral of Christ the Saviour in the centre of Moscow.

It remains now only to analyse the fall of Ceausescu's power, and in particular the role played by ethno-religious pluralism and by voluntary religion on the Transylvanian periphery, and the role of generic Christian symbolism.

The Urban Theatre of State Violence

The violence deployed by the 'enlightened' state met the protests of the people precisely in the public spaces (or urban theatres) where Ceausescu had harangued cowed crowds to the accompaniment of orchestrated cheering. The protest itself began along the hairline

crack in the structure located in Timisoara, the capital
of the periphery, and—as already emphasized—it was
sparked off by Lazlo Tokes, a Reformed Hungarian
pastor. So a geographical periphery in alliance with
ethnic and religious pluralism provided the first base of
change.

The centre of Timisoara is a vast oblong space capable of holding the whole population of about a third
of a million. At one end is the opera house, from the
balcony of which Ceausescu had spoken from time to
time. At the other end is the Orthodox Cathedral,
marking the edge of a park. But the seismic rumble
began in a side street outside the unassuming façade of
the Hungarian Reformed Church, before it moved into
the city centre. Tokes, as its pastor, had made broad-
casts in Budapest about the unhappy state of the Hungarian minority, and had spoken in favour of human
rights. He was, therefore, descended upon by the
Securitate, and the revolution began because a group of
elderly ladies attempted to protect their pastor. Somehow this little group grew into an extensive crowd which
ended up as a vast assemblage in the city centre crying,
'We want bread and we want warmth.' This assemblage
found itself faced with the army and the Securitate, and
in the carnage which followed at least 700 people died.
Crosses now mark where they fell.

After a weekend of chaos and confused fighting, the
factory sirens sounded on Monday morning and over a
quarter of a million people came into the square. They
flowed up the steps of the cathedral, but no priest
appeared, and for long no bell rang. They faced directly

into the tanks and guns gathered in the park on either side of the cathedral, and in the mounting tension large numbers knelt, repeating the Lord's Prayer. What they did not and could not know was that Ceausescu had ordered the assassination (suicide?) of the commanding officer for inadequate violence in shooting only a few hundred people three days before, and had demanded the elimination of any other protestors by chemical warfare. They were equally ignorant of a possible rift between the army and the Securitate and of what may have been Gorbachev's influence in the army. Whatever the reasons, the tanks turned and trundled away and the crowd took over Timisoara. The mayor went to the opera house balcony and declared Timisoara a free city, and was followed by two pastors, one Baptist, one Pentecostal. One of these shouted 'God exists' and was greeted with answering shouts of 'God exists.'

The sparks ignited at Timisoara then flew to Sibiu, in the centre of Romania, where some ninety people, mainly students, were shot, and to Bucharest. The confrontations in Bucharest took place in front of Communist Party headquarters and from the outset were broadcast on television. Ceausescu emerged on the balcony of Party HQ to make his usual style of speech and was greeted by hisses and shouts of derision. He then fled by helicopter and there followed a confused attempt by the Securitate to rescue him and to regain control, especially of the television station. This attempt was foiled only after days of fighting and extensive casualties. Ceausescu with his wife was captured, tried, and shot, and on 25 December Romanian television announced, 'The tyrant has died on Christmas Day.' Christmas trees were placed on the balcony from which he had spoken and carols broadcast for the first time in decades.

The narrative of events is not here a central concern. What is evident is the way a series of cracks in the organic structure on the periphery suddenly widened to produce cumulative reinforcements which brought the structure down, or at least dismantled the most oppressive part of it, since it is well-known that the 'National Salvation Front' masked opportunist sections of the Communist Party which manipulated the revolution to their own ends and have managed to retain or regain substantial power. The cumulative reinforcements included the generic Christian repertoire of symbol embedded in all the Christian traditions, but carried for most people by the Romanian Orthodox Church. So, while many in the upper echelons of the Romanian Orthodox Church remained assimilated to the power structure, including the Patriarch, the language of Christianity was available for use. The flowers, processions, prayers, and crosses became part of the resources of protest, and they fused with other resources not tainted by association with the regime but expressing the spirit of the nation, such as the old national song and the national flag shorn of its hammer and sickle—the famous 'hole in the flag'. In other words, the ecclesiastical institution might remain captured by a reactive organicism but the language of Christianity floated freely as a popular resource. In the huge but unsuccessful secondary protests of spring 1990, for example, the crowds shouted 'Christ is risen.'[2]

None of the details above implies that the potential for political oppression has been finally removed or that the more dangerous aspects of a fusion of free-floating Christian symbolism with nationalism have been eliminated. The ethnic tensions in the north-west of Romania remain and it may well be that ancient hostilities towards Jews and Gypsies are reviving, in spite of the minute numbers of the former. But the most restrictive forms of control have been removed and religion has emerged as a relatively autonomous and functionally specific power able to create large-scale associations between State and individual. And the voluntary denominations, while undoubtedly stressing their national loyalty, also promote a peaceable psychology, resistant to statist ideology, to militarism, to the culture of revenge, and to the macho personality.

What has been the main objective of this argument? It has been to show how even under cumulatively disadvantageous circumstances there can emerge significant cracks in the union of religion and society. Though the spirituality of the Romanian nation emerged in the current of nineteenth-century nationalism there were, nevertheless, alternative possibilities. These came out into the open in 1989 as part of a protest against State violence and enforced political homogeneity under the

[2] Dan Antal, *Out of Romania* (London, 1994), p. 185 in chapter 8, 'The rose that did not bloom'; cf. also pp. 30–1 for the eruption of Christian symbols in December 1989.

aegis of an 'enlightened' ideology. They took off in the Transylvanian periphery and had significant bases in ethnic minority faith and the voluntary denominations. They were able to deploy a free-floating Christian symbolism alongside other resources for protest.

This is not to say that the hegemony of the Communist Party and the Securitate has finally been overthrown or that religion cannot be co-opted once again. There are disturbing signs that the ancient hostility towards Jews and Gypsies has resurfaced.[3] Nevertheless, within strict limits, and with a crippled gait, Romania is changing, and among those changes is a decline in the relation of religion to coercive control and its emergence in functionally specific and autonomous forms.

[3] Radu Florian, 'The resurgence of anti-Semitism in Eastern Europe', *Sociological Review* (Institute for Community Studies, Bar Ilan University), 4/1 (April 1995), pp. 1–9.

4

Second Example: England

TO map in detail the transition to a differentiated society and to a voluntary religiosity in England is a difficult enough task. To weave into that the relation of religion to peace and war in English culture is virtually impossible. So all that can be attempted here is a specification of elements and of the more important shifts and sequences.

Of course, when we compare England with Romania the breakdown of the organic unity of religion and society in England began very early and it has worked itself out over some four centuries. Voluntary religious groups had certainly emerged by the late sixteenth century and there were clear intimations of voluntarism in the late Middle Ages. England is a country which has changed at a *relatively* slow and even pace, in spite of times of turbulence like the Civil War and the Glorious Revolution. This is true not only in matters of religion but economically and politically. Being an island helps, and so does having an empire. The fact that England (or more strictly Britain) is an island means that you have some room in which to experiment, and also that you have some natural protection against invaders who would disrupt the stability and the continuity of culture.

Having an empire is a way of exporting war rather than experiencing it at home. And apart from all this, England (Britain) was for a variety of reasons the first society to be industrialized, and that meant problems could often be surmounted one by one rather than encountered in rapid succession by importation from more advanced societies. England has, in short, been safer and/or more powerful than other countries and it has therefore been possible from time to time to have and to imagine peace.

Most of the advantages just referred to have some bearing on the fact that in England pacific and pacifist traditions have a more continuous and influential history than almost anywhere else. The only comparable case is British North America, later to become the USA and Canada. The United States enjoyed equivalent advantages to England. It too experienced several centuries of voluntarism or virtual voluntarism and, in addition, disposed of vast space for religious and social experiment. It too gained some protection from the ocean and by the export of war elsewhere. In any case, such enemies as it had on the broad face of the continent were not particularly formidable. And, of course, the USA was, with Britain, a pioneer of industrialization, picking up the initial British advances. By the 1880s it had surpassed them, as had Germany.

But what more specifically is it about the religious cultures of England and the USA which places them at the propitious end of a spectrum of routes into modernity by contrast with countries like Romania or Serbia? What elements can we point to as crucial? One quite central element was the institutional damage sustained by the Church of England in the troubles of the Reformation period. Elizabeth tried to make the Church inclusive and comprehensive and to curb extremes, but the thrust of the Reformation meant that the Church had lost some of its power to patrol its boundaries. The open Bible was a constant source of conflicting ideas and in a few decades a large part of the radical repertoire of Christianity had escaped ecclesiastical control. By the late sixteenth century the Bible was agitating the hearts and minds of many of the most active and curious citizens. That they were far from a majority hardly mattered: they were a very vigorous minority. The Christian repertoire, combined with ideas of Covenant, became the early seed-bed of British North Atlantic culture in the seventeenth century and provided enough radical potential for centuries to come. Among these ideas were some that undercut two universal attributes of human society: internal control and external means of defence (or indeed attack). Some Christians objected both to magistracy and to war, and their objection was not to particular forms or acts of magistracy or particular forms or acts of war, but to the institutions of law enforcement and to the power-based dynamic of international relations as such. As an established Church, assimilated to the average conditions of human sociation, the Church of England inevitably condemned both positions in her fundamental Articles.

But it was too late. The Church lacked adequate control of its social and doctrinal boundaries and, in any case, the organic link of Church and State, whereby each perfectly replicated the other, was weakening, and the necessary attributes of sovereign bodies, including powers of compulsion and automatic inclusion, were slowly passing to the State. Heresy was turning into treason and a space was opening up in the religious sphere which presaged individual conscience and personal decision. Indeed, virtually every cultural and political possibility was canvassed in the organizational experiments and doctrinal positions taken up by Christians in the late sixteenth and seventeenth centuries: anarchism, local autonomy, individualism, pacifism, antinomianism, perfectionism, the rule of the elect, the rule of the elected, and so on. The climax of this ferment came in England with the Commonwealth, when a Republic was established and Church separated from State.

But in England the range of experiment was severely checked by the Restoration, whereas in British North America experimentation took advantage of space and distance and local autonomy, and along with other facilitating changes and ideas helped prepare the way for the American Revolution. Thus the counter-culture of Britain became the founding culture of the United States.

The difference between the two countries was not so great as that formulation suggests. In Britain the current of radicalism and voluntarism was not only carried along the narrowing institutional channels of dissent but lodged in heads. Individuals were able to exploit the comprehensiveness of the Established Church. In both countries then, there was a relatively free movement of ideas, among which were the ideas of a semi-Christian Enlightenment. And this relatively free movement derived from the original weakening of the boundaries of the Church, the loosening of the union of religion and State, faith and nation, and the huge hole torn in the protective dykes by the torrent of radical ideas.

More has to be said about this shift from Church to nation, because the underlying argument is that the system properties (as we have to call them) of society as such—social control, military violence, boundary maintenance, reduction of dissonance, cohesion, identity, geopolitical dynamics—were being gradually concentrated in 'the nation' and the nation state, though this was masked by the role the Church continued to play as the faith of the governing classes and of a majority of the people. However gradual this process might be in English (and American) culture it was, nevertheless, more advanced than almost anywhere else. The various expulsions of non-Catholics from Spain in the period after 1492 and from France in 1685 could not and did not occur in England, though events in Ireland, especially in the seventeenth century, were versions of the same drive to organic unity, carried out under the aegis of the nation.

The end result in England, and also in the USA, was the idea of a Protestant nation assembled under a mixture of Protestant and Enlightenment aspirations. This was very different from the idea of a Church-nation. And the mixture of Protestant and Enlightenment motifs drew quite heavily on the Old Testament precisely because that was the production of a tribal group. The

Hebrew Scriptures were combined with ideas of the New Jerusalem, the 'heavenly city of the philosophers', and Virgilian concepts of the Novus Ordo Seclorum. The realities of power were now mobilized behind the hopes, myths, and legitimations provided by progress. They could therefore be simultaneously Machiavellian in their actual operation and naïvely idealist in their stated long-term objectives. US foreign policy retains this dual character to this day. Progress provided ideological cover for power, as other nations were quick to note and complain. A good example is the way the Presbyterian President McKinley justified the American war in the Philippines by reference to democracy and 'the gospel'. And the point is worth stressing because what the Enlightenment plus the notion of a Protestant nation attempted in the way of social mobilization exhibits some parallel with what the Enlightenment tried to do in harness with varieties of *secular* nationalism in twentieth-century Eastern Europe. The organic impulse is renewed time and again, as shown even by the examples of England and the USA, where the voluntary principle has achieved its maximum realization. Breakthroughs activate 'system constraints' and the pressure of change creates its own counterweights.

As for the voluntary tradition, it has to be stressed that it only makes *possible* the aspiration to universal peace and peaceability. There is no inevitable connection. This is crucial from a theoretical point of view. Put into sociological language, a change which reorganizes the net impact and mutual interaction of the system properties of human sociation is not easily arrived at or maintained. Voluntarism only secures a space: it does not guarantee an outcome. Indeed, it may itself be swept into the currents of national feeling or, as in the American South and Ulster, acquire a militant defensiveness. And it does, of course, encounter the dilemmas of international politics from time to time, and has to devise a response. A characteristic example of the pressure exerted by geopolitical dilemmas on the pacific tradition could be provided by the career of Bishop Oxnam. Oxnam was the kind of ecclesiastical statesman found very frequently in the contemporary World Council of Churches. For him the issue of peace was a crucial criterion of any Christian politics. As the crises of 1933–41 built up, he consistently tried to evade the narrowing range of viable choice, and sought short-term solutions likely soon to collapse, as well as likely to ensure the crunch came under conditions of maximum disadvantage. This period pitilessly exposed the lack of a mundane 'practical wisdom' in the Christian Churches, and their over-reliance on generalized moral opinions. Of course, everything was further complicated by the moral reaction against Versailles and the reinforcement this gave to suspicion of allied policy and intentions.

The example of Bishop Oxnam, under the impulsion and logic of events, comes from a situation where the religion in question—Methodism—had lost the protective boundaries of its initial period and was wide open to liberal culture. Such a loss is exemplary. It very often happens that groups, like the Society of Methodists or the Society of Friends, protect radical possibilities for generations. But then, eventually, the boundaries weaken, the possibilities spill out and then maybe mutate, sometimes travelling far from their original base. Emerson provides an individual example of this mutation. After absorbing both Anglican and Unitarian influences, it was precisely his own religious culture which led him to dissatisfaction with his Church. In other words, Churches as cultures generate dissatisfactions with Churches as institutions. The result in Emerson's case was that in 1832 he resigned from the ministry, in part over the issue of Christian participation in war.

Ethno-religion

Are there British and American analogues to ethno-religious pluralism as analysed earlier in Romania? That analysis suggested that ethno-religious minorities concentrated in peripheries, such as Transylvania and the Banat, can under particular facilitating conditions cooperate with voluntaristic pluralism. Have Britain and the USA their own versions of ethno-religion in Transylvania? Do these cooperate at times with voluntarism? And are there examples of the situation found so frequently in Eastern Europe, where the ethnic minority on the periphery is not only at odds with the national 'centre' but also at odds with enclaves inside its own territory?

In the case of Britain (strictly the United Kingdom) there is, indeed, an ethno-religious pluralism rooted in the northern and western peripheries. Scotland, Ulster, and Wales have all been non-Anglican cultures made up in varied proportions of Presbyterians, Methodists, Baptists, Episcopalians—and Roman Catholics. These alternative religious traditions are woven into vigorous non-English cultural identities, or (if one prefers) into micro- or proto-nationalisms. Over centuries they have, at different junctures, alternately counterbalanced and joined with the nationalism of England within an overall British nationalism, and have also counterbalanced the Established English Church. Indeed, it was migrants of the Scottish and Ulster traditions who mingled with migrants from the voluntary sector in England, not only to lay down the future pattern of American culture but to take a disproportionate role in the patriot armies. Again, it was the weight of Scotland which in all likelihood tipped the balance in the confrontation between King and Parliament in the English Civil War. Today, if we look at the political and religious cultures of the three 'peripheral' nations, one notes that the internal balance of religious and political traditions is still contrary to that obtaining in England. Indeed, it can be demonstrated that the ethnic or religious differences based in these peripheries have, in combination with English voluntarism, made a disproportionate contribution to Liberal and Labour Party leadership. If one looks at particular countries, for example, Wales, one can also see how pacifist traditions find a niche in the overlap of voluntary religion and local ethnic loyalty. Why that is not so in Presbyterian Ulster or Scotland is material for a book rather than an aside.

As for the United States, the early separation of Church and ethnicity, Church and State, Church and territory, facilitated—as already suggested—a generalized relation between the nation as such and the legitimations offered by the idea of a Protestant nation and Enlightened Progress. When fresh waves of migrants arrived later, bringing with them their ethnic religiosity, there was no way they could hook that particular identity either to territory in the New World, or to the State, or to a mythic history relating only to themselves. All these connections had already been preempted by the national idea.

What would have happened had they been able to make these connections and so constitute a society in embryo is illustrated by Quebec. There ethno-religion did, indeed, establish itself on a territory and hooked it to a particular institutional Church up till as late as the 1960s. Thereafter, the ecclesiastical component partially dissolved in a secular concept of the nation under the aegis of language and of a (semi)-mythic history. No sooner had that happened than minor versions of ethnic and linguistic cleansing got under way, as English-speakers in Quebec found to their cost. Whether such developments ever occur in the USA depends on how far American culture retains its absorbent power and its ability to promote Americanism at the expense of any ethnic group constructing a separate (semi)-mythic history and staking a plausible territorial claim. The Catholic Irish-Americans showed what could be done with a (semi)-mythic history, but were controlled by the context of Americanism. More recent semi-mythic histories may be less pliable partly because claims to territory put forward by Hispanics or Native Americans—or Afro-Americans—have in their different ways some genuine political potential.

England: A National Church in a Protestant Nation

As indicated earlier, the slow transfer from a Church state to a nation state was partly masked by the way the Church of England retained a hold on the governing classes and was thus, to some extent, aligned with the national culture, especially its literature, architecture, and music. In so far as the Church was rooted in monarchy and in subsequent ruling oligarchies (e.g. in the period 1689–1837) it was also aligned as an institution to the 'system properties' already discussed, including social control and the armed forces. The incidentals of these alignments do not much matter. It is self-evident that when the nation rejoiced or mourned or remembered it did so through the ceremonies of the Church of England, and that in the more privileged classes the careers of soldier or priest jostled as rival options. Generals, ministers of the Crown, and archbishops came from the same nurseries. At the same time, the focus of loyalty and indeed of idolatry was the nation, so that Westminster Abbey and the crypt of St Paul's became arsenals of national losses and victories. The history of the British Empire can still be read off the walls of thousands of churches, especially the chancels where the privileged presumed to take up spaces in closest proximity to the sacred. England was a nation under covenant viewing itself as a second Israel—as well as a second Greece and Rome. Thus, when the Stewarts were finally defeated in the rebellion of 1745, Handel's *Judas Maccabaeus* associated England (or Britain) with victorious Israel and apostrophized 'Peace' and plenty as the fruit of English liberty and piety. Social criticism too could be focused through the lens of Jerusalem, Athens, and Rome, as when the morals of the Court were indirectly criticized through the classical myth of *Semele*. Both England and the USA enjoyed and deployed the varied inheritances of the classical world, by turns senatorial and evangelical. And their leaders were usually educated enough to know precisely what they were about. They knew the sources of their own rhetoric.

Anglican religion (and in those days Protestant Christianity generally) went with the flag from Jamaica to Sydney to Simla. At the same time, Protestant Christianity did not merely follow the flag but remembered other priorities. Sometimes it was in tension with the priorities of soldiers or traders, sometimes in tension with the imperial idea itself. That is well illustrated by the tradition of protest in Victorian Britain which centred on Exeter Hall, London, and focused much anti-colonialist sentiment. Those in this tradition sought to separate Bible and Sword and represented the kind of religious and political alliance found later in the Peace Pledge Union of the 1930s and the Campaign for Nuclear Disarmament in the 1960s. Perhaps it should be remembered that it was educational institutions with roots in Victorian Christianity which nourished the largely non-violent cadres of black leaders which took over the newly independent states of Africa.

Though in Victorian England the Established Church had a rather tenuous hold with respect to regular practice, it remained a focus of affection for a large section of the English population. Indeed, at the apogee of imperial power its ecclesiastical culture was probably not far removed from the popular sense of Englishness. In his book *God and Greater Britain*, John Wolffe suggests that round about 1900 the everyday meanings popularly attached to the idea of 'Christian' probably approximated the everyday diffuse Christianity of many Anglican clergy.[1] This was not at all the old organic union of Church and society, but it did represent a consonance of attitudes between people and Church, nation and popular religious sentiment. The national idea simply acquired expression in religious form as, for example, in hymns like 'Land of our birth' and 'I vow to thee my country'. In 1913 Robert Bridges, the Poet Laureate, wrote a poem about Christmas Day which referred to the spires of English churches standing up 'straight and tall' for England.

And here we have a difference between England and the USA since the same kind of national sentiment in the USA could not possibly have attached itself to the buildings of a particular historic Church. But perhaps 1913 was, in any case, the last moment when such a sentiment could be expressed. Though in the First

---

[1] John Wolffe, *God and Greater Britain* (London, 1994).

World War following most clergy joined in the fervour of identification with the national cause, sentiment shifted from the early enthusiasms of a Rupert Brooke to the sombre reflections, and even repudiations, of Siegfried Sassoon or Wilfred Owen. In any case, as will be indicated below, the Church of England was itself coming somewhat closer to the status of a voluntary denomination, and that had important implications.

Voluntarism: A Potential for Peace

Though the first stirrings of a peace sentiment emerged in the late Middle Ages, the strongest challenge came from some of the separated groups which sprang up in the early seventeenth century, though no doubt there were also pacific humanists in the mould of the Swiss Reformer, Conrad Grebel. Baptists, for example, included a pacifist wing in the 1620s and 1630s. During the Civil War itself there was a wide range of positions, some opposed to war, some quietly expecting God's millennial Kingdom, some helping the Kingdom forward with their strong right arms. Milton himself, as the pre-eminent literary figure on the Puritan side, sketched an apotheosis of the nation under Divine Providence that eventually fed into American as well as British mythology. Milton believed that God spoke 'as his custom is' first to his Englishman.

Very soon after the restoration of the monarchy and the Church in 1660, the Quakers issued a statement declaring they would not fight either for the kingdoms of 'this world' or for the kingdoms of Christ. At this juncture the radical egalitarian and pacifist strains of dissent were gathered up in small 'sectarian' capsules. They went underground and over time their ideas gradually seeped through to the cultural surface. Yet one thing did not return at the Restoration. In the course of the Civil War, English people as a whole had acquired a dislike of standing armies that remains to this day.

As already mentioned in Chapter 2, many dissenters felt considerable sympathy for their co-religionists in the American colonies in their rebellion against the London government, and they were joined in this by many Irish and Scottish Presbyterians. But these alignments, whereby Anglicans in England and North America often tended to support the loyalist cause and Protestant 'dissenters' to support the patriot cause, were very partial. George Whitefield, for example, an Anglican clergyman deeply involved in the great awakening in North America and in the evangelical revival in England, was a major voice for the patriot cause.

The war itself was in no sense about disagreements over theological doctrines, though the patriots were, as it happens, seriously put out by British generosity towards Catholic Quebec in 1775. Naturally, preachers on both sides invoked Biblical analogies, implored divine aid and expressed gratitude for it where appropriate, and debated the application of Paul's injunction to obey the civil power. Perhaps the circumstances of the War of Independence allow us to measure a shift from the situation obtaining in 1588 when Protestant Englishmen faced the Spanish Armada. In that conflict there *were*

specifically religious issues at stake, even though intimately woven into issues of national independence.

Before continuing the history of dissent and peace
with regard to the French Revolution and the Napoleonic wars, it is worth making a brief excursion forward
to the American Civil War because it raises a further
issue of some importance. As in the case of the War of
Independence, the American Civil War was not a religious war. It was a war about the right of secession
which became also a war about slavery. But in so far as
it was a war about slavery, the anti-slavery clergy of the
North have been blamed (or credited) with being major
propagandists for its prosecution. They felt a theological issue was at stake, and preached to that effect. By
the same token, those in the South who believed otherwise took a contrary theological view. So there was an
element of theological disagreement present among the
various reasons for prosecuting the war even though the
primary reasons, especially at the beginning, had mostly
to do with national unity along with certain economic
issues. But if the cause of the North was a just one—
or became a just one—are the northern clergy to be
blamed for supporting it? Does the argument which
blames religion for causing wars include just wars?
Would Dawkins blame those clergy who supported the
Second World War, for example?

Returning to the chronological sequence, we come to
the period 1789–1815. To begin with, many English dissenters were disposed to support the French revolutionary cause. It was, after all, a sermon in support of the
revolutionaries preached in 1789 by a prominent

dissenter, the Revd Richard Price, which sparked off Burke's sombre and hostile *Reflections on the Revolution in France* (1790). But with the accelerating incidence of violence and then with the advent of Napoleon, support among dissenters swiftly diminished. More particularly among the evangelically included, there emerged a mixture of apolitical and millennial attitudes sometimes combined with expressions of loyalty to the constitution and with increasingly sombre reflections on the lamentable consequences of war. The wars ended in 1815 and dissenters, especially Quakers and Unitarians, then became prominent in the peace societies founded almost immediately in both Britain and the United States.

In the course of the rest of the century, the cause of British nonconformity and of a considerable segment of American Protestantism strongly overlapped with the peace agitations. British nonconformists were often located in the commercial classes and easily identified with the liberal view that free trade and international harmony went together. Methodism and Liberalism became very closely allied, and both contributed to a climate where peace was a major priority and where political issues were adjudged in terms of conscience. In such a climate, the notion of conscription was unthinkable, so much so that even in the First World War conscription could not be imposed until half-way through the conflict. Four million men volunteered, much encouraged in doing so by many of the clergy.

It is interesting that Herbert Spencer in his *Ecclesiastical Institutions* identified the Free Churches as carriers of peace and pacific sentiment. Certainly a case can be made out along such lines by tracing the liberal and liberal-socialist traditions which run from John Bright to Arthur Henderson and Philip Noel-Baker. If we except the periods of the Indian Mutiny, the Boer War, and the First World War when national chauvinism was very widespread indeed, the Free Churches have shown a consistent concern for peace; and for many Free Church people after the First World War, peace became the touchstone of all other issues. Traces of that preoccupation can be found in the overlap of the Free Churches with the Liberal and Labour Parties up to the present day.

Indeed, British Liberal and Labour politics have been infused with attitudes towards peace derived from religious nonconformity, even though there are today many fewer Nonconformists involved in these two parties. That once again underlines the way in which religious symbols and innovations presage developments in the political sphere. As ideas draw free from their institutional carriers, they can mutate and come to suffuse a whole culture of moral aspiration. Vegetarianism has roots in religious nonconformity and so have concerns for pure food. One could easily document a radical Protestant involvement in the original production of foods designed to promote both spiritual and physical health and wholeness: jams, soaps, cereals, chocolate, and fruit. The model communities established at Port Sunlight by Lord Leverhulme and at Saltaire by Sir Titus Salt provide exemplary anticipations of contemporary tender-mindedness. Both entrepreneurs were

Congregationalists. At Port Sunlight, William Lever not only created a model Village, with an art gallery and without a pub, but set up employee benefits, such as pensions, medical care, profit-sharing, and free insurance. There are literally hundreds of such examples of the overflow of piety in charitable innovation.

The extensive influence exercised about a century ago by the views of T. H. Green is another example of a moral atmosphere generated out of evangelical Christianity. It underpinned British liberalism, provided a prelude to the welfare state, and articulated a *Politics of Conscience*.[2] A parallel instance, bearing specifically on the peace sentiment is charted by A. L. Rowse in his study of *All Souls and Appeasement*.[3]

However, there is a further twist in the moral and political dialectic of peace and war to be traced in the context of liberal Protestantism and liberalism more generally. It arises from the hyper-moralism of some varieties of religious and secular sentiment, especially in the Nonconformist and Anglo-Saxon world but now, of course, widely diffused in the culture of ecclesiastical bureaucracy and the World Council of Churches. Hyper-moralism first of all establishes a moral viewpoint sufficiently elevated above all the concrete choices to be made in proximate situations in which it never has to pay the costs of given policies. It remains firmly ensconced in the role of moral observer and

[2] Melvin Richter, *The Politics of Conscience* (London, 1965).
[3] A. L. Rowse, *All Souls and Appeasement* (London, 1960). Cf. also G. P. Gooch, *The Life of Lord Courtney* (London, 1920) and V.de Bunsen, *Charles Roden Buxton* (London, 1948).

critic. Indeed, in relation to issues like nuclear weapons, it can actually combine a secular and religious apocalyptic in order to 'flee to the mountains', that is, to declaim concerning the likely end. At the same time, however, one never knows when this moralism may not go into reverse and demand exemplary and condign destruction of the enemy. At the point where the rapid and limited deployment of violence can avert future conflict, say in the Rhineland in 1936, it refuses to act because it is paralysed by generalized guilt. In numerous situations it refuses to recommend a viable policy based on 'practical wisdom' because it views 'the West' as somehow the deeper long-term source of current ills and therefore morally equivalent to (or worse than) whoever is the current opponent. In this way, hyper-moralism can lead to moral irresponsibility by obfuscating relevant distinctions of relative good and evil.

It is as if the ghost of Woodrow Wilson permanently haunts the councils of nations, and more especially the World Council of Churches. This is the Wilson characterized by J. M. Keynes in 1919 in his *The Economic Consequences of the Peace*. In that book Keynes traced Wilson's approach back to his liberal Presbyterianism, and no doubt were he alive today Keynes would find plenty of material with which to trace the continuing travail of Wilson's soul. The problem is that liberalism, whether Protestant or secular, can eventually recognize a situation has become irretrievable, at which point it converts limited conflict into 'a war to end all wars'. The comments on 'the Hun' by H. G. Wells in the First World War amply illustrate this particular moral temper. The polar opposite is the Panthéon in Paris: a secularized church dedicated to *la gloire* with every Christian constraint jettisoned. (But then hypermoralism is not the besetting sin of French foreign policy. France has, after all, been a Catholic country in its time and after 1685 found a very short way to deal with Protestant dissenters.)

The Established Church as Voluntary Denomination

As for the recent history of the national Church, it remains heir to natural law traditions of the 'just war', but all that matters here is to note a transition from a semi-organicist body strongly aligned with the political classes to a social condition similar to that of the free Churches. It is not an all-explanatory factor among the various cultural changes of the mid-century, including the end of empire, but it is a relevant consideration. With space and time one might trace shifts from an Anglican position which in the First World War accepted the bare possibility of conscientious objection to the appearance between the wars of a considerable pacifist minority associated with such names as Charles Raven and Dick Sheppard, and thence to a sad recognition of the unavoidability of the Second World War and the rather generalized pacific attitudes of today. Since the mid-century there has been a shift to the positions of the centre, even sometimes the centre left, and the adoption of a political ethos close to that of the welfare professions. The report dealing with the Church and the nuclear deterrent and the careful archiepiscopal comment on the Falklands War are simply markers of this change. Even in the Second World War, Archbishop William Temple commented that it was a war not for 'Christian civilization' but for a civilization which could become Christian. The distance travelled since can be measured by the fact that Coventry Cathedral offered itself for a memorial service for an animal rights campaigner, Jill Phipps, accidentally crushed by a lorry in the course of a protest, and the Bishop of Dover blessed the activities of animal rights groups assembled by Dover docks.

There are many ways in which older traditions are maintained, for example, the association of churches with ex-servicemen's organizations, the celebration of 'mateship' on Anzac Day, and the remaining ceremonies of Remembrance Day. But the tone of these is hardly triumphalist. The Churches are conspicuously reserved towards patriotic fervour and there is a distinct unease among many clergy about acting as chaplains and about State prayers. This unease manifests itself in a rejection of military metaphors based on the notion of *milites Christi*. Certainly it would have to be a very assiduous researcher who could adduce much evidence from contemporary Anglican or English Christianity to support Dawkins's contentions.

There is a web of reverberating changes here: unease about establishment, monarchy, nationalism, chaplaincies, uniformed organizations, and militant or military imagery. Parallel changes could be documented throughout Western Christianity as, for example, the report of the American Catholic bishops on peace and war, and the pronouncements of the Dutch Churches. The process of differentiation is virtually universal and contemporary evidence indicates the shifts which occur as religion ceases to be locked into the core processes of cohesion, power, and control.

These sketches are schematic and simply indicate kinds of changes, but it will be abundantly clear that the historical period when religion might plausibly be indicted as *itself* an issue about which men or monarchs might go to war is long past. Since the seventeenth century the involvement of religion in wars has been largely as one marker of national identity, though a major one. In the eighteenth century the wars between 'Protestant' England and 'Catholic' France were not *about* religion.

The extent of the shift to voluntarism and its inevitability can both be overstated. The Church retains its relation to territory and history, to national belonging and to death. These are constants which all the sometime established Churches continue to pick up and express. Even in secular Sweden one person in three attended the Lutheran State Church when the *Estonia* sank with the loss of over 900 lives. Obviously, there have been no crises in Britain comparable to those in Romania, where mass assemblages faced directly into the armaments of an oppressive government, but the same signs used in Romania—crosses, wreaths, processions, flowers, candles—are used in Britain when there are occasions of national mourning and in the course of religio-political protest.

An example of the tension between the continuing

social and psychological reality of establishment and the religious element in the culture of protest was provided by the clash over the statue recently erected to Air Chief Marshal 'Bomber' Harris outside the RAF Church of St Clement Danes in the Strand, London. The Queen Mother, as a symbol of resistance to aerial bombardment on London, unveiled the statue and ran into a protest organized by (*inter alia*) Bruce Kent. The same tension emerged at the service in St Paul's marking the successful conclusion of the Falklands War in 1982. The Church arranged the service, but insisted on the theme of reconciliation to the considerable chagrin of some members of the government. Parallel problems marked the celebration of the anniversary of 'Victory over Japan' taking place in August 1995.

Conclusion

What, then, has this argument tried to establish? First, it has aimed to show that even under the most favourable conditions, such as obtained in the United Kingdom and the United States (and perhaps also in Scandinavia and Australasia) the achievement of a peaceable temper is not easily maintained. Progress in this respect activates frustrating counterweights.

The argument has also aimed to show how a radical and peaceable universalism embodied in the foundation documents of Christianity becomes embodied in the general conditions of organic society so as to produce a symbolic suspension (or iconographic refrigeration) of radical signs in the Church at large, and a culture of experimentation among the religious orders and dissident Christian groups. However, this symbolic suspension, which is socially inevitable, and the culture of experimentation vary in form and incidence with particular social conditions, and especially they vary at the onset of modernity as differentiation takes a distinctive course in the relatively protected spaces of Britain and North America.

Under such favourable conditions radical ideas undermine the established ecclesiastical system from the 1580s onward. The institutional container of the Church, holding in the explosive materials in the Christian symbolic repertoire, becomes damaged, and there is a massive leakage of radical notions into the wider society for which dissident groups are major carriers. In England, even after the Restoration of 1660, there is a good deal of free space in which to pick up these notions, and in the culture of North America there is even more. Experiments occur in religious forms which anticipate a wider generalization into political language, and religious ideas mutate freely, often at some distance from their original institutional base. The Nonconformist conscience, for example, becomes Nonconformity and conscience.

Throughout the early phases of differentiation, religion remained in partial alliance with organicist ideologies, for example, monarchical absolutism, enlightened autocracy (or oligarchy), and secular populist nationalism. It also retained a collectivism, which may be of left or right but could be illustrated in traditions which prefer Edmund Burke to Tom Paine, James Stephen—

or William Morris—to J. S. Mill, and T. S. Eliot to Bertrand Russell. Eventually, however, all denominations acquire some of the characteristics of voluntary bodies. Though not an all-explanatory factor, this in differing degrees allows a certain amount of distinctively Christian socialization to be undertaken, able to regain some of the tensions between primitive Christianity and 'the world' of established 'principalities and powers'. The statements and ceremonies of the Established Church over the past two or three decades offer ample examples of this tension.

However, one further point has to be made, and it is that the contrast between the peaceable message of Christianity and the 'principalities and powers' is not the only relevant contrast. The problem of contemporary Christianity, in particular as represented by many of those in the international clerical bureaucracy, is not at all as Dawkins conceives it. It is rather that too much Christian comment has retired to an apocalyptic view that conceives the 'World', and especially the West, as a domain of political sin, and of pollution and violence, without trying to understand how it and all the other extant political systems actually work. The World Council of Churches has embraced this muted apocalypticism for decades. The missing category between the peace of the Gospel and the 'principalities and powers' has to be the Aristotelian notion of practical wisdom. Thus, the criticism which Dawkins might properly pursue is not the connection between religion and war but an *undiscriminating* invocation of peace and with that the neglect of a practical wisdom in political affairs. The analysis provided by Reinhold Niebuhr in the mid-century waits to be done all over again.[4]

[4] I have made this point in different ways ever since the publication of my book, *Pacifism: An Historical and Sociological Study* (London, 1965). The same point is made in a contemporary and vigorous form by John Kennedy as, for example, in his essay on 'The Church and the European model of political economy', in Jon Davies (ed.), *God and the Market Place* (London: 1993), pp. 83–110. Kennedy starts from the premise that the Church has 'an inadequate model of how society functions'. In an insightful passage, part of a defence of the social market, he refers to the Church's powerful 'instinct to allocate' based on the monarchical nature of its texts and a kind of extension from monarchy to command economy. Kennedy's own interpretation of 'the Kingdom' is one where nobody is absolutely in charge, and where people are idealistic about possibilities but canny about failings. I am grateful to John Kennedy (Secretary of the Methodist Board of Social Responsibility) for recovering the concept of 'practical wisdom' and recalling me to the argument of my early book on *Pacifism* concerning the ambivalences of liberalism.

Anyone interested in the peace stance of Continental Churches, more particularly in the Netherlands, can consult Ronald Jeurissen, *Peace and Religion: An Empirical-Theological Study of the Motivational Effects of Religious Peace Attitudes on Peace Action* (Kampen, 1992).

PART III

Signs of Peace: Christian Semiotics

5

Recapitulating the Argument in Sign Language

THE argument so far can be recapitulated in dramatic shorthand, using systematic changes in the sign language of Christianity, including its rites and ceremonies. When St Paul said he determined to know nothing but Christ and his cross he meant something rather different from what Constantine meant when he said, 'In this sign conquer.' When Christ himself said, just before his sacrifice on the cross, 'Thy will not mine be done,' his meaning was very far from what the assembled crusaders meant when they greeted the prospect of crusade with *Deus lo volt*—God wills it. Christianity remains the same through the centuries by its retention of a canonical point of reference which cannot be expunged, but it alters greatly according to who believes it and its distance from or proximity to the structure of power. The faith of an obscure voluntary group in Galilee is likely to differ from the faith espoused by a universal empire. The distance is as dramatic as between two different kinds of power and two different understandings of power. 'The Word came with power' is not a political statement.

But we fail to draw the obvious inference from this

entirely standard observation. It makes little sense to devise some balance sheet of what Christians have done in history, totting up St Francis against Louis XIV. What has to be asked is *what kind of understanding and practice of Christianity might one reasonably expect from a typical member of this or that social caste or country at such and such a period of social development?* What are recently converted Norsemen likely to make of such a faith? What will a Dutch seventeenth-century merchant facing the embarrassment of riches make of selling all his goods and giving them to the poor? This is not to say Christianity makes no difference to warriors or to merchants but it is to ask a question about how groups engage in selective readings according to time and place, social position, and the implication of religion in a social structure. Thomas of Canterbury imitated Christ in his acceptance of martyrdom but he did so within the limiting frame of feudal presumptions.

In what follows, then, I observe just four typical situations: the faith of the obscure fraternity; of the imperial cult; of the national religion; and of the voluntary group. But there is obviously a much wider range of situations into which the Christian sign of peace may be inserted and thereby acquire a particular kind of expression and ambiguity. The ironies of the sign of peace in differing situations of violence exhibit almost infinite variety. What else could one expect?

Before setting out the original deposit of faith it is useful to illustrate the maximum degree of contrast and irony. As Donald Davie has reminded us, Christianity turns on the oxymoron, the first being last, the lord being servant, God becoming Man, strength achieved in weakness, and life saved in self-giving.[1] The primary oxymoron is the warfare of the cross and the whole armour of salvation. Christianity captured the language of war for the purpose of peace. But no victory of that kind is fully secure. Recently a Serb soldier took a Croat prisoner. He then forced him to make the sign of the cross from right to left in the Orthodox manner, rather than from left to right in the Catholic manner before slitting his throat. The spectrum of 'Christian' practice runs from redemptive self-giving to slitting throats in the name of Christ. But if the original marker had not been set down outside the city wall of Jerusalem, the range of irony would never have become available. 'See how these Christians love one another' is an irony ultimately dependent on having some knowledge, direct or indirect, of the first epistle of John: 'Beloved, let us love one another.'[2]

The Original Deposit

What, then, was the original deposit of faith espoused by the obscure Galilean fraternity? It was a promise of deliverance from 'the world', the principalities and powers. Christianity proclaimed a revision of the self by

[1] Donald Davie, *The Eighteenth Century Hymn in England* (Cambridge, 1993). Cf. the working out of this oxymoron in David Martin, *The Breaking of the Image* (Oxford, 1980).
[2] First epistle of St John, chapter 4, verse 7.

a second birth; it relativized family, and State, and the aggrandisements of wealth and power by setting out the prior claims of God's Kingdom; it countered the secular orders of power and status by the Lord of all becoming of 'no reputation' and the servant of all; it advanced on the secular city by a redemptive offer of self, rejecting the sword and commending peace, forgiveness, and reconciliation; it replaced the nexus of imperial power in Babylon the Great by a New Jerusalem inhabited by all nations, tribes, and tongues.

Yet this faith became the official cult of an imperial system and the hinge of expansive empires. What had been preached by wandering artisans and fisherfolk now provided spiritual furniture for the interior lives or, at any rate, the external observances of judges, senators, and consuls. And this was the more extraordinary because Christianity lacked a jurisprudence (unless we count St Paul as a Roman jurist), and lacked also the regulative principles of everyday practical wisdom. What was missing in these respects had to be made up from the storehouse of the ancient world, including the Hebrew Scriptures. The result was ambiguity and the *double entendre*, meaning by that an established iconography or sign language which simultaneously sustained the powerful, juxtaposing them with the power of God, and subverted them by proclaiming that they, too, were under judgement. Potent ambiguity was woven into the fabric of civilization. The Virgin was both protectress of the secular city and the lowly woman who sang, 'He hath put down the mighty from their seat and exalted them of low degree.'

Christian Empire and the Middle Ages

A good example can be found in the earliest century of
the Christian empire. In a discussion of Augustine on
the 'just war', R. A. Markus illustrates the potent ambiguity that remained even after Christianity was fully
established and had faced the question of imperial
defence.[3] By this time the pacifism advocated by such
Christian thinkers as Lactantius had already been subject to a severe scrutiny, and the legitimacy of war was
widely accepted. What Augustine confronted was a contemporary tendency to fuse the roles of the emperor
with the kingship of Christ. That, in turn, implied that
the wars of Theodosius were holy wars pursued in the
promotion of a Christian empire. In confronting and
discarding such a view, Augustine retained the dialectical ambiguity donated by the foundation documents of
his faith. He related the appalling necessity of war to
the need to pursue justice and execute it both within
a society and between societies. Augustine offered a
vision of the social order which recognized conflicting
purposes, uncertainties of direction, divergent loyalties,
irresolvable tensions, and an underlying precariousness.
Warfare, and killing in warfare, had to be subject to the
standard norms governing human conduct. Thus he retained the ambiguity inserted into human affairs by the
tension between the goods of the eternal city and the
goods of the human city. The Christian icon of 'another
city' remained as a sign of a different order and of other

[3] R. A. Markus, 'Saint Augustine's views on the "Just War"' in
W. J. Sheils (ed.), *The Church and War* (Oxford, 1983), pp. 1–13.

possibilities. Through Augustine it provided a constant reference point for debate about war in subsequent centuries.

Further witness to the wide-ranging tension introduced into society by Christianity can be drawn from Peter Brown's study of *The Rise of Western Christendom* (1996). He shows how this tension still acted as a social leaven even after Christianity became established. Established Christianity both absorbed and utilized the realities of power and signalled a radical reserve towards its pride of rank, its luxury, and its inbuilt violence. Just how the absorption and the reserve found expression depended on the time, the social context, and the kind of accumulated spiritual resource locally available.

Thus in some situations in the post-imperial times described by Peter Brown, the bishop might reflect or emulate the worldly style of the powerful and himself be a man of power. His basilica and its liturgy might be religious versions of regal architecture and ceremonial. As for the Christian sovereign, he might still make triumphal entries in the old imperial manner but now in the name of the 'Lord mighty in battle'. All such Christian potentates would share the universal assumption that power and victory validated truth and it would follow that truth could extend little tolerance to 'pagan superstition'. Zeal to convert by persuasion or by force was fuelled by a sense of cultural superiority. In any case, the issue usually came down to one of brute survival as Christianized Europe faced centuries of incursion by nomadic tribes and confederations from the east.

Yet this picture of an embattled and intermittently expansive Christendom has to be qualified by the way Christian faith also pursued other priorities. Peter Brown suggests we set aside the standard notion that the Church was principally forged in the crucible of persecution and powerlessness. At the same time, it did imprint a model of relationships between the divine and the human whereby the highest was identified with those of no account through the lowly agency of Mary. All were equal in sin under God's law, in their capacity for salvation, and in sharing in Christ's victory over the demonic and fateful powers. Moreover, the Christian Church unified the hitherto disparate spheres of ceremonial, ethical conduct, and philosophical belief; and it also expended the hard-won fruits of personal discipline in gestures of mutual care and public charity. Often the bishop would act as the ombudsman of the community, administering justice and dispensing charity.

The austerities of the 'athletes of God' carried their own message of equality between rich and poor, clerical and lay. The examples set by monks and hermits were even capable of undermining the psychic security of the proud and inducing men of noble station in (for example) fifth-century Provence morally to confront the body politic by a renunciation of ease and by the way they reformed their own bodies in vesture and gesture.

Gregory the Great exemplified in his own life and

person the working of a Christian leaven in society. For the young Gregory lay people might embrace the same vocation as monks and so meet in their full force the tension of the cares of the political world and social obligation. In that context women were able to surpass men and indeed provided the unspoken model of behaviour. For Gregory the creative alternation of public eminence and personal reflection on the Gospel was taken for granted, and this meant that the interior of the soul was never fully colonized by the imperatives of politics. In his own life he moved from being Prefect of Rome to the disciplines of the monastic life and then back again to the public world of the Bishop of Rome. The ascetic disciplines of devotion bred in him a capacity to analyse the paradoxes of power and its exercise, so that in the long run the intellectual fruits of his disquiet became decisive for the whole future of Western Europe. In his view power encompassed a concern for the greatest and the least mirroring the universal and omnipotent power of God, and the merciful condescension of his Son. In this way what had been a creation of austere personal space spilled over into the practice of justice and responsibility, and the building up of peaceable consensus.

The retention of ambiguity can again be illustrated from the early Middle Ages. On the one hand the Church of the eleventh and twelfth centuries strongly disapproved of internecine conflict between lay rulers, and it could on occasion launch a holy war precisely to contain endemic conflict. On the other hand, as Elizabeth Hallam has documented, monasteries could be founded as 'war memorials' in celebration of martial victory.[4] Moreover, there was a liturgy of knighthood deriving from ninth-century Frankish roots. Elizabeth Hallam comments that the medieval Church was entirely clear in its condemnation of war, but adds that 'the special powers of the king in the church as a patron of monasteries ensured that even when ecclesiastical castigation of war was at its most emphatic, powerful lay rulers could still use religious houses, the symbols of peace and prayer, to commemorate martial victories.'[5] This clearly illustrates a continuing ambiguity and also the consequences inherent in a close and organic relation between temporal and spiritual powers such as one finds in a poorly differentiated society.

Another contrast is that between the notion of holy war and the sacred militarism which attended the crusades, and the central affirmations of the liturgy. Prayers for peace normally followed the canon of the Mass, thereby placing the desire for peace next to the most sacred moment in the rites of the Church. Of course, the strict letter of the New Testament injunctions against killing was usually restricted to subterranean groups like the Albigensians and Waldensians. According to Peter Biller, the Waldensians in the last two decades of the twelfth century extended their New Testament literalism to an absolute rejection of killing in all circumstances.[6] However, the fact that this

---

[4] Elizabeth Hallam, 'Monasteries as war memorials' in W. J. Sheils (ed.), *The Church and War*, pp. 47–58.

[5] Ibid., p. 57.

[6] Peter Biller 'Medieval Waldensian abhorrence of killing pre-c.1400' in W. J. Sheils (ed.), *The Church and War*, pp. 129–46.

outright pacifism belonged to subterranean traditions does not mean that it cannot be viewed as yet another witness to the continuing ambiguity written into Christian civilization.

The case has to be that even when Christianity was woven into a poorly differentiated society, where the roles of cleric and soldier might well on occasion be confused, and where cleric and soldier often came from the same social estate, the fundamental tension set up by the foundation documents constantly resurfaced, both in established and subterranean traditions. What is surprising is its existence, not the limited extent to which it was embraced. And it allows a further reflection about Christianity as compared with Islam, and about the ambiguities fostered in the former which are absent in the latter.

An Aside on Islam

Clearly Christianity can be read in such a way as to provide the official cult of empire or the religion of a feudal system, but it is arguable that Islam could provide a faith for such societies which was much more immediately serviceable. Each major faith creates a flexible but distinctive logic and a grammar of transformations, but the logic of Christianity lies at a greater distance from social and civilizational dynamics than Islam. The distance has to be reduced to a bearable ambiguity and irony, but there is no such necessity in Islam. Islam removes the ambiguity about the family and (to some extent) about the State, and above all it removes the stain of blood, the stigma of criminality, and the imputation of suffering and weakness from divinity. There is, as Max Weber argued, less rejection of 'the world' in Islam compared to Christianity and, therefore, less of a dialectic contrast between the peace given by faith and the regulated peaceability and enforced order of the State.[7] That need not mean that the politics of Christian civilizations operate so very differently from Islamic ones. What it does mean is that the iconography of Christianity, even when part of established Churches, creates a different kind of subversive ferment and a different kind of subterranean protest. There are no Waldensians or Anabaptists within Islam.

Christianity Appropriated by Secular Nationalism

In looking back at the early imperial period and at medieval society, we can see quite clearly the juxtapositions of temporal and spiritual power and the ambiguous counter-cultural iconography. The mosaics at Ravenna show emperor and divinity in proper proximity; the cross surmounts the medieval crown. It also surmounts the crown of the 'godly prince' in the Renaissance period. In the Anglican Church there was a time when the royal arms replaced the rood. But the ambiguity is less obvious when it comes to nationalism because we are still within hearing of its withdrawing roar, if indeed it is withdrawing.

[7] Max Weber, 'Religious rejections of the world and their direction' in H. Gerth and C. W. Mills, *From Max Weber* (London, 1948), pp. 323–59.

The most obvious sign of the subsumption of Christianity by secular nationalism is the place of the cross on the flag. What had been the cross on the crown becomes (or is joined to) the cross on the national flag of Britain or Norway or wherever. But the association of Christianity with secular nationalism need not be overt. It can occur in the USA without any such obvious symbolism or any connection between Church and State. Furthermore, Christianity is just as much part of established nationalism in Catholic countries as it is in Protestant countries with more openly Erastian traditions.

If one reads the sign language of the American republic there is a rich and complex annexation of elements of Christianity to national pride and identity. In the American Air Force chapel at Colorado Springs the central icon exuberantly exploits the ambiguity of Christianity. The chapel is dominated by a cross which is also an ascending plane of justice and a descending dove of peace. In the Episcopal church at Valley Forge, where the patriot army lingered out the dreadful winter of 1777–8, one sees the meaning of covert establishment. First the prayer of George Washington aligns the cause of the infant republic with divine Providence. Then, before the altar, there kneels a patriot soldier cradling a sword which is also a cross. 'The Battle Hymn of the Republic', written some three-quarters of a century later, deploys a parallel set of images around the theme

> As he died to make men holy
> Let us live to make men free.

Clearly, God 'marches on' in some partial lock-step with manifest destiny—as Cherokees found out.

Even today a book on *The American Religion* by Harold Bloom can argue that the American dream is drenched in faith and has generated its own specific religiosity.[8] What is more, Bloom, though a Jew and an agnostic, seems half to lend his assent to this American faith. Significantly, he claims it barely needs a cross of suffering. It is enough to possess an American gnosis of the Spirit and a promise of the millennium offered to 'this our evening land'. In this case, it seems the central sign of Christianity is sufficiently at odds with the secular faith to be dispensed with.

An interesting variant on the partial annexation of Christian signs to the ends of romantic and/or liberal nationalism is found in Norway, especially in the way its founding myth was re-used to symbolize the re-emergence of the nation in 1905. Norway is, of course, a country noted for its warrior past and its pacific and peace-making present, and both have to be reconciled within the national self-understanding. Norway also has several dissident religious traditions, mostly pietistic, which are analogous to Nonconformity in Ango-Saxon countries, and have generated the same moral temper, but they have nearly all remained within the state Church of Norway. These traditions were particularly strong in the Bergen periphery and fed into the protest against Swedish domination from 1814 to 1905. The

---

[8] Harold Bloom, *The American Religion* (London and New York, 1992).

point is important in that pietism flows in the current of national revival.

The details are complex and are bound up in regional loyalties, internal religious divisions, and linguistic variety, but the overarching charter myth is that of St Olaf and his role in the Christianization and unification of the country between the late tenth century and 1030. His predecessor, Olaf Tryggvason, was a Viking whose understanding of Christianity paralleled Clovis: for him the cross was also a sword. From 995 onwards he quite literally rammed Christianity down the throats of people who did not want it. Olaf Haraldsson (St Olaf) continued the forcible Christianization from AD 1024 onwards, but at the Battle of Stiklestad in 1030 he was defeated and almost immediately became a saint. In death in battle he achieved victory. So, in the iconography of his death and in battle, the figure of Olaf is assimilated to the Christian pattern of suffering, redemption, and resurrection, and in the church at Stiklestad the central mural, painted in 1930, portrays Christ as armed both with a sword and a lily. In other words, the annexation of Christian symbols by nationalism has generated an ambiguity and an irony parallel to that in the Air Force Chapel at Colorado Springs. We read off the equivalences: Olaf, Christ, Norway. The themes of peace and power are woven together and the result is that Christianity subverts nationalism and nationalism subverts Christianity. A rather similar annexation has occurred at the Nidaros Cathedral in Trondheim nearby, since the cathedral was restored as part of the restoration of the nation and in the process its dedication was changed from 'Christchurch' to 'St Olaf's Cathedral'. In the grounds of the cathedral stands a monument perfectly summing up the undergirding assimilation of themes: *Norskdom og Korstendom*. Nor is this assimilation confined to an emotionally extinct iconography, though the irony can hardly be missed. Every year thousands of Norwegians, irrespective of Church commitment, watch a historical play in the open air, reconstructing the myth of Olaf.

France offers yet another variant, in spite of the long history of anti-clericalism and the separation of Church and State in 1905. The two world wars created emotional wounds so deep that the Church had, once again, to be called upon to heal and redress. Thus the woman who broods over her children *morts pour la patrie* might be France, or she might be all mothers, or she might be the Virgin of the Sorrows. When De Gaulle entered Paris in 1944, the tricolour billowed from the Arc de Triomphe and the general went straight to Notre Dame, invoking *La France éternel*.

In Britain, and perhaps more specifically England, our secular nationalism generated a vernacular semi-Christianity, partly inside but mostly outside the Church. This faith reached its apogee in late Victorian and Edwardian times and achieved a terrible poignancy in the horror of the two world wars. However, this was not at all a matter of religion causing war. Religiously, Britain had more in common with Germany than with France and the lines of theological contact remain Anglo-German to this day. It was rather that religion was the one remaining language capable of framing so dreadful a collective sacrifice. The redemptive cross of Christ became that vast multitude of crosses marking the graves of those, whether truly heroes or not, whether willing or not, whether virtuous or not, whose lives were lost in battle. Death in battle was for them an all-sufficient grace, and treason or cowardice was the one damnation. And this iconography is not only to be judged ambiguous because it transferred the grace of redemption to combatants *en masse* but because it could also carry the freight of passionate religious protest against war and the pity of war. In Burghclere Chapel, the murals of Stanley Spencer show the dead of the Macedonian campaign casting down their myriad crosses before the crucified Redeemer. The same sign blesses the combatants and protests against their immolation.

In an excellent analysis, Jon Davies maintains that the Reformation contempt for medieval martyrology left Christ as the only model to frame mass immolation in the twentieth century.[9] This was the one public option available apart from total cynicism or adamant pacifism. Just as paganism had once re-imbued Catholic saints with martial valour so a secular and semi-pagan nationalism admixed the Christian faith with the comradely Calvaries of Normandy and Flanders. It even subsumed death in war to the eucharistic narrative, 'Do this in remembrance of me' . . . 'Greater love hath no man than this that he lay down his life for his friends.' Davies

[9] Jon Davies, 'Lapidary texts: a liturgy fit for heroes?' in Jon Davies and Isabel Wollaston *A Sociology of Sacred Texts* (Sheffield, 1993), pp. 26–36.

concludes that 'War memorials are in essence collective and doomed attempts at mutual forgiving between those who asked for the killing and those who did it.'[10] Perhaps our growing inability to read these poignant signs is the real disestablishment of our times, or at any rate a real parting of the ways of secular nationalism from Christianity.

Ambiguity Supplemented by Irony

The poignant ambiguity of all these examples is clear, but there is also a Swiftian irony. In English culture the irony is perhaps present as far back as Chaucer, perhaps at its most potent in the late Victorian period just when the imperial cultus of Britain had most extensively appropriated the sign language of Christianity, melding it with aristocratic Stoicism. In 1900 the use of irony and its impact depended precisely on an implicit knowledge of the embodiment of peace in the central enactments and phraseology of the Christian liturgy: *Dona nobis pacem*, 'Give peace in our time O Lord,' 'Peace be with you.' An example can best show how such an irony might work, and the one now offered derives appropriately enough from the dissident tradition of English culture. It is found in J. A. Hobson's *The Psychology of Jingoism*[11] and is a letter to the *Manchester Guardian*, written in the course of the Boer War after the writer

---

[10] Ibid., p. 36.
[11] J. A. Hobson, *The Psychology of Jingoism* (London, 1901), pp. 61–2. A later version of the same Christian irony can be found in A. A. Milne, *Peace with Honour* (London, 1934).

had heard a bishop maintain that virtue is watered by the red rain of blood shed in battle. Perhaps Swiftian laughter is a direct descendant of Gospel hyperbole and evangelical oxymoron.

To the Editor of the 'Manchester Guardian'

Sir,—I see that 'the Church's duty in regard to war' is to be discussed at the Church Congress. That is right. For a year the heads of our Church have been telling us what war is and does—that it is a school of character, that it sobers men, cleans them, strengthens them, knits their hearts, makes them brave, patient, humble, tender, prone to self-sacrifice. Watered by 'war's red rain', one bishop tells us, virtue grows; a cannonade, he points out, is an 'oratorio'—almost a form of worship. True; and to the Church men look for help to save their souls from starving for lack of this good school, this kindly rain, this sacred music. Congresses are apt to lose themselves in wastes of words. This one must not—surely cannot, so straight is the way to the goal. It has simply to draft and submit a new Collect, for war in our time, and to call for the reverent but firm emendation, in the spirit of the best modern thought, of those passages in Bible and Prayer-book by which even the truest of Christians and the best of men have at times been blinded to the duty of seeking war and ensuing it.

Still, man's moral nature cannot, I admit, live by war alone. Nor do I say, with some, that peace is wholly bad. Even amid the horrors of peace you will find little shoots of character fed by the gentle and timely rains of plague and famine, tempest and fire; simple lessons of patience and courage conned in the schools of typhus, gout and stone; not oratorios, perhaps, but homely anthems and rude hymns played on knife and gun, in the long winter nights. Far from me to 'sin our mercies', or to call mere twilight dark. Yet dark it may become. For remember that even these poor makeshift schools of character, these second-bests, these halting substitutes for war—remember that the efficiency of every one of them, be it hunger, accident, ignorance, sickness or pain, is menaced by the intolerable strain of its struggle with secular doctors, plumbers, inventors, schoolmasters and policemen. Every year thousands who would once have been braced and steeled by manly tussles with small-pox or diphtheria are robbed of that blessing by the great changes made in our drains. Every year thousands of women and children must go their way bereft of the rich spiritual experience of the widow and the orphan. I try not to despond, but when I think of all that Latimer owed to the fire, Regulus to a spiked barrel, Socrates to prison, Job to destitution and disease—when I think of these things and then think how many of my poor fellow-creatures in our modern world are robbed daily of the priceless discipline of danger, want and torture, then I ask myself—I cannot help asking myself—whether we are not walking into a very slough of moral and spiritual squalor.

Once more, I am not alarmist. As long as we have wars to stay our souls upon, the moral evil will not be grave; and, to do the Ministry justice, I see no risk of their drifting into any long or serious peace. But weak or vicious men may come after them, and it is now, in the time of our strength, of quickened insight and deepened devotion, that we must take thought for the leaner years when there may be no killing of multitudes of Englishmen, no breaking up of English homes, no chastening blows to English trade, no making, by thousands of English widows, orphans and cripples—when the school may be shut, and the rain a drought, and the oratorio dumb.

Yours &c.

A Patriot.

August 30, 1900.

As for the contemporary stage when Christianity is largely embodied in voluntary groups, I have already sketched what that involves and have also suggested that religion still retains a relationship to time and place even as it relinquishes a relationship to power and social control. There is plenty of evidence available to show the extent to which religion provides an important focus for neighbourly associations and for the maintenance of what Robert Putnam has called 'social capital'.[12] But since the concern here is with mutations of sign language, perhaps it is best to conclude with an overview of how the 'sign of peace' expressed in liturgy alters its meaning according to the kind of society in which it is embedded.

The Freight Carried by the Sign

Liturgy is the dramatic enactment of the fundamental Christian message. It is 'the gift relationship' expressed in the offer of free grace and reconciliation through the self-offering of Christ. He comes in peace to break down the partitions of difference and to inaugurate a unified kingdom of righteousness and love. However, the inauguration of the kingdom comes only as the powers of violence overwhelm the Prince of Peace and do him to death. It is then that his brokenness makes his people whole. 'Blessed is He that cometh in the name of the Lord . . .' 'Grant us thy peace.'

That is the shortest possible summary of the encoun-

---

[12] Robert Putnam, 'Bowling alone: America's declining social capital', *Journal of Democracy*, 6/1 (January, 1995), pp. 65–78.

ter of the Prince of Peace with the powers of violence and it is re-enacted throughout Christian history. But, of course, it is embedded in precisely the kinds of structural relationship just outlined. It is found in the voluntary groups in the early Church prior to establishment and in those which now exist after establishment. In between lie periods of structural implication in imperial cultus, feudal system, monarchical rule, enlightened absolutism, secular nationalism, and so on. Conditions of structural implication ensure that many of the key issues of history are filtered through the prism of liturgical enactment. Thus the question of whether the laity should receive both the bread and the wine, which was proposed by the moderate ('Utraquist') party in the Hussite revolution, carried the weight of full availability to all rather than restriction to a privileged caste. The principle is capable of constant extension outside what look like issues of ceremonial. Similarly, the controversies over Baptism in the time of Zwingli bore directly on whether Christianity is acquired quasi-automatically by right of birth in a natural community or by voluntary choice, and that issue portends the separation of Church and State, and of spiritual and temporal. Again, inside the question of whether to wear vestments, which arose in the 1570s and 1580s in England, lay differences to do with open access to spiritual power rather than an approach to God through mediation. Underlying all such issues is a problematic of individual conscience and interiority over against the authoritative, the collective, the objectified, and the consensual.

So, even the issues that are often regarded as

illustrating an *odium theologicum* have been, in terms of their historical and social structural meaning, carriers of issues of central importance to human welfare. That apart, the analysis indicates that war conducted solely for religious reasons is a relative rarity. The most obvious instances of wars with a strong religious component arise from the clash between Christians and Islam. In the course of that clash there arose a form of sacred militarism. But even the crusades were carried on for a great variety of reasons, and the same is true of the so-called wars of religion from (say) the 1530s to the 1640s. Thereafter wars occurred between ethnic groups in part defined by religion, but not between religions over matters of religious faith. In the most recent period, religion in the West has been largely a hinge of voluntary association and has mostly expressed the message of the liturgy concerning peace, goodwill, and conciliation. As argued elsewhere, it is characterized by an unequivocal peaceability, both in its local manifestations and in its public utterances.

6

The Peace Code Itself and the Inevitability of Violence

Assumptions and Presumptions

The key to any understanding of a faith is its original code. That does not mainly mean, of course, its moral rules and prescriptions but the horizon within which those rules and prescriptions are set. The fundamental rules are in large measure shared among the major faiths and turn on our mutual courtesy to each other as human beings. But rules need to be placed and situated against landscapes of signs and horizons of anticipation and aspiration. Morality has to be part of a story or stories. There has to be a pathway laid down and prescribed and some sense of a destination to be reached or a condition to be achieved. Life is a matter of departures and anticipated arrivals. It follows that religions are maps showing how we may best come and go.

It is important to set out the code because we are, after all, concerned with the social consequences of religion, and for present purposes of one religion in particular. We cannot ignore its central message. If the message declares beyond all doubt that the kingdom of God does not come by violence, we have to identify a sub-text where that injunction is subtly reversed. Or else we have to identify the special circumstances under which those who profess peace will, in fact, practise violence. From everything that has been said so far these special circumstances occur when religion becomes virtually coextensive with society and thus with the dynamics of power, violence, control, cohesion, and the marking out of boundaries. These are permanent characteristics of all societies of any size, however much such characteristics vary in rigour and in form. So the questions to be asked are very simple. First, what happens to a code of non-violence when joined to a society where violence is inherent? Second, what elements in the code will lend themselves to reinterpretation and reversal? That second question can be rephrased. How will a code which contradicts a given social reality be supplemented by other material more suitable to such requirements?

A religious code has two sets of elements, one set necessary and having to do with the fundamental options of social organization, the other set metaphysical and having to do with fundamental attitudes to the world, or what Max Weber rather oddly called 'religious rejections of the world and their direction'.[1] The first set involve options between authority and equality, representation and participation, closure and open access, focused authority and dispersed authority, locality and universality. The second set involve options between

[1] Max Weber, 'Religious rejections of the world and their directions' in C. Wright Mills and Hans Gerth, *From Max Weber* (London, 1948).

transcendence and immanence, law and grace, and differing approaches to suffering. The two sets meet in the
question of how the community of faith relates to the
natural community, and how the City of God relates to
the City of Man. Both are crucial for what follows.

The options which relate to social organization
such as authority and equality naturally cut across the
boundaries of religion and politics. Politics, like religion, is a field structured by different ways of relating
authority and equality, closure and access, and so on.
What remains deeply problematic is the relationship
between their religious expression and their political
expression. My own position is clear; it is that religion
can prefigure the political realization of these options in
the symbolic realm, but there remains an irreducible
religious realm of transcendent possibilities that cannot
be straightforwardly realized on the plane of politics.
Religion erects symbolic platforms in consciousness,
above all the protected sacred texts, and conducts
miniature experiments in social living which anticipate
and reflect (or are analogous to) realizations in politics.
The Benedictine Order, for example, devised an early
experiment in democracy; the Oneida Community conducted a late experiment in communal sexuality. In neither case was religion some illusory shadow merely
waiting to acquire its true social substance. But why is
the transcendent lake of religious power partly suspended behind a protective dam rather than released
and dispersed along the irrigation channels of society?

For one thing, the plenitude of possibilities cannot all
be realized at once: every alternative, even in the best of

all possible worlds, imposes its opportunity cost. For another, there are conciliations and harmonies, and a vision of complete humanity, simply beyond the capacity of the political realm to deliver. They live in the sign language of liturgy. Above all, they live in the signs of the Presence which evoke the response of worship. Presence signifies Plenitude.

Yet, there is a common dynamic or pressure shared by the two realms which is the persistent human struggle to secure peace, to acquire access, to institute equality and ensure that communication takes place as far as possible between persons of equal worth and dignity. This presence provides the dynamic of successive transformations. But each transformation encounters its own specific, inbuilt opportunity costs and is by no means a simple possibility. It goes without saying that opportunity costs will be related to the social circumstances of the time and place. It is central to the whole project of the human sciences.

The Code: Putting Matters to Rights

Concerning the nature of the code, Christianity has to be asked to speak for itself. I say 'asked' to speak for itself because a faith can appear to be a somewhat opaque and incoherent jumble, when in fact it embodies a supple but precise socio-logic with its own characteristic forks and branches. The horizon set up by a faith derives from a unique, discrete angle of vision, and there is a strictly limited number of such angles. For example, John Bowker explored this limited number of angles in relation to the problem of suffering, but the same is true of the relation of the sacred realm to whatever is defined as 'the World'.[2] These fundamental angles of vision, these basic grammars, do overlap, and we observe similar contents at the point of overlap. But the meaning of those contents is donated by the unique and distinctive angle of vision.

If we come closer to the Christian cluster of motifs and signs, what do they imply about the internal dynamic governing their transformations? They imply that liturgy arranges signs, pointers, and markers in order to put ourselves and the world to rights. The pointers are not simply inert indications but storehouses of power, since what they indicate is already implicitly present. Gestures and enactments half-create what they intend. The placing of hands in gestures of offering and reception is part of an enactment of the gift. It resembles the making and signing of a solemn treaty or compact. After all, the shaking of hands is a large part of the process of pacification and conciliation. Amity has to be initiated and concluded in the symbolic realm.

If the dynamic of liturgy is a setting to rights then that will be achieved in several dimensions. Past, present, and future need to be reconciled; so, too, do the wrongdoer and the wronged, who are simultaneously the same person in both roles as well as different persons. Moral aspiration needs reconciling with moral failure, and justification with a sense of sin. All lesions and wounds, external and internal, need to be put to rights. And this

[2] John Bowker, *Problems of Suffering in Religions of the World* (Cambridge, 1970).

can best be done by each of the wounded being ushered by others of the wounded to the point of delivery or the pool of healing and there bathed in the restorative powers of Being itself. Since each must carry the other, liturgy cannot be fully achieved in isolation. If priesthood is to be pared down to its essentials, it is a shepherding of the hurt down the steps to a pool of Siloam at the moment when the angel stirs the waters.

This may seem a rather devotional and idealized way of putting it, but if we put a question to Christianity the answer must come from within its own resources. There is no higher language into which images may be translated and so acquire their proper clarity. All that is possible by way of elucidation is significant and pointed juxtaposition, accompanied by the rubric: watch carefully to see how it connects. The imagery is itself clear and cumulative. As Deutero-Isaiah puts it: every one that is thirsty is invited to come to the waters. All those who are diseased are invited to descend the steps to the pool. The crowd that stands by the river-bank is asked to walk into the river and be carried across from death to life and from darkness to light. The woman standing by the well is offered water which will slake her thirst even for eternal life. The gestures of sacrament and the images of hymn and of scripture are of being covered, recovered and purified, and made whole. They are all in the active-passive tense: cast your burden elsewhere and you will find it already lifted. Take my yoke upon you: my yoke is easy and my burden is light. You are commanded, but it is for you to pick up your bed and walk. None of this need be understood as external magic but as alteration and redress by the power of the gesture and the sign: active beneficence and potent benediction.

All these images and get-well messages are addressed to one end: peace and the offering of the perfect gift. The gap in the Man–God relationship can be closed by the perfect gift which, since you yourself do not possess it, is placed in your hand. The wounded do not have it in them to offer a perfect gift. They need only stretch out their hands to show they want to recover. Liturgy, then, is the placing of the perfect gift in their hands to heal their wounds and relieve their distresses. This fundamental gesture of pacification is accompanied by its own recitation, about how the offering of the perfect gift was first initiated. As the gift is given, the foundation story of gift-giving has to be told: how He that was rich became poor that the poor might be rich, and how He that was whole became mortally wounded that the mortally wounded might inherit eternal life. This recitation expresses the true cost of the gift and shows that the gap cannot be closed unless the true cost is fully accepted and paid. Nothing is for nothing: free grace was bought by self-giving. There is no peace without a terrible encounter on the battlefield of the spirit.

So, here we see an imagery of battle transferred to the realm of the spirit, but capable of migrating back to the material world. *Pange Lingua*, sing my soul the glorious battle; *Vexilla regis*, the royal banners forward go. The material meaning of war has been reversed and put at the service of peace. But what has been reversed once can be reversed again. *Deus lo volt*: God wills it. The crusaders put up their bright swords and set out for an earthly Jerusalem. The pacific *milites Christi* spring up again as armed men. Thousands of allied soldiers stand on a battleship in the Pacific embarking for actual war, and singing 'Onward Christian Soldiers'. It happened in 1942 and it *was* a just war. But the meaning of the sign had migrated, because these were real soldiers. Crosses stand in Dresden: the sign of the battleground of redemptive love is now a sign of irredeemable loss and the futility of war. The meaning has migrated again. In 1995 on the fiftieth anniversary, candles are carried to those Dresden crosses as signs of returning life and reconciliation: part of the original meaning has returned.

All enactments and gestures to secure the perfect gift are made in order to bring peace. According to the Christian narrative, there is an aboriginal enmity set up between humans and a turbulent alienation which has radically reduced our access to the resources of life, love, and peace. So what is given in liturgy is a sign of peace, a Pax or a *Pax vobiscum*, asking for a response: 'And with thy Spirit'. For that matter, *shalom* and *salaam* also lie at the heart of Judaism and Islam, though differently framed. Once peace is offered and received, through the medium of the One who *is* our peace, all those present are incorporated as brothers and sisters. They are renamed as part of a spiritual family. All are brothers because the ill will of the brother who murdered a brother has been replaced by the goodwill of the Son who gave his life to make all bondmen into sons and heirs. They may now enter once again into the

Paradise Garden, walk by the healing stream, and eat of the fruit of the tree of life.

But, of course, the deep recalcitrance remains and even the signs of new life may be partly expropriated and the perfect gift temporarily compromised. Perhaps elaboration has destroyed the simple efficacy of the gesture; perhaps the priestly shepherds who conduct the wounded to the pool have begun to restrict access; perhaps the powerful have established privileged rights over grace; perhaps some who might participate have become dehumanized and rendered of no account and so have become absences; perhaps the act of giving has been impaired by being made mechanical or external or even magical. So, one way or another the gift has been in practice cancelled by the manner of giving, and can only be restored by a return to the foundation story written as authoritative scripture beyond erasure. And that return will depend on facilitating social circumstances, since internal dynamics have to take off from bases in external conditions, even though they help shape those conditions. Diseases in the body politic have an intimate relation to diseases in the body of Christ. The diseases in the body politic which complement and interact with diseases in the body of Christ can be of many kinds. It might be that part of a population is deprived of legitimate anticipations in the sharing of goods and this is reflected in restricted access to the Lord's Table. Or it might be that there is a tide of rising expectations that expects all the good things of the Kingdom of God now, and so bypasses the Lord's

Table. Not everything can be had now. Humans may for brief precious moments experience their own wedding feast at Cana or their own last supper when the true Vine is present and received by all the guests, but these moments cannot be prolonged and made part of the everyday economy of the sacrament. They are given against a background of the dissipations of time, the reality of deterioration, and the fragility of all hopes. They are just singular hours of feasting when the heavenly banquet enjoys a real presence without necessarily requiring invocation or explicit liturgical setting.

So the fullness of the sign is normally placed in reserve on the other side of time. And the pressure of time on the present will vary a great deal. Sometimes we will be safely ensconced in a congenial liturgical rota; sometimes time will press very hard, announcing the urgency of the Kingdom. The Kingdom of Heaven is 'at hand'. But the Kingdom in its fullness always remains eschatological, glimpsed or overheard in music but never fully realized and emptied out into human history. If it were, then religion, according to the New Testament, would become otiose. The Son would have delivered the Kingdom up to the Father, and the Lamb would be there in the centre of the city, taking the place of the Temple.

The Offer of the Gift of Peace

Supposing we revert to the image suggested earlier of Pentecost as not simply the assembling of disciples but the coming together of all the combustible material of

Christianity and its catching fire. The material catches fire and obliterates all the normal boundaries of language and local identity. But then, Christianity has once more to be contained, for its own conservation and for the safety of society. The Church becomes as much the lightning conductor as the lightning, reducing the tension between the Kingdom of God and the kingdoms of this world. The shut-off power now reaches the mundane world either by underground sectarian transmission or else because the sign language of original Christianity cannot be erased from the iconography of the Church. The signs are only partly expropriated: they also infiltrate and are there to be picked up as conditions and situations give them relevance. And that would be the core of any sociological understanding: situations come into being which bring alive particular elements in a symbolic repertoire and those elements then help shape these situations.

We can now reconstruct the Christian narrative around the theme of the Perfect Gift. We can see how that relates to the migration of the Christian signs away from geography and biology, from an earthly Jerusalem and a birthright membership, to a Jerusalem which is above and a baptism in the spirit. And we can see, too, how the Christian signs migrate *back* to geography and biology, that is, to place and to the continuity of the generations. The parish and the diocese never disappear.

The migration begins in a new Exodus which crosses a dangerous and deadly sea from captivity 'to the powers' to resurrection on the further shore. What had been under the old dispensation a migration to a land becomes under the new dispensation a migration from the land; what had been a forty-year sojourn in a real wilderness becomes a testing pilgrimage through a barren spiritual landscape. Geography becomes biography.

In the same way, what was given biologically at birth and marked on the body by circumcision becomes a spiritual event in biography marked by the gentle gesture of baptism. Whereas the people of the Jews crossed old Jordan to gain a land of milk and honey, so the New Man stands in the waters and receives a baptism in the spirit to gain a heavenly kingdom. He or she is no longer linked simply to the family of generation but has founded a fraternity of those regenerated in the spirit. The twelve families of Israel are now every family under heaven, all named by God. Naturally, the twelve disciples half misconceive their mission as really to the twelve tribes. They believe it is their destiny to sit on twelve real thrones. They do not know the true spirit animating their mission because they recognize all the similarities between the old dispensation and the new, and miss the essential differences.

And that being the case they do not quite grasp the meaning of entering into Jerusalem meekly and riding on an ass. Originally King David took Jerusalem and made it his capital by force of arms, but the Son of David seeks to take Jerusalem by spiritual conquest and sheds tears as He foresees His rejection. The cry in the Book of Lamentation, 'Jerusalem, Jerusalem, turn to the Lord your God'—*convertere ad Dominum Deum Tuum*—becomes 'Jerusalem, Jerusalem how

often would I have gathered you . . . but you would not.'
This city is not taken physically to fulfil a destiny, but
offered a choice. However, it is inevitable that the
choice will be refused. The city cannot accept what belongs to her peace. She belongs to the realm of violence
and is established, as are all cities, on power and violence. From the viewpoint of the city an unarmed man
walking towards its gates is barely a threat, let alone a
promise. Jerusalem cannot receive what will in the end
set her aside and make her redundant and ensure that
God is worshipped neither in Jerusalem nor on Mount
Gerizim but anywhere in spirit and in truth. The physical destruction of the Temple is as nothing compared
with the erasure of the idea of the sacred place. It is no
wonder then that the Dome of the Rock is now superimposed on the site of the Temple, since the universal faith
of Islam retains the old relation to the whole natural
community, to biology, to circumcision, and to the
sacredness of the place.

The terrible conclusion at Golgotha of the migration
from Galilee to Jerusalem reverses the triumphant conclusion of the migration from Egypt to Israel: 'He came
unto His own but His own received Him not.' And this
refusal is not simply of the people of the Jews or the city
of Jerusalem but of the whole world of the *polis* and
politics. The constitution of the political world is inherently dependent on the arrogation of power, on the
deployment of violence, and on the physical defence of
borders and boundaries. What is unbounded will be
expelled and obliterated outside the city wall. The violence that lies in the foundation stones of the city will be

visited on the body of the Saviour. He came from the outside, from a remote and unconsidered region, and will be immediately cast outside and hung on a gibbet. The sign of peace will have become a sign of what violence has to do and will do. This is a necessity; it is written. 'The Son of Man goes as it is written of Him.' The Saviour who comes from the mountains with the gospel of peace must be the scapegoat cast out from the human community, despised and rejected of men. His broken body will be the first foundation stone in a new universal city, and the figure of the scapegoat will be built into the fabric of its banners and icons. *Vexilla Regis prodeunt*: the royal banners advance on a *New* Jerusalem.

The new citizens of the universal city are about to separate from all those whose birthright membership is in Israel and in Rome. The new cell first implanted in the body of Mary by the operation of the universal spirit has constituted the body of a universal Humanity through the Representative Man, cast outside the particular city to found the universal city of all nations, tribes, and tongues. The new fire crossing all borders at Pentecost speaks to anyone who may hear, whether from Cilicia or Cyrenaica or anywhere to 'the ends of the earth'. The Representative Man is the first among many brethren bound together in unbounded fraternity, all of whom have been baptized again out of the natural community and regenerated in the Spirit.

But this unbounded fraternity must also have its own boundary, between those who live within the old city and those who seek a city which is to come. There is bound to be mutual hostility all along that boundary, and even incomprehension, because the similarities on either side of the border will be so striking and the difference so total. Warnings are posted up about the dangers of cross-border institutions. The new border will require defending, partly because the life and integrity of the new cell is constantly at risk in its early stages, partly because it has no existence in biology or geography. It lacks any natural defendability or any of the weight of ordinary time and place. It is opening dangerously onto a new time outside the ordinary rotating temporalities of the local and natural community. Indeed, it announces by anticipation that their time is at an end. This is, symbolically, the end-time for the family and the nation, because a break has been made by those born not of the flesh or the will of man but of God. So the promise in St John about the shift from physical birth to spiritual birth foreshadows the end of the current world order. It is inherently eschatological because 'The former things have passed away.'

This is no ordinary time. An explosion has occurred, cracking all the old categories of time and place in order to establish the new dispensation of universal love, separated out from the dispersed communal solidarities of the Jewish diaspora (though drawing on the diaspora for recruits) and also separated out from the political world order of imperial Rome. That border of love, so carefully manned because so difficult to maintain and so newly drawn, will attract intense pressure from the established cities of Jerusalem, Athens, and Rome. That pressure will unleash such insane terror that New

Jerusalem will only emerge after a holocaust of pain and suffering in which it must appear that the evil powers have gained control and have free rein to shed the blood of the saints and to tread the grapes of wrath. The new time of the New Jerusalem can only be ushered in by a time of troubles, revealing the horrors that always lie in wait. The earthly city is Babylon the Great, and the powers of the evil *polis* are not the authorities in Jerusalem at the margin of empire, dealing with a tiny dissident fraternity at the margin of Israel, but the central powers at the heart of the world imperium. Just as Pharaoh set out to take back the escaping Israelites, so the Emperor harrows and terrorizes the liberated saints.

But this is not the final trial of the new and peaceful city. After all, ordinary clock time continues according to the imperial calendar, and does so for another five hundred years. Even AD is not yet. The proper strategy of Babylon the Great is to confiscate the powers of the New Jerusalem by converting them to her own use. The cross might be made the sword of state, in which case the sign of the scapegoat might be expropriated by the sign of the king. *In hoc signo vinces*—in this sign conquer—could then be used for victory in real physical warfare and peace itself would be defeated. Christianity would be incorporated in the kingdom of violence and the saying 'the kingdom comes not by violence' rendered of no effect. The sword of the spirit will now be a real sword and the helmet of salvation a genuine helmet. The imagery captured by Christ from the powers of this world will be restored to them and they will be equipped by the physical armour of light. They can, in due course, set out to aid the cross with the cross on their shields once more to capture a real Jerusalem. The city into which the unarmed man entered, only to be expelled as a scapegoat and killed, can now be forcibly entered by a Christian empire and its faithless infidel inhabitants slaughtered in the name of Christ. The cross will now be on the flag and the flag raised over the city with the image of the Virgin. The words of Fortunatus great hymn *Vexilla regis*—'The royal banners advance'—which once accompanied the cross into sixth-century Poitiers, capture precisely this ambiguity: triumphal entry or redemptive humiliation. The humble Hebrew maiden is now Our Lady of Victories. When she fails to protect Constantinople many of her servants desert her. There is no icon for Our Lady of defeats. For that one must return to the humble mother by the cross: *Stabat mater dolorosa.*

So, the earthly king will place his image on the mosaic next to the King of Kings and the Good Shepherd of souls, and the humble Eucharist will be assimilated by the courtly ceremonies of Constantine's empire. A Justinian will now erect a new Temple to the Divine Wisdom, Sancta Sophia, in a new earthly Jerusalem, and cry 'Solomon, I have surpassed thee.' But Solomon will only have been surpassed architecturally; in terms of spiritual dispensation, he will partly have returned and converted the body of Christ once again into the body politic. But only *partly*: that is crucial. The return of the old dispensation is not complete.

It is important to remember that the secular is not *necessarily* Babylon the Great, and not *merely* the arena of violence, power politics, confusion, and blood-letting. There is a viable secular city, nurse of sciences and arts and home of a proper civility. The Christian city is not an impossibility. Christianity itself inserts into the Christian city the knowledge that its promise is other than its performance. That is why the images of the Virgin and the statues of Christ crowning the city are so often clouded in a distinctively Christian irony. At the same time, the seed of blood is at work in civilizations as well as in voluntary groups. Precisely when the blood of death-dealing violence has sunk into the stones the blood of life-giving sacrifice is memorialized and celebrated. That too has to be explored. As Auden put it, 'Without a cement of blood (it must be human, it must be innocent) no secular city may safely stand.'

Of course, this new earthly Jerusalem and this new earthly temple can be rebuilt anywhere, in central Africa, or seventeenth-century London, or even Utah. Any Christian group, defending itself or, indeed, setting out on colonizing adventure, can be another Chosen and Elect People. Boston, Massachusetts, can be the City 'set on a hill which cannot be hid'. From now on conversion, which had been the transmission of a new Spirit, can be achieved by automatic biological membership in a Christian nation, or can be accomplished *en masse* by mere command of the King: Birinus of Wessex, or Charlemagne in Aachen, or Philip the Second in Nueva España, or the Tsar of all the Russians progressing toward the eastern shores of Kamchatka.

The holy family can now be set up to secure the continuity of the generations under the aegis of the Virgin Mother herself.

This means that there is now available a double reading of all the images, a *double entendre* or symbolic whispering gallery working throughout Christian civilization. That civilization is informed by *both* Testaments, since both represent valid principles: spirit and body, universality and locality, fraternity and family, the eschatological break and the continuities and rotations of time. Indeed, the New Testament will retain the Old, and the Old anticipate the New. Baptism will henceforward be read simultaneously as a spiritual choice to enter into the waters of 'death to sin' and resurrection to life, *or* as the conferment of a status from the store of grace held in trust by the Church. Which reading asserts itself will depend on the social circumstances, and as the Church emerges as a voluntary group, the Christian meaning will recover something of its original salience. Baptism will no longer be subject to Kierkegaard's accusation of being Christianized circumcision. In the same way, the cross as the sign of peace will lose some of its absorption in the systematic kingdom of violence, though (given that violence and power are in fact inherent) it will be read both as a sign set over the city next to the proper signs of power *and* as a sign outside the city set over against the misuse of power. The figure of the scapegoat and the outsider will constantly be read as standing for all those in any way excluded from full citizenship. All signs will retain the potential of their New Testament meaning. They will be partly incorporated by the institutional powers, partly stand outside as the power of the spirit. They will help ensure that no city of Man is unequivocally identified as a city of God on earth. Jerusalem remains 'above', in the last resort untranslatable into a set of human social relationships and also beyond time. The icon of the heavenly feast by staying 'above' protects all earthly eucharists from being dissipated and converted without remainder into the everyday, and so finally destroying the reserve powers of the spirit and the dialectic pressure of the kingdom.

What, then, of the Eucharist? How is it to be read, as the complement and completion of the Baptism? The imperial reading is clear. The priesthoods control access. They open and close the gates of grace, because they have confiscated the keys of the Kingdom. Look up at the dome of St Peter's and read their claim to control the keys. This is not to say that priests are unnecessary. They too are constitutive of the social world and guard the treasury of images and signs, ensuring their availability and even controlling some of their radical power to disrupt. The sign of violence still present in the imperial eucharist is to be located in the political way it interprets the invitation 'Compel them to come in.' Forcing people in means the border of the spiritual Church has been moved dangerously close to the border of the physical kingdom. The American Indians will be forcibly converted by the Spanish and sometimes enslaved as well, in spite of the lonely protests of Fra Bartolomé de Las Casas and a few other missionaries and protagonists of natural law. The moral sanctions of the original voluntary group are now virtually fused with the compulsory powers of the natural community. After all, the Roman Catholic Church is now in its Constantinian condition. It is the Holy Ghost of the Roman Empire, and the Holy Father has become a variety of Pontifex Maximus, a temporal father as well as a Father in God. This, again, means that the Eucharist is under the control of the Father but, nevertheless, the Christian meaning can still be read, because the sacred fathers are not the elders of the people, not wise ancients, not biological fathers. They cannot but represent the powers of the Son. The Fathers protect the revolution of the Son in spite of themselves.

In the same way, the Eucharist cannot really be erased as a sign of peace, or obscured as a genuine Pax. The Eucharist represents the perfect gift offered to bridge the alienation between man and God (expressed in loss of access to the Garden) and between man and man (expressed in the felling of one man by another). It restores all these relationships to perfection. The Eucharistic sacrifice represents the cost of love's unarmed appeal to the city and of what followed from the rejection of the sign of the peace. Violence breaks the body of the Representative Man. And this is always understood because everyone knows what has happened. It is general knowledge. It corresponds with universal experience and cannot be obscured by any degree of expropriation whatever. It follows that all the ordinary citizens of the city are able to become a brotherhood by a sharing in the broken body and the shed blood. They are made whole and peaceful again by absorbing and imbibing its brokenness and its violence. They are simultaneously those who have committed the violence and those who are made whole by the perfect gift and the sacrifice. In a similar way the Victim is both priest and victim: offered and offering.

The citizens do not need to accept the perfect gift any more than they need accept regeneration by baptism in the spirit. They belong to a community called to a free response. The response is to the perfect costly gift and to the free offer of a grace which 'has cost not less than everything'. They are the People of God celebrating their Christian liberty and freedom of the Spirit, not the Chosen People celebrating their Exodus from the land of bondage. So the milk and honey of the Promised Land in the old dispensation have become the bread and wine of the new. They drink it anew with the Son who is the first born of many in the Father's Kingdom. The imagery of that Kingdom is an imagery of a peace not secured by violence, a country ruled by the vulnerable Child and the broken Man. Henry Vaughan put it in the imagery of war converted to the uses of peace:

> My soul there is a country
> Afar beyond the stars
> Where stands a winged sentry
> All skilful in the wars.

> If thou canst get but thither
> There grows the Flower of Peace
> The Rose that cannot wither
> Thy fortress and thy ease.

Coda[3]

What has just been provided is the symbolic logic of Christianity as it is transformed under social pressure. But it would be possible to offer many much closer readings with specific reference to the canonical text of the Bible. So what follows now is a short coda tracing the fundamental logic of Christianity from particular Biblical sources. I take a passage from the Old Testament and parallel passages from the New and aim to show that we exaggerate the contrast between the two Testaments. Judaism in the Old Testament (or Hebrew Scripture) is already pregnant with universalism, if not with the Christian version of it.

The two scriptural reference points are the Book of Jonah and chapters 10 and 11 of the Book of the Acts of the Apostles. These run precisely in parallel and establish the peaceable logic of universalism. The point of the humorous tale of the whale is that Jonah (literally little 'dove' or 'son of truth') is commanded to go east to Nineveh, which is the chief city of the imperial power currently oppressing the 'people of God'. Jonah is to give the people of Nineveh a stern warning of God's judgement on account of sin. However, Jonah's own will is quite contrary to God's. He fears what may befall him in Nineveh and decides instead to go in a diametrically opposite direction, taking the sea route west to

---

[3] The following treatment of Jonah is much indebted to James Ackerman, 'Jonah', in Robert Alter and Frank Kermode (eds.), *The Literary Guide to the Bible* (London, 1987), 234–43.

Tarshish. The city of Tarshish symbolizes a chaos located at the furthest margin of God's sovereignty.
Clearly Jonah is now (literally) embarked on a downward course: he 'goes down' to the seaport of Joppa, he
enters the 'innermost parts' of the ship, he sinks into a
deep sleep, and ends up (or down) in the furthest deep
of the sea where the cavernous maw of the whale awaits
him. He is now about as low as he can get. This is sheer
hell, as he clearly realizes, but (as the Psalmist also says)
even in hell man cannot escape God. God is everywhere
and his temple and salvation are always available.

In the Providence of God, the whale violently ejects
Jonah after three days (a symbolism later embraced by
Jesus concerning his own burial and resurrection) and
Jonah again hears the Word of God telling him to go
east. This time he takes care to do as he is commanded.
He goes east and delivers his message to the Gentiles of
Nineveh. They repent with almost comic alacrity, they
and their cattle, and they *stop the violence.* By so doing
they have passed from judgement to mercy, which it so
happens is very annoying to Jonah because it makes him
look silly and he expects God to be consistently judge-
mental, especially perhaps to foreigners. (At this point
it is worth remembering that Jesus in St Luke, chapter
11 verses 29–32, points out that it is the *Jews* who will
receive 'the sign of Jonah', that is, the sign of judgement, and that it is the people of Nineveh and Ethiopia
who are more open to signs of mercy.)

The dramatic point of this Gentile repentance, which
even goes so far as to clothe the animals in sackcloth
and ashes, is the contrast it makes with the attitude of

God's own People. There is an obvious contrast between the prompt response of Nineveh and the stiff-necked resistance of Judah. That is particularly evident, for example, in Jeremiah, chapter 36. Like the people of Nineveh, the people of Judah receive a warning of condign judgement by the stammering mouth of the prophet Jeremiah, but written on a scroll. But unlike the King of Nineveh, the King of Judah takes his penknife, cuts up the scroll, and casts it on the fire.

Here, then, we have a humorous satire which criticizes the particularism of an Ezra or a Nehemiah. Jonah is a tale of the essential unity of Jew and Gentile in relation to God's judgement and mercy. There is a message of peace between man and man, man and God, and the people of Nineveh 'stop the violence'.

The Book of the Acts, chapters 10 and 11, offers a direct parallel to the Book of Jonah, because it shows a Christian Jew, Peter, hesitating about the universal scope of redemption and therefore about the relevance of Jewish law concerning separation, food, social distance, and circumcision. The symbolic focus in this case is food (whereas for Paul it is circumcision).

In the course of the dramatic dialogue of Jew with Gentile, Peter preaches a sermon in which he sets out the basis of redemption as pacification and forgiveness through the Passion of Christ (who submitted Himself to be murdered by the unjust) and through His Resurrection. The key text here is chapter 10, verse 35, concerning 'the good news of peace by Jesus Christ'. This peace complements the attitude of peaceability recommended in the Sermon on the Mount (St Matthew, chapters 5–7) and the beatitude pronounced on the peacemakers, but it is more comprehensive because it negotiates and establishes peace between Jew and Gentile, man and man, man and God.

The meaning of this is immediately illustrated in the parallel pages of the Acts of the Apostles where Peter the Jew encounters Cornelius the Roman. In one way Cornelius takes the role of the people of Nineveh, but he is an active seeker after God who sends messengers to Peter on his own account to find out the truth. The question of particularity and universality is firmly in focus. Even while the messengers are on their way, Peter is on the roof terrace of a tanner's house in Joppa and, being both sleepy and hungry, he has a dream of food. In this dream the food is of *every kind*, but Peter feels he cannot eat because it is against the law of his people. At that point God speaks to him and confirms the unity of all creation. Nothing God has made is to be rejected. And the same clearly applies to the approaching meeting with Cornelius. There is now no separation between Cornelius and Peter because 'all are one in Christ.' There is one God, one creation, one humankind, and it immediately follows that the one holy spirit can fall on everyone alike. At this point, Jews and Gentiles are baptized together, they speak in the universal tongue of Pentecost and unite in receiving the Spirit.

What takes place in Acts 10 and 11 by way of filling out and realizing Jonah's message in a Christian form is summarized in the second chapter of Paul from Rome (itself a latter-day Nineveh) to the Ephesians. Christ is 'our peace', who has abolished 'the enmity' in his own body, erased the category of stranger and foreigner, and joined the conflicting parties in a single citizenship. Glossing that from the rest of the New Testament, it means that Christ in His human vulnerability as the image of God embodied in our flesh, has taken the full force of violence and thereby neutralized and reversed it. The 'cost' is written on his face and his outstretched hands. His—and our—restored and resurrected humanity bears the scars of the spiritual warfare with violence and takes them 'up' into God Himself. Therefore, 'Christ *is* our peace.'

There remains just one sociological comment on this pattern of buying back or recovering human being and unity by taking the force of the violence. It is that once you break down the barriers between groups (tribes or nations or whatever) you must logically create a further barrier or boundary between those who accept this way and those who do not. Thus universality itself sets up a boundary. When Christianity inaugurates a voluntary fraternity (and sorority) outside the territorial 'grounding' of the natural biological group it sets a myriad counterweights in motion. The announcement of peace sets off a profound tension.

Furthermore, there is more than one solution to the problem of peace and universality, though the various solutions can probably be arranged in a limited set. Each member of the set exhibits a coherent logic, and not (as Dawkins seems to believe) a collection of arbitrary and mutually contradictory pre-scientific illusions. The logic of Islam, for example, represents a recovery in its canonical texts (and not, as in the Christian case, in

later adjustments) of the involuntary 'territorial' principle, together with the acceptance of collective force.
As such it can be seen as a built-in and inevitable recovery of 'social nature' and a potent counterweight to
Christianity. Islam aims to include all 'Ummanity'
under the same universal law, and is therefore on a
collision course with the other principal paths to universality, not only Christianity and Buddhism but liberal Enlightenment and Marxist Enlightenment. The
great world religions together with the two or three
secular universalisms (themselves metamorphoses of
religious logic) are all mutually irreconcilable. To that
extent the aspiration to peace is itself a source of conflict. Secular ideologies, like religions, find themselves
fighting for peace, and their rival semiotics richly illustrate precisely that paradox. We are all of us trapped in
the paradox of 'wars to end wars'. It is our human
condition.

PART IV

Religion and Politics

7

Politics and Religion: Complementarities and Differences

IN giving an account of the Christian code I tried to lay out the theo-logic and the socio-logic behind the text 'The Kingdom comes not by violence.' The Lord tells his servant Peter to 'put up' his sword and explains that his servants do not fight. At the very least, this suggests that Dawkins's theory of the inherent bellicosity of religion is the reverse of what the Gospels actually teach, and Dawkins would need to explain why this is so. There is, after all, not a ghost of a suggestion that the Gospel should be spread by warfare. There is, of course, God's judgement on those who do not recognize the presence of the Kingdom in the imprisoned, the sick, and the beggars, and who do not repent. But nobody is invited to fit out a military expedition to ensure that judgement is enforced here and now. The powers of restitution are entirely eschatological.

But, of course, my whole argument so far has dealt with the question as to why Christianity as a state religion harnesses itself to the means of the violence, engages in compulsory conversion, and persecutes or harasses heretics and deviants. Clearly, once Christianity has been adopted as the ideological vesture of the body politic (and indeed even before that, once it has gained some acceptance among the political classes) its foundation documents undergo reinterpretation. Doubtless it is significant that it has a very specific appeal to women and can be accused of undermining the military ethos of the empire. But, in due course, Christian members of the political classes and bishops who double as imperial administrators reinterpret the gospels according to political requirements. That is how the Gospel invitation to bring in anybody to the messianic banquet comes to be interpreted as a political directive to convert by force and to ensure the religious homogeneity of the realm.

This shift in interpretation is not simply to be regarded as cynical readjustment on the part of the worldly wise. A more complicated analysis is required and one which examines the nature of the political. This chapter aims, therefore, to examine the nature of 'the political' and the collusion of 'the religious', especially Christianity, in structures of authority, social cohesion, social control, and the maintenance of boundaries. But it also aims to show that, once some social differentiation has occurred and once Christianity can provide some measure of independent religious education, then the themes of the original charter documents gain greater resonance. These themes become even more resonant wherever the various Christian churches cease to be coextensive with a territory. The New Testament, after all, seeks for a universal spiritual country beyond any particular relationship to the land. This means that Christianity will find it easier to pursue that theme once the tie between territory and adherence has been weakened or broken.

The argument is this. As social differentiation and the internal pressure of the Christian message play one into the other, the Christian religion divides into some sectors which are still active among the political classes and inured to the presumptions of power, and other sectors which (mostly) lie outside those classes. With the extension of this process, Christianity acquires a greater capacity to provide an independent and distinctive socialization. Other things being equal, that produces a modal evangelical personality with a strong emphasis on conciliation and peaceability and a distinct resistance to the warrior spirit. (The exceptions to this, where other things are not equal, are themselves well worth careful analysis, in particular the existence of the evangelical soldier, for example, General Dobbie who inspired the defence of Malta in 1940–2, General Montgomery of El Alamein, and in an earlier generation Henry Lawrence and Henry Havelock, both of them involved in the Indian Mutiny of 1857.) Alongside the creation of this modal personality there emerges an individualized, humanized, even to some extent feminized discourse, in which the issue of peace is of particular importance. A Christianized politics, fostered by distinctive socialization, not only attaches particular importance to the question of peace but gives an account of the political in personal terms. The contrast between that account and the partly impersonal nature of political process is central to what follows. It will be argued that Christianity, in order to pursue the religous goal of the redemption of the human, cannot give up its personal images and adopt impersonal political discourses. However, some Christians with strong political commitments do, from time to time, try to apply the dynamics of human redemption to politics, for example, the need for forgiveness, and find themselves trapped in distressing paradoxes. Consider, for example, the problem of forgiveness as a judicial principle.

Only one thing further needs to be added. It is perfectly possible to observe the effects of a distinctive Christian socialization in contemporary society and these seem to be that the inner core of committed Christians differ from marginals in their concern with peace and other matters, like tolerance for aliens. Again, it is very difficult to control for all factors but it would, for example, be worth examining contemporary evidence of this from both Catholic and Protestant populations in Holland and Belgium. What now follows, then, is first an account of the political in general, and an illustration of the relationship between the pacific evangelical personality and the political realm, drawn from my own research in Latin America.

Politics is the arena within which authority, violence, cohesion, and the maintenance of boundaries are conspicuously at play. All these elements are inherent in society as such and, indeed, they are constitutive of social organization. Of course, authority may be more or less oppressive, cohesion may be more or less exacting, and boundaries more or less vigorously maintained.

But they do not wither away. They are the source of much suffering, but they are also the necessary conditions of civilized and humane living. For example, authority has certainly provided the basis of inequality, inequity, and oppression, and its very existence requires unequal access to the instruments of power. But without authority there is not even the remotest chance of establishing minimum equalities, of creating a regime of modest equity, or of protecting the weak from the strong. Without authority we are each of us threatened by a war of all against all. By an extension of this fundamental social paradox, all movements aiming to secure some measure of equality themselves require internal discipline and depend on the exercise of authority. This is sometimes so strict that, when those movements finally gain control of the state, they transfer their own internal discipline to the whole society and virtually turn it into an armed camp. Jean-Paul Sartre was entirely correct in his description of the mutual terror implicit in disciplined comradeship, but did not envisage the long-term consequence of comradeship once enforced on a whole society. You have only to ask with Lenin, 'What is to be done?' rather than put the easy question 'What would make a comprehensive list of approved social desiderata?' for all the paradoxes of social organization and all the opportunity costs of policy to emerge. The demands of social organization are inexorable. They may be eased and partially circumvented but cannot be refused.

But easement and circumvention themselves require the mobilization of a sufficiently large and cohesive social constituency with some real interest in bringing about change. You will, in short, need disciplined 'force' to achieve peaceable and egalitarian ends. That paradox always returns in every context, whether we are concerned with internal politics or external foreign relations.

That means that the established political classes will not only pursue their own interests in power, wealth and the spoils of the system (within such checks as may be available) but will also have written on their minds and hearts the stigmata of political viability. By political viability I mean, first of all, what can be done at any given moment in any given situation. At the point of political delivery freedom is exercised in respect of a very restricted range of options, particularly perhaps in a democracy. But political viability also has to do with the general limits on what power may achieve and the strict opportunity costs attendant on every option. To govern is to choose.

This sketch of the constitution of social organization as such and of the nature of the political has been tentatively offered simply as a preliminary to understanding what is involved in a religion becoming comprehensively involved in a political system and equally to understanding what may become possible as religion partially emerges from that system, particularly when equipped with the kind of code found in Christianity. If put in the language of sociobiology, there is a social programme essential for existence and survival which religion supports but also qualifies, in particular by generating counter-societies.

What, then, does the partial release of Christianity from the embrace of the political classes make possible, through partial disestablishment, through distinctive socialization, and the generation of independent voluntary religious groups? Well, that varies, of course, with the degree of distance from the 'habitus' of the political classes and from the psychic imprint imposed by belonging to them and being socialized by them. One possibility, among several, is the adoption of the critical stance often associated with what Karl Mannheim called the 'unattached' intelligentsia. The idea that the intelligentsia lacks interests is vastly exaggerated, but it does enjoy unusual scope for appraisal and for long-term review, prospectively and retrospectively, and for engaging in free-ranging moral accountancy. That scope can come to be enjoyed by the Church, and especially by its clerical intelligentsia. Indeed, as social space is continuously enlarged, all sorts of people can increasingly exercise personal predilections, and can decide to take a special interest in the intellectual vocation, including the opportunity it offers for moral accountancy and political criticism. This choice will be open to some clergy just as it is open to intellectually-minded people in general. It offers a different experience of the possible and a different kind of moral accountancy to that practised in the political classes. These different kinds of experience and moral accountancy complement one another, however great the tension between them may be from time to time. There is, after all, no unequivocal 'real world', enabling us to judge between them, in spite of the existence of vigorous outer limits.

[169]

What is of particular value in the viewpoints of Christians, whether these are members of the clerical intelligentsia or simply individual believers, is the invocation of broad principles embodied in fundamentally human imagery. Moreover, these principles continue to retain some authority, provided they are not constantly used to bludgeon those actually responsible for policy with moral imperatives. Politicians and policy-makers cannot easily dismiss such principles as ill-adjusted to what they construe as *the* 'real world', since that 'real world' is demonstrably constituted by their own sharp apprehension of collective and personal interest. After all, most politicians recognize that religious principles have been fundamental to the very civilization of which they are a part. They also know that churches socialize segments of the population in the reciprocities and respects essential to civilized living, and they prefer those reciprocities to be promoted, even if only for pragmatic reasons.

In due course the partially disestablished sectors of Christianity and the independently generated voluntary groups will move towards each other. They will now have rather similar group status and that will greatly assist ecumenical cooperation. However, the formerly established Churches will still retain elements of their long-term political stance and that means easy psychological and intellectual access to casuistries, to concepts of natural law, to ancillary philosophies like Stoicism, and to notions about the most amicable way to settle Church–State tensions. In relation to violence and foreign affairs, their representatives will refer with practised ease to Augustine, Aquinas, Grotius, and other exponents of what constitutes the just war, of the rights of conscience, and of obedience or resistance to authority. By contrast the emergent voluntary groups, at least prior to becoming socially mobile, will have less access to such resources and tend to rely more on the simple application of moral maxims, and on reference to the Bible. Being themselves schooled in effective voluntary action, they may have a high estimate of what can be achieved politically, by individual probity, peaceability, and compassion. There are many possibilities. They may equally well have a strong sense of how difficult it has been to defend their Zion against worldly subversion. In that case they may view politics as part of 'the World', inherently corrupt and occupied by people who regard their simple virtues with contempt.

This is not the place to work through the full range of political and apolitical options most easily available to voluntary Christian groups below the level of the political classes, or to provide a complete anatomy of how their pacific attitudes intersect with the political realm. The important point is that both formerly established Churches and voluntary groups entertain perspectives informed by personal images of political process derived from the fundamental Christian narratives, and this is the case along the whole political spectrum. It is also important to understand that the pacific attitude is a potential inherent in voluntary status, not a necessary corollary, as witness the overlap of evangelical moral fervour and belief in Providence with both British and American imperialism.

All this is certainly *not* to assert that religion has to do with the individual and politics to do with the collective. It is, however, to suggest that religious understandings of collective action are informed by precisely those images which can deal with the fundamental problems of the human condition, such as purpose, meaning, hope, vision, suffering, and death. They are tuned more to 'moral man' than to 'immoral society'. Christian imagery is not cast in terms of immediate political exigency or the manipulation of opaque and non-human processes like the PSBR, or framed with respect to long-term developments in social structure. If it were, it would be as dead as yesterday's political programme.

If Christian imagery were composed of semi-abstract political calculations, then pastors would be politicians. A pastor may act politically from time to time, to defend an essential human dignity, but if he adopts the political role full-time then his religious role is almost inevitably deformed. Worse still, the proper complementarity between the broad moral vision and the immediate political exigency will be lost. Once again, this is certainly *not* to say that political action must of its nature lack moral vision. Indeed, it depends for motive force on mobilizing both ideal and material motives in collusive alliance. But it does have to focus on the exigencies of policy, on the most advantageous dispositions of party propaganda and self-promotion, and on alliances of convenience to buttress alliances of principle. The one thing necessary is survival and viability. Politics cannot avoid a pervasive contrast between its proclaimed moral vision or promise and its actual performance. At the same time, politics must, for its own survival, and for the sake of the political good, avoid accepting that such a contrast exists, except in relation to opponents and rivals. It is for 'the other' to make public what is really your own confession. Political man must never ask forgiveness of opponents or of 'the people' for mistakes and malpractices. Those who ask for forgiveness will never be forgiven. The Lord's Prayer does not apply across the floor of the House. Indeed, were a minister openly and always to obey the ninth commandment against false witness he would be expelled. William Waldegrave, currently (1995) at the British Treasury, told the truth when he said lying was a political necessity, and he was criticized even for that. It was wrong even to tell the truth about lying.

That is precisely the difference between the realm of the Christian religion and the domain of politics. A politician must not so forget his political duty as to act like a human being face-to-face with another human being. If he wants to be fully truthful he must reserve that for private, personal conversations with his God or for the posthumous publication of his memoirs. He— or she—cannot practice the dynamics of redemptive grace, except when disgraced and excluded by the specific moral standards of the political realm itself, that is, when expelled and returned to the realm of the personal.

The problems inherent in the transfer of the human dynamic of redemption to the opaque collective realm of politics are well illustrated in the contemporary practice of ecclesiastical leaders who ask forgiveness of other countries for the sins of their own. Of course, this is not the full dynamic of redemption wrought in and through the self-giving of the innocent Redeemer, but simply a formal statement of the principle of concilia- tion with no attendant costs. Nevertheless, it is fraught with difficulties because relations between collectivities are manifested over generations in terms of reified his- torical actors, such as *the* Germans, *the* British, *the* Irish. The real historical actors are unavailable, buried in the geopolitical 'agency' of class and national interest, itself not entirely identifiable in terms of individual persons.

The question therefore arises as to whom precisely an ecclesiastical leader thinks he is that he should apolo- gize on behalf of a reified national entity to members of another reified national entity for deeds he did not com- mit to persons who themselves did not suffer from those deeds. And if he asks for forgiveness, who precisely on the supposed 'other' side has power to pronounce abso- lution? In what sense can the Cardinal Archbishop of Armagh 'accept' an apology from the Archbishop of Canterbury for British policy and then himself balance the moral account by apologizing for the deeds of the IRA? Such notions are based precisely on quite recent historical concepts whereby multicultural and multi- ethnic entities have been dubbed '*the* British' and '*the* Irish' and retrospectively credited with collective moral agency over centuries, thereby involving whole populations in transferred obloquy. Of course, these mythical transferences are the stuff of politics, but they are not moral realities and as such cannot be cancelled by quasi-liturgical requests for forgiveness. For that matter, King William of Orange cannot be resurrected and named as *the* guilty party, when in the circumstances of the time he did what he had to do as the defender and representative of the 'Glorious Revolution' of 1688–9. He was not responsible for the train of events following his victory at the Boyne.

It can be argued, of course, that the public display of good intentions by a well known person acting in a plausibly representative capacity can have a conciliatory effect, given enough publicity. That might be true at the margin, and it certainly provides evidence that contemporary Christian leaders are mostly of a pacific rather than a militant frame of mind. But since it is not rooted in moral realities it remains a distortion of Christianity and a misapplication of redemption to the political sphere. The peace that follows from forgiveness in Christ *cannot* be transferred to international relations, and in particular it cannot be transferred by some doubtfully representative functionary apologizing on behalf of a reified collectivity for remote (or even for relatively proximate) historical events.

The implications of this type of transference are both offensive and ludicrous. They would be offensive because the German baby born this moment is already eligible to ask forgiveness for the sins of the Nazis. They would be ludicrous because the dynamic of the original sin of the Old Adam and the cost of redemption borne in the body of the New Adam would collapse in an absurd series of spiralling gestures, whereby everybody apologized to everyone else for everything in history and then, of course, carried on exactly as before. After the Pope has apologized to a mixed entity of contemporary 'Mexicans', to whom do the mixed descendants of Aztecs, Toltecs, and the rest apologize? In short, the moral accountancy of the collective is profoundly opaque. It can only be summarized in the universal mark of Cain, and in the sheer generality and inclusive scope of 'general confession'.

It follows that the full range of the dynamic of redemption cannot be disclosed in the human city. This is not to say that the dialectic relation of love with justice, righteousness, and equity cannot be let into the foundations of the human city in such a way that the opaque order of power and interest is countered and criticized from a higher vantage point. It is to say that in the ordinary course of governance the highest viable morality concerns the trustworthiness of contracts and calculated reciprocities based on respect for neighbours. For commentators and practitioners like Alan Clarke, even that is pitched somewhat too high. At any rate, it seems clear that even religiously motivated politicians like John Smith, Tony Blair, Douglas Hurd, William Waldegrave, Alan Beith, and Shirley Williams restrict their Christianity to the second commandment concerning love of, and respect for, 'your neighbour'. And even that has to operate under rather strict limits *vis-à-vis* 'members of the bench opposite'. (As for international relations, the limits appear even stricter and severely qualify the ninth commandment. Thus in the Scott Report of February 1996 into the covert sale of equipment to Iraq—presumably to protect the oil sheikhdoms from

Iran—Parliament was 'misled' but apparently no one did the misleading.)

A Particular Illustration from Latin America

I now turn to an illustration which works out the argument so far in the context of my own research in Latin America. I focus on evangelicals, more particularly Pentecostals, as a voluntary group numbering some forty million, far below the level of political classes. They maintain strict boundaries over against the wider society in order to protect their attempt to build an enclave of honesty, discipline, and dignity, and to shut out the intrusive power of a corrupt and often dissolute society, and its corrupt political systems. Above all, they cultivate a peaceable personality, and reform the macho character. They have walked out of what they, like the early Christians, see as a realm dominated by 'the powers'; and their relationship to the political and to peace and violence is instructive. From time to time, I try to highlight their position by comparison with that of Catholics and Liberal Protestants, partly to show that *all* Christians are constrained by their imagery of conciliation even when they offer political analysis and engage in political activity.

Pentecostalism is apolitical in the sense that it is simultaneously about peace and power: personal peaceability and personal empowerment. It has tamed the macho personality, feminized male discourse, and restored mutual respect within the family. This empowerment is realistic rather than fantastic, because it offers wholeness, reform of life, disciplines of survival and betterment. It offers to release the captive and the possessed, to inspire the despairing, reconcile the hostile, pacify the aggressive, and relocate the wells of hope. It addresses the person by a personal name which confers uniqueness and the ability to be redeemed; and it bestows confidence in the face of suffering and death. Compared with the political aims currently pursued in Latin America, like control of inflation and, above all, removal of corruption, their aims are realistic and attainable. For them political change is pie in the sky. Indeed, my own observation of the believers suggests their aims are often attained. But were believers to convert themselves into political animals they would encounter a quite different dynamic of power at odds with the dynamic of their perfectly real and practical redemption. They would enter what Christians have always called 'the World' and would have to devise extraordinary strategies to circumvent its ubiquitous corruption. They pose a counter-culture of austerity against the dissolute tolerances of a civilization.

The power which Pentecostals need and desire for the betterment of their lives comes to them *as* persons *through* persons. People face God and face each other with respect to the meaning, quality, and purpose of their lives. Thus in the church one may observe an intimate concourse of persons continually facing God and facing each other solely as human beings with respect to the issues of life and death. Within that concourse they are addressed by names, called by their Christian names, so it is no wonder one of their favourite books is entitled *You Have a Name Writ in Glory*. Nowhere else are they, or could they be, addressed heart to heart, face to face, by name and in entirely personal language. It is through this personal language that the divine power manifests itself.[1]

That comes about by the rehearsal of Biblical stories about people and by the way those stories are renewed and (*mutatis mutandis*) retold in the personal lives and testimonies of believers. The constant retelling of stories enables believers to traverse moral landscapes saturated in personal meaning and to locate well-trod paths of righteousness. Pentecostalism, like Christianity itself, is sacred history as story. It is autobiography living off sacred biography. Once the divine power has manifested itself on this human scale in homely tales of innocence and experience, there is a rebirth or reappropriation of self and personhood, by re-identification. Once the lost or threatened self is found again there is an outburst of praise, an overflow of joy, a vital circulation of healing influences and positive thoughts and feelings, and a renewed capacity to order priorities and circumstances.

By contrast, political power is exercised through collective weight externally applied. It operates in terms of social categories and interest groups, it offers an analysis and calculates political strategies in terms of forces and alignments, and to some extent understands history as structures of transformation. This is not to say that

[1] The pages immediately following are self-quotation in that they are also to be included in a book on Latin American Protestantism.

politics resolutely excludes the personal and cannot appeal to the heart by stories and narratives about persons, or indeed through semi-fantastic myths in the meaning of myth proposed by Sorel. Indeed, politicians are often so impressed and depressed by the opacity of the impersonal forces in which they deal that they agonize to express themselves and illustrate their problems in personal language. They make individual trust an issue. Nevertheless, politics aims above all to change societal not individual circumstance through policy and not personal will, and to manipulate entities and structures through an extended and close analysis of causes and reasons, typical actions and reactions.

Furthermore, the political horizon is proximate, located in more or less foreseeable and calculable time, for example, five years, whereas the horizon of faith (building plans apart) is now and for ever. The religious appeal, in terms of today or else *sub specie aeternitatis*, is the consequence of the use of personal language. By contrast, the political appeal in terms of proximate outcomes is the consequence of collective analyses. Neither politics nor religion can abandon their distinctive and separate natures without severe and immediate lesions. Thus, if a pastor were to evade eye-to-eye contact in favour of political discourse about (say) financial base rates he would induce immediate bewilderment. If a political boss were to offer his enemies forgiveness or humbly request forgiveness of them, he would immediately be ousted as a traitor or someone who failed to understand his assigned role and the basis of his responsibilities and activities.

Inevitably, these distinctions and differences are heuristic devices for separating out kinds of power without any detailed attempt to pursue exceptions. It is enough to assert that differences of this kind and magnitude bear down on social ontologies which fail to recognize the autonomy and permanent distinctive character of religious action. They simultaneously render implausible claims that the expressed desire of believers for spiritual empowerment is *sotto voce* a thwarted or dislocated ambition to achieve political power or even a compensation for social powerlessness. The pursuit of personal and spiritual empowerment is so specific, so *sui generis*, so humanly natural that it is well nigh impossible to imagine the warrant for its reduction to some other category of activity.

The point even bears repetition. Religion and the power of religion deal primarily in a personal mode, whatever overlaps there may be with power in the political sphere and whatever the overflows from time to time between the religious and the political. Even those who exercise quasi-political power within religious institutions and ecclesiastical polities have—at least in modern differentiated societies—to go about their occasions and conduct their business in terms of an unction quite distinct from the clout of the political boss. And that is significant for the occasions on which pastors meet bosses, because their discourses, like their powers, are largely incommensurate. Their conversations cannot continue long beyond immediate exigencies or beyond a delimited sector of issues, for example, the moral aspects of public order. The most extended exigency occurs where priest or pastor is able to speak for a whole oppressed people or tribe. But even that takes place within limits derived from religious inhibitions which notoriously jar on political activists, and has to be seen in the last analysis as existing only for the time being.

Those who do not observe the momentary and delimited character of religious involvement in politics are usually lay, and in so far as they enthusiastically espouse a moral agenda, as do most Pentecostals and some Catholics, they run into persistent dilemmas, dramatically illustrated, for example, in contemporary Brazil. In contemporary Brazil evangelical deputies recently elected have found themselves compromising their essential character by wheeling and dealing and using their churches as clienteles, or else they find their innocence misused and themselves bypassed, or they try to move along a tightrope, maintaining integrity and acknowledging the dynamics of power while still attempting to use it responsibly.

These problems and turbulences and dilemmas affect Catholic and Pentecostal alike, and illustrate how the logic of the relation between religion and politics (the autonomy and specific character of the two spheres) has consequences for everybody in a Christian culture. Yet there are, of course, specific problems attaching to Pentecostals and it may be useful to set these out in a brief parenthesis for the sake of completeness.

It is, for example, clear that Pentecostals constitute a relatively undifferentiated group and are, therefore, unlikely to generate specialized agencies of political

activists, or to give house room to ecclesiastical bureau-
crats with portfolios in social responsibility. Pentecostals have no leaders ensconced in the political
class, habituated to comment on affairs, and protected
for most of the time by traditional prestige and international visibility. Again, they have not experienced centuries of establishment during which the turbulence
affecting the transition from religion to politics has been
channelled by understood rules of engagement and
spheres of activity, and by theories that can guide the
lay Catholic in executing his role as a member of the
political classes. Pentecostals are persons remote from
such classes, knowing they feature politically only as
potential clients in a culture of corruption suffused with
Catholic presumptions. They are aliens who are regarded as such, and unlikely to risk their new-found
sense of dignity in places where they count for less than
nothing. Their conceptual equipment consists solely of a
sense of the historic separation of Church and State
located in their origins, and of the damage done to
religion and specifically to them by all the manifold
connections between Church and State in Latin
America. Their sole guide in translating this combination of normative history and unhappy experience is the
Bible, with its sharp distinction between the arena of
lovingkindness within the Church and the arena of the
World, where the principalities and powers are in full
and maleficent occupation. That distinction is in fact
less a guide than an image conveying in minatory
terms precisely the turbulence originally experienced
by first-century persons, who, like twentieth-century

Pentecostals, were well below the level of political notice.

The aim of any Pentecostal group is holiness and righteousness. That is the primary object of their existential search, though they happen to know by raw experience that it is the only way in which they have been raised above the dirt floor. To the extent that this primary object is adamantly pursued, the turbulence in any transition from the religious to the political increases. Love finds itself confused by having to deal in images of generalized hostility framed in terms of opposing categories and embattled collectives, evil is accorded a specific political name and address, peaceability has to contemplate coercion, truthfulness has to succumb to virulent propaganda, and humility has to reclothe itself in political self-righteousness. Pentecostals are above all lovers of peace, and reviled as such, industrially and politically, and it is precisely on entering the political sphere that lovers of peace find they have to revile their war-mongering adversaries and the protagonists of militancy, and the doves find themselves propelled to savage the hawks. Each and every one of these kinds of turbulence has but one consequence. It is that any cultural resistance to corruption framed in the moral terms supplied by religion has to repudiate any cultural resistance to oppression framed in accordance with everyday political strategies and tactics. Otherwise the love, peace, truthfulness, and humility so hardly won in the church as between Christian persons (the very basis of all the betterment they know) is corroded from within and sapped from without.

Supposing one had to summarize the turbulence central to this analysis. It could best be done showing how the concept and reality of peaceful and redemptive martyrdom has to mutate as groups negotiate the defile from religion to politics. The issue of what happens to martyrdom is peculiarly relevant, given that peace and redemption are at the heart of evangelical experience, but as the whole of this argument would suggest, it also has profound relevance for committed Catholics, including members of base communities, as they enter more and more fully into the primitive meanings of Christianity and leave behind the cultural inhibitions on Christianity associated with establishment.

Christian martyrdom is voluntarily undertaken by single and unarmed individuals to redeem the other, by forgiveness and by absolution, through pure witness. Political martyrdom, by contrast, is undertaken for the most part by armed groups, who endure it rather than embrace it, and who seek the elimination of the other by the generation of communal hatred. Clearly there are many resemblances across this stark divide, otherwise it would be quite impossible to reassemble the death of soldiers in war under the icons and texts of Christian sacrifice. Nevertheless, the metaphor 'the Son of God goes forth to war' can never lose the force of paradox because the Gospel adamantly requires that 'his servants do not fight.' The moment they do fight the cost of redemption is converted into the casualties of a mêlée. There was only one 'casualty' at Calvary. This means that the literal crux of Pentecostal living, their peaceability and self-sacrifice in all its dimensions, would be thrown into confusion by indiscriminate violence. This is in no way to be understood as a theological point, but arises quite simply by way of existential accounting and costing. It has practical consequences in that Pentecostals can be relied upon, once mobilized in an industrial dispute, but they resolutely refuse to involve themselves in a violent mêlée.

Again, it has to be emphasized that the costs of confusion and violence are also part of the moral accountancy of base communities. They too are more inclined to martyrdom than to murder, because like Pentecostals they are fundamentally religious and not political. This firm religiosity as opposed to politicization is further reinforced by the fact that both Pentecostals and members of base communities are more often women than men, and thus reinforced in a personal understanding of the world.

This analysis could be pursued further in terms of those issues where either Pentecostals or members of base communities have dramatized an injustice by exposing themselves to martyrdom. A priest defending the forest rights of Indians is exposing himself to death, not conducting guerrilla warfare. A Torres is quite atypical. Archbishop Romero, like Thomas à Becket, symbolically 'unbarred the door'. He was archetypal. In Peru at the present time Pentecostals and members of base communities alike are murdered and (in terms of moral meaning) martyred because they represent islands of leadership and stable improvement contrary to the planned immiseration pursued by 'Shining Path', not to mention the depredations of the official army.

These martyrdoms are a special kind of religious politics essentially different from military sweeps or the policy of arming the peasantry. It has to be understood as a particular kind of personal witness which encounters a barrier and an inhibition at the point where it enters the turbulence inherent in political action. Catholics can and do more frequently negotiate that turbulence. That follows, of course, from their long-established history, the theoretical bridges available to them, and their more frequent membership in the political classes.

Of course, religious images can refer to and provide comprehensive cover and legitimation for whole communities and regimes, particularly in undifferentiated societies. By the same token, they can provide comprehensive legitimation for the opposition of a people or a tribe or a nation to oppression in the way already referred to above. It is in this context, it must be said, that Pentecostals can be tempted into the political by being asked to exchange recognition of a military regime in return for a state recognition of their presence such as has never before been offered them. They are, so to speak, tempted to quasi-political action by long-delayed justice utilized as a ploy. But this, where it occurs, as in Chile, lacks the wholesale character of normal political action but works rather at the level of mutual recognition between Church and State. The action certainly takes place in the political realm but in no way commits Pentecostals at large to the dynamic of political action. Indeed, the action is almost entirely confined to defensive strategies on the part of a pastorate concerned to maintain institutional survival, and in that strictly limited sense the pastorate does act politically.

Religious images, whether offering cover to states or to oppressed nations, remain broad and lack tactical or strategic content. For example, the aspiration to 'build Jerusalem' in the British national hymn cannot be converted into a rolling programme. It is precisely the generality and open texture of such aspirations that keeps them available and allows them to motivate and inspire. Once they are deployed for too specific a purpose they are rendered impotent. Indeed, at the very moment a condensed symbolism is harnessed for too specific a purpose, it slips the harness and makes its way back to its original home in the broad iconography of faith where, indeed, it can be used to criticize its misuse. Perhaps the prophetic critique of the use (or misuse) of Zionism would provide a case in point from a Jewish rather than a Christian context. It is only as an aspiration is held up as an icon and suspended on high in sacred space that it retains its latent ability to inspire. That is exactly how icons or rather stories and pictures are suspended in the sacred space of Pentecostalism. Icons live by nature in broad landscapes saturated in permanent meanings, not in momentary catch-phrases and political slogans. At most they can confer general positive auras such as have gathered around ideas like shared sacrifice or universal welfare, that is, fairness. They are, in short, not waiting for politicization and a chance for real power, but exerting and retaining real power by resisting politicization.

8

Recapitulations and Mutations: Differentiation and Peace Code Together

THE argument just made does *not* confine religion to the individual and assign politics to the collective. That would be absurd. Nor does it *confine* the positions espoused by religious groups or by individual believers to arguments of a broadly based kind, touching on issues of principle or on fundamental human rights. It aims solely to show that *in so far* as religious groups or individual believers advance deep into the opaque calculations of politics and propose to play the political game on a full-time basis, they lose hold on the specific religious role. And that is because the dynamic of Christian redemption is conducted in terms of a narrative which is personal and which in addition summarizes the resistance of the political realm to moralization under a permanent image of 'the World'.

The argument up to this point also suggests that in so far as religious groups emerge from the comprehensive embrace of society and from establishment, they develop broad political perspectives which are informed to an unusual extent by the special focus of redemption, which is peace and reconciliation. Such groups may even experiment in a transfer of the dynamics of redemption from the religious to the political realm, for example, by advocating mutual forgiveness between nations or between other collectivities. This application of Christianity is likely to be defeated by the special nature of 'responsibility' in the political realm because one cannot locate who is to blame and who is innocent on either side. Who forgives whom for what when?

However, the focus on conciliation and the occasional attempt to transfer the dynamic of redemption to the political realm do both derive from the fundamental Christian 'peace code'. It follows that Dawkins's theory of the inherent warlike aggression which derives from the presumed 'certainties' of religious belief would need to offer some explanation as to why this is the case, or alternatively show it is not the case. One further point needs to be stressed again before taking the argument further, and it is that the Christian approach to the *polis* and to its mode of operation in terms of power, cohesion, and the maintenance of boundaries is not one of unequivocal rejection. The secular city is not damned comprehensively. It contains profoundly evil potentials, but it is open also to those neighbourly and peaceable reciprocities which are the foundation of any civilized living. If Christian politics cannot proceed beyond these reciprocities to full-scale redemptive reconciliation without encountering severe costs, equally it cannot do less than press for everything implied by neighbourliness. What this means in practice is, of course, endlessly complex, and further exploration would be a diversion from present concerns towards a religiously informed political philosophy. But the sheer generality of these considerations helps make the essential point: the political values derived from Christian images are not precise policies but outer limits and broad perspectives. They embody a dialectic of the perfect as it engages with real situations, and as it pays a full and proper respect to the realities governing the political realm. Without that respect, religious witness degenerates into the kind of sentimental invocation of inner peace proposed by gurus. By gurus I mean the people who believe that their particular therapy offers a quick solution to world problems, and advertise as much on the walls of underground stations.

The Prerequisites of Society and the Old Testament Code

We can now move the argument on by selecting a somewhat different point of departure. Supposing we raise the standard sociological issue of the prerequisites of social existence, that is, those conditions which have to be met for a society to exist and survive. Probably in Dawkins's terminology these prerequisites of survival would count as the fundamental 'programme', though that is not a vocabulary I intend to deploy. But some prerequisites are obvious and uncontentious. There needs to be a secure physical habitat, which is usually a territory, but can be demarcated more loosely, for example, among roaming groups like gypsies and hunter-gatherers. This establishes the primary importance of the land and a title to the land. Land in turn implies some kind of boundary, properly maintained, and that minimally involves resistance to incursion. Within that boundary there will need to be some alternative to the war of all against all, a canalization of violence, and some agreed channels of authority and decision-making. Peaceability will be further stabilized by codes of practice, involving minimal reciprocities, and by sanctions against those who ignore them. These codes of practice must include arrangements which help ensure biological and cultural reproduction. In other words, there must be provision for imprinting and reprinting the cultural pattern.

It will also be very helpful, though perhaps not strictly necessary, if these prerequisites are bound up together in a collective narrative, explaining the origin of the group, its relation to the powers of nature and of the spirit, and identifying the sources of difficulties and troubles. Such a narrative should also commend the group to itself as valuable and worthy of continuance. And it will also be helpful, though I suppose not necessary, for some understanding to be built in to the group narrative which can carry it through severe trials and threats to identity, and even appear to guarantee a good end to the story. Clearly, there will be a strong pressure for the group to defend all these elements, so helpful with respect to its future, by sanctions and by more or less strict instructions as to their retention into the future. Or, to put it another way, those groups which do not embody such a defence may well expose themselves to a more limited future than those who do.

Now, if this brief sketch of those things which are
requisite and those things which are helpful is translated
historically, maybe we can see the Hebrew Bible as
embodying them. The Bible is much else besides. This is
a minimal account, not an exercise in reduction; it is
social bones, not existential flesh. But as a narrative and
a code of practice with sanctions it does embody the
elements just set out. The Hebrew Bible is not the only
possible social print-out but it is one of the most effective, and because it is a 'Word' reproducible from
generation to generation it helps ensure that one generation does indeed successfully follow another. A
'word', guarded and maintained by sanctions, constantly reproduces the cultural pattern and maintains a
recognizable identity over time, so that the group is
further aided by an ability to locate itself in history and
know itself in terms of past and present and future. So
far as the Hebrew Bible is concerned, that ability to
locate itself in history is framed in a universal destiny
and a sacred narrative of salvation.

This means that some of the social features complained about by Dawkins are indeed faintly visible in
the Hebrew programme of survival. I mean there exists
an enlistment of God in favour of the Jews, a presuppo-
sition in favour of the group's own perspective rather
than some other perspective, a resistance to intrusive
elements which might unhinge its arrangements for survival, and a legitimation of violence and of a defence of
its own integrity. To this may be added a cosmic guarantee generating the necessary collective confidence. And,
as it has turned out, this has worked, even under the

terrible trials of the Holocaust, when an attempt was made to destroy both the bodies of Jews and their story. That story had, nevertheless, provided for so appalling an exigency, though it might well not have seemed so to those who endured it. The narrative held, especially the narrative that promised a recovery of the link between nation and land. Again, land matters. In the contemporary world there continue to be movements within Judaism which aim to renovate and to reinforce that fundamental redemptive narrative, and simultaneously to save faith and people. The Hassidim, for example, are trying to replace the biological losses of the Holocaust, but they would not be able to do so if they did not respond to the rigorous precepts of Halakah. In *their* situation, if they once slacken those demands they may live physically, but culturally and religiously they die.

It is perhaps important to stress that this literally 'saving' narrative as presented here is not coextensive with the religion of Judaism. *That* is a very complex phenomenon and it has generated many expansions and revisions of its narrative (Christianity among them, as well as all the partial inclusions of strangers and the Gentiles by Judaism itself). Nevertheless, the narrative remains a persistent resource, which is, and has to be, canonically guaranteed, 'written in'. Canonicity ensures perpetual availability.

But what, then, of Christianity as a second-stage 'programme' (or narrative) which retains these powerful resources but reapplies them through a massive revision of Judaism on a universal scale? Clearly, this revision on a universal scale, symbolized in Pentecost, cannot immediately be implemented. It has to work its way in and through enormous resistances which partially confiscate it to the needs of social survival and the continuing prerequisites of that survival. So there is a dialectic upheaval which is controlled and kept in minimal order by 'the Church'. Various 'nations', using that term anachronistically, re-use the resources of the narrative as revised by Christianity. Indeed, the narrative is itself powerful enough to generate nations out of next to nothing. But characteristically 'nations' lean for survival on the conserving resources of the original 'covenant' narrative, and it is these resources which provide a viable platform for carrying forward 'on the books' the radical Christian notion of a New Israel. *The key Christian concept of the New Israel is kept alive by being partly redesigned on the model of the Old Israel.* Among other things, this allows expansive empires to deploy the universal Christian idea for their own quasi-universal purposes, fusing and confusing the kingdom of Christ with their own imperial jurisdiction. In an exactly parallel manner, the eschatological and universal 'city set on a hill' as envisaged by Christianity becomes a quasi-Judaic city set on real hills, in Boston by the Charles River, in Utah, or in central Zaire or Brazil; or it is transmogrified as Rome, second Rome, third Rome, and so on.

To turn aside for a moment: how then would one conceptualize Islam from the perspective of this model? In its essentials Islam represents a reversion to the original Jewish narrative. But this time it is semi-universalized in a Perfect Word expressed in the sacred language of Arabic. Alongside this reversion from Word made flesh to Word as text and Word as sacred, untranslatable language, there is a parallel reversion to the sacred city, but transferred from the old centre in Jerusalem to a new centre in Mecca. Jerusalem is retained as the necessary link with the original territorial genealogy but, at the same time, made subordinate to a new focus in the territory of Arabia. The sacred geography of 'the land' is, therefore, reorganized and Jewish 'property' in land expropriated. At the same time, the dangerous elements and dialectics set in motion by Christianity are stabilized and reined in, in particular the humanization and individualization of the Father in the person of the Son, So too is the freedom of the Holy Spirit to 'lead into all truth', to extend canons, and to translate the Word literally and figuratively into any language whatever. The physical markers of identity are restored, such as circumcision, and the unitary principle restated with authoritative forcefulness. As a result, the secular city and the community of faith will become fully differentiated only with great difficulty, and the community of faith itself will be fully equipped to resist its own internal fission. The Old Testament programme of taboos, practices, implantation by rote and memorization, and by markers of difference, is very firmly re-established. As for the Jews and the Christians, they are to be excluded by the markers of difference, but since both of them retain elements of the basic narrative stabilized in sacred texts, they can, nevertheless, be accorded second-class citizenship.

Once this return to the holistic, unitary principle has

been achieved, the means of violence are recovered from the eschatological realm of God's judgement and again made straightforwardly available for the effective pacification of the community. There is, for example, no question of believers not taking each other to law. Alongside divine judgement and alongside spiritual jihad there is physical jihad, for use in the 'House of War' outside Islam and for the vigorous restraint of those who would leak across the boundaries of the community and so weaken it.

The recovery of legitimate violence as a means to secure a religious peace as well as to establish a secular peace (the two being only marginally distinguished) has clear implications. It means that elements of redemptive suffering to secure peace in both Judaism and Christianity are now otiose and have to be removed. The collective suffering of the Remnant as envisaged in the Old Testament and the individual suffering of the Word made flesh portrayed in the New, both become unacceptable, except in the form of martyrdom for the collective cause. The human blood shed in the Christian narrative and representing the cost of redemptive self-giving has to be redefined as a pollutant. It is dangerously individualized, it implies a subversive rejection of violence in the pursuit of redemption, it suggests the separation of Church from State, and it compromises the power of the unitary Father by the exposure of God to human violence. From an Islamic viewpoint, for God to receive rather than to use violence is the wrong way round and quite inappropriate. The unitary Father has to retain the means of violence both as a spiritual threat and as a physical threat placed in the guardianship of his servants. Islam does not need to reinterpret the eschatological text 'Compel them to come in' when it is perfectly able to deliver that message without equivocation. In Islam the *double entendre* of Christianity is rendered otiose.

Of course, in practice a Christianity which has partly reverted to the initial programme and has become (virtually) coextensive with the social whole will behave in a very similar manner to Islam. The Catholic Church will try to secure its borders with as much severity as may be required. It will retain an interest in the physical city of Jerusalem to symbolize its link to the Old Israel but will transfer ultimate authority to the physical city of Rome and for centuries cherish Latin as yet another sacred language. As for the advance of the Pilgrim People towards a new spiritual Jerusalem, it will be reduced to pilgrimages to real places, each of them a physical city 'set on a hill': Zaragoza, Rocamadour, Cologne, Santiago, Canterbury. However, because established Christianity lacks concepts of either first- or second-class citizenship, which at least serve to define and stabilize the place of Christians and Jews in Islamic societies, it treats the awkward fact of second-class citizens, above all the Jews, with crude and intermittent violence. Indeed, it uses the original markers of identity and of defence with added animus, given that it recognizes itself in the supposed 'enemy'.

Nevertheless, these reversals to a sacred city, to a sacred language, and to a religiously sanctioned violence are only partial. The revised Christian code is too deeply incised in the new canon to be repudiated. Even though held in symbolic suspension, it can speak in two voices to whoever has ears to hear, and can make signs with a contradictory content. Some of the signs are obvious: the quasi-sacrament of foot-washing always hints at the equality of master and servant. But celibacy is also a sign. Celibacy can imply the temporary and relative character of the patriarchal order. The Virgin is not only our Lady of Victories but also the Jewish mother who released the freedom of the Spirit in the incarnation of her son. She is also the sign of a new body outside the continuities of biological reproduction and outside the limits of the local tribe, and that body is simultaneously the corporate body of brothers and sisters in Christ and the body of the resurrection, these two bodies being intimately related. The socio-logic is subtle and complex. The Virgin understood as a pre-eminent sign of locality and of a boundary as she presides over Santiago de Chile or Guadalupe or Paris, is also the secret sign of the breaking of all boundaries, whether these are the boundaries of the natural group or of physical, bodily locatedness. Peter Brown has brilliantly illustrated this kind of connection in his study of the relation between virginity and resurrection in fifth- and sixth-century Christianity.[1] The body of the resurrected Christ is everywhere.

Perhaps it is in this context that we may best understand the remarkable ambivalence of Christianity's treatment of sexuality. On the one hand there is a

---

[1] Peter Brown, *The Body and Society* (London, 1989).

---

proper acceptance and validation of marriage, and of time, place, legitimate violence, and reproduction, and on the other hand there is a breaking of the bounds of the family and of local language, and a validation of those who are 'eunuchs for the sake of the kingdom of heaven'. Clearly, the opportunity costs of a universal code, reversing, or at least expanding the initial code of local survival, are high. But that is the nature of human society: all options impose severe and condign costs. The history of Christian civilization is therefore a history as to how Church and society have exercised control over those costs and, for the most part, opted instead to pay the costs of the original Jewish code. Nevertheless, as social developments, especially differentiation and globalization, offer opportunity, the universal code comes into play and, indeed, expands the social base that makes it relevant and viable. The changes in contemporary Catholicism illustrate precisely that process, however strongly the brakes are applied.

The First Differentiations: Church and State, Church and Nation

The principal step in the process of differentiation is that separation of Church from nation, of faith from land and natural community, which was the keystone of the original Christian code. As differentiation progresses and accelerates in the post-Reformation centuries, it involves a transfer of the compulsory powers of the semi-unitary Church State, so well articulated in

Hooker's *Ecclesiastical Polity*, to the nation. This can be traced through a shift in the locus of the sacred from the holy father to the monarchical father of his people (or, in the cases of Elizabeth and Mary II, the mother of her people) and thence by another shift to fatherland or motherland. These migrations of the sacred have recently been described by David Starkey and earlier by Werner Stark.[2] Each migration is likely to involve both psychological and actual violence, first of all in the repudiation of the holy father, then in the executions and vilifications of sacred monarchs. It is these shifts which help provide opportunity for Christianity to reactivate its original status as a cross-cultural voluntary group. And in the working-out of such changes a set of complex relationships is set up between religion and nationality. Whether these are mainly positive or negative depends on contingent historical circumstances. Just as the shifts from holy father to fatherland may entail violence, so these relationships of religion and nation may entail violence. I mean that it is possible to set out conditions under which violence is more or less likely as the body of the Church separates from the body of the nation. One can analyse precisely what happens as the nation seeks to establish its own plenary powers in relation to cohesion, homogeneity, boundaries, and sovereignty in general. It is the nation which now disposes of the power to 'Compel them to come in' and to decide

---

[2] David Starkey, 'Parallel or divergence: monarchical symbolism in England', *Acts of the 14th Conference of the C.I.S.R. (Strasbourg 1977)* (1978). Werner Stark, *The Sociology of Religion* (volume 1, *Established Religion*) (London, 1966).

---

what degrees of heterogeneity are compatible with its cohesion and what groups are to be suppressed or even ejected. This constitutes the ancient power of 'ethnic cleansing'. It was begun (mythologically or actually) in ancient Egypt with the assault on and ejection of the Jews, continued in Canaan by the Jews themselves in relation to 'the peoples of the land', operated by the Church State in medieval times, and then transferred by stages from monarch to nation in the modern period.

Perhaps a cross-over point occurred in Spain in the period after 1492 with the expulsion or forced conversion of Muslims and Jews, which was simultaneously an act of the realm and of the Church. Perhaps the complete sequence of these changes is to be observed in the effective devolution of the powers of the *patronato* first from the Pope to Spanish monarchs, and then from Spanish monarchs to the independent successor states of Latin America. These plenary powers, of which the *patronato* is only one, have been constantly deployed in association with the fundamental social programme as it relates to the inviolability and inherent title of the people to the land, to the identity and integrity of a people over time and in place, to criteria of cohesion and acceptable degrees of divergence, and to the maintenance of boundaries. To recognize the operation of this programme one may look anywhere from Cyprus to Burma and from Japan to Armenia. What needs to be recognized is that *religion is not necessary to this programme.* It inheres in social process as such and, as already indicated, religion actually provides a variant coding which undermines it and subjects it to critical strain. But it remains powerful nevertheless, just as the defences of the individual self remain powerful even when overridden by religion. After all, the self-proclaimed successors of the Enlightenment enthusiastically operated it, as when Stalin dealt with 'the nationalities problem'—or the Sandinistas with the peoples of the Atlantic coast of Nicaragua.

The Several Tensions and Easements of Differentiation

The next intellectual task is the most complicated. What has to be provided is an analysis of the many-sided and often thwarted advance of differentiation, first of all through the transfer of the powers of violence and 'ethnic cleansing' from religion to the nation state, and then through the appearance of religion in the form of the voluntary group.

With regard to these changes, much depends on whether the nation state emerges in the early stages of its existence with a positive or a negative relationship to the majority religion in its territory. Obviously this bears crucially on whether or not Church and nation are in conflict, and on what kind of tension is aroused by the initial appearance of voluntary groups interrupting the religious homogeneity of the nation. These conflicts, as and when they occur, will be part of the process of differentiation itself and inherent in it. There will be initial tearings of tissue with this emergence of the nation state and as new 'forms of religious life' come into being.

Often, of course, there will be a positive relationship between the nation state and the majority religion in its territory. Other things being equal, it suits both politicians and ecclesiastical leaders to cooperate. In colonial situations nationalist politicians will often have been in alliance with ecclesiastical leaders, though in Christian societies the latter will tend to be subordinate partners in the actual struggle and they will display less militancy once it is successfully concluded. Much depends on local circumstances. In Ireland, for example, ecclesiastical leaders tended not to be in the forefront of actual struggle, and not to countenance violence; in Poland they have been the pre-eminent symbols of national will to survive, but nevertheless inclined to politic compromises provided these do not undermine that survival or the institutional integrity of the Church.

But the main point concerns the existence of a positive relation between a particular religion and a particular nationalism, because where that exists there will be pressures against minority religions, and these may give rise to overt conflicts. The factors which make for conflict can be set out quite succinctly. Conflict is most likely where the minority religion is found among an ethnic and/or linguistic group which occupies a peripheral territory, which has a sizeable power base, and can call upon allies across the border. An example would be the Tamils of northern Sri Lanka, who are a minority of about 20 per cent and can call on support from southern India. However, this type of conflict has little to do with religion *as such*, since, as argued earlier, it occurs just as easily when the religious factor is absent. Turks, Iraqis, and Iranians can slaughter Kurds, and vice versa, with an enthusiasm entirely unaltered by the presence or the absence of religious difference. In Turkey Turks are largely Sunni, Kurds often Alawite. In Iraq Kurds are Sunni, like most Iraqis, and in Iran they are Sunni and the Iranians mostly Shia. But the degree of conflict remains fairly constant.

Of course, the salience of religion in identity does vary, and it is probably high, for example, when the territorial minority is Muslim and the majority religion Catholic, as is the case in Mindanao in the Philippines. It is also high where the territorial minority has adopted a religion different from the majority faith, in part as a measure of cultural defence and in part as a move which renovates cultural identity. This is the case among many tribal groups in South-East Asia, for example, the Karens and others on the Burmese–Thai border, who have adopted Christianity rather than the majority religion of Buddhism, and it is also a factor in the conversion of Maya, Quechua, and Aymara to evangelical Protestantism in Latin America.

By contrast, conflict is rather unlikely where a religio-ethnic minority lacks a territorial base, or has one in the centre of the national territory where it is mixed with the overall majority population, as is the case with the Muslims of Tatarstan. Conflict is even less likely when the minority is simply a voluntary grouping with no ethnic or linguistic base. Overall, the effective factors governing conflict are how long a minority has been present, how much power and wealth it possesses (for example, the semi-Christianized Chinese of Malaysia), how far its practices jar on majority susceptibilities, and the extent to which it is relatively anonymous and invisible in the town rather than all too visible in the countryside.

And it really is important to take account of the economic factor. Conflicts in Chechenya and Kuwait have a lot to do with oil. Equally, a great deal turns on whether a minority is perceived as the cultural fifth column of a foreign power. In Latin America, for example, there are many nations where people identify their culture as inherently Hispanic and Catholic, and this means that the expansion of voluntary religious groups is roundly identified as cultural intrusion from North America. However, one should note this view is at least as likely to be held by members of the secular nationalist intelligentsia as it is by pious Catholics. The point is crucial because it underlines the collusive relation of nationality and majority religion during the early phases of differentiation. What happens in later phases is rather variable and the focus of tension is often seen to shift to language and to culture in general. Quebec firms up its boundaries in terms of ethnic and linguistic criteria, not religion.

So much for patterns emerging when the nation state and the majority religion are in collusion. What happens, then, when a nation (or its government) frames its identity in secular terms or in terms overtly opposed to the majority religion? Basically, a secular government does everything it can to secure dominance over what it calls the national territory, and that means dealing with regional redoubts in part defined and defended by religion. In such situations religion is often an element in regional resistance to cultural expropriation, and often the policy of central government is over-determined, even counter-productive, as it was with Stalin and Mao. Situations vary. Central government may persecute the majority religion of the central territories but, nevertheless, prefer it to minority religions rooted in fissiparous national peripheries. Clearly once the autonomy of a peripheral region is at issue, the central secularist authority may respond by force or else by intruding new populations from the majority ethnic groups, as in Tibet.

What is most at issue here is not some question of inherent religious militancy but the thrust of the nation state to secure its integrity and dominance, often through the superimposition of a secular ideology. But whether the state is secular or secularist or religious or in collusion with the majority religion, it will act against any perceived threat. The Greeks of Smyrna were expelled by the secular government of Ataturk and the Turks of eastern Thrace were ejected by a Greek government well disposed to religion according to exactly the same socio-logic. Counter-examples, such as the benign attitude of the Czech Republic to Slovakian independence, are rare. One can normally assume that any nation, big or small, imperial or ex-colonial, will refuse to others the autonomy it demands for itself. This leads to conflict (a) where a nation expands over cultural and religious frontiers and (b) where those frontiers have been drawn solely for economic and geo-political reasons. An example of (a) is the attempt of the secular French government, in the course of long-term historic expansion, to subdue the linguistic identity of Brittany as reinforced by Catholic piety, and also to ignore the specific constitutional, religious, and cultural traditions of Alsace on its re-incorporation in 1918. In both cases an 'enlightened government' acted according to the socio-logic of 'Compel them to come in.' An example of (b) might be Nigeria or Lebanon–Syria. The borders of Nigeria were drawn around a complicated set of ethnic and religious demarcations. Peace was established, as it sometimes is, by a 'third party', in this case Britain, but with independence from Britain the potential for conflict returned. It occurred, first of all, in relation to the largely Catholic 'periphery' of Biafra and it could occur in the future between the north and the south of the country. Given that the north is mainly Muslim and the south partly Christian, with proportions each of about 40–45 per cent, there could be a conflict in which constitutional, economic, regional, tribal, and religious components were all mixed up together. But how much do any of the conflicts just canvassed owe, if anything, to the kind of mechanisms posited by Dawkins?

Probably the most serious conflicts occur where the secular government faces religious peripheries large enough to challenge its total dominance or counter-assert a religious dominance. This is what happened in Mexico in the civil war beginning in 1910 and the chronic disequilibrium led to seriously over-determined militancy on both sides. The residue of that conflict has led subsequently to tacit alliances between the secular

State and minority religions on the grounds that they are more amenable and weaken the majority religion. That policy has been adopted towards Protestantism in Latin America both by Liberal governments who saw it as democratic in ethos and by military governments who saw it as obedient to the powers that be.

These instances illustrate the substantial tearing of the social fabric as the nation state comes to exercise plenary powers of sovereignty, cultural cohesion, and of inclusion or exclusion in relation to its borders. They also illustrate the relatively minor lesions which occur as voluntary religious forms emerge without a territorial, ethnic, and linguistic base, though here again some contemporary Muslim states appear to be an exception, as Pentecostals and Bahais discover to their cost in Iran, and heterodox Muslims and Christians in Pakistan. It is worth emphasizing that where the demarcation within a sovereign nation state is solely religious and lacks an ethnic or linguistic base, the likelihood of conflict is enormously reduced. This is true even where there is some degree of territorial concentration as between different religions, such as is found in Holland and Germany. Conflicts in these countries during the period of industrialization were partly over differential access enjoyed by Protestants and Catholics to State power and to resources, partly over the maintenance of cultural and regional identities, partly over the thrust of the State to secure unequivocal sovereign power. All the same, these superimposed and reinforcing conflicts were solved by political negotiations between élites, and by redistributions of power through the ballot box. Only in Switzerland was there overt conflict in the Cantonal war of 1847–8. The converse has also to be noted in that as differentiation shifts the burden of territorial identity to ethnicity and language, as in Quebec, tension over borders continues at a high level.

What has been argued thus far is that with social differentiation the fundamental social programme is partly transferred from the religion state to the nation state and that religion exists in a series of positive or negative relationships to that nation state. These are distributed in a complex manner according to relationships of centre and periphery, defined in different combinations by ethnicity, territory, language, economic resources, and religion. Such relationships are in turn affected by the placing of borders. With further differentiation, the peace code written into original Christianity emerges in partial association with the religious voluntary group, and the tension aroused by that emergence is not all that long-lasting. Running in parallel with such differentiations is a migration of 'the sacred', shifting from Church to monarch to nation, though in differing combinations of mutual reinforcement or rivalry at various stages in the process. The further implication of this argument is that rather little in the instances of conflict or tension cited has to do with an inherent militancy associated with doctrinal certainty.

Before turning finally to the condition and role of religion as a voluntary group in a modern differentiated society, some interim examples need to be offered of societies in various stages of differentiation. These interim examples are intended to help illuminate the kinds of disaggregation which can occur: historical contexts filter differentiations along different channels.

Suppose we begin with Russia and its traditional proxy Serbia in order to illustrate two different kinds of differentiation in societies which historically have cherished unitary traditions of Church and nation. In Russia the collusion of Church and State is maintained only by the mainly pragmatic concerns of the new ruling élites and by an overlap between a sector of the clergy and a sector of nationalist opinion. It is in that overlap that opposition is generated to religious voluntarism, and that voluntarism (for example, of American evangelicals or New Age groups) is defined as cultural invasion. So far as the rest of the society is concerned, the 'spirit' walks abroad quite freely and with some volatility, though it often comes to rest in the religious shapes and havens carved out by the sometime national Church, and in the invocation of place and continuity with which that Church is associated.

In Serbia, however, a long-term siege mentality has been exacerbated by the instability of borders since the break-up of the former Yugoslavia and the existence of substantial pockets of Serbs outside those borders. This mentality has subsumed both communist and Christian universalism into a nationalist ideology which is simultaneously defensive and aggressive. Serbian society is aggressively directed by opportunist ex-members of the communist apparatus wearing the garments of nationalism, and they are to some extend aided, though at a less stentorian level, by many of the leaders of the Serbian Orthodox Church. Religion and ethnicity are for the moment barely distinguishable in that a Serb *has* to be an Orthodox (meaning, in part, *not* a Muslim and *not* a Catholic). A non-Orthodox Serb is likely, therefore, to be regarded with some suspicion.

The signs of this near-identity can be found in the magnificent new cathedral recently erected in Belgrade, in the obsession with Kosovo as a pilgrimage centre set in territory now mostly occupied by non-Serbs, and in a constant almost mythic invocation of lands lost and Serbs expelled. It is in the cause of recovering these historic lost lands that a Serb may seek a quasi-religious martyrdom. Yet, in spite of this union of national and religious identity, differentiation is in practice far advanced. The religiose version of nationalist fervour only marginally overflows into regular religious worship or communion or belief. Investigation of Serb belief shows it floating fairly freely around a repertoire of Orthodox and other motifs.

If one wanted to cite parallel examples of besieged cultures where religion and nation are still closely aligned, the obvious cases would be the Protestant Scots-Irish of Northern Ireland, the Israelis, and the Afrikaaners. The Israelis maintain their original narrative in relation to a territory given by God, and are (understandably) concerned over the defensibility of its borders, the precise defintion of God-given territory, and who is to count as in and who as out. The Afrikaaners are a people defined to some degree by ethnicity, language, history, and religion—and by a narrative of expulsion and pilgrimage—but unlike the Israelis they have no territory where they form a viable majority. First they tried erecting internal borders and herding people of colour into reservations, but with the collapse of such a policy they were left with no 'homelands' of their own. In Ulster there are three semi-territorial churches, Catholic, Anglican, and Presbyterian, each attached to a semi-ethnic base. The relationship between these three groupings (usually reduced to two, Catholic and Protestant) is in permanent disequilibrium because in many areas they are mixed together, because each is large enough to threaten the other (as well as to counterbalance the sovereign powers of the State), and because they identify with powers outside present borders.

In all three cases a group with the sense of having been elected as a covenant nation has been on the move, sometimes more than once, and in the Jewish case over centuries. Through all vicissitudes these peoples have retained the crucial narrative of a land set aside for them, only to find the niche chosen by them and/or by God is too constricted, or partly occupied by other peoples, or just not viable. As a result the definitions of nationality and religion have historically been pushed together, in particular by the question of boundaries, but in all three there is a partial separating out of those engaged in the practice of piety from those merely identifying themselves in religio-ethnic terms. Thus, in Israel there is both a non-religious nationalism and a religiosity opposed to the state of Israel. Indeed, there is a religiosity nourished in the Yeshivot which specifically rejects violence in the appropriation of the land given by God.

The next two examples are towards the voluntaristic end of the spectrum, though both contain substantial religo-ethnic enclaves. They are South Africa *taken as a whole*, and the United States. These two examples are selected to show that where voluntarism is established as the main principle of religious organization, and ethnic concentrations do not simultaneously correspond to territorial and religious differences, then it is possible to achieve a reconciliation of differences which is in part facilitated by religion. It is very unlikely that conflicts will arise over religious differences *per se*.

If we take South Africa first we observe a society cast in the Anglo-American model of voluntary religious bodies. There are many different ethnicities, many religious bodies, but few if any instances of a religio-ethnic combination situated in a viable territory. Given this basic configuration, it has been possible to move to a democratic, multi-ethnic society with relatively little violence, and there has been very little by way of a militant fusion of ethnicity and religion. The main problem relates to the territorial concentration of the Kwa-Zulu, but that is not reinforced by a particular distinctive religiosity unless the Zulus were to attempt the erection of a national religion. In South Africa the Afrikaaners were the 'senior' white ethnic group, and their culture was nourished by Calvinist Churches. But their power was qualified and checked by the British, whose culture was in turn nourished by the Anglican Church, and by other British denominations, notably the Methodists. All these churches had constituencies across the colour line. Indeed, in the Anglican, Methodist, and above all the Roman Catholic churches, the black membership outnumbered the white. With this kind of mixed constituency, it was possible for large numbers of clergy to become critics of apartheid, and so inhibit polarization, even though local churches generally tended to be of one colour rather than another. Beyond that, it was also possible for charismatic movements to move across barriers both of denomination and ethnicity, even though their political content was often apparently conservative. Perhaps that even helped, since a combination of religious and political radicalism might have aroused fears and inhibitions.

There were two other principal players on the South African scene, excluding for the moment substantial communities of Jews, Indians, Orientals, etc. The Zulus have already been mentioned. They had a partial ethnic base but belonged to various denominations. And then there were the Christian Zionists, and others who derived from voluntaristic denominational traditions, some of them Pentecostal, and numbering anything up to six million. Politically these were the sleeping giants of black consciousness. Just as among American blacks, religion brought them together and created a social space where they could be themselves. It even organized them in quasi-military formations, but it was conspicuously non-violent. The Zionists found a voice, but they were soft-spoken.

Given this configuration, the negotiations could be carried out by people nurtured in pacific denominational traditions and within cultural talking distance and hearing distance. De Klerk came from a 'Dopper' background which emphasized a conservative Calvinism, but he experienced a religious conversion as to the need to abolish apartheid and attempt reconciliation. Mandela came from a Methodist background. Oliver Tambo was an Anglican, as was Desmond Tutu, and Alan Boesak was Reformed. Buthelezi, as leader of the Kwa-Zulu, was—and is—potentially the most recalcitrant player, but he happened to be a devout evangelical Christian and was persuaded at the crucial moment by Kenyan evangelical friends through a prolonged session of prayer. Joe Slovo is an obvious exception, coming from a Jewish background and being both an atheist and a communist. However, the overall atmosphere was dominated by a culture of voluntaristic religiosity, without any direct correspondence of a given ethnic group with a given religion.

In the United States the proportions of black and white were almost the reverse of those in South Arica, which certainly facilitated peaceful change in the American case, at least outside the South. It is not necessary here to repeat the standard analyses of American religion in terms of Judaizing elements relating to territory, pilgrim journey, promised land, covenant people, and so on. These have certainly been present historically, but the crucial point relates to the way voluntarism provided the original cultural motive and absorbed successive migrations of groups partly defined in religious and ethnic terms. Thus tensions rarely broke into overt conflict and, in any case, had no territorial bases from which conflict might be organized. In a similar manner the mobilization of black consciousness was begun in the social space cleared by religion and led by black ministers on a basis of principled non-violence. As in South Africa, denominations crossed the colour line, even though in the South, these denominations, notably Methodists and Baptists, split into black and white variants. Thus negotiations could be carried out within cultural hearing distance and aided by the mobility of black leaders within a partly shared social system of American aspiration, opportunity, and constitutional rights.

It is crucial that the lines of ethnicity were partially crossed by the religious organizations, even though there was sufficient alienation to generate the Nation of Islam, and so hint at a greater polarization and a separate black consciousness, at increased cultural distance, and possible militancy. But note that black militancy both in South Africa and the United States, meaning by militancy the threatened use of violence, was a tactic of *political* groupings. In the USA the non-violent religious leadership was much more successful, but what is interesting in South Africa is that as apartheid collapsed the leadership on both sides was able to shift into a religious mode and deploy the language of brotherhood, peace, and reconciliation. The new national anthem of South Africa is an old Methodist hymn.

Before proceeding to the last interim example, which is Brazil, it is worth indicating in passing the possibility of hybrid cases where a Judaizing group can be independently generated by the original narrative within the context of voluntarism. These are fascinating mutations of the basic code as well as migrations of the sacred. Three groups illustrate this possibility, the Mormons and Jehovah's Witnesses in the USA and La Luz del Mundo in Mexico. The Mormons actually created a territorial base, the Witnesses constituted a nation, outside the secular nation, and La Luz del Mundo has acquired a specific district in Guadalajara.

The final example is drawn from Brazil. Brazilian Catholicism was nationalized by 'enlightened' Portuguese autocracy over two centuries ago, but it remained effectively nationalized under the Brazilian empire and then again under the republic up to the early twentieth century. Even after Rome recovered control, the nationalist theme was emphasized and the Virgin proclaimed Queen of Brazil. However, the Brazilian Virgin never had the power of our Lady of Guadalupe in Mexico or of our Lady of Czestochova in Poland. The identification of Catholicism with Brazilian nationalism was far from militant and coexisted alongside an extensive Afro-Brazilian spiritism. Nowadays Brazil offers hospitality to any number of voluntary groups.

When evangelicalism began to expand in the northeast early in the twentieth century, it encountered relatively modest opposition on the grounds of being culturally alien. Now evangelicals, especially Pentecostals, comprise a massive constituency of over twenty million and within their communities they have successfully reformed and pacified most aspects of the Brazilian macho personality. Brazilian evangelicals, like evangelicals elsewhere in Latin America, are industrious, disciplined, and highly pacific. Their characteristic personality is highly resistant to any kind of collective military organization of left or right. They are devout and they offer violence to none. Nor do they expect to encounter violence from others on grounds of religion. Brazil is a society thoroughly animated by the presumption of a spiritual world but not on that account generating violence, either internally between faiths or externally. The predicted consequences of religious belief are notably absent. The same is true of other forms of social differentiation in Brazilian religion, notably charismatic Catholicism and the base communities. The base communities do, indeed, shift their theological emphasis to the Exodus and the liberation from Egypt but their critique of society is mainly applied in local politics, and the sanctions they apply, even the occasional occupations, are always carried out according to non-violent norms. The patron saint of liberation theology is not the deviant case of Camillo Torres, the guerrilla, but Archbishop Romero of El Salvador, the man who suffered exemplary martyrdom.

Reference to Brazil introduces the final point to be made about the role of religion in a differentiated society. I make it shortly, but I regard it as a major qualification to standard secularization theory. If we suppose, as I do, that differentiation is the most universally widespread element in secularization, it is perfectly possible to view the voluntary condition of Christian churches as a release from a Babylonish captivity to the nation state. That does not mean, as has been frequently emphasized in the course of this argument, that it loses all contact with place, time, continuity, and history. Equally it does not mean that the religion becomes privatized. As José Casanova has recently argued in his important book *Public Religions in the Modern World*, contemporary religion is able to mobilize broadly humane sentiments in order to make a major contribution to debate in the public forum.[3] Casanova argues vigorously that the temple has not finally been made irrelevant to the forum. Whether we consider the critique mounted by the Catholic Church in Brazil, the public debates in the United States, or Holland or Brazil, the concept of subsidiarity in the construction of the European Community, the role of the Churches in changes in Eastern Europe and Africa and the Philippines, the contribution of religion has been of signal importance. And it has been almost entirely directed to peaceful reconciliation internally and peace in foreign affairs. If Dawkins's arguments were correct then the separating out of believers and clergy from the general population ought to reveal them as major proponents of violence towards each other and violence in international affairs. This is far from being the case. The evidence does not bear out the contention. The case falls.[4]

[3] José Casanova, *Public Religion in the Modern World* (Chicago, 1994); for a rather different view cf. Gilles Kepel *The Revenge of God* (Oxford, 1994).

[4] For accounts of the approaches of Judaism and of Christianity with respect to war and violence such as might fill out the argument in this chapter cf. Susan Nidich, *War in the Hebrew Bible* (Oxford, 1993), and Roland Bainton, *Christian Attitudes Toward War and Peace* (London, 1961).

BIBLIOGRAPHY

Alter, Robert, and Kermode, Frank (eds.), *The Literary Guide to the Bible* (London, 1987).

Aron, Raymond, *Peace and War: A theory of international relations* (London, 1962).

Bainton, Ronald, *Christian Attitudes to War and Peace* (London, 1961).

Beales, A. C. F., *The Catholic Church and the International Order* (Harmondsworth, 1942).

Bloom, Harold, *The American Religion* (London and New York, 1992).

Bowker, John, *Is God a Virus? Genes, culture and religion* (London, 1995).

——*Problems of Suffering in Religions of the World* (Cambridge, 1970).

Brock, Peter, *Pacifism in the United States from the Colonial Era to the First World War* (Princeton, NJ, 1968).

Brown, Peter, *The Body and Society* (London, 1989).

Bruce, Steve, *God Save Ulster!* (Oxford, 1986).

Burnside, Jonathan, and Baker, Nicola (eds.), *Relational Justice* (Winchester, 1994).

Carlton, Eric, *War and Ideology* (London, 1990).

Casanova, José, *Public Religion in the Modern World* (Chicago, 1994).

Ceadel, Martin, *Thinking about Peace and War* (Oxford, 1987).

Clark, Jonathan, *The Language of Liberty* (Cambridge, 1993).

Davies, Jon, and Wollaston, Isabel, *A Sociology of Sacred Texts* (Sheffield, 1993).

Dawkins, Richard, *The Selfish Gene*, 2nd edn. (Oxford, 1989).

Ferguson, John (ed.), *Studies in Christian Social Commitment* (London, 1954).

Frost, Brian, *The Politics of Peace* (London, 1991).

Hinsley, F., *Power and the Pursuit of Peace* (Cambridge, 1963).

Jacoby, Susan, *Wild Justice: The evolution of revenge* (New York, 1983).

Jeurissen, Ronald, *Peace and Religion* (Kampen, The Netherlands, 1991).

Kepel, Gilles, *The Revenge of God* (Oxford, 1994).

Lewis, C. S., *The Allegory of Love* (Oxford, 1936).

Malcoln, Noel, *Bosnia: A Short History* (London, 1994).

Martin, David, *The Breaking of the Image* (Oxford, 1980).

——*A General Theory of Secularization* (Oxford, 1978).

——*Pacifism: An historical and sociological study* (London, 1965).

——*Reflections on Sociology and Theology* (Oxford, 1996).

Martin, David, and Mullen, Peter (eds.), *Unholy Warfare: The Church and the bomb* (Oxford, 1983).

Nidich, Susan, *War in the Hebrew Bible* (Oxford, 1993).

Niebuhr, Reinhold, *The Children of Light and the Children of Darkness* (London, 1945).

——*Moral Man and Immoral Society* (New York, 1932).

Niebuhr, Richard, *Christ and Culture* (New York, 1951).

Ramsey, Paul, *The Just War: Force and political responsibility* (London and New York, 1968).

Richter, Melvin, *The Politics of Conscience* (London, 1965).

Sheils, William (ed.), *The Church and War* (Oxford, 1983).

Wallensteen, Peter (ed.), *Peace Research: Achievements and challenges* (London and Boulder, Col., 1988).

Walzer, Michael, *Just and Unjust Wars* (Harmondsworth, 1977).

Wilkinson, Alan, *The Church of England and the First World War* (London, 1978).

Wolffe, John, *God and Greater Britain* (London, 1994).

World Council of Churches, *World Conference on Church and Society* [Geneva, 1966] (Geneva, 1967).

Yinger, J. Milton, *Religion in the Struggle for Power* (Durham, NC, 1946).

—— *Religion, Society, and the Individual* (New York, 1957).

—— *The Scientific Study of Religion* (New York, 1970).

Zahn, Gordon, *German Catholics in Hitler's Wars* (New York, 1962).

INDEX

Gender,
Ideology, and
Action

GENDER, IDEOLOGY, AND ACTION

HISTORICAL PERSPECTIVES ON WOMEN'S PUBLIC LIVES

EDITED BY

Janet Sharistanian

CONTRIBUTIONS IN WOMEN'S STUDIES, NUMBER 67

Greenwood Press
NEW YORK • WESTPORT, CONNECTICUT • LONDON

Library of Congress Cataloging-in-Publication Data
Gender, ideology, and action.

(Contributions in women's studies, ISSN 0147–104X ;
no. 67)
Produced in the University of Kansas Research
Institute on Women's Public Lives.
Bibliography: p.
Includes index.
1. Women in public life—History—Congresses.
2. Women in public life—United States—History—
Congresses. 3. Women—History—Congresses. 4. Women—
United States—History—Congresses. I. Sharistanian,
Janet. II. University of Kansas. Research Institute
on Women's Public Lives. III. Series.
HQ1390.G45 1986   305.4′0973   85–27257
ISBN 0–313–24273–9 (lib. bdg. : alk. paper)

Library of Congress Catalog Card Number: 85–27257
ISBN: 0–313–24273–9
ISSN: 0147–104X

First published in 1986

Greenwood Press, Inc.
88 Post Road West, Westport, Connecticut 06881

Printed in the United States of America

∞™

The paper used in this book complies with the
Permanent Paper Standard issued by the National
Information Standards Organization (Z39.48-1984).

10 9 8 7 6 5 4 3 2 1

This book is dedicated to the memory and legacy
of Michelle Zimbalist Rosaldo and Carolyn Wood Sherif,
pioneers and leaders in the development of women's studies

Contents

Gender,
Ideology, and
Action

1

Introduction: Women's Lives in the Public and Domestic Spheres

JANET SHARISTANIAN

During the summer of 1980 fourteen researchers selected in a national competition came together to work individually and collectively at the University of Kansas Research Institute on Women's Public Lives. The institute was designed to explore the subject of women's public—that is, extradomestic—lives and the connections between their activities in the public and private spheres. This general framework was chosen partly as a corrective to the common tendency to see women as synonymous with the family and partly as a test of some generalizations about women's status and social roles that have emerged from feminist scholarship.

The participants, all women, represented a wide range in terms of age, class, race, ethnic background, and sexual orientation and came from the humanities and the social, behavioral, and biological sciences (though not all are represented in the two volumes that have resulted from the institute). Thus they represented many kinds of connections to the field of women's studies. Diversity was also evident in their topics, which were not predetermined but instead emerged out of the researchers' varied interests, methodological backgrounds, and conceptual frameworks.

Vocabularies and conceptual storehouses were additionally enriched by eight visiting scholars who gave lectures and seminars and held informal discussions on aspects of and approaches to women's public lives.[1] By the end of the summer it was apparent that a complex, often intense, fusion of the public and the private had taken place in the institute itself—in the group as a whole, among participants, and for individuals—and that these spheres overlapped, intersected, and sometimes conflicted with one another.

Such public/private connections were renewed at the follow-up meeting held the next year, when the researchers' presentations were commented on in writing by all of their institute colleagues and session leaders from the university, as well as orally by the audience.[2] The nearly invisible, highly private editorial and rewriting cycles that followed particularly pointed out the limitations, difficulties, and rewards of attempting to think, create, and "talk" across disciplinary boundaries and languages. Though information, concepts, terms, and methodologies characteristic of one discipline can be integrated into study done in another, and even symbiosis is possible, the demands on researcher and editor are heavy. Ideas must be "translated" across disciplines, which may range from the particularistic to the universal, the abstract to the concrete, the qualitative to the quantitative; and even individual disciplines often speak in a Babel of tongues.

In both public and private ways the institute has continued, since friendships made there endure and many individual and collaborative research projects have been entered into because of it. Yet this volume and its companion (*Beyond the Public/Domestic Dichotomy: Contemporary Perspectives on Women's Public Lives*, ed. Janet Sharistanian, Greenwood Press, 1987) comprise its most obvious public product and as such should be set into the context of ongoing debate on the opposition and connections between public and private domains that has constituted a significant theme in the recent study of women.

Concepts of public and private entered feminist theory primarily through the medium of cultural anthropology. In her influential theoretical overview to the volume *Women, Culture, and Society*,[3] Michelle Z. Rosaldo posited the separation of, or opposition between, domestic and public realms as a way of explaining comparable studies of women emerging from a wide variety of historical and social settings. She based this model on a number of key points. First, despite matriarchalist assertions, wide cultural variation, and the fact that women are frequently "important, powerful, and influential,"[4] in all known societies male activities are more highly valued than female activities.[5] Second, universal sexual asymmetry is also evident in the fact that "everywhere men have some authority over women, . . . a culturally legitimated right to [their] subordination and compliance."[6] Third, though women "exert important pressures on the social life of the group,"[7] they generally do so through informal influence and power rather than through formal authority.

Rosaldo suggested that sexual asymmetry be understood not in terms of biology per se but in terms of "the fact that, in most traditional societies, a good part of a woman's adult life is spent giving birth to and raising children"; that because of these responsibilities women participate relatively less than men in public life; that this leads to "a differentiation of domestic and public spheres of activity"; and that such structural differentiation affects men's and women's relative psychological, cultural, political, and economic experiences in given societies.[8]

Arguing that such opposition underlies rather than determines sexual asymmetry in particular societies, Rosaldo offered several suggestions for the improvement of women's status. They might enter the public world of men or form a public world of their own, or men might enter the domestic world. In general, she hypothesized that "women's status will be lowest in those societies where there is a firm differentiation between domestic and public spheres of activity and where women are isolated from one another." Conversely, the most egalitarian societies will be "those in which public and domestic spheres are only weakly differentiated," with women and men sharing authority in both domains.[9]

Though the domestic/public model advanced by Rosaldo, Louise Lamphere, Sherry Ortner, Nancy Chodorow, Peggy Sanday, and others[10] has had substantial impact on the development of women's studies, various arguments against it—or, at any rate, reinterpretations of it— have been advanced. In effect, all of these criticisms amount to a perception of the model as overgeneralized and too homogeneous, though it ostensibly accounts for variety. Such disagreements can be divided into three rough and sometimes overlapping categories: cross-cultural diversity, transhistorical variation and change, and arguments arising from consideration of different classes and races within a given society. From these, more generalized objections can be drawn.

For example, Niara Sudarkasa, arguing from a cross-cultural perspective, contends that in preindustrial, precapitalist, and precolonial societies generally, traditional West African societies in particular, and even, to a considerable extent, contemporary West Africa, many political and economic activities are embedded in domestic units. Thus power, authority, and influence are not dichotomized into spheres for either sex, and female leaders operating in the public domain are not thereby entering the world of men. In short, though such societies may appear to fall into the category of weak differentiation between private and public spheres, domestic and public domains are not distinguished as such, so that analyzing them in these terms is misleading.[11]

Another cross-cultural denial of the model has come from Sharon W. Tiffany. While commending recent studies of peasant women's exercise of informal political power, she has also pointed out that to assume that women in most societies exercise only covert, indirect influence on male decision making can make it impossible for observers to recognize women's formal political and administrative roles where these exist.[12] This methodological warning has been expanded into a more comprehensive rejoinder by Susan Carol Rogers in an overview of anthropological approaches to the study of women. She argues against the use of the public/private domain distinction on both cross-cultural and epistemological grounds. First, a general theory of sexual differentiation "based primarily on the constraints of woman's physiological functions and childrearing responsibilities is . . . a clear reflection of our cultural priorities,"[13] and second, "the fact that women are assumed from the outset to be subordinated introduces considerable tautology."[14] And on a yet more general level Erika Bourguignon, in introducing a wide-ranging collection of anthropological essays, points to the confusing diversity in definitions of what is included in the domestic and public domains and insists that the researcher's first task is "to seek to discover what domains are, in fact, recognized in particular societies."[15]

None of the arguments discussed so far need be limited to the study of contemporary settings, and additional objections to the public/private model have come from historians and sociologists concerned with the accuracy of the historical record and with social change occurring over time. For instance, historian Louise Tilly has expressed dismay at what she considers the normative and prescriptive nature of much anthropological endeavor, which, in describing a particular culture at a given time, may be both overgeneralizing the picture and fixing it in a static frame. Her point is that unless attention is paid to "negative or anomalous cases,"[16] such as unmarried or childless women, the complexity of a given historical and social situation will go unrecorded. In effect, she is arguing, the exception may disprove, not prove, the rule. In addition, she asserts that sexual asymmetry does not necessarily imply subordination. One might elaborate on her discussion; to define women mainly in terms of their status relative to that of men is in effect to judge them externally and from a masculine point of view. When women are viewed from their own perspective, the value to them of female solidarity, quite aside from its usefulness as a tool to influence men, or even of sexual segregation may be revealed.

Looking at recent historical change, sociologist Gaye Tuchman objects that the domestic/public domain approach obscures not precapitalist societies but contemporary capitalist ones. Pointing out that since the late nineteenth century the meanings of *public* and *private* have become thoroughly confused, that over a third of women with preschool children work outside the home, and that the conventional nuclear family is becoming increasingly rare, she considers it more sensible to see women as "people with two jobs" rather than identifying them with the domestic sphere.[17]

On the intrasocial level, Diane K. Lewis, in an influential study of black women's responses to feminism, has modified the domestic/public model. Specifically, she argues that it is "of limited applicability to minority women subjected to the constraints of both racism and sexism";[18] more generally, that it is not discriminating enough for studying complex societies in which dominant and subdominant groups, male and female roles, and different aspects of the dominant public sphere must be both distinguished from and correlated with each other.

For instance, insofar as the public sphere is defined as paid employment, black women have traditionally had high levels of labor-force participation, albeit frequently in menial and low-paying jobs. Moreover, this has given them "power over the limited resources available to a racially excluded group."[19] On the other hand, if the public domain is taken to mean political and legislative authority, then both black women and black men have systematically been excluded from that sphere—despite which, and in direct contrast to the model, researchers find "growing evidence of strong egalitarianism in black sex-role relationships."[20] Lewis concludes, from her example, that "differential participation in the public sphere is a symptom rather than a cause of structural inequality. While inequality is *manifested* in the exclusion of a group from public life, it is actually *generated* in the group's unequal access to power and resources in a hierarchically arranged social order."[21] And if the root issue is the hierarchical ordering of society, then her enlarged categories are applicable to other complex societies, to other racial minorities, and to the analysis of class differences.

Given these responses to her original formulations, it is not surprising to find Rosaldo herself questioning and revising the domestic/public model in a 1980 essay entitled "The Use and Abuse of Anthropology: Reflections on Feminism and Cross-Cultural Understanding." She reasserts the significance for their public status of women's reproductive role, again argues that "in all known human groups . . . the vast majority of opportunities for public influence and prestige, . . . are all recognized as men's privilege and right,"[22] and points out that to focus on situations in which women enjoy the use of power is to forget "that men and women ultimately live together in the world."[23] However, she also breaks with her earlier formulation in stating that women's status in society is "not in any direct sense a product of the things she does (or even less a function of what, biologically speaking, she is) but of the meanings her activities acquire through concrete social interactions."[24] Since " 'women's status' is itself not one thing but many things," gender must be studied "in political and social terms, with reference . . . to local and specific forms of social relationship."[25]

In fact, among the most productive contributions to the study of women are those which have looked at definitions of and interactions between public and domestic not in universalist, biological, and ahistorical terms but in terms of social and political interpretations of women's and men's activities in specific historical contexts. For instance, as Rosaldo herself noted,[26] Western political philosophy since the time of the Greeks and the Victorian ideology of separate spheres are particularly dependent upon assumptions about the location of male and female in public and domestic domains, respectively. Jean Bethke Elshtain has unpacked the many layers of meaning—social, economic, psychological, epistemological, even metaphysical—that such assumptions have led to in *Public Man, Private Woman: Women in Social and*

Political Thought.[27] Susan Moller Okin, in *Women in Western Political Thought*, has shown that these assumptions are so central to our canonical political theory that an attempt to redefine it so that women are equals to men pulls the foundation out from underneath the foundation.[28] Katherine Kish Sklar has shown how Catharine Beecher both was molded by domestic ideology and, as a powerful public figure, made use of it to help create a female domain with substantial impact upon national life.[29] By tracing the shifting meanings of *public* and *private* in nineteenth-century feminism, Ellen Carol DuBois has been able to locate the radicalism of the women's suffrage movement in its challenge to the very basis of American political institutions.[30] Elaine Showalter has documented the exclusion of women from the masculine realm of literature and their formulation of what amounts to an intermediate public domain in *A Literature of Their Own: British Women Novelists from Brontë to Lessing*[31]—and then has gone on to develop a theory of women's writing as occupying two different, but overlapping, verbal cultures: dominant and mute.[32] And Zillah Eisenstein has argued in *The Radical Future of Liberal Feminism* that the particular kinds of conflicts between public and domestic being experienced by contemporary American women who are both mothers and members of the labor force will form the basis of future feminism.[33]

Such studies, which in effect if not intent are applications of Rosaldo's revised model, show that the domestic/public paradigm continues to be of value, when it is given precise definition and tested by a specific context. And it is in the spirit of these studies that the essays in this volume should be read. Each asks whether, in studying women's activities outside the home, concepts of domestic or private and public can be useful analytical tools. None makes large-scale generalizations about the origins of women's status cross-culturally and transhistorically, and no absolute definitions as to the content and meaning of women's and men's activities can be drawn from them. Rather, some common themes emerge from these studies, with provocative corollaries and disagreements both between essayists and with Rosaldo's model becoming evident as essays are read in conjunction with one another; one version of such a reading is given in the concluding chapter. In all of them, however, connections between the ideology and the actuality of men's and women's lives, and connections between women's private and public lives, are complex in themselves and in relationship with one another.

NOTES

Members of the Research Institute on Women's Public Lives owe a debt of gratitude, first of all, to the Ford Foundation and its former program officer Mariam Chamberlain, without whom the individual and collaborative activities that made up the institute would not have taken place. The institute also benefitted enormously from the efforts of the seminar leaders and follow-up meeting commentators and from the cooperation of knowledgeable staff members throughout the University of Kansas Libraries, especially Mary Finnegan, then women's studies bibliographer, and Sherry Williams, curator of the Kansas Collection. A special word of thanks goes to the institute's graduate assistant, Susan Watts, who handled tasks from the sublime downward with aplomb. We would also like to honor the memory of institute participant Cheryl Allyn Miller, to whom the companion to this volume, *Beyond the Public/Domestic Dichotomy: Contemporary Perspectives on Women's Public Lives*, is formally dedicated, but who also understood the connections between past and present.

1. The seminar leaders were Margot Peters (biography), Clair (Vickery) Smith (economics), Nona Glazer (sociology), Elaine Showalter (literary criticism), Carolyn Sherif (psychology), Joan Scott (European history), Jacquelyn Hall (American history), and Carol Stack (anthropology and public policy).

2. The commentators were Karlyn Kohrs Campbell (communication studies), Regina Morantz (history), Shirley Harkess (sociology), and Aletha Huston (psychology).

3. "Women, Culture, and Society: A Theoretical Overview," in *Women, Culture, and Society*, ed. Michelle Zimbalist Rosaldo and Louise Lamphere (Stanford, Calif.: Stanford Univ. Press, 1974), pp. 17–42.

4. Ibid., p. 17.

5. Ibid., p. 19.

6. Ibid., p. 21.

7. Ibid.

8. Ibid., p. 23.

9. Ibid., p. 36.

10. See Louise Lamphere, "Strategies, Cooperation, and Conflict among Women in Domestic Groups," pp. 97–112; Sherry Ortner, "Is Female to Male As Nature Is to Culture?," pp. 67–87; Nancy Chodorow, "Family Structure and Feminine Personality," pp. 43–66; and Peggy R. Sanday, "Female Status in the Public Domain," pp. 189–206 in Rosaldo and Lamphere. See also Nancy Chodorow's *The Reproduction of Mothering: Psychoanalysis and the Sociology of Gender* (Berkeley: Univ. of California Press, 1978).

11. Niara Sudarkasa, "Female Employment and Family Organization in West Africa," in *New Research on Women and Sex Roles*, ed. Dorothy G.

McGuigan (Ann Arbor: Univ. of Michigan Center for Continuing Education for Women, 1976), pp. 48–61.

12. Sharon W. Tiffany, "Women, Power, and the Anthropology of Politics: A Review," *International Journal of Women's Studies* 2, no. 9 (Sept./Oct. 1979):430–42.

13. Susan Carol Rogers, "Woman's Place: A Critical Review of Anthropological Theory," *Comparative Studies in Society and History* 20, no. 1 (Jan. 1978):137.

14. Ibid., p. 143.

15. Erika Bourguignon, "Introduction and Theoretical Considerations," in *A World of Women: Anthropological Studies of Women in the Societies of the World*, ed. Erika Bourguignon (New York: Praeger, 1980), p. 7.

16. Louise A. Tilly, "The Social Sciences and the Study of Women: A Review Article," *Comparative Study in Society and History*, 20, no. 1 (Jan. 1978):171.

17. Gaye Tuchman, "Some Thoughts on Public and Private Spheres," *Centerpoint: A Journal of Interdisciplinary Studies*, special issue "Women: The Dialectic of Public and Private Spaces," ed. Rosette C. Lamont, Flora S. Kaplan, and Susan Saegert, 3, nos. 3/4 (Fall/Spring 1980):111–13.

18. Diane K. Lewis, "A Response to Inequality: Black Women, Racism, and Sexism," *Signs: Journal of Women in Culture and Society*, 3, no. 2 (Winter 1977):339.

19. Ibid., p. 345.

20. Ibid., p. 342. However, Alison Bernstein questions Lewis's assertion that black women's substantial responsibilities in the (occupational) public sphere have led to equality in sex-role relationships. See her "Comment" on Lewis's article in *Signs: Journal of Women in Culture and Society* 3, no. 3 (Spring 1978):733–36, and Lewis's "Response" to Bernstein in the same issue, pp. 736–37.

21. Lewis, p. 343.

22. Michelle Zimbalist Rosaldo, "The Use and Abuse of Anthropology: Reflections on Feminism and Cross-Cultural Understanding," *Signs: Journal of Women in Culture and Society* 5, no. 3 (Spring 1980):394.

23. Ibid., p. 396.

24. Ibid., p. 400.

25. Ibid., pp. 400–401.

26. Ibid., pp. 401–2.

27. Jean Bethke Elshtain, *Public Man, Private Woman: Women in Social and Political Thought* (Princeton, N.J.: Princeton Univ. Press, 1981).

28. Susan Moller Okin, *Women in Western Political Thought* (Princeton, N.J.: Princeton Univ. Press, 1979).

29. Katherine Kish Sklar, *Catharine Beecher: A Study in American Domesticity* (New Haven, Conn.: Yale Univ. Press, 1973).

30. Ellen Carol DuBois, *Feminism and Suffrage: The Emergence of an Independent Women's Movement in America, 1848–1869* (Ithaca, N.Y.: Cornell Univ. Press, 1978).

31. Elaine Showalter, *A Literature of Their Own: British Women Novelists from Brontë to Lessing* (Princeton, N.J.: Princeton Univ. Press, 1977).

32. Elaine Showalter, "Feminist Criticism in the Wilderness," *Critical Inquiry*, special issue "Writing and Sexual Difference," ed. Elizabeth Abel, 8, no. 2 (Winter 1981):179–205.

33. Zillah Eisenstein, *The Radical Future of Liberal Feminism* (New York: Longman, 1981).

2

Public and Private: Some Implications for Feminist Literature and Criticism

PATRICE CLARK KOELSCH

Compared with the reality that comes from being seen and heard, even the greatest forces of intimate life—the passions of the heart, the thoughts of the mind, the delights of the senses—lead an uncertain, shadowy kind of existence unless and until they are transformed, deprivatized and deindividualized, as it were, into a shape to fit them for public appearance. The most current of such transformations occurs in story telling and generally in artistic transposition of individual experiences. But we do not need the form of the artist to witness this transfiguration. Each time we talk about things that can be experienced only in privacy or intimacy, we bring them out into a sphere where they will assume a kind of reality which, their intensity not withstanding, they never could have had before.

Hannah Arendt[1]

The personal is political. This is now such a familiar phrase that its truly revolutionary significance for philosophy may not be fully appreciated. From the standpoint of the classical philosophical tradition, this idea is perhaps the most radical premise of feminism. From a feminist standpoint, it is absolutely fundamental. This essay is an examination of the implications of this premise for a feminist theory of literature and literary criticism.

Literature has functioned as a particular kind of interface between the private and public spheres. My claim is that allegiance to the traditional formulation between these spheres has been inimical to the development of a literature (and a critical approach to literature) that is able to come to terms with the privatized nature of women's experience.

I shall begin by discussing the classical Greek distinction between the public and private realms, arguing that the formulation of the distinction implicitly denigrates women and excludes truly personal concerns from political legitimacy.[2] I shall then argue that the role of the arts in general, and literature in particular, as mediator between public and private has served historically to reinforce traditional misogynous ideologies. Finally, I shall present the implications of this phenomenon for feminist literature and criticism.

Historically, the private sphere is the realm of necessity. It is concerned with the creatureliness of persons, the producing, consuming, and reproducing of the persons and things required to sustain us as creatures. It is both cyclic and dualistic. Cyclically, there is the perpetual recurrence of events—seasons, patterns of growth and deterioration—even the body has its own daily cycle of energy and fatigue, hunger and satiation. Dualistically, the cyclic aspect is often experienced as the alteration between two opposites—birth and death, sickness and health. The private sphere is one in which no thing endures but, rather, all things are continually used up and replaced. This is the sphere of physical labor and laborious production. It was in large part because of the extreme physicality of this realm that the ancient Greeks regarded it with disdain.

In the private sphere relationships between individuals were inevitably hierarchical, and these hierarchies were seen as natural (e.g., husband/ wife, father/son, master/slave). Thus this sphere was fundamentally inequitable and authoritarian.

The realm of the polis, the political sphere, was distinguished by its apparent escape from the realm of necessity. The political realm was unconcerned with the satisfaction of specific and constant creaturely needs. The real existence of the polis was predicated on the fact that those who participated in it were in a position that freed them from the creaturely concern for themselves. Only those persons who did not have to labor to meet immediate creaturely needs would be able to take part in the life of the polis. Hence, freedom from such material concerns was the condition, not the consequence, of participation in political activity. One could not be bound to labor in the realm of necessity and also be free to act in the polis.

The polis was the sphere in which one became most individualized by speaking. In contrast to the hierarchical relations of the household, persons in the polis were ostensibly equals. The individual was distinguished by his actions, particularly the act of speech making. Immortality of a kind came to an individual as that individual was remembered for speeches and actions that moved the whole body of the polis. In contrast to the apparent insignificance of any particular individual in the realm of necessity, individuals have endured in the collective memory of the polis. Paradoxically, then, the physical being of an individual had a certain ephemeral quality that was grounded in its quantitative impact.

Two things must be emphasized here. The first is that freedom, as the condition for the political sphere, required that other, nonfree persons provide the care and commodities, the necessities of life, for the free and publicly active persons. The work of the polis was then contingent upon the productive and reproductive labor of persons who could not participate in it. In short, there had to be nonfree persons who could maintain the creaturely needs of others as well as themselves. The second point is that given the biological fact of the essential and inevitable labor of female reproduction, women not only were de facto excluded from activity in the public realm but, perhaps more insidiously, were graphically tied to the realm of necessity through the physicality of pregnancy, birth, and nursing. Consequently women, as a biologically laboring class, were devalued.

It is important to note that the historical association of the female with the private, domestic realm is more than accidental. The inequity of the two spheres is clear. The public almost literally stood on the shoulders of the private. The private supported the public and lifted it out of the realm of necessity. One could breathe the rarefied air of the polis only if there were others consigned to live always among the varied animal odors of necessity. It was not only women's intimate and obvious manifestation of the realm of necessity (a cycle begun at menarche and characterized by menstruation, gestation, parturition, lactation, and menstruation again until the cycle is completed at menopause and women return to the original nonfertile state) but also the assumption that their connection with necessity rendered women unfit for political activity that was so pernicious. For surely the most recurrent, obvious, and pressing instances of necessity are exhibited by both men and women: both sexes consume and excrete organic matter. It may even be the case that male needs exceed female needs quantitatively; men are generally larger than women and thus are likely to have larger appetites and to need more food.

It is crucial to appreciate how pervasive and fundamental this dichotomy of the public and private spheres was and how thoroughly women were relegated to the common, less human private sphere. It is also significant that the arena of rational argument and persuasion was the public sphere, the sphere of purported equals (i.e., persons equalized by freedom). There was no real role for persuasive discourse in the private realm insofar as it was characterized simultaneously by urgency and routine—a fundamental paradox that seems to exclude reasoned discourse by its very nature. One cannot persuade necessity to loosen its bond, nor can one persuade creatures to ignore the demands of nature.

In the ancient world it was in the public sphere, the arena of reasoned discourse among theoretical equals, that a person became most individualized. This calling attention to oneself as an individual was accomplished by speaking well. In the private realm one performed one's role adequately or inadequately. The person in the domestic realm was (and perhaps still is) evaluated primarily on how well he or she functioned within the domestic hierarchy in meeting the always urgent and always routine demands of necessity. An exemplary wife and mother was one who exhibited the virtues suitable to her position. She was not distinguished by any particular act; she was simply a model instance of her kind.

The same was not true in the public realm. What it meant to be an exemplary citizen was not so clear, because an exemplary citizen was not simply an instance of someone enacting a role. Simply obeying the law did not make one an outstanding citizen, although there are outstanding examples of obedience (e.g., Socrates in the *Crito*). In contrast, the obedient, faithful, prudent, and restrained woman was likely to be thought an exemplary wife. Thus Odysseus's wife Penelope is the epitome of this ideal, while Socrates' wife Xanthippe is her antithesis. (It is interesting to note that the zenith of wifeliness is a creation of fiction; the nadir is a victim of biographical caricature.) A citizen, on the other hand, was remembered for speaking in such a way as to cause his fellows to act. Even now the public person is remembered for affecting the common good, for changing the course of events, for making a difference in the contingent realm of the state. One cannot, however, change the course of necessity; one can only meet its demands in ingenious and inventive ways.

The traditional construction of the private and public realm was and still is ultimately destructive to women. The conception of self that women develop under patriarchy is of self as Other. Simone de Beauvoir has pointed out how destructive this construction is to a woman's autonomy, to a woman's ability to act on the premise that "humanity is not animal species, it is an historical reality. Human society is an *antiphysis*—in a sense it is against nature, it does not passively submit to the presence of nature but rather takes over the control of nature on its own behalf."[3]

Men who have had access to the public sphere have assumed this to be true for themselves, but women have always been seen as determined by their female animality or spirituality. However, this idea of women as Other goes hand in hand with the classical and later classic (i.e., nineteenth-century class and caste) formulations of the public and private spheres.[4] It is essential to recognize that the public/private distinction is an aristocratic male construct and is rooted in the oppression of women and nonaristocrats.

Moreover, this oppression was further justified by the ancient bias against the animality of physical labor. Hence, women were ontologically unfit for the public sphere whereas slaves and male laborers were only circumstantially excluded. A woman was in her physical being the very paradigm of labor insofar as she reproduced her kind and produced the nourishment of her offspring. She produced a product that in turn consumed her. Ontologically, then, women could never meet the political condition of freedom. Since the public/private distinction was epistemically grounded in aristocratic male value assumptions, the distinction ignored the actual experience of women. This meant that the women's experience of the private sphere was ideologically irrelevant to how that sphere would be regarded. Women's privatized experience was denied any conceptual legitimacy.

Because the public realm was and is the realm of action, of language, of naming, the ideology of the private realm has always been publicly constructed. The values of both spheres continue to be publicly defined. The essential quality of the private sphere, necessity or the creatureliness of persons, is a given and beyond dispute. However, the accidental qualities of that realm (such as health and sickness, prosperity and plague) are subject to revision and reconstruction. Unfortunately, what is merely customary may be (and often is) confused with what is apparently natural.[5] The creatureliness of female persons in particular is misconstrued.

I have suggested that the values of the private sphere continue to be determined by the public sphere insofar as the public sphere is the realm of purported reasoned discourse, of ideology, of naming, and of language itself.[6] But the problem is larger, since literature—as a manifestation in and of the values of the public realm—assumes a role that is inevitably both descriptive and normative. Furthermore, this role is particularly significant because of the special function of literature as the intermediary between the public and private spheres, between society and the individual. This was in fact suggested by both Plato and Aristotle but with rather different implications for each.

The aesthetic conservatism that characterizes classical theories of art is consonant with the bifurcation of the public and the private. Plato's famous castigation of the poets in the *Republic* is perhaps the most obvious instance of the belief that art can contribute to the public good by undergirding the political ideology and organization of the state.[7] Plato especially feared the formative power of literature upon the very young. Consequently, in the ideal state, storytellers were to be restrained in the tales that they told to their eager and gullible listeners.[8]

Aristotle, on the other hand, emphasized the heuristic pleasures of imitation:

It is clear that the general origin of poetry was due to two causes, each of them part of human nature. Imitation is natural to man from childhood, one of his advantages over the lower animals being this, that he is the most imitative creature in the world, and learns at first by imitation. And it is also natural for all to delight in works of imitation. The truth of this second point is shown by experience: though the objects themselves may be painful to see, we delight to view the more realistic representations of them in art, the forms for example of the lowest animals and of dead bodies. The explanation is to be found in a further fact: to be learning something is the greatest of pleasures not only to the philosopher but also to the rest of mankind, however small their capacity for it, the reason of the delight in seeing the picture is that one is at the same time learning—gathering the meaning of things.[9]

According to Aristotle, then, art informs us about the reality of our world and ourselves. Art acts upon the individual. (Aristotle's most celebrated example is the morally therapeutic value of tragic catharsis.) Because art often depicts both the microcosm (the individual) and the macrocosm (the individual's social structure), it implicitly presents the norms for both. Consequently Aristotle, like Plato, constantly underscores the importance of the moral values portrayed in a given work. In this way a work would maintain the assumed values of the public sphere. The themes appropriately depicted in the arts became universal insofar as they support and justify the prevailing ideology. Literature has continued to function in this manner up to the present. The issue is not that these dominant themes are misguided or even misogynous (though many clearly are), but rather that they are partial and, because of this partiality, have often had a pernicious effect on generations of readers.

Plato's insistence on the dichotomy between the poets and the philosophers (and his apparent repudiation of the former) was based on his acknowledgment of the seductive power of poetry to persuade the hearer that the mere representation of appearance is more than that. In his critique, Plato implies that art does not imitate reality but rather apes it. In doing so, as Iris Murdoch puts it, art "subtly disguises and trivializes" the spiritual.[10] Unfortunately, it does so with utterly bewitching charms.

Because the Greeks understood art as essentially mimetic, it followed that what art presented was a representation of reality. Plato believed that the poet especially had a moral imperative to portray an idealized reality, for at its best, art could teach how things ought to be by providing dispassionate models for emulation. Plato was heir to a tradition that emphasized an ideal of nobility and dignity in the visual and dramatic arts. Reason and serenity were exalted and exemplified. However, this tradition was being supplanted in Plato's own lifetime by a more naturalistic tendency in which states of violent emotion were depicted in sculpture and in which bawdy farce appeared on the stage. Despite this shift from an idealized representation to a more naturalistic portrayal of human behavior, Greek art never abandoned the assumption that art was basically imitative. Art inevitably presented the realm of appearance as the substance of reality.

In fact, Plato was right, but for the wrong reasons. Plato claimed that one danger of an indiscriminate production of and exposure to the arts was an often metaphysically adulterous seduction by the particular. He feared that an infatuation with the appearances made manifest by an individual exemplar would distract the observer from approaching the ultimate reality of the less apparent, more universal realm of truths. The early romance of the learner (noted, as above, by Aristotle) with the mere particular in the insubstantial realm of appearances is likely to become a liaison that rules out a mature fidelity to the objects of transcendent reality. Plato emphasized that the representation of the particular is seductive, for art objects are, in Murdoch's words, "completed by the fantasizing mind in its escape from reality."[11] Plato asks, "is not this dreaming, namely, whether asleep or awake, to think that a likeness is not a likeness but the reality which it resembles?"[12] However, the seductiveness of the particular ought not to be confused with the particularity of seduction. My point is not only that various particulars (among them particular classes such as genres) seduce as metaphysical sirens but that the seduction affects particular individuals in significantly different ways.

It is not the mere fact of the particular but the normative partiality of the particular as it becomes canonical that has been most oppressively seductive. Male experience becomes the human experience; men's portrayal of women becomes women's own self-image. Literary genres and types have an informing and formative effect on social norms and individual psyches. The picaresque novel, for example, celebrates and therefore invites and sanctions youthful, roguish adventure.[13] Social structures and values are often reinforced or challenged by works of literature. (A familiar example of the former is Feodor Dostoevsky's *Crime and Punishment*; of the latter, Harriet Beecher Stowe's *Uncle Tom's Cabin*.)

Literature often implicitly suggests limits for the possibility of an individual's realizing his or her desires and values. In presenting, or by some lights representing, the particular satisfactions, triumphs, and failures—the fates, in short—of individuals, families, and nations, the models in literature describe, prescribe, and proscribe. Although other cultural institutions (such as religions and governments) also shape norms, literature is particularly effective as a broker of values because it is a diversion. It interests and entertains because it allows us to get away from ourselves. The values implicitly espoused in a work (or even by a genre) can easily be assimilated because the work of literature does not, strictly speaking, require us to do anything. We are open to it in a way that we are not when, for example, we are confronted by the imperatives of a sermon. Literature enables us to turn away from ourselves only to return to and refocus on ourselves. We often see ourselves differently in the afterglow of some particularly absorbing literary work. In this way, literature shapes our apprehension of ourselves and our world.

Insofar as literature has an undeniably public existence and function, and inasmuch as the particulars in literature function as universals, the "private" life is publicly constructed by literature. For women especially, this public literary construction of the private is often radically incommensurate with the actualities of private experience. The public literary construction of women informs (though not exclusively) the expectations of literate and literary men and women about women. The actual lived (i.e., privatized) lives of women seem unreal because they are unrepresented or misrepresented by a literary tradition that is predominantly male and patriarchal.[14] Suppose, for example, that the fictional Molly Bloom is taken to be the definitive statement on the private life (i.e., the consciousness) of one kind of woman—the "earthy" type. Joyce's construction of the sexuality of the character Molly Bloom becomes an archetype not only in literature but also for actual women's lives. When an actual woman has been identified or categorized as this type (by herself or by others) she will be expected to conform to the norms and conventions appropriate to Molly Bloom. If she apparently doesn't, she may be seen as shamming, either deliberately or because she is lying to herself about what she really wants. The literature produced is partial and incomplete, yet, as it suggests the possibilities for women's human existence, it assumes a crucial public function. Here again is the conflict between appearance and reality. The catch is that we often depend on art to tell us what appearances really mean. Traditional (i.e., patriarchal) literature has served to confirm the masculine construction. Unfortunately, the "felt contradiction" is likely to be explained in terms of personal inadequacy or distortion on the part of the woman so affected. It is important to understand that both women and men explain the contradiction for women in this way. This shows clearly how potent the public literary models are. To say that "the personal is political" is to repudiate the patriarchal construction of public and private and to claim a legitimacy for the unconcealment of the privatized.[15]

It was exactly this discrepancy between the public literary construc-

tion of women and their existential situation that prompted Virginia
Woolf's ironic remark:

A very queer, composite being thus emerges. Imaginatively she is of the highest
importance; practically she is completely insignificant. She pervades poetry
from cover to cover; she is all but absent from history. She dominates the lives
of kings and conquerors in fiction; in fact she was the slave of any boy whose
parents forced a ring upon her finger. Some of the most inspired words, some
of the most profound thoughts in literature fall from her lips; in real life she
could hardly read, could scarcely spell, and was the property of her husband.[16]

It might be argued that art (and literature in particular) has never been
loyal to the reality of ordinary lives, that until fairly recently the great
works (i.e., those in the canon) have focused on aristocratic heroes and
figures of mythic stature, thus excluding the experiences of the vast
majority of men. Surely this is true, and I do not want to minimize the
ways in which Western literature has upheld the legitimacy of the
oppression of men who were not Caucasian, Christian, or affluent by
those who were. However, for women there has been a difference not
just in degree but also in kind. Men from particular socially oppressed
groups and women as a group do find themselves routinely subjected
to the rigid polarities of stereotyping. Women are traditionally portrayed
as either completely chaste and self-sacrificing (i.e., the stereotype of
the Madonna), or as evil and sexually voracious (i.e., the temptress/
whore stereotype). Analogously, men of color have been depicted as
either stoic "noble savages" or ignorant "jungle bunnies." The similarities in stereotyping indicate that stereotyping is a politically useful
strategy for trivializing oppression. But the parallel ends here abruptly.
The implications of gender differences outweigh the similarities in stereotyping. Simone de Beauvoir puts it this way:

It amounts to this: just as for the ancients there was an absolute vertical with
reference to which the oblique was defined, so there is an absolute human type,
the masculine. . . . [woman] is defined and differentiated with reference to man
and not he with reference to her; she is the incidental, the inessential as opposed
to the essential. He is the Subject, he is the Absolute—she is the Other.[17]

It is this reduction to the ontological (as well as the biological) category of the Other (consequently, the dependent, the lesser) that is so
degrading to women. The language and the structure of this traditional

framework make it virtually impossible for women to achieve any conceptual autonomy. The private realm of female experience has been forced to lie in the Procrustean bed of patriarchal public ideology.[18]

I am not arguing for a mimetic theory of art that would simply include works by and about women that accurately represent the privatized aspects of women's experiences. It is important that women find their voices and visions, but mere imitation, however skillful, is too narrow an aesthetic. Instead, I want to emphasize the dynamic aspect of literature as a liberating and transforming agent that cannot be restricted to an ostensibly representative technique. The work of literature becomes part of the reality that is the life history of the person who encounters it, confirming, affirming, denying, and expanding that person's ideas. Sometimes the apparently fantastic touches us with startling immediacy and intimacy; thus the impact of Franz Kafka's "Metamorphosis," Samuel Beckett's *Waiting for Godot*, and Toni Morrison's *Sula*. This literature engages us in a rather different way by inviting an expanded apprehension of the very meaning of possibility and limitation.

In a slightly different context, Wallace Stevens claimed that "the truth seems to be that we live in concepts of the imagination before the reason has established them. . . . In [this] statement . . . the word 'concepts' means concepts of normality."[19] Stevens believes that the work of the imagination is to enable the individual to understand and order experience. Literature not only is a manifestation of the imagination of an author, but it also nourishes the imagination of the reader.

This dynamic, transforming aspect of literature is a particularly important feature in the modern period. Catharine Stimpson puts it this way:

Literary texts do have the strength to subvert ordinary modes of consciousness. Naming the strange, unfamiliar, unpalatable, and alarming, they can, potentially, rearrange habitual modes of thought and feeling. In much modern literature and literary theory, this ability is construed less as one option for the text than as a necessity.[20]

The transforming effect of literature depends upon both what exists in the work and what the reader brings to the work (i.e., the critical framework through which the reader interprets the work). The critical framework can be either a formal, scholarly method or a more informal inductive approach based on other literary and nonliterary experiences and expectations. Northrop Frye has claimed that the enterprise of the scholarly literary critic is "scientific," whereas "it is the task of the public critic to exemplify how a man of taste uses and evaluates literature, and thus how literature is to be absorbed into society."[21]

As a critical ideal, Frye advocates the separation of the subjectivity of the critic (i.e., the personal) from the practice of scientific criticism:

The critic has a subjective background of experience formed by his temperament and by every contact with words he has made, including newspapers, advertisements, conversations, movies and whatever he read at the age of nine. He has a specific skill in responding to literature which is no more like this subjective background, with all its private memories, associations, and arbitrary prejudices, than reading a thermometer is like shivering.[22]

Frye's ideal critic is impersonal, highly skilled, and able to take the universal perspective. What this actually amounts to is that criticism becomes an exercise practiced by an elite for its own benefit. In this theory, process and feeling, those personal, "feminine" elements, are impurities that the critic must filter out. In effect, Frye sanctions only those critics who speak from the pulpit of Beauvoir's Absolute.[23] But this purportedly objective and disinterested stance is in reality neither; moreover, objectivity and disinterestedness are false patriarchal idols. Indeed, not only the impersonality of literary criticism but that of science itself can be questioned. The label "scientific" is a misleading but politically effective honorific. Contemporary philosophers of science and sociologists concerned with the sociology of scientific knowledge have argued that the fact-value distinction is not substantive and that scientific "progress" is not a linear accumulation of objective knowledge.[24]

Claims of critical impartiality, objectivity, and disinterestedness have enabled traditional critics to ignore or justify the social and political implications of their critical work. Feminist critics have attacked this interpretation of the nature and function of literary criticism as benign defense of the status quo. Criticism (whether popular or academic) teaches us how to read the text. Thus even when women have written about the experience of women (paticularly when they have written about the existential meaning of being female), the literature is read in ways that confirm patriarchal structures and judgments.

For example, Jane Austen's *Emma* is often read as a prenuptial variation of the taming-of-the-shrew tale rather than as a treatment of the way in which the social approbation of feminine beauty, wealth, and position nearly blinds a young woman to what is valuable to herself and others. Traditional critics of *Emma* usually emphasize how Emma must be taught the folly of her own vanity and self-serving matchmaking without putting Emma in her patriarchal social context. Emma is thus interpreted as an exemplar of a female stereotype. Even such a generally humane and sympathetic critic as Wayne Booth sees Emma as

deficient both in generosity and in self-knowledge. She discovers and corrects her faults only after she has almost ruined herself and her closest friends. But with the reform in her character, she is ready for marriage with the man she loves, *the man who throughout the book has stood in the reader's mind for what she lacks* [italics mine].[25]

On this reading Emma must prove herself worthy of the superior Knightley, and this is accomplished by her humiliation and subordination, her devaluation of herself. She must recognize the inadequacy and stupidity of her judgments. Her marriage to Knightly assumes that she will forever afterward be guided by her mentor, "the completely reliable" Knightley. Compare this patriarchal interpretation with that of the late Ellen Moers:

Because she cared deeply and primarily about young women, because she suffered from a rooted disrespect for parents, especially fathers, because she saw the only act of choice in a woman's life as the making of a marriage upon which alone depended her spiritual and physical health, Austen turned a severe and serious eye . . . on the economic life of her heroes. . . . What I am suggesting is that Austen's realism in the matter of money was in her case an essentially female phenomenon, the result of her deep concern for the quality of a woman's life in marriage.[26]

Feminist critics ask how Emma could be otherwise than she is, given her rigorous training in the cultivation of material appearances and the failure of her society to encourage the intellectual discipline that would allow Emma's abilities to be usefully engaged.

In her landmark essay "Dancing through the Minefield: Some Observations on the Theory, Practice, and Politics of a Feminist Literary Criticism" Annette Kolodny claims that "literary history (and, with that, the historicity of literature) is a fiction," based on her analysis of the nature, function, and interpretation of the idea of a literary canon.[27] She declares that "an established canon functions as a model by which to chart the continuities and discontinuities as well as the influences upon the interconnections between works, genres, and authors." This claim seems to be safely descriptive, for surely this is how an established canon is used. Kolodny points out, however, that in effect, the way in which a canon is established and used depends upon the conceptualization of just what kind of an instrument the arbiters of the canon think that it is. For instance, its arbiters may create a canon based primarily on internal developments, with "new literary forms result[ing] from some ongoing internal dialectic," or they may operate on the assumption that nonliterary events should determine interpretation of, and inclusion in or exclusion from, the canon.[28]

Kolodny reminds us again how the literary experience of women has often been an intensely personal disappointment. The study of literature precipitates "a painfully personal distress at discovering whores, bitches, muses, and heroines dead in childbirth where we had once hoped to discover ourselves."[29] Thus literature has failed to function for women as it has for men, and this failure is experienced as personal failure, denying confirmation of a successfully emergent self (i.e., a self that is female and self-determining) and withholding affirmation for personal possibilities uncontaminated by one's female nature.[30]

The humanistic tradition teaches us to come to literature with the highest expectations; it is to be our guide out of the cave, offering safe, if difficult, passage. The Great Books tradition does not, however, easily accommodate women. For us, literature has more often seemed a writ of execution for the personal aspirations that are antithetical to the Great Books models of whore, bitch, muse, and dead heroine. The limits and hazards of being female are clear. While the male protagonist usually seeks and often realizes some degree of freedom or autonomy, the female protagonist is routinely defeated or compromised. In the Eve and Pandora stories the woman who is curious and seeks knowledge— activities usually culminating in adventure and reward for male protagonists—brings about disastrous consequences for humanity. Moreover, the "exceptional" woman is shown either to be not so exceptional (for instance, Portia ultimately assumes her natural feminine place), or really not to be a woman after all (as in the question of the sanity, sanctity, and sexuality of Joan of Arc).[31] Since literature is the interface of the public and the private, and since "art" has traditionally been credited with embodying ideals of public and private virtue, it is particularly distressing to discover that this cultural stamp of approval denies the full humanity of women.

Because it is the interface between the ostensibly private and public realms, we expect literature to confirm our deepest, most private hopes for a meaningful life as individuals and not to offer instantiations of gender limitations. Especially for the modern reader, literature is the public confirmation of private aspirations. It is precisely because women experience the contradiction between the "conventional wisdom" (i.e., the official social reality) and the lived experience that we turn to literature for confirmation of our private feelings. It is because of literature's personal voice ("Reader, I married him"), and incidentally because of the materially private existence of books (which can be read privately, even secretly), that we expect—originally—our personal feelings to be respected. This, however, has not been the case for women in the way that it has been the case for men. Feminist critics have shown conclusively that relatively few women have had the intellectual, social, or economic resources that would enable them to formulate and communicate an artistic vision effectively.[32] The very language that constructs women as Other implicitly denies women the imaginative autonomy that is needed to participate, even by abstention, in the great fraternity of literature. As Other, women lack the conceptual freedom to imagine playing the prodigal son (or even his brother) within the patrimony of an established literary tradition.

Literature is a mediator between public and private, and the warp and woof of literature is language and power. Patterns and textures may change, but the very stuff of literature is politics. All literature thus becomes susceptible to a feminist critique insofar as feminist criticism is one aspect of the larger task of facilitating what Cheri Register describes as "the illumination of 'female experience,' which will help to decide *how* to transform the world. Feminist critics look at how literature comprehends, transmits, and shapes female experience."[33] This emphasis on literature as it discloses and transforms brings us back to the fundamental aesthetic issues concerning the "real" nature and function of the work of art.

In order to address these issues, let me suggest that a work of literature can be criticized for failing to express or embody some perspective because that failure or omission misleads or fails to disclose. As an example take the critical response to Norman Mailer's *An American*

Dream.[34] The narrator and guiding consciousness, Stephen Rojack, expresses and embodies a view of sexual relationships between men and women that is degrading to women. The degradation is portrayed as natural and inevitable because women are constructed as genitally and congenitally inferior to men. According to the "reliable" Rojack, women need to be kept in their supine place, and they are grateful to men who insist, however brutally, that they stay there. The reader is shown that this is the secret to Rojack's success. *An American Dream* is the misogynous dream of murdering one's wife and getting away with it. It is part of an established literary and critical tradition which assumes that as sexual Other, women are inferior. Moreover, women purportedly know this and secretly despise men who do not pass the test of masculinity by sexually bullying them. Sadism is justified in men because masochism is inherent in women. The possibilities for male and female selves are thus "illumined."

Mailer's book is defended against feminist criticism in two ways. First, it is defended on the grounds that one cannot impute the values portrayed or espoused in a work to its author. Second, the claim is made that one cannot criticize an artist on the basis of the vision that he (or she) has. The first kind of defense supposes that the work is to be judged strictly on its "formal" qualities, that form is separable from content, and that the values expounded in the work or those held by its creator are irrelevant to aesthetic merit. This would mean that the work of art is to be evaluated entirely as an instance of *techne*, or formal skill, and does not disclose any truth about reality. This notion of the work of art denies the agency of the work in reflecting and formulating reality. It entails an absolute dichotomy between aesthetics and ethics. The second kind of defense is exactly the opposite. It supposes that the primary criterion for evaluation is how honestly or accurately the artist expresses his or her own personal vision. In this view, the work must be an instance of self-exposure.

Both defenses are fallacious. Each defense presupposes a different conception of the nature of the work of art, and both are mistaken insofar as the former maintains that the work of art is both objective and autonomous, while the latter entails a narrowly representational and narcissistic understanding. Both conceptions fail to take into account the cultural and dialectical context from which the work emerges.

The case, then, is a complicated one. The artist must have freedom to be expressive, but freedom in itself is not the ultimate value to be embodied in the work of art. The artist needs to be free from the debilitating intellectual, social, and economic constraints discussed previously, but at the same time, humanly speaking, the artist does not create in a moral vacuum. Art is not simply self-expression. The work qua work is the embodiment of this essentially human dialectic. As such an embodiment, it appears in the world to act upon and be reacted to. The work of art is not just fabrication, the making of something new; the making is making unconcealed. That is, I think, what Adrienne Rich describes as "the true nature of poetry. The drive / to connect. The dream of the common language."[35] Thus, a work of art that falsifies or conceals (as opposed to portraying falsification and concealment for what they are) is essentially flawed. Because literature has usually reflected and often served the ideology of the patriarchal public sphere, the ways in which women have experienced the human condition have been ignored, falsified, and left concealed.

Sensitive to misogynous acts of omission and commission, feminist critics interpret and evaluate works *in part* on how they express or fail to express certain social, moral, political, or psychological perspectives as well as on how those works invite or discourage transformation and disclosure. In this way, feminist critics take into consideration the dialectical agency of literary works. As authentic dialectic, works of art should not attempt to falsify or conceal. Works that omit certain perspectives may be significantly flawed, but this is a less serious offense than concealment or falsification. One particularly illustrative example of omission occurs in Leo Tolstoy's *Anna Karenina*. Levin's bewilderment and anxiety while awaiting the birth of his child are carefully and sympathetically presented; Kitty, however, is simply a shrieking creature giving birth. The "privatized" nature of Kitty's lived experience is not significant. But the effect of that privatized experience on the reader's consciousness may well be. Certainly it was for Rich, who writes:

The fear of pain in childbirth in literate or in non-literate societies may come (and often does) from verbal tales, phrases, anecdotes: it is further reinforced by literature. As a girl of twelve or thirteen, I read and reread passages in novels which recounted births, trying to imagine what actually happened. I had no films, no photographs of childbirth to enlighten me, but in my favorite novel, *Anna Karenina*, I found the account of Kitty Levin's labor, as perceived by her husband.[36]

Feminist critics look at a text in terms of its place in a culture, its past and present function in conveying meaning. Feminist critics read in part by asking what is in the text, what is not, and why the work is what it is and not something else. The task of revealing what has been hidden or obscured or falsified may require diverse analytical skills and interpretive strategies. In order to show how literature has functioned to maintain the ideology of patriarchal culture, feminist critics may expose the implicit biases in a text and demonstrate the place of the text in the lineage of its genre. An especially effective example of this is Judith Fetterley's analysis of American literature, *The Resisting Reader*. Fetterley shows that the masculine American ideal of prolonged adolescence and rugged individualism is portrayed as inevitably threatened by the demands of women incapable of noble action, from Dame Van Winkle to Gatsby's Daisy. Fetterley argues persuasively that in American literature the female is constructed as shallow, unimaginative, and doomed by her sexual function (which is, in masculine terms, sexual dysfunction).[37]

A different exercise in feminist criticism is to provide new readings of old texts. The remarkable susceptibility of old texts to new readings has been particularly useful in demonstrating again how the very personal experience of reading a book is structured by the dominant public ideology. In reading old texts without the patriarchal blinkers, feminists try to uncover perspectives and values in the narrative structure of the work or in the treatment of the subject matter that have been ignored or suppressed in interpretations accepted by the dominant patriarchal culture.[38] As the earlier example of Ellen Moers's analysis of *Emma* indicated, feminist critics are particularly sensitive to the public/private distinction insofar as it denies the lived reality of women's privatized lives.

Just as the old texts have been illuminated by the new readings of feminist critics, so do new works by feminist authors require that the reader jettison traditional critical approaches.[39] Because of the experience of raised consciousness, feminist critics are often able to discover in new texts what is not apparent to those who come to new texts with traditional stylistic or thematic expectations. For example, feminists have pointed out that the standards of literature of the heroic tradition generally have been inimical to the disclosure of women's privatized experience.[40] The social and economic conditions supported the public production of literature in which subject and mode conveyed the values and ideas of patriarchal cultures. New works that are implicitly critical of those patriarchal values and ideas in both form and content are likely to be judged by the nonfeminist critic according to the very standards that those works are critical of.[41]

Thus the practice of feminist criticism is clearly pluralistic rather than monolithic. Some feminist critics have chosen to examine the inherent limitations of patriarchal aesthetic standards; some have shown how the exclusion of certain subjects has resulted in a very partial account of human experience (I am reminded here of Virginia Woolf's comment in *A Room of One's Own* to the effect that the most remarkable sentence in English literature is "Chloe liked Olivia"); and still other feminist critics have suggested alternative approaches emphasizing analyses of female imagery, style, and language in women's writing. What unites these diverse critical interests and approaches is the realization that both literature and the enterprise of literary criticism express and shape values. They acknowledge that a critic always makes judgments as a subject but insist that this subjectivity in no way impugns the validity of the critical enterprise.[42] Instead, feminist critics consider the subjectivity of the critical process essential.[43]

The interpretation and evaluation of works written by feminist authors is a particularly exciting and complicated task for feminist critics. As one who "sees the same things differently,"[44] the feminist author is likely to be skeptical of genres, modes, and conventions that have seemed to be particularly suited to maintaining the exclusion of women as authors, readers, and authentic characters. Thus epic poetry, heroic literature, and formalist fiction are suspect. Contemporary feminist authors are wary of the accepted and even expected devices and techniques that make much highly praised literature intelligible only to academic specialists (e.g., Ezra Pound's *Cantos*, James Joyce's *Finnegans Wake*). Many feminist authors deliberately use language and forms that make their work accessible to a larger audience, specifically to persons who are not specialists in literary studies. The poetic development of Adrienne Rich is a clear illustration of this. Her early poems were tightly and brilliantly constructed according to the best academic models; her mature poems are looser, simpler, and more powerful.

Rich's poetry also exemplifies another prominent concern of feminist authors: that of including those privatized experiences which have been routinely denied or distorted in literature. Feminist literary works often emphasize and analyze the difficulties of women dealing with the il-

lusions of a changing society. For example, a woman in a story may
experience the popularly accepted myths of contemporary culture as
fundamentally false and oppressive. In Agnes Smedley's autobiographical novel, *Daughter of Earth*, Marie Rogers learns that her comrades
and brothers in revolution mouth equality but harbor a double standard
for sexual behavior. The apparently "new" society is covertly riddled
with the old patriarchal norms. And once again the woman recognizes
her position as marginal, as that of Other. Thus the privatized nature
of women's experience is disclosed. As in this case, the feminist writer
often uses her own experience as subject matter, and critically evaluating
the artistic adaptation of intimate autobiographical materials may present
special challenges to the feminist critic sensitive to women's struggle
for authentic disclosure.[45]

Feminist authors and critics have been particularly concerned with
the issue of artistic responsibility, of artistic accountability for the work
as it invites us to construct reality through its presentation of experience,
values, and ideas. Style is scrutinized as well as subject. Consequently,
some feminist poets and critics have called attention to the pernicious
use of the literary persona as a device that enables an author to evade
any personal responsibility as speaker or seer.[46] We thus return to the
philosophical concern of the ancient Greeks regarding the moral implications of art making.[47]

Within feminist criticism, however, there seem to be two very different general positions that, predictably enough, mirror the political
distinction in the women's movement between reformists and revolutionaries. Since the women's movement is a critique of culture in the
broadest and most basic sense of the word, disagreements about critical
frameworks should not be unexpected.[48]

Reformist critics believe that feminism is at least not incompatible
with the basic ideology of humanism. This is not to say that reformist
critics endorse the historical or cultural manifestation of the humanist
tradition in patriarchal Western societies. Minimally, however, reformists see in some humanistic ideals values that are consonant with a
commitment to ending the oppression of women. Some reformist critics
might even argue that in feminism humanism realizes its full philosophical potential.[49] In contrast, revolutionary feminist critics repudiate
all allegiance to a literary tradition conceived and nurtured under the
auspices of patriarchy. Revolutionary critics argue that not only the

traditional categories of critical approbation but even the category of literature is essentially oppressive.[50]

In essence, then, reformists and revolutionaries disagree about the reality of aesthetic categories. Reformist critics seem to allow that the categories and distinctions involved in aesthetic evaluation may have been misconstrued or used manipulatively or oppressively, or even that the formulations have been unfair, yet the reformist critics maintain that evaluative distinctions get at ultimately real distinctions even if the traditional characterizations of those distinctions have been flawed. Reformists show how literature has been used to oppress and distort, as well as how literary criticism has sanctioned oppressive and distorting interpretations. They expect feminist literature and literary criticism to transform or complete or restore literature so that it becomes a genuinely humanistic accomplishment. According to reformists, there are great books; they just may not be the canonical Great Books.[51]

Revolutionary feminist critics reject traditional artistic categories and the aesthetic distinction between popular and high culture. They argue that such distinctions are entirely reducible to their functions in maintaining and promoting the oppressive structures of capitalist patriarchy. Revolutionaries claim not only that what we know as literature is partial but that such partiality has been deliberate in its oppression and exploitation of women. The very notion of literature itself is taken to be an instantiation of elitist, exploitative, and therefore illicit categorization. The existence of aesthetic categories is symbiotic with the existence of patriarchal social, political, and economic categories. It is not only that aesthetic categories are invoked to oppress women, but that the very belief in the validity and reality of such categories is antithetical to liberation. Revolutionary critics claim that traditional evaluative and interpretive categories are inherently hostile to the disclosure of women's privatized experience. One cannot speak truly using the language of these categories because the categories do not have any real referents beyond their functions in patriarchal society. The categories merely sanction an oppressive organization of human and material resources. They are metaphysically null.[52]

Despite these important differences, feminist critics have tended to emphasize the common grounding of their efforts in the knowledge that the privatized lives of women have not been authentically disclosed in patriarchal culture. Both reformist and revolutionary critics recognize that an artistic effort to disclose the privatized nature of women's experience is always a public and political act. Feminist scholarship and pedagogy have self-consciously tried to avoid the adversarial mode characteristic of patriarchal scholarship in which "colleagues" attack and defend positions. Instead, there is a respect for the diversity of efforts to publicly explore what has been private and concealed. As feminist politics and criticism become more diverse and sophisticated, feminists have become increasingly concerned with disclosing the racist and heterosexist biases in feminist work.[53] One of the most difficult and important tasks of all feminists is to make public the extent to which we have assimilated and acted on these oppressive attitudes and the extent to which we have materially benefitted from privileges of race, class, or sexual orientation. This is another very clear instance in which the personal is political.

The complex effort to describe the diversity of feminist critical projects and to draw the connections between them is an ongoing and increasingly rewarding task. A particularly important example of this is Elaine Showalter's theoretical essay "Feminist Criticism in the Wilderness." Showalter identifies four theories of sexual difference in women's writing: the biological, the linguistic, the psychological, and the cultural.[54] Though each, in her view, has the limitations inevitable to its special emphasis, all show that writing by women has characteristics special to women which are foreign or invisible to men. Showalter understands women's writing as "a double-voiced discourse, containing a 'dominant' and a 'muted' story."[55] Both discourses are present in texts by women; the task of the feminist critic is to disclose the latter and to enunciate the connections between the two. The result is a dialectical interplay between the private and the public which presumes that each is part of the other.

In this way, feminist critics facilitate disclosure by putting the work in a dialectical context that acknowledges the personal and political nature of the work and the critical process. In part, this means that the critic is open to be acted upon by the work and, in turn, reacts to it through interpretation, analysis, and evaluation. The critical response should invite further dialectical exploration. It seems entirely appropriate for feminists to insist on the moral vocabulary of engagement, authenticity, and good faith to name what ought to go on in the critical process.[56] The feminist critic must employ a discerning imagination and empathetic scrutiny to discover how and whether the work accomplishes its work of unconcealment and transformation and thus gives those intimate things, in Arendt's words, "a kind of reality which, their intensity notwithstanding, they never could have had before."[57]

NOTES

1. Hannah Arendt, *The Human Condition* (Chicago: University of Chicago Press, 1958), p. 50.

2. My interpretation of the nature and significance of the private/public distinction in classical antiquity has its roots in the scholarship of Hannah Arendt. See especially the second chapter of *The Human Condition*, "The Public and Private Realm," and the essay "What Is Authority?" in *Between Past and Future* (New York: Viking Press, 1968). Arendt's analysis virtually ignores the implications of this distinction for women and must be supplemented by chapters 4 and 5 of Sarah B. Pomeroy's *Goddesses, Whores, and Slaves: Women in Classical Antiquity* (New York: Schocken Books, 1975), "Women and the City of Athens" and "Private Life in Classical Athens."

3. Simone de Beauvoir, *The Second Sex*, trans. and ed. H. M. Parshley (New York: Random House, Vintage Books, 1974), p. 58.

4. An interesting discussion of the nineteenth-century exclusion of women from public life is Jean Bethke Elshtain's "Moral Woman/Immoral Man: The Public-Private Distinction and Its Political Ramifications," *Politics and Society* 4, no. 4 (1974):453–73.

5. This point is made repeatedly by John Stuart Mill in "The Subjection of Women": "So true is it that unnatural generally means only uncustomary and that everything which is usual appears natural" ("The Subjection of Women," in *Essays on Sex Equality*, intro. and ed. Alice S. Rossi [Chicago: University of Chicago Press, 1970], p. 138).

6. Aristotle endorses the popular maxim "Silence is a woman's glory" while maintaining that this is "not equally the glory of man" (*Politics* I, 13 [1260a], 30 [trans. Jowett]). This is later echoed in the Christian tradition by Paul's prohibition "As in all congregations of God's people, women should not address the meeting. They have no license to speak, but should keep their place as the law directs. If there is something they want to know, they can ask their husbands at home. It is a shocking thing that a woman should address the congregation" (1 Corinthians 14.34–35 *New English Bible*, Oxford Study Edition [New York: Oxford University Press, 1976]).

7. Plato, *Republic* II–III (377–94).

8. See Iris Murdoch's convincing interpretation of Plato's philosophy of art, *The Fire and the Sun: Why Plato Banished the Artists* (Oxford: Clarendon Press, 1977).

9. Aristotle, *Poetics* I, 4 (1488b) 5–15 (trans. Bywater).

10. Murdoch, p. 65.

11. Ibid., p. 66.

12. *Republic* V 476c (trans. Grube).

13. In English this genre embraces Tobias Smollett's *Roderick Random* (1725) and Jack Kerouac's *On the Road* (1955). The picaresque protagonist is almost always male; until very recently the authorship was uniformly male. The recent exception is Erica Jong, whose *Fanny: Being the True History of the Adventures of Fanny Hackabout-Jones* (1980) is an attempt to reconstruct and chronicle the episodes in the life of a female Tom Jones. The form is cleverly mock-eighteenth-century, but the perspective is clearly post-Beauvoir.

14. Even when women have tried to participate in the critical tradition their efforts have been abused. Susan Sniader Lanser and Evelyn Torton Beck have uncovered a history of crimes against women critics in "Why Are There No Great Women Critics? And What Difference Does it Make?" in *The Prism of Sex: Essays in the Sociology of Knowledge*, ed. Julia A. Shuman and Evelyn Torton Beck, (Madison: University of Wisconsin Press 1979), pp. 79–91. Their appendix lists 21 women critics writing between 1700 and 1900.

15. Sandra Bartky argues that the perception of the contradiction between the publicly constructed "social reality" and the existential reality of women's situation is the beginning of feminist consciousness in "Toward a Phenomenology of Feminist Consciousness," reprinted in *Feminism and Philosophy*, ed. Mary Vetterling-Braggin, Frederick A. Elliston, and Jane English (Totowa, N.J.: Littlefield, Adams and Co. 1977), pp. 22–34. I am grateful to Professor Bartky for her generous and helpful comments on a very early draft of this essay.

16. Virginia Woolf, *A Room of One's Own* (New York and Burlingame: Harcourt, Brace and World, A Harbinger Book, 1929), pp. 45–46.

17. Simone de Beauvoir, *The Second Sex*, pp. xviii–xix.

18. As an aside I would suggest that the barrier that is supposedly assaulted by the intrusion of (patriarchal) social science into the "private" sphere is, in reality, often an attack on the authenticity of the "privatized" lives of women. The paradox is that these privatized lives were, in large part, shaped by the public ideology of the private realm. This public ideology (about the "sacredness" of the household, for example) has constructed the private realm in such a way that the reality of women's lives was denied and distorted so that the appearances of the private/public distinction were maintained. Women lead privatized lives because the false (oppressive) construction of the public/private distinction is maintained. The reality is denied to save the appearances. I am suggesting that the new ideology of patriarchal social science—the scientific intervention of professional "helpers" (therapists, counselors, etc.) in the private sphere to make it work—is often just a different (albeit more subtle) attack on the authenticity of women's privatized lives.

19. Wallace Stevens, "Imagination as Value" in *The Necessary Angel: Essays on Reality and the Imagination* (New York: Random House, Vintage Books, 1951), p. 159.

20. Catharine A. Stimpson, "The Power to Name: Some Reflections on the Avant-Garde" in *The Prism of Sex*, p. 56.

21. Northrop Frye, *Anatomy of Criticism: Four Essays* (Princeton, N.J.: Princeton University Press, 1957; Princeton paperback ed., 1971), p. 8.

22. Ibid., p. 28.

23. Compare this critical stance with Virginia Woolf's charming and imaginative critical persona, "The Common Reader," *The Common Reader* (New York: Harcourt, Brace and World, 1925) and *The Second Common Reader* (New York: Harcourt, Brace and World, 1932).

24. The classic revisionist text is Thomas S. Kuhn's *The Structure of Scientific Revolution* (Chicago: University of Chicago Press, 1962). Two important feminist collections are *The Prism of Sex*, cited above, and *Discovering Reality: Feminist Perspectives on Epistemology, Metaphysics, and Philosophy of Science*, ed. Sandra Harding and Merrill B. Hintikka (Dordrecht: Ridel, 1981). For a very personal account of sexism in science read "The Anomaly of a Woman in Physics," by Evelyn Fox Keller, in *Working It Out*, ed. Sara Ruddick and Pamela Daniels (New York: Alfred A. Knopf, Pantheon Books, 1977), pp. 77–91.

25. Wayne Booth, *A Rhetoric of Fiction* (Chicago: University of Chicago Press, 1961), pp. 244, 254.

26. Ellen Moers, *Literary Women: The Great Writers* (Garden City, N.Y.: Doubleday and Company, Anchor Books, 1977), p. 107.

27. Annette Kolodny, "Dancing through the Minefield: Some Observations on the Theory, Practice, and Politics of a Feminist Literary Criticism," *Feminist Studies* 6, no. 1 (Spring 1980):1–25.

28. Ibid., p. 8.

29. Ibid., p. 1.

30. Beauvoir points out that "[woman] is simply what man decrees; thus she is called 'the sex,' by which is meant that she appears essentially to male as a sexual being. For him she is sex—absolute sex, no less" (*The Second Sex*, p. xix).

31. In *Joan of Arc: The Image of Female Heroism* (New York: Alfred A. Knopf, 1981), Marina Warner traces the political and social motivation for the successive popular interpretations of the Joan legend.

32. For contemporary women writers reflecting on the woman writer's heritage of social and economic constraints see Tillie Olsen, *Silences*, a Delta/Seymour Lawrence Edition (New York: Dell Publishing Co., 1978), and Adrienne Rich, *On Lies, Secrets, and Silence: Selected Prose 1966–1978* (New York: W. W. Norton and Company, 1979). The apparent popular success and

critical failure of many nineteenth-century British women novelists is discussed by Elaine Showalter in *A Literature of Their Own: British Women Novelists from Brontë to Lessing* (Princeton, N.J.: Princeton University Press, 1977). Showalter's investigation of the effect of the double critical standard on the work of George Eliot is especially helpful in understanding the milieu of intellectual resistance to female genius. Sandra Gilbert and Susan Gubar have theorized that while a male writer struggles with what Harold Bloom has called "the anxiety of influence," a woman writer experiences a more visceral "anxiety of authorship—a radical fear that she cannot create, that because she has never become a 'precursor' the act of writing will isolate or destroy her" (*The Madwoman in the Attic: The Woman Writer and the 19th Century Literary Imagination* [New Haven, Conn.: Yale University Press, 1979], p. 49). Virginia Woolf's plea for *A Room of One's Own* is the classic text for exposing the hypocritical public formulation of women's private lives.

33. Cheri Register, "Review Essay: Literary Criticism," *Signs: Journal of Women in Culture and Society* 6, no. 2 (Winter 1980):269.

34. Norman Mailer, *An American Dream* (New York: Dial Press, 1964). Kate Millett's discussion of Mailer's work in *Sexual Politics* (Garden City, N.Y.: Doubleday and Company, 1970) is a pioneering exercise in feminist criticism.

35. Adrienne Rich, "Origins and History of Consciousness" in *The Dream of a Common Language: Poems 1974–1977* (New York: W. W. Norton and Company, 1978), p. 7.

36. Adrienne Rich, *Of Woman Born: Motherhood as Experience and Institution* (New York: W. W. Norton and Company, 1976), pp. 158–59.

37. Judith Fetterley, *The Resisting Reader: A Feminist Approach to American Fiction* (Bloomington: Indiana University Press, 1978).

38. See, for example, Carolyn G. Heilbrun's reading of the *Oresteia* in *Reinventing Womanhood* (New York: W. W. Norton and Company, 1979), pp. 152–61; Coppelia Kahn's "*The Taming of the Shrew*: Shakespeare's Mirror of Marriage" in *The Authority of Experience: Essays in Feminist Criticism*, ed. Arlyn Diamond and Lee R. Edwards, (Amherst: University of Massachusetts Press, 1977), pp. 84–100; and "The Women of Cooper's *Leatherstocking Tales*," by Nina Baym, in *Images of Women in Fiction: Feminist Perspectives*, ed. Susan Koppelman Cornillon (Bowling Green, Ohio: Bowling Green University Press, 1972), pp. 135–54.

39. Two articles by Suzanne Juhasz are especially helpful: "The Critic as Feminist: Reflections on Women's Poetry, Feminism, and the Art of Criticism," *Women's Studies* 5, no. 2 (1977):113–27, and "The Feminist Mode in Literature and Criticism," *Frontiers* 2, no. 3 (Fall 1977):96–103. Ruth Yeazell cautions against critical zealotry in "Fictional Heroines and Feminist Critics," *Novel* 8, no. 1 (Fall 1974):29–38.

40. The issue of female heroism is a matter of some controversy among feminists. See Lee R. Edwards, ''The Labors of Psyche: Towards a Theory of Female Heroism,'' *Critical Inquiry* 6, no. 1 (Autumn 1979):33–50; Joanna Russ, ''What Can a Heroine Do? Or Why Women Can't Write,'' *Images of Women*, pp. 3–26; and (in the same anthology) ''Heroism in *To the Lighthouse*'' by Judith Little, pp. 237–42.

41. For a good treatment of the difficulties involved see Annette Kolodny, ''The Lady's Not for Spurning: Kate Millett and the Critics,'' *Contemporary Literature* 17, no. 4:541–62.

42. On the nature and function of subjectivity in aesthetic judgments see especially Hans-Georg Gadamer's 1964 essay ''Aesthetics and Hermeneutics,'' in the Gadamer anthology *Philosophical Hermeneutics*, trans. and ed. David E. Linge (Berkeley and Los Angeles: University of California Press, 1976), pp. 95–104.

43. See Dorin Schumacher's ''Subjectivism: A Theory of the Critical Process,'' *Feminist Literary Criticism: Explorations in Theory*, ed. Josephine Donovan (Lexington: University Press of Kentucky, 1975), pp. 29–37.

44. Bartky, ''Toward a Phenomenology of Feminist Consciousness,'' p. 6.

45. See Vivian Gornick, ''Feminist Writers: Hanging Ourselves on a Party Line,'' *Essays in Feminism* (New York: Harper and Row, 1978), pp. 164–70, and Julia P. Stanley, ''Fear of Flying?'' *Sinister Wisdom* 1 (December 1976):52–62.

46. Marilyn R. Farwell, ''Adrienne Rich and an Organic Feminist Criticism,'' *College English* 39, no. 2 (October 1977):191–203.

47. Wayne Booth concludes *The Rhetoric of Fiction* with a chapter called ''The Morality of Impersonal Narration.'' He claims that ''an author has an obligation to be as clear about his moral position as he possibly can be'' (p. 389) and that ''when human actions are formed to make a work of art, the form that is made can never be divorced from the human meanings, including the moral judgments, that are implicit whenever human beings act. And nothing the writer does can be finally understood in isolation from his effort to make it all accessible to someone else—his peers, himself as imagined reader, his audience'' (p. 397). Booth's sentiments are admirable, and twenty years ago even women acted as if the masculine pronoun were generic.

48. The internal struggles within the women's movement concern class, race, sexual preference, and political orientation. Some useful and diverse sources are Alison Jaggar, ''Political Philosophies of Women's Liberation'' in *Feminism and Philosophy*; Janet Radcliffe Richards, *The Skeptical Feminist: A Philosophical Essay* (London and Boston: Routledge and Kegan Paul, 1980); Shulamith Firestone, *The Dialectic of Sex: The Case for Feminist Revolution* (New York: William Morrow and Company, 1970); and from *Building Feminist Theory: Essays from 'Quest'* (New York: Longman, 1981) see esp. Lucia

Valeska's "The Future of Female Separatism" (pp. 20–31) and two essays by Charlotte Bunch: "Beyond Either/Or: Feminist Options" (pp. 44–56) and "The Reform Tool Kit" (pp. 189–201).

49. See "Theories of Feminist Criticism: A Dialogue" by Carolyn Heilbrun and Catharine Stimpson in *Feminist Literary Criticism* (pp. 61–73); Sandra Gilbert, "What Do Feminist Critics Want? A Postcard from the Volcano," *ADE Bulletin* 66 (Winter 1980):16–24; and Annis V. Pratt, "The New Feminist Criticisms: Exploring the History of a New Space," in *Beyond Intellectual Sexism: A New Woman, A New Reality*, ed. Joan I. Roberts (New York: David McKay Co., 1975), pp. 175–95.

50. See Silvia Bovenschem, "Is There a Feminine Aesthetic?" *New German Critique*, no. 10 (Winter 1977):111–37; Julia Penelope Stanley and Susan W. Robbins, "Towards a Feminist Aesthetic," *Chrysalis*, no. 6 (1977):57–71. Mary Daly's *Gyn/Ecology: The Metaethics of Radical Feminism* (Boston: Beacon Press, 1978) is in its form and language an embodiment of the repudiation of traditional categories. The introduction ("The Meta-patriarchial Journey of Exorcism and Ecstasy," pp. 1–34) is especially illuminating. Lillian S. Robinson's compelling essays have been collected in *Sex, Class and Culture* (Bloomington: Indiana University Press, 1978). One can follow the evolution of her position from academic critic in "Dwelling in Decencies: Radical Criticism and the Feminist Perspective" (1970), pp. 3–21, to popular critic in "Criticism: Who Needs It?" (1975), pp. 69–94. See also Barbara Smith, "Toward a Black Feminist Criticism," *Conditions: Two* 1, no. 2 (October 1977), pp. 25–44.

51. Among the critics cited in these notes, I would identify Gilbert, Gubar, Fetterley, Heilbrun, Juhasz, Moers, Pratt, and Showalter as reformist critics.

52. Radical critics would include Daly, Kolodny, Rich, Robinson, and Penelope (formerly Stanley). It is obvious that the term *literary criticism* is far too narrow for the projects of these feminists, and this itself might be taken as evidence for their position.

53. Again, see Smith's previously cited "Toward a Black Feminist Criticism." In addition to reprinting the Smith and Kolodny essays, *The New Feminist Criticism: Essays on Women, Literature and Theory*, ed. Elaine Showalter (New York: Alfred A. Knopf, Pantheon Books, 1985), contains Deborah E. McDowell's "New Directions for Feminist Criticism," pp. 186–99, and Bonnie Zimmerman's "What Has Never Been: An Overview of Lesbian Feminist Literary Criticism," pp. 200–24. Also see *Black Women Writers (1950–1980): A Critical Evaluation*, ed. Mari Evans (Garden City, N.Y.: Doubleday and Company, Anchor Books, 1984).

54. Elaine Showalter, "Feminist Criticism in the Wilderness," *The New Feminist Literary Criticism: Essays on Women, Literature and Theory*, p. 249.

55. Showalter, p. 263.

56. See Marcia Holly, ''Consciousness and Authenticity: Toward a Feminist Aesthetic,'' in *Feminist Literary Criticism*, pp. 38–47. I have been enormously influenced by Martin Heidegger's ''The Origin of the Work of Art,'' in *Philosophies of Art and Beauty: Selected Readings in Aesthetics from Plato to Heidegger*, ed. Albert Hofstadter and Richard Kuhn (Chicago: University of Chicago Press, 1964, Phoenix ed. 1976), pp. 650–703. Sandra Bartky's analysis of Heidegger's work in ''Heidegger's Philosophy of Art,'' *British Journal of Aesthetics* (1979), pp. 353–71, is especially helpful in understanding and appreciating Heidegger's ideas.

57. Arendt, p. 50.

3

Queens and Claimants: Political Insecurity in Sixteenth-Century England

CAROLE LEVIN

Through biological accident sixteenth-century England was a century of queens. Henry VIII's two daughters, Mary and Elizabeth, ruled successively from 1553 to 1558 and from 1558 to 1603. For the first time women ruled undisputed in their own right; such rule had a number of social, political, and psychological repercussions. Queenship provoked questioning of the legitimacy of the ruler, a questioning that coincided with the further turmoil brought on by the Reformation. Just at a time when ceremonies that had brought comfort for centuries were being stripped away, so too the familiar figure of the king, God's annointed, was being replaced by that of a woman. The issue of legitimacy was brought even more sharply into focus because neither Mary nor Elizabeth had sons to succeed them. England had been lucky in its succession for centuries; from Henry II in the twelfth century to Richard II there had been a direct line of male heirs. The end of that line in 1399 with Richard II's deposition was one cause of political unrest in the fifteenth century. With childless queens ruling this unease continued into the sixteenth century as well. This essay will examine certain related aspects of the insecurity caused by women ruling, especially in a time of religious upheaval: rumors of the survival of the last Tudor king, male impostors, and stories of illegitimate children.

Rumors of the survival of kings and impostors claiming to be the rightful heir occurred at other times in English history as well, when kings rather than queens were ruling. While not arguing that these rumors and impostures appeared only in the reigns of women rulers, I would like to suggest that they do appear with some regularity at times when the legitimacy of the sovereign is in question. Given the attitudes of the sixteenth-century political nation, the fact of a queen regnant was in itself enough of a departure from what was perceived as the proper form of rule to bring about such phenomena.

Moreover, not only were Mary and Elizabeth both queens, but they were both childless, so that the populace could not even console itself with the expectation that though a woman was ruling now, eventually her son would succeed to remedy the constitutional irregularity and restore the proper order. Mary at least attempted to follow this more traditional path; she married (though disastrously) and pathetically hoped for a child. But this marriage to her younger cousin, Philip of Spain, robbed Mary of the power that ought to have been hers. Though queen, she was also wife to the man she and her counselors saw as the real ruler.[1] Her sister, Elizabeth, watching from the wings, would not make the same mistake. Despite flirting with the concept of matrimony for twenty years after ascending the throne, she never married. Courtship was a useful political tool; marriage would have made her a figurehead, as Elizabeth was well aware. But by not marrying, Elizabeth also refused the most obvious function of a queen, that of bearing an heir. And it was during the last years of her reign, when she was too old to conceive a child and the charade of marriage proposals had finally been exhausted, that the whisperings of King Edward VI's survival, which had occurred in Mary's time, were heard again.

As queens regnant in the sixteenth century, Mary and Elizabeth had few examples of appropriate behavior for them, particularly in the public aspect of their rule. While both made attempts to deal with this issue— and clearly Elizabeth was a more effective politician than Mary—the very existence of a woman ruler was difficult to accept for a people who perceived the monarch as God's representative and thus, by definition, as a male. Writing in the 1530s, Stephen Gardiner, bishop of Winchester, expressed it thus: "The king represents the image of God upon earth."[2] In describing the succession at the beginning of Mary's reign, Carolly Erickson writes, "Mary was now raised to a political status that conflicted with her sexual status at every turn."[3] The same, of course, could later be said of Elizabeth.

To deal with this conflict, both queens tried to assume masculine (i.e., kingly) characteristics while still exhibiting feminine qualities where appropriate. Sir John Neale suggests that with political astuteness Elizabeth turned the court, which prior to this time had functioned as an exclusive male club, into an adoration of herself.[4] Elizabeth and her ministers carefully developed the cult of the Virgin Queen in part to replace the cult of the Virgin Mary, which had been destroyed by the Reformation.[5] Elizabeth also clearly separated her behavior from how she expected other women to behave, thus distinguishing herself from general expectations about women. The Homily on Marriage, which was added to the original 1547 set of homilies when they were reissued by Elizabeth's government, praised marriage as the only acceptable state for women and told women, "as for their husbands, them must they obey, and cease from commanding, and perform subjection."[6] Yet Elizabeth herself refused to be so guided. Quite early in her reign, Melville, the ambassador from Scotland, told the queen that he could see she would never marry, since if she did she would be but queen of England, whereas now she was "both king and queen." When she had been queen for only a few years, Elizabeth told another ambassador who came with a marriage proposal "that in England there was a woman who acted like a man, and did not need . . . [one] to guide her." She reminded Robert Dudley, the man she came closest to marrying, "I will have here but one mistress and no master."[7] Elizabeth would never have followed Mary Stuart's example of silently doing embroidery during Council meetings. Yet even though Elizabeth attempted to delineate this clear distinction between herself and other women, and between her public function as ruler and whatever private role there was for her as woman, others refused to accept this dichotomy. Foreign ambassadors bribed the women of Elizabeth's bedchamber for intimate information about her life, and their reports home are filled with such details as Elizabeth's light and irregular periods; it was even rumored she had been bled in the foot to correct this problem. However effective a ruler Elizabeth in particular might be, the fact that she was a woman was in some sense insurmountable—and thus in part cause of the longing for the king that was manifest in the belief of Edward VI's survival.

The motif of the woman ruler, the generalized sense of insecurity, and the consequent appearance of a male impostor pretending to be the supposedly dead king can be found as well in thirteenth-century Flanders. In the 1220s the Countess Joanna ruled Flanders under the domination of the French. At this time people in Flanders, in the midst of a famine and wishing to throw off French influence, were in an uneasy state. Rumors began to circulate that Joanna's father, Count Baldwin, killed while on a Crusade twenty years before, was not really dead. After years of wandering, he would return home to free his people from bondage.

With wild delight many people recognized a wandering hermit as the returned count. He admitted his "identity" and then proposed to take Flanders by force from his daughter. After losing in battle Joanna fled, and "Baldwin" was crowned with great ceremony. It was seven months before he was identified as a serf, Bertrand of Ray, and executed. Yet Joanna was spoken of with hatred for generations for having caused her "father's" death.[8]

We can see the link between lack of legitimacy of the ruler and belief in rumors of survival and pretenders in earlier periods of English history as well. In one case this belief pattern occurs when a woman is ruling.[9] After the deposition and murder of Edward II in 1327, though the crown theoretically passed to his fourteen-year-old son Edward III, the real rulers were Edward's wife Isabella and her lover Mortimer. There were a variety of rumors that Edward was still alive and would reclaim his throne from the rule of an obviously inappropriate person—namely, his wife. These rumors of Edward's survival were strong enough to convince Edward's own half brother, Edmund of Woodstock. Mortimer considered Edmund's conviction dangerous enough to have him executed, yet the rumors persisted.[10]

These beliefs in a deposed king's survival appear as well in the reign of Henry IV, who had caused the deposition and murder of his cousin Richard II in 1399. These rumors, which plagued Henry IV throughout his reign, were still current in the reign of his son. People whispered that Richard had escaped to Scotland but that unfortunately the whole experience had had a detrimental effect—he had lost his wits.[11]

These rumors attending the reigns of the early Lancastrians make a great deal of sense if legitimacy was a key issue in their appearance. Though Henry IV was Richard's cousin he was not his legal heir, and when Henry had broken his banishment in 1399 he had said he was returning to England only for his rightful inheritance, the duchy of

Lancaster. Instead, he had deposed his cousin and taken over England without just claim (which, of course, led to the War of the Roses in the fifteenth century).

In the late fifteenth century, England suffered through the War of the Roses: thirty years of civil war, of questioning the legitimacy of the king. By 1485 kingship rested its title primarily on the incumbent's ability to seize and maintain authority. Though the number of people who died during the War of the Roses was small, for people in the sixteenth century looking back on their history the instability, lawlessness, and lack of justice were frightening to all classes of society. In the early sixteenth century there was, argues John William Allen, an "urgent sense of the need for order."[12] Moreover, writers throughout the Tudor Age exaggerated the troubles of the previous century as a way to expound on the necessity of legal kingship and good order.[13] The problem of instability was all the more severe in England because the crown had never quite attained the mystical, religious overtones associated with the French monarchy, which explains in part why incompetent French kings were less likely to be deposed than their English counterparts.[14]

The War of the Roses ended in 1485, when Henry Tudor defeated Richard III. But Henry VII's claim to the throne was dubious, and a number of people believed that Bosworth Field was simply another event in the continuing struggle for control of England by the great lords. As a result, Henry VII had his own share of pretenders claiming to be the nephews and sons of Edward IV.[15] Henry defeated Lambert Simnel's supporters at Stoke in 1487. "In spite of the flimsiness of Simnel's imposture the danger [he posed to Henry VII] had been very great because of the fragility of Henry's own position," suggests D. M. Loades.[16] The second pretender, Perkin Warbeck, posed a far more serious threat. In the 1490s a number of foreign sovereigns and some of the nobility of England gave Warbeck intermittent support. Sir William Stanley, who only a decade earlier had crowned the young Henry Tudor after the battle of Bosworth Field, died on the scaffold after asserting that if Warbeck were really the son of Edward IV, then he (Stanley) could not fight against him. As it turned out, Warbeck was not.[17] But Warbeck paid dearly for his impersonation; in 1499 it cost him his life.

The appearance of Simnel and Warbeck, and of at least three other "feigned boys" who got little support in early Tudor England, was understandable, even to be expected.[18] Henry had become king after thirty years of civil war, and his claim to the throne was weak. In the late fifteenth century people could hardly foresee that the dynasty Henry had founded would endure for over a hundred years, through a period of great change and of great cultural achievement. It must surely have seemed worth the chance to an adventurer and his backers to try for the big prize at a time when the king was new and the line shaky. The fact that Henry chose to shroud in mystery the fates of the sons of the House of York only helped such schemers use substitutes when no actual claimant was available.

By midcentury, however, the question of the succession was rather different. Although Henry VII's reign began with turmoil and uncertainty and the appearance of pretenders to his throne, there was a peaceful and triumphant transition to his son. By 1509 Henry VIII and the Tudor line were firmly in control. And during his reign, Henry VIII promoted more and more belief in the mystique of kingship. Henry VIII, unlike earlier rulers, was addressed as "Majesty." The lessons of the War of the Roses and the jeopardy of the kingship must have been very much on the new king's mind, however. One way we can ascertain this is by his ruthless elimination of anyone who might have exercised a claim to the throne, such as the Duke of Buckingham, the Poles, and the Earl of Surrey. But even though Henry VIII tightly controlled the kingship, the only way for his line to continue was a male heir. J. J. Scarisbrick suggests: "English experience of the queen regnant was remote and unhappy, and Henry's conventional mind, which no doubt accorded with his subjects', demanded a son as a political necessity."[19]

Henry believed he had to have a son for his line to be secure and in order to save his subjects from renewed civil war, but his first marriage to Catherine of Aragon had produced only Mary, their one child to survive infancy. Though historians such as Lacey Baldwin Smith suggest that Henry might have neatly solved all his problems by marrying his daughter to her cousin James V, thus uniting the crowns of England and Scotland a half century before this actually happened,[20] Henry was horrified by the thought of having no legal son to succeed him. Henry obviously considered the idea of placing his illegitimate son Henry Fitzroy (son of Bessie Blount, later Lady Talboys) in the succession. With this option in mind he created the boy Duke of Richmond—his own father's title.[21] Yet with the haunting experience of what had happened in the previous century when legitimacy was questioned, Henry clearly doubted this course of action and never fully pursued it. What he needed was a son who also was his legal heir.

As is well known, Henry's conscience suggested to him that the reason all his sons had been still-born or died in infancy was that God was punishing him for his invalid marriage; he should never have broken the religious injunction against marrying his dead brother's widow. By this time Henry had also fallen deeply in love with Anne Boleyn, who had refused to become his mistress. What effect this had on his decision to seek an annulment of his marriage is conjectural. What is most significant for this study is the effect of Henry's decisions on the people of England in their attitude toward kingship. Because of the rise of Martin Luther and the spread of Protestantism, Pope Clement VII feared antagonizing Catherine of Aragon's nephew, the Holy Roman Emperor Charles V. Yet he hesitated to deny Henry VIII his request. For six years the pope attempted to stall, hoping events would somehow resolve themselves naturally. This did not happen, and Henry eventually took the tumultuous step of breaking off from the Catholic church and opening the floodgates of the Reformation in England.[22]

By Parliamentary decree, "this realm of England" had become an empire, and no outsider—not pope, not emperor—could tell its king or its people what to do. Henry was now not only king but supreme head of the church as well. Thus rituals that had given comfort for centuries were cast into doubt. And with this confusion, the figure of the king became ever more significant in the minds of the people.

Henry had broken with the church, turned his world upside down, and married Anne Boleyn, all to have yet another daughter, Elizabeth. This second marriage lasted only three years, produced another still-born son, and ended dramatically with Anne's execution for adultery. Henry's third wife, Jane Seymour, finally gave him the legitimate son he had so long sought, although she died of disease contracted during childbirth. Henry married three more times, but none of these unions produced any more children.

Thus in 1547 Henry VIII, despite all his marital adventures, had only one son; all the other close heirs were women.[23] When Henry made his will—in 1536 Parliament had decreed he could leave the throne to whomever he wanted—he had to decide upon alternatives if Edward should chance to die without sons of his own. Though he had had both his daughters declared illegitimate and never legally altered their status, this did not stop Henry from restoring them to the succession; should Edward die without heirs of his body, the crown would pass to Mary, and in turn to Elizabeth. For good measure, Henry added a further contingency: should Elizabeth also die without children, the line would pass to the descendants—also all women—of his younger sister Mary. Mary's only surviving children were her daughter Frances, Duchess of Suffolk, herself the mother of three girls, Jane, Katherine, and Mary Grey; and Eleanor, Countess of Cumberland. Eleanor had yet another daughter, Margaret Clifford. In this will Henry ignored the Scottish branch, descendants of his older sister Margaret, of whom the most famous was yet another woman, Mary Stuart.

Yet it is doubtful that Henry really considered that a woman would be the ruler. Henry's idea of the function of a ruler was a strong military commander, and the battlefield, he once remarked, was "unmeet for women's inbecilities." (Perhaps Henry, judging from his own experience, believed it was "meet" for men's imbecilities!) Erickson tells us that "no provision was ever made to prepare Mary to handle affairs of state."[24]

But though Henry never trained his daughters to be rulers, in 1553, with the death of Edward VI this possibility became reality. In the mid-sixteenth century the English people not only had to deal with the new phenomenon of a woman ruler,[25] but had to deal with it at a time of great religious unrest. England, within about thirty years, under Henry VIII was to be Catholic, maintain Catholic dogma but without allegiance to the pope, become far more Protestant in ritual under Edward VI, return its allegiance to the pope under Mary, and with Elizabeth's accession return to an Anglican church hierarchy. At the same time as this religious confusion came queenship. Women were to rule in England for the rest of the century, and one of the many results of this change in the sex of the monarch was the rumor that Edward VI was not really dead. Concurrent with the rumors were the impostors who claimed that they were the king.

I am arguing that gender as well as legitimacy is a significant factor in the emergence of pretenders. Yet the issue is an exceedingly complex one, and sorting through the belief patterns of people from earlier centuries is difficult. For example, though during Mary's reign the rumors and impostures all centered on her brother Edward, Mary herself was once the object of such an impersonation. In 1533 in the north of England an eighteen-year-old woman, Mary Baynton, was arrested and examined for impersonating Mary. She had gone around begging money so that she might use it to seek the protection of Emperor Charles V. She explained to her listeners that her aunt and namesake Mary, the French queen, had once read a book of prophecies and had told her, "Niece, Mary, I am right sorry for you, for I see here that your fortune is very hard. Ye must go a-begging once in your life, either in your youth or in your age." Being of the temperament to get something unpleasant accomplished immediately, she decided to do it in her youth. It is not clear from the examination whether Mary Baynton really belived she was the Lady Mary or had merely figured out a useful method of gaining money, but she was apparently successful enough at finding people to accept her claim to bring her to the attention of the magistrates. The year 1533 was, of course, a particularly stressful one not only for the Lady Mary but for those who believed in her cause: Archbishop Cranmer had finally declared the marriage between her parents invalid, and Henry as a free man had publicly announced his marriage to Anne Boleyn.[26] The imposture of Mary Baynton was an isolated event and not part of the series of rumors and impostures that linked questions of gender and legitimacy.

Before discussing the pretenders in the reigns of Mary and Elizabeth specifically, there is another general issue to be raised on the subject. In the sixteenth century it was much easier for rumors of the king's survival to flourish because of the lack of precision in the distribution of news. There were no newspapers, magazines, or television. Few people would have seen the king when he was alive, and portraits were often stylized to represent an ideal. As a result, few people would really know what the king looked like.

Moreover, the *image* of the king had become immensely powerful. As a result, it was more and more difficult for people to accept the mortal, physical aspect of the ruler, and his death somehow had to be marked appropriately.[27] For example, people claimed that on the night Henry VIII died there was a storm such as no one had ever experienced before. Only six years later people whispered of other happenings on the death of Edward VI—that the grave itself opened up and Henry VIII walked again in fury over the breaking of his will.[28]

When Edward died, despite the provisions of Henry's will, there was not a smooth transition to Mary. Encouraged by the Duke of Northumberland, who had been ruling England in Edward's name, the young king had made a will of his own, disinheriting both his sisters in favor of his cousin Jane Grey. Fortuitously, Jane was soon to be married to Northumberland's youngest son, Guilford Dudley.[29] Without the force of Parliament, this new will was patently illegal. As it happened, it was also dynastically unsound, since even if Edward's sisters were excluded, Jane's mother Frances was still alive. People rallied quickly around Mary, who had adroitly escaped capture, despite Northumberland's attempts to trick her. (Northumberland had, in the king's name, asked Mary to come to London, claiming that the boy king wanted to die in his sister's arms. Luckily Mary had been warned that this message was a trap and that Edward was already dead, and she fled to Framlingham in Suffolk and proclaimed herself queen.) As Mary was the true heir, even many Protestants who had distrusted Northumberland supported her. In fact, Northumberland was so disliked that Mary began her reign with an abundance of goodwill. Mary's success also rested in large measure on the fact that her rival—the figurehead Northumberland was forced to use—was also a woman.

In August 1553, Mary triumphantly entered London as the first queen since the Conquest. Yet by November, when it was known that the queen would soon marry the hated Philip of Spain, people were saying that Edward was still alive.

Margaret Cornfield suggests that the rumors of the king's survival may have had something to do with the mystery surrounding Edward's death and with Protestant fears of a Catholic ruler.[30] Northumberland had kept Edward's death secret for a few days while he attempted to lure Mary and Elizabeth to London. The confusion this caused, as well as the bizarre treatment Edward received at the hands of the quacks Northumberland hired in a desperate attempt to keep Edward alive when he was clearly dying, produced rumors that Northumberland had had Edward poisoned. This was the last thing Northumberland would have done in the circumstances; events were already moving too quickly for him.[31]

It is less clear how the rumors of poison would eventually lead people to believe that Edward was not dead at all. Yet within a few months this was exactly what happened. In November 1553, three men, Robert Tayler, Edmonde Cole (or Coles), and Thomas Wood, were brought before the Council for their "lewde reportes" that Edward was still alive. Wood was a servant, and the other two were dealers in textiles— men of the tradesmen class. After their appearance before the Council they were ordered to appear before the Star Chamber, so the Council obviously viewed these rumors with some seriousness. In January, Tayler was forced to pay 500 marks in good behavior so that he would be available if called upon. Coles was later asked to pay £500.[32]

These rumors were beginning to appear at a time when Mary's government had other disturbances to worry about as well. For example, a mysterious wailing wall prophesied against Mary; only later was it found out that a carefully coached child was inside. Mobs broke up sermons and threw daggers at preachers. Libelous pamphlets and ballads were available on every street corner. The belief in Edward's survival appears to have been part of a larger crisis in the people's confidence about the queen's rule. This belief in the king's presence was a fundamental attack on Mary's legitimacy. If Edward were still alive, she had no business claiming to be queen.

It was distressing enough to Mary's government that men of the tradesmen class would repeat such a rumor. The response to Robert Robotham "of the wardrobe of the robes" shows even more alarm. Even though he was himself a part of Mary's government, in January 1554 he repeated talk that could have drastically undercut it. "For his lewde talke that the kinges majestie deceased shulde by yet lyving" he was committed to the Fleet as a close prisoner. But the rumors continued to spread. The very next day Joan Wheler "for her devellishe sayeng that King Edward was styll lyving" was committed to Marshalsea, yet another prison. Cornfield suggests that the three may all have been sent to different prisons to keep them isolated from each other, in an attempt to stop the rumors. Certainly none of them were publicly punished by being put in the pillory, which may have been the government's way of trying to keep these rumors from spreading.[33]

This isolating of prisoners apparently was effective for a while. For more than a year after this the rumor does not appear in any official records. During that time Thomas Wyatt attempted his futile rebellion against the coming Spanish marriage and died on the scaffold before Philip came to England. The Spanish marriage was solemnized with great ceremony in 1554, and by the end of October of that year Mary was convinced she was pregnant. Despite all the upsets earlier in her reign which had been aimed against the Spanish marriage and the restoration of Roman Catholicism, "the news of [her pregnancy] had a strangely calming effect on the turbulent citizens of London," D. M. Loades states. "Any child born to Philip and Mary would have been three-quarters Spanish but the evidence all suggests that English people

were prepared to welcome such a child."[34] Perhaps the calming effect
is not strange when one looks at it from the perspective that Mary in
childbirth would serve the approved function of a woman. This was
even more important than the fact that a child by Mary would mean
the continuation of Catholicism in England.

When it became painfully obvious the next May and June that this
was a false pregnancy, there was another rash of disturbances, including
rumors of Edward's survival and impostors claiming to be the king.
This time it was impossible for Mary's government to keep the matter
quiet. Realizing this, they tried different means of suppression. The
reaction over Mary's false pregnancy was especially acute because on
April 30 rumors had spread all over London that Mary had been safely
delivered of a son. The celebration turned to sullenness when it became
clear that this had not occurred. "In London disillusionment . . . led to
mounting agitation. New libels against Mary were thrown into the streets
every few days, stirring up fears and encouraging rebellion. . . . Seditious talk was everywhere—in taverns, in the streets, anywhere gentle-
men met to eat and gamble."[35]

In mid-May 1555, two men were apprehended in Essex for spreading
rumors of Edward's survival. Also at about this time at least two young
men actually claimed to be Edward.[36] One of these was eighteen-year-
old Edward (or William) Featherstone, alias Constable, son of a miller
and servant to a Sir Peter Mewtas. Instead of simply passing along a
rumor that Edward was still alive, Featherstone claimed that *he* was the
king. He was brought before the Council at Hampton Court for examination but when asked for an explanation of his behavior "coun-
terfetted a manner of simplicitie, or rather frensie, and would make no
direct answer." He was committed to jail at Marshalsea as a "lunatike
foole," though historians writing thirty years later believed this to have
been feigned as a defense.[37] The Council wondered if there were more
important people behind Featherstone coaching him. Though this seems
quite likely it was never proved, and no other names are given in the
accounts.

This case gained enough publicity for the London citizen Henry
Machyn to record it in his diary.[38] Apparently Featherstone had found
a number of people willing to express belief in him, whether genuine
or not. The Venetian Ambassador Michiel reported, "Being believed
to be such, both in the country and here . . . he raised a tumult amongst
the populace." Michiel concludes, "Nor is this a novelty in England,

as of youre there was a similar impostor who represented himself as one of the sons of Edward the 4th, . . . which I mention that your Serenity may comprehend what strange fancies prevail amongst these people, and how much their ideas differ from those of other nations.''[39]

If the government had decided to keep earlier rumors about Edward's survival quiet, they had a different approach with an actual pretender. On May 22, 1555, Featherstone was ridden throughout London in a cart and wearing a fool's coat with derisive statements attached to it. After being thus paraded he was whipped and had his ears cropped. When this painful and humiliating punishment ended he was banished from London.[40]

Yet in January 1556 more rumors were heard, and handbills were circulated in London and the countryside. One such handbill, in effect inciting rebellion, assured readers that Edward was alive and well and waiting in France for a demonstration of support that would enable him to recover his crown.[41] At least some of these communications could be traced back to Featherstone, who had certainly not learned his lesson. In fact, his supporters were keeping very busy. ''One Laurance Trymmyng of Grenewich committed this daye to the Towre for a seditious bill conteyning King Edward to be alive'' that had been delivered to him by Constable. The same month William Cockes, one of the officers of the Pantry, was arrested, relieved of his office, and commanded to appear before the Council on a weekly basis simply for ''receiving a lewde bill surmysing that King Edward was still lyving.''[42] Michiel for one considered the matter ''ridiculous and unimportant'' but assured the doge that Mary's Council ''viewed it in a different light.''[43]

After Featherstone's followers distributed his handbills, he again made an appearance claiming to be Edward. This time there was no leniency. He was arraigned at the Guildhall in London, found guilty, and condemned to be hanged, drawn, quartered, and beheaded. This grisly sentence was carried out, and as a stern reminder his head was set on London Bridge. By this time Mary would accept no question of her legitimacy as queen. Nor were there further rumors or impostors during her reign, judging from the official records. ''The affair is consigned to silence,'' Michiel correctly wrote the doge.[44]

Yet the rumors that had disappeared by 1556 resurfaced again nearly thirty years later, well into the reign of Elizabeth. Their reappearance might at first glance be surprising, since such allegations should have ended in the reign of Catholic Mary if religion had been the motivating factor in their development, as Cornfield has suggested. True, Edward had been a Protestant, and Mary was enforcing Catholicism at a time when many people resisted the return of English allegiance to the pope. Religious uncertainty might well have encouraged the emergence of rumors concerning Edward's survival. If this were their whole motivation, however, one might question why these rumors also emerged in the reign of the Protestant Elizabeth. Religious insecurity was still very much a problem in her reign, especially with Catholic Mary Stuart as the alternate possibility for ruler; in their Protestantism, however, as opposed to their gender, Edward and Elizabeth were very similar. Yet the fact of a woman's rule is not enough to explain the reemergence of these rumors and impostors, since for the most part this did not happen until late in her reign. The crucial factor was that by the time the rumors of Edward's survival resurfaced, the problems of a successor for Elizabeth were acute. With Mary Stuart an enforced "guest" in her country, she still refused to name a safe Protestant heir. Moreover, she was finally too old to marry and have a child, which would have solved the succession problem in the way most people had originally wanted.

The mid-to-late sixteenth century was a time of considerable disturbance and insecurity. C. W. Previte-Orton says that in the years following Edward's death and well into the reign of Elizabeth predictions of some supernatural happening "were particularly rife. Each religious party, Romanists and Protestants, hoped for a final revolution in their own favor. . . . It was to be miraculous."[45]

There was enough concern in the late Elizabethan period over prophecies in general and the rumors of Edward VI's survival in specific for John Harvey to write in 1588:

Alas what fond and vaine expectations hath a long time rested in the minds not of one or two, of a few, but of great multitudes of the simpler sort in England about King Edward the Sixth, as though they were sure either of his arising from death, or his returne from I know not what Jerusalem, or other strange land: A mad conceit. . . . And what counterfeit suborned marchants of base perentage, have thence ranged abrode in the countrie, presuming to terme themselves by the roiall name of king Edward? Such is the rash and blind credulitie of the common people, and such is the desperate insolencie of some brainsicke presumptuous runnagates.[46]

We know about one of the "runnagates" referred to by John Harvey. He was Robert Blosse, who used the name Mantell while trying to find supporters for his claim. One such supporter was Elizabeth Vessie, who had her fortune told by Jane Standlie in 1578. The fortune promised Vessie was certainly an impressive one—nothing less than that "she should be the chief instrument in reinstating, 'the king' of this realm" to his proper place. We notice here that the wily Mistress Standlie did not mention who this king was to be. She did, however, add the warning that while her efforts would bring Vessie into great favor with the king, they would cause her serious problems with the queen and her counselors.[47]

Mistress Standlie did not tell her patron exactly when all this would come to pass, but she did give her a grisly way to mark the time, by enumerating the many children and servants she would bury before the king's return. By the early 1580s Vessie had apparently buried enough. In London she met a stranger calling himself Mantell, who, she was convinced, was the person to whom Standlie had referred. Vessie asked Mantell who he was, at the same time confiding Standlie's prophecy to him. Mantell admitted he was indeed Edward VI; he had not died in 1553 after all. Mantell then "made much of her, calling her ever after 'sister.'" Elizabeth Vessie was apparently a far better sister to this "Edward VI" than Elizabeth Tudor. While Mantell did not concern Vessie with his past impostures, they may explain how she had been able to recognize him; he had already been brought before Robert Fleetwood, Recorder of London, in 1572 for spreading rumors that Edward VI was still alive, and also that Elizabeth was the mother of four children by Robert Dudley. Fleetwood had dismissed him in 1572, so that some years later he was able to take the rumor another step and claim he was himself the king.[48] Unfortunately, soon after his meeting with Elizabeth Vessie, Mantell confided his secret to a less sympathetic listener, a Mr. Collins of Essex, who promptly informed against him, at least partially in hopes of receiving special privileges in his trade as victualer.[49]

Elizabeth's government did not originally take Mantell with the same seriousness with which Mary's Council had regarded Featherstone thirty years earlier. Regarded as the victim of "frenzies," he was merely sentenced to a year's imprisonment. Despite his frenzies he managed to escape, perhaps with the connivance of Vessie, who visited him soon before the event. Elizabeth's government, like Mary's, viewed a repeated offense far more seriously than a first one. Mantell was recaptured and, like Featherstone, eventually executed as a traitor.[50]

Mantell's execution, however, did not end the rumor. There are several other reported cases. In 1587 William Francis, a smith of Hat-field Peveral, claimed that Edward was still alive. In fact, he said, he personally knew the man who had carried Edward "in a red mantle into Germany in a ship called the *Harry*."[51] Edward's elaborate tomb, claimed Francis, was really empty. (It is interesting in symbolic terms that the ship supposed to have carried the boy king to safety should bear the name of his father.) The same year a Leicester embroiderer named Sawford suggested the possibility of Edward's survival.[52] In March 1588, a Francis Nevell returned from serving in the Low Coun-tries and while discussing preparations for possible invasion with his drinking companions confided to them that Edward VI was still alive. They were sufficiently surprised by this information to pass it on to the Justice of the Peace. When questioned in a more sober state, Nevell explained "that he had heard [King Edward] was alive by a thousand of his fellow-soldiers in the Low Countries some of whom said he was in France and some in Spain," either of which would be a dubious sanctuary for a Protestant king.[53]

The rumor made its last appearance in Elizabeth's reign in 1599, when Thomas Vaughan made the statement that Edward VI was not dead. Instead, he claimed, another child had been substituted for him and Edward had been safely spirited off to Denmark, where he married the queen and "now is king there." Recently, asserted Vaughan, the king had saved the poor in England, Wales, and Ireland by giving them corn and provisions. Vaughan, with touching faith in family feeling, added that "he heard that her Majesty did say she would gladly hear whether her brother King Edward were dead or alive."[54] By 1599 Edward was almost a mythic religious figure who provided for his people in need. Accounts of the rumor in the seventeenth century are far more vague; for the most part, when Elizabeth died, the belief in her still-living brother died with her.[55]

Although the rumors of Edward VI's survival greatly lessened in the early Stuart period, there appears to be more to this development than the mere fact of their appearance during the reign of women. The timing of these rumors under Elizabeth may provide a clue to the social and psychological functions they served. They appeared in the 1580s and 1590s, reflecting not only doubts over female rule but uncertainty con-cerning a woman who would soon be leading her country to war with Spain, who was too old to have a child of her own, and who yet refused to name her heir. An analogous situation is the recurrent rumor that Elizabeth herself had one or more children.

If the rumors about Edward VI's survival are connected not only with a woman ruler but with an infertile one, then this anxiety may well have expressed itself in these related stories of Elizabeth's illegitimate children. There may have been both a wish that Elizabeth would completely fulfill her womanly responsibility and have a child and an attempt to diminish the queen in the most traditional way—by dismissing her as a whore.

In the first years of her reign Elizabeth was seen everywhere with Robert Dudley, who was eventually created Earl of Leicester. Especially after the mysterious death of Dudley's wife, Amy Robsart, many people around Elizabeth were desperately afraid she would forget everything in a moment of passion and marry him. Throckmorton, the English ambassador, wrote from Paris that the French gossip about Elizabeth's morals made him wish he were dead. Had Elizabeth married Dudley, she might well have gone to bed one night as queen and awakened the next morning as plain Mistress Dudley, the Spanish ambassador predicted. In such a climate it is not unexpected for the government to hear of people gossiping about Elizabeth and Dudley's relations. "The evidence available from so many trustworthy sources leaves no doubt," writes Martin Hume, "that the relations existing between the Queen and her lover were very intimate and even compromising for at least ten years after her accession. It is not surprising that, as a natural outcome . . . rumors were set afloat that children had been born to the pair."[56] We have already noted that the troublemaker Robert Blosse (alias Mantell) had been one of those spreading the rumor.

Throughout these comments so carefully gathered by a worried government is a definite thread of malice—the sense that Elizabeth, this unmarried woman no better than she ought to be, had no business ruling. In 1560, for instance, Mother Anne Dowd was committed to jail for "openly asserting that the queen was with child by Robt. Duddeley."[57] The mix of scandalmongering and anger at having a woman ruler was expressed even more openly three years later by Edmund Baxter, who said "that Lord Robert [Dudley] kept her Majesty, and that she was a naughty woman, and could not rule her realm, and that justice was not being administered." His wife added that when she saw the queen at Ipswich "she looked like one lately come out of child-bed."[58] The ability to administer justice was one quality by which a people judged a medieval or early modern monarch able or not. By being called unchaste, Elizabeth was also being charged in general with not being a good ruler in ways that had no connection with her sexuality. Also, the concept of honor and its relation to behavior was markedly different for women and men. For males, honor had to do with keeping one's word and with not being shamed on the battlefield. For women, honor was remaining chaste not only in body but in reputation. In accusing the queen of sexual improprieties people were charging her with dishonorable behavior in a way that would not be the case with a similar rumor about a king.[59] The linking of a woman's generally inappropriate behavior and the charge of sexual incontinence was very common in the sixteenth century, appearing often in witchcraft and heresy trials. The gossip of Mother Dowd and the Baxters is more comprehensible than the later rumors, since Elizabeth was young, unmarried, and in the early 1560s indiscreet in some people's eyes in her displays of affection for Robert Dudley.

In the 1560s and 1570s the rumors of Elizabeth's illegitimate children continued to crop up amid hostile foreign Catholics. One example occurred in 1574. Antonio de Guaras, acting Spanish agent in London, reported there would be a marriage between the son of Catherine Grey and ''a daughter of Leicester and the Queen . . . who, it is said, is kept hidden, although there are bishops to witness that she is legitimate.''[60] Guaras's only source of information was the gossip of the Catholic party. His meddling in conspiracies, by the way, eventually led to his expulsion. In November of the next year, the Venetian ambassador in Spain reported that Elizabeth had an illegitimate daughter of thirteen, whom Cecil hoped to marry to his son.[61]

In 1581 Henry Hawkins explained Elizabeth's frequent progresses (or tours) throughout the countryside as a way for her to leave court and have her illegitimate children by Dudley—five all told. Said Hawkins of the queen, ''she never goethe in progress but to be delievered.''[62] The rumor was also mentioned several times around the turn of the century.

In 1598 Edward Fraunces attempted to seduce Elizabeth Baylie (or Boyle) by telling her the queen had three illegitimate children. Why should not Baylie have a sexual relationship without marriage, he asked her, when ''the best in England, i.e. the Queen, had done so.'' Elizabeth Baylie's refusal made Fraunces angry not only with her but with the woman he had urged on her as a model, for he added, "that the land had been happy if Her Majesty had been cut off twenty years since, so that some noble prince might have reigned in her stead." Elizabeth Baylie testified about this conversation before the magistrates. Fraunces further amplified his misogyny when he attempted to discredit her testimony with the statement that "women are base creatures and of no credit."[63]

In 1601 the rumor surfaced several times.[64] The most interesting version is from a man named Hugh Broughton, who again wove together the themes of hostility toward her rule and Elizabeth's lack of chastity. William Knyght was horrified by the monstrous speeches Broughton was making about the queen, including one that is Gothic in its melodrama. According to Broughton, a midwife was taken to a secret chamber where she was told to save the mother (Elizabeth, of course) at whatever cost to the child. The midwife was too skilled; she saved both.

And after [delivering] . . . a daughter, [the midwife] was brought to another chamber where was a very great fire of coals, into which she was commanded to cast the child, and so it was burnt. This midwife was rewarded with a handful of gold, and at her departure, one came to her with a cup of wine, and said, Thou whore, drink before thou goest from hence, and she drank, and was sent back to her house, where within six days after she died of poison, but revealed this before her death.[65]

Just as the rumors of Edward VI's survival finally brought about actual impostors, so did the rumors of Elizabeth's own illegitimate children. In 1587 a young Englishman in pilgrim's garb was arrested in the north of Spain on suspicion of being a spy. He was sent to Madrid and confronted with Philip II's English secretary, Sir Francis Englefield, who was at first inclined to believe the young man, who claimed he was Arthur Dudley, illegitimate son of Robert and the queen. He gave a detailed account of childhood in the household of Robert Southern, who had confided to the boy his real identity on his deathbed. Dudley detailed meetings with high-level members of Elizabeth's government after he had tried to leave the country. In the mid–1580s, he told Englefield, he had finally fled to the continent and wandered about in the company of disaffected English. He primarily lived off of the enemies of his supposed mother. Arthur Dudley proposed to Englefield that Philip II take him under his protection and use him in the coming attack on England. "The poor foolish young man [was] apparently under the impression that King Philip was an amiable altruist, who would help him to a crown for the sake of his *beaux yeux*."[66] Though at first Englefield had believed Dudley's story, in his later letters he wondered if Dudley were actually a "simple instrument in the hands of Elizabeth herself."[67] His final suggestion to Philip was:

For this and other reasons I am of the opinion that he should not be allowed to get away, but should be kept very secure to prevent his escape. It is true his claim at present amounts to nothing, but . . . it cannot be doubted that France and the English heretics, or some other party, might turn it to their own advantage.[68]

Alarmingly for Dudley, the letter by Englefield has a notation by Philip stating that it would be "safest to make sure of [Dudley's] person until we know more about it."[69] And with that Dudley disappears from the records.

Though Dudley's story has enough plausible details to suggest that he had been well coached by people who were intimately connected with the court twenty-five years earlier, its basic premise is impossible. Elizabeth's illness in 1562 is well attested to as smallpox rather than childbirth. Also, as Hume points out, "It is . . . beyond belief that a boy in the condition represented would have been allowed to run about the world at his own free will."[70] Hume suggests further that it would hardly have served Arthur Dudley's own best interests, if he actually were Elizabeth's son, to wander about the continent consorting with her enemies. Hume is convinced that he was a spy who used this story to try to gain access to important people and to save himself when caught. Elizabeth Jenkins adds that he may well have been willing to spy for either side.[71]

The belief in Edward VI's survival and the actual appearance of pretenders were only several aspects of a very complex system of beliefs that flourished in the second half of the sixteenth century. Yet these belief patterns were troubling nonetheless. The rumors of the king's survival, the gossip about Elizabeth's children, and the impostors who eventually emerged all reflect the uncertainty of having a woman ruler. But I believe the idea can be taken further. The rumors were most frequent, and were coupled with the appearance of an actual impostor, in Mary's reign after it was evident that she would not have a child. In Elizabeth's reign, for the most part, the rumors of Edward VI's survival did not emerge for nearly thirty years, and most of the rumors of her illegitimate children and the appearance of Arthur Dudley took place in the last two decades of her reign as well.

I believe the rumors and pretenders of the 1580s and 1590s reflect the people's sense of instability over not only the rule of a woman but the rule of an elderly, childless woman who refused to name a successor. And this woman without a direct heir was ruling at a time of great change and potential crisis. For the fifty years preceding, the state had kept changing the official religion back and forth between Catholicism and different forms of Protestantism. The English could look to their neighboring countries such as France and see the ravaging effect of religious civil wars. Mary Stuart's presence in England until her execution in 1587, and the attendant assassination plots against Elizabeth, made it vividly clear to many of the English people how close they were to political chaos. And though Mary Stuart's death removed one danger, Philip II's threatened invasion of England as a holy war provided another. Elizabeth was aware of this sense of precariousness when she gave her Armada speech in 1588: "Although I have the body of a weak and feeble woman, I have the heart and stomach of a king, and of a king of England too."[72] But while her words could stir patriotism, they could not deflect this deeper insecurity.

Mary and Elizabeth never had to face a pretender with an army behind him, as Joanna of Flanders did. Neither Featherstone nor Mantell had great support, nor did the queens evoke commensurate hatred for refusing to accept these impostors as their brother. Nonetheless, for the English people in the second half of the sixteenth century, a woman ruling in her own right—and without a son of her own to succeed her and reestablish the male order—was unsettling. These male pretenders were one example of how the insecurities the English people felt demonstrated themselves. The pattern of the male monarch as savior echoes through sixteenth-century England, so that the fears caused by female rule manifested themselves in a longing for the safety and tradition of the king.

NOTES

I would like to thank the other members of the Research Institute on Women's Public Lives, University of Kansas, 1980, for their help and support, and especially the director, Janet Sharistanian. Retha Warnicke, Stanley Rolnick, Dennis Moore, and Mary Beth Rose also gave me very helpful suggestions. Thanks as well to Mary Strottman and Maxine Fredericksen.

1. For a discussion of both Philip's legal position and his actual influence, see D. M. Loades, *The Reign of Mary Tudor: Politics, Government, and Religion in England, 1553–1558* (New York: St. Martin's Press, 1979), pp. 122–23, 252–55.

2. *De vera obedienta oratio*, printed in 1535; English version in 1553, cited in John William Allen, *A History of Political Thought in the Sixteenth Century* (London: Methuen, 1957), p. 126; Keith Thomas discusses how this image of king as God's representative affected family life in women's status in "Women and the Civil War Sects," in *Crisis in Europe, 1560–1660*, ed. Trevor Aston (New York: Basic Books, 1965), pp. 317–40.

3. Carolly Erickson, *Bloody Mary* (New York: Doubleday, 1978), p. 304.

4. J. E. Neale, *Queen Elizabeth I* (1934; reprint ed., New York: Doubleday Anchor Books, 1957), pp. 64–65.

5. Louis Adrian Montrose, " 'Shaping Fantasies': Figurations of Gender and Power in Elizabethan Culture," *Representations* 1, no. 2 (Spring 1983):61–94.

6. John Griffiths, ed., *The Two Books of Homilies to Be Read in Churches* (Oxford: At the University Press, 1859), p. 504.

7. Lacey Baldwin Smith, *Elizabeth Tudor* (Boston: Little, Brown, 1975), pp. 122–58; Martin Hume, *The Courtships of Queen Elizabeth* (London: E. Nashe Grayson, 1926), pp. 59–60.

8. Norman Cohn, *Pursuit of the Millenium* (1963; rev. expanded ed., London: T. Smith, 1970), p. 79.

9. There are of course many parallels in Russian history as well: the false Dimitris of the Time of Troubles, Pugachev calling himself Peter III during the rebellion of 1773 against Catherine II, and the rumors of the survival of the last czar's daughter Anastasia after 1917. I think, however, that these may well be part of a rather different tradition, and I am not sure how fruitful a comparison can be made with the medieval/early modern English examples.

10. Harold Hutchinson, *Edward II: the Pliant King* (London: Eyre and Spottiswoode, 1971), p. 144; Caroline Bingham, *The Life and Times of Edward II* (London: Weidenfeld and Nicolson, 1973), pp. 215–17. Interestingly enough, there was also a madman impostor during Edward II's lifetime. John of Powderham claimed to be Edward I's true son, saying Edward II was not, as was obvious from his unkingly behavior with Piers Gaveston. Powderham was executed in 1318. Bingham, *Edward II*, pp. 123–25.

11. Harold Hutchinson, *The Hollow Crown* (London: Eyre and Spottiswoode, 1961), pp. 235–37.

12. Allen, *Political Thought*, p. 121.

13. For a discussion of this, see D. M. Loades, *Politics and the Nation, 1450–1660* (London: Oxford University Press, 1974), pp. 126–27.

14. For an analysis of this phenomenon, see William Huse Dunham and Charles T. Wood, "The Right to Rule in England: Depositions and the Kingdom's Authority, 1327–1485," *American Historical Review*, vol. 81, no. 4 (Oct. 1976):738–61, and Charles T. Wood, "Queens, Queans, and Kingship: An Inquiry into Theories of Royal Legitimacy in Late Medieval England," in *Order and Innovation in the Middle Ages*, ed. W. C. Jordan, C. B. McNab, and T. F. Ruiz (Princeton: Princeton University Press, 1976), pp. 385–400. Another illumination of this difference was explicated by Marc Bloch in *The Royal Touch* (London: Routledge and Kegan Paul, 1973). Touching for the king's evil, scrofula, began spontaneously in France, and was deliberately copied by the monarchy in England.

15. These of course are the boys supposed to have been slaughtered by Richard III, and the debate still rages over whether Richard was guilty or a victim of Tudor propaganda. See, for example, Paul Murray Kendall, *Richard the Third* (London: Allen and Unwin, 1955).

16. Loades, *Politics and the Nation*, p. 99.

17. From the confession printed and published shortly before his execution, he was a native of Tournay, the son of John Warbeck and Catherine de Faro. A hundred years later Sir Francis Bacon suggested that Warbeck might well have been an illegitimate son of Edward IV. *The History of the Reign of King Henry the Seventh*, ed. Roger Lockyer (London: The Folio Society, 1971), p. 131.

18. Paul Murray Kendall, *Richard the Third*, p. 402.

19. J. J. Scarisbrick, *Henry VIII* (Berkeley and Los Angeles: University of California Press, 1968).

20. Smith, *Elizabeth Tudor*, pp. 19–20.

21. But Henry Tudor was Earl, not Duke, of Richmond before his own elevation to the kingship.

22. Obviously, this is a very quick overview of a long, complex, and often written about series of events. For a more detailed discussion, see, for example, the works by G. R. Elton, Lacey Baldwin Smith, and J. J. Scarisbrick.

23. His illegitimate son Henry Fitzroy had died a decade previously. While John Perrot claimed to be Henry VIII's son, he was never so acknowledged by Henry.

24. Erickson, *Bloody Mary*, pp. 302–57.

25. The one other attempt at having a woman rule had been disastrous. Henry I had attempted to force his barons to accept his daughter Matilda as his heir in the twelfth century. After Henry's death most of the barons abandoned Matilda for her cousin Stephen, leading to a civil war that was only resolved when Matilda's son became Henry II.

26. *The Letters and Papers of Henry VIII*, ed. James Gardiner (London: H.M.S.O., 1888), VI, 1193.

27. For a lengthy discussion of this concept and its ramifications, see Ernst H. Kantorowic, *The King's Two Bodies: A Study in Mediaeval Political Theory* (Princeton, N.J.: Princeton University Press, 1957).

28. Smith, *Elizabeth Tudor*, p. 43.

29. However, in *Edward VI: The Threshold of Power* (Cambridge: Harvard University Press, 1970), p. 515, W. K. Jordan does suggest that it was Edward himself who thought of excluding his sisters, and presented it to Northumberland.

30. Margaret Cornfield has discussed this phenomenon in her article "A Legend Concerning King Edward VI," *English Historical Review* 23 (1908):286–90. There are a number of instances she does not report, and my conclusions are rather different from hers. Keith Thomas also discusses this issue in *Religion and the Decline of Magic* (New York: Charles Scribner's Sons, 1971), pp. 419–22. Thomas sees this rumor as part of the system of ancient prophecies of the returned hero-king at a time of great need, that Edward VI here is another reincarnation of the Arthur myth. While Edward VI might have been transmuted into this mythic hero-come-again by the mid-seventeenth century, it seems to me to be a very different formula for people to believe that he was still alive within the same generation of his death. Erickson's *Bloody Mary* was also very useful in giving sources of this belief. Cynthia Chermely, in an unpublished paper, "From Melancholy to Murderous Psychosis: The Scope of Madness in Tudor England" (1985 Sixteenth-Century Studies Conference) throws interesting light on Mantell.

31. John G. Dubois, ed., *Chronicle of the Grey Friars of London* (Camden Soc., Old Series LIII, 1852), p. 78; John Clapham, *Elizabeth of England*, ed. Evelyn Plummer Read and Conyers Read (Philadelphia: University of Pennsylvania Press, 1951), p. 54.

32. *Acts of the Privy Council*, ed. J. R. Dasent (London, 1890–1907), IV, pp. 363, 364, 367, 390, 391–92.

33. Ibid., p. 390.

34. Loades, *Politics and the Nation*, p. 235 and 235n.

35. Erickson, *Bloody Mary*, p. 415.

36. *Calendar of State Papers and Manuscripts, Relating to English Affairs, Existing in the Archives and Collections of Venice*, ed. Rawdon Brown (London, 1877), VI, p. 85.

37. *Holinshed's Chronicles*, ed. Henry Ellis (London: J. Johnson, 1807–1808), IV, p. 75.

38. *The Diary of Henry Machyn*, ed. John Gough Nichols (London: Camden Society, 1848), p. IX.

39. *CSP, Venetian*, VI, p. 85.

40. Charles Wriothesley, *A Chronicle of England During the Reign of the*

Tudors, ed. William D. Hamilton (Camden Society, New Series, XI, XX, 1875–1877), II, p. 129.

41. *CSP, Venetian*, VI, p. 324.

42. *APC*, V, pp. 221, 228.

43. *CSP, Venetian*, VI, p. 324.

44. *CSP, Venetian*, VI, p. 339.

45. C. W. Previte-Orton, "An Elizabethan Prophecy," *History* 2 (1918):209.

46. John Harvey, *A Discoursive Probleme* (London, 1588), p. 61.

47. *CSP, Dom. Eliz.* clxxvi, no. 91, 72 cited in Cornfield, "Legend," pp. 288–89.

48. John Strype, *Annals of the Reformation* (Oxford: Clarendon Press, 1824), II, pt. II, p. 503.

49. *Calendar of State Papers, Domestic Series of the Reigns of Edward VI, Mary, Elizabeth, and James I, 1547–1625* (London: Longman, Brown, Green, Longmans, and Roberts, 1856–72), clxxxvii, no. 64.

50. Thomas, *Religion*, p. 420.

51. Ibid.

52. Ibid.

53. *CSP, Dom. Eliz.* ccix, no. 34, cited in Cornfield, "Legend," p. 289.

54. Hist. MSS, Comm. *Report of the Marquis of Salisbury*, IX–167, 187, cited in Cornfield, "Legend," pp. 289–90.

55. A Puritan minister named Gervase Smith did, however, talk in 1606 of prophecies that included the eventual restoration of the true faith by someone named Edward, possibly Edward VI, "'who was either dead or living 'in Africa' and would be miraculously raised again'" (Thomas, *Religion*, p. 421). Smith was known in his neighborhood for his obsessive interest in prophecy. By this time, suggests Keith Thomas, Edward VI had taken on something of the sleeping emperor, who would come back when his people needed him most. As late as 1652 a published collection of prophecies declared, "Up Edward the Sixth . . . the time is come" (cited in Thomas, *Religion*, p. 422).

56. Martin Hume, *The Courtships of Queen Elizabeth* (London: E. Nash and Grayson, 1926), pp. 335–36.

57. *CSP, Dom. Eliz.* xiii, p. 157.

58. *CSP, Dom. Addenda Eliz.* xi, p. 534.

59. Lawrence Stone, *The Family, Sex, and Marriage in England, 1500–1800* (New York: Harper and Row, 1977), pp. 503–4. See also Mervyn Jones, *English Politics and the Conception of Honour, 1485–1642 Past and Present*, Supplement 3, 1978.

60. Quoted in Hume, *Courtships*, p. 346.

61. *Calendar of State Papers related to English affairs preserved principally at Rome*, ed. J. M. Riggs (London: H.M.S.O., 1916–26), ii, p. 238.

62. *CSP, Dom. Eliz.* cxlviii, p. 12.

63. *CSP, Dom. Eliz.* cclxix, no. 22, pp. 136–37.

64. *CSP, Dom. Eliz.* cclxxxi, no. 60, p. 86.

65. *CSP, Dom. Eliz.* cclxxix, no. 48, p. 24. The concern over Elizabeth's fertility, manifested by these rumors, has a parallel in Mary's reign as well. Mary was clearly infertile; her false pregnancy ended in humiliation and despair. Despite the fact that she could not produce a child, a rumor surfaced during her reign that she had an illegitimate child by Stephen Gardiner, bishop of Winchester. John Strype, *Memorials of the Reverend Father in God, Thomas Cranmer* (Oxford: At the University Press, 1840), p. 456.

66. Hume, *Courtships*, p. 341.

67. Ibid.

68. *Calendar of the Letters and State Papers Relating to English Affairs Preserved in, or originally Belonging to, the Archives of Simancas*, ed. Martin Hume (London: H.M.S.O., 1899), IV, pp. 101–12.

69. Ibid.

70. Hume, *Courtships*, p. 345.

71. Elizabeth Jenkins, *Elizabeth and Leicester* (New York: Coward-McCann, 1962), p. 334.

72. Quoted in Joel Hurstfield, *Elizabeth I and the Unity of England* (New York: Harper and Row, 1960), p. 157.

4

Voyages Out: Nineteenth-Century Women Travelers in Africa

KATHERINE FRANK

For the Western imagination Africa has always been much more than
a geographical place. It is also the mythic kingdom of Prester John, the
land of fabulous beasts, gold, and diamonds, the Dark Continent, the
White Man's Grave and White Man's Burden, the Garden of Eden and
the Heart of Darkness. Great treacherous rivers snake their way through
the Western vision of Africa, and deep within the interior they penetrate
are ancient cities whose very names conjure impulses of mystery and
desire: Timbuktu, Kano, Khartoum. Even the bare outline of Africa on
a map or globe can transfix the European much as it does Joseph
Conrad's Marlow at the beginning of *Heart of Darkness*. To the Western
mind the entire vast continent seems a hallucination, from the west coast
mirror image of South America, round the Cape of Good Hope, past
Zanzibar, and up to the Suez Canal.[1]

More than America, more than the frozen wastes of the polar regions
or any of the other great arenas of human discovery, Africa has functioned as a sort of fantastic Rorschach test for those who have fallen
under its spell. The very "darkness" or "blankness" that the great
African explorers of the nineteenth century hoped to illuminate or fill

in was the source of Africa's enormous appeal. For onto this geographical tabula rasa could be projected all manner of human dreams and desires. Often the real drama of the Victorian "opening up" of the continent was not so much the individual struggles of a Speke, Baker, Livingstone, or Stanley—struggles with hostile "savages," dangerous swamps, or deadly tropical diseases—as it was the collision of these men's myths of Africa with the reality of the land they were forced to confront. As they sometimes painfully discovered, the psychic landscape of Africa had only the most tenuous connection with its physical outline on their maps.[2]

This psychic landscape, the myth of Africa, was almost exclusively a male creation, and not surprisingly, the written accounts in which it was delineated constitute a preeminently masculine literary form. The sturdy, multivolume, copiously illustrated, gilt-bound books of the nineteenth-century explorers of Africa relate the same tale over and over again with only the hero, location, and dates changed. The plot of this tale involves the initiation of the hero-explorer into the world of archetypal male experience, and it is related in the terms and images of sexual conquest. From James Bruce at the end of the eighteenth century onward, Africa was portrayed as an irresistible femme fatale. To restless, unhappy, frustrated men imprisoned by class or circumstance in England, "she" offered exotic temptation—the promise of either extraordinary fulfillment or heroic death.

Though the sexual nature of the allure undoubtedly remained suppressed beneath conscious impulse and the acceptable exploration motives of scientific discovery, imperialistic gain, or missionary zeal, there was no denying this essential erotic vision of African exploration. Margery Perham describes it well in her introduction to an anthology entitled *African Exploration*:

Africa is allowed at times her beauties, but the general impression given by the explorers is one of caprice, of treachery, of violent extremes, and of hostility to men, which, combined with the allure which held them, has suggested the ready analogy of the dark slave, ravished, beautiful but untameable. She was still at the height of her power against these first intruders [in the nineteenth century] and . . . she guarded to the last the secret of the great waters in her rivers and lakes, which had been hidden from the civilized world for thousands of years.[3]

One can take Perham's implicitly Freudian analysis even farther. The most ubiquitous verb in the story and discussion of African exploration is *penetration*: penetration of the continent via dark, sinuous rivers such as the Nile, Niger, and Congo, rivers that either empty into womblike inland lakes or flow through forest, savannah, and desert and finally coil back into the salt sea. To negotiate this penetration and try to reach the interior lakes or return to the ocean scores of men risked their lives, and more than a few perished in the attempt.

But for those who succeeded the rewards were enormous: fame, fortune, and a secure niche in the rolls of history. All of them were, as Robert Rotberg insists, hopeless romantics, and their African adventures at bottom profoundly egotistical dramas.[4] Every voyage of discovery to Africa was at heart a voyage of self-discovery, so that the "opening up" of the continent for a Park, Clapperton, or Du Chaillu was essentially a journey of self-revelation.

Browse through the books of these men and the Dark Continent is indeed dark, overcast as it is by the giant shadows of the hero-explorers. Africa itself, in fact, is merely an appropriate stage for their self-centered adventures, a vivid, exotic backdrop like an endless Henri Rousseau painting. On the banks of rivers or among the trees one dimly glimpses the dusky shapes of Africans, light glancing off an upraised spear, the glowing eyes of some monstrous beast crouched in the gloom. But these are only momentary distractions, for the focus remains relentlessly fixed on the male explorer as he proceeds through forest and bush, his line of carriers trailing into the distance behind him. In his solar topee and khaki drill he looks like a conqueror leading a black army.

In their own day the African explorers were idolized by the Victorian public for their scientific and geographical discoveries, their anthropological and religious activities, and perhaps most of all their daring and bravery. But as Rotberg again points out, the explorers' actual impact on Africa—for good or ill—was negligible. Despite all the talk of civilizing "benighted" and "savage" "natives," the explorers almost entirely failed to alter the lives of Africans. They introduced nothing, and they were only rarely deemed important enough to be incorporated into African oral traditions. The real, discernible, and largely destructive impact of the West came only with empire, to which exploration was a kind of handmaiden. Thus Rotberg concludes that at best the explorers were merely "intellectual middlemen, . . . precursors but not progenitors of imperialism."[5]

The great saga of the Victorian exploration of Africa, then, was a preeminently masculine history, a history of penetration, conquest, and romantic self-fulfillment. But although one would scarcely gather it from *Through the Dark Continent*, *Journal of the Discovery of the Source of the Nile*, or any of the other major exploration narratives, a small number of mostly British women also journeyed through Africa in the nineteenth century. Some were there simply because they accompanied their husbands, as did Florence Baker to the shores of Lake Albert or Mary Moffat Livingstone to the banks of the Shire River, where she found her final resting place under a baobab tree. Others came to Africa alone—willingly, eagerly, and after surmounting a barrage of criticism, stunned disbelief, and even obstruction at home. Whether on their own or with husbands, these women in nineteenth-century Africa were an awesome, hardy band. But what is most striking about them is how little they share with their male counterparts. For as various as their backgrounds and motives were, all of them attempted to journey to the real, not the mythic, Africa. And their explorations involved neither penetration nor conquest but a kind of vocation or dedication to service that was the antithesis of romantic, self-projecting egoism.

This female motive of service originated in part from the need for justification, for in an age when a woman could scarcely ride alone in a railway carriage from Brighton to London, she would certainly be called upon to explain why she was off for the mouth of the Niger or the source of the Nile.[6] Male explorers might go to Africa solely in pursuit of personal gain and private fulfillment, but women clearly needed a public, selfless rationale for their journeys. Hence Mary Kingsley, for example, explained that she went to Africa in order to fulfill her "duty" to carry on her dead father's study of sacrificial rites and to collect fish for the British Museum. In contrast, she played down her own strong desire to study little-known peoples living in the Gabon and also the sheer pleasure she found in "skylarking" up and down the west coast. Similarly, the Scottish missionary Mary Slessor justified her many years in Calabar, Nigeria, in terms of the numerous Ibo she brought into the fold of the church.

Women in Africa, then, felt they had no business going there unless they could perform some sort of public service by studying, observing, nurturing, healing, even saving. But paradoxically, such service was not dedicated to that deity of Victorian womanhood, Duty. Duty, as the novels of the Brontës and others so graphically show, was the scourge of nineteenth-century women, and one could not serve it without stifling or even killing private needs and dreams within. Instead, the vocation of service that drove women to Africa a hundred years ago actually protected and was fueled by these vital, inner impulses. And because of their ability to reconcile public and private—to study *and* skylark, to use Kingsley's formulation—the Victorian woman in Africa was not the Angel in the House writ large but instead, whether she acknowledged it or not, a harbinger of the twentieth-century New Woman.

From Anna Falconbridge in the 1790s to Mary Gaunt and Rachel Watt in the first decade of this century, women in Africa, far from martyring themselves to a public Duty, embarked on journeys of private self-discovery no less than the male explorers. The crucial difference between the two groups of travelers is that the women found liberation in the discovery of a large enough sphere for all their pent-up energies, gifts, and capacities. Their African sojourns always involved an extensive and intense relationship with the land and its peoples. Rather than imposing or projecting their private needs and fantasies upon Africa through violation and conquest, they all to some extent could have subscribed to the contemporary anthropologist Laura Bohannan's description of her African experience in her book *Return to Laughter*: "I have written simply as a human being, and the truth I have tried to tell concerns the sea change in oneself that comes from immersion in another and savage culture."[7]

The private, psychic liberation that nineteenth-century women discovered in Africa was not, however, simply a matter of immersion and the finding of a field commensurate with their capacities. Perhaps Africa's greatest appeal and gift to European women sprang from the highly paradoxical position in which it placed them. On the one hand, as Patricia Lamb has cogently argued, white women in Africa were perceived and perceived themselves in terms of race rather than gender.[8] For the first time in their lives they transcended their sexual identities and experienced the exhilaration of functioning and being treated—by Africans and other Europeans alike—as white "men" rather than as women. Some, like Mary Kingsley, Rachel Watt, and Helen Caddick, nervously joked about being called "Sir" or "Bwana" or cloyingly protested that they would rather have perished on a public scaffold than don trousers or omit wearing stays in the bush. But beneath the defensive jests we glimpse an incipient pride, for all shared what Mary Gaunt described as her "desire to be out of leading strings and to be allowed to take care of myself.'"[9] None of them can entirely disguise or suppress this heady sensation of being released from the long habit of inferior sexual station.

And their physical and social freedom in Africa aptly reflected these women's psychological liberation from sexual definition and oppression. They habitually traveled on their own, with no European companions and only a small party of African carriers, because they lacked the large governmental, missionary, or private funding that enabled a Baker or Stanley to hire literally hundreds of African porters. Their tiny entourages were necessitated by paltry means produced from small legacies or years of patient saving. But whatever hardships such small parties brought, they also meant that the women who headed them were accountable to and overseen by no one. They were free to go where they willed and do what they desired, an intoxicating mobility that Mary Kingsley referred to as "skylarking in Africa."

The entrenched Victorian conviction of white racial supremacy, then, was responsible for nineteenth-century women's extraordinary freedom in Africa, where their identity derived from their white skins rather than their female bodies. But at the same time, the legacy of sexual oppression paradoxically fostered these women's identification with the subjugated Africans whose lower station facilitated their own liberation in Africa. Here again we see the reconciliation of public and private in these women's experience: they were liberated by their new freedom as public white "men" and also powerfully moved by their personal empathy with Africans. In England or Europe women had long been victims, in Kate Millett's phrase, of an "interior colonization," and when they came to Africa, most of them sensed on some level that the colonial "scramble" for Africa in the nineteenth century was not unrelated to, and indeed sprang from the same source as, the patriarchal rule of women at home. This crucial recognition of a shared bond with Africans took several forms. Missionaries such as Rachel Watt and Mary Slessor embraced the African on religious grounds, as a fellow and inherently equal child of God, while ethnographers such as Kingsley and D. Amaury Talbot realized that Africans were no "benighted savages" but the possessors of a highly developed and complex culture of their own. But however they came to this vision of racial equality, the result was the same: in a manner somewhat analogous to that of nineteenth-century women abolitionists in America, British women in Africa felt an affinity with oppressed Africans and in various ways shouldered their cause and worked for their good—as missionaries and anthropologists, or merely through private acts of kindness and generosity as travelers and officials' wives. With very few exceptions, all the women rejected the virulent racism that blights most of the male accounts of Africa.[10] And this lack of prejudice is all the more remarkable considering the popularized Darwinian and other so-called scientific theories that sanctioned racism in the nineteenth century in even the most enlightened and humane circles.

Such are some of the more salient observations to be made about nineteenth-century women in Africa and how and why they are such a strikingly different species from their male counterparts. But the only way really to comprehend their African sojourns is to turn from generalizations to the women themselves and the books in which they recorded their experiences. As a group, they span roughly 125 years, from Anna Falconbridge in 1791 to D. Amaury Talbot just before the First World War—an era that extends from the founding of the first British African colony in Sierra Leone to Lugard's doctrine of the Dual Mandate and the consolidation of Nigeria. (See the chronologically arranged bibliography at the end of the essay.)

Broadly speaking, there were four distinct classes of nineteenth-century women in Africa, and though there were representatives of each class throughout the 125-year span, there was something of a historical progression as first one and then another type predominated in various periods. In the early years of the century, for example, most of the women in Africa were government wives or daughters such as Anna Falconbridge, Mary Church, Elizabeth Melville, Katherine Petherick, and Florence Baker. (John Petherick and Samuel Baker, in addition to their official government positions, were also explorers of the sources of the Nile.) Mary Alice Hodgson and Constance Larymore are two later, twentieth-century examples of government wives. Missionaries such as Mary Slessor and missionary wives such as Rachel Watt were also on the scene early and remained active throughout the century. Women explorer-travelers and ethnographers or anthropologists, however, followed in the footsteps of the government wives and missionaries, and understandably so, for their motives for coming to Africa lacked the acceptable feminine justifications of their predecessors'. Women like Alexine Tinne (the only pure explorer in the lot), Mary French Sheldon, Mary Kingsley, Helen Caddick, and Mary Gaunt came neither as wifely helpmeets nor as maternal missionaries but instead, as Kingsley put it, in pursuit of "fish and fetish" and "to skylark and stalk the wild . . . African idea."[11] There had to be some degree of initial scouting by government agents, missionaries, and male explorers before women could come to Africa in quest of scientific and anthropological information. Thus the explorer-travelers and anthropologists dominate in the latter half of the nineteenth century and the early decades of the twentieth.

Important as these four groups are, however, perhaps the key factor to be noted about each of these women in Africa is the same unfortunate determinant in so much of women's history: namely, whether or not they were married. Other characteristics were important, such as age (most of the women were in their twenties or thirties), class (usually middle- or upper-middle-class), and whether or not they had children (only Elizabeth Melville, Annie Hore, and Rachel Watt did, and Melville and Watt promptly shipped theirs back to England). But marital status was decisive because it automatically determined a particular women's role in Africa and how she was treated there. And it is crucial to us because it indicates whether her sojourn in Africa was voluntary or involuntary—whether she went as a dedicated, obedient spouse or as a convention-flouting, solo woman traveler.

However, with that said, it must be admitted that the first woman to leave a record of her African experience, Mrs. Anna Falconbridge, blurs all such nice distinctions between married and unmarried women in Africa. Yet one could not hope for a better or more intriguing initiator of this female literary-historical tradition. Mrs. Falconbridge went to Africa in 1791 because her husband was commissioned by the St. George's Bay Company to relieve and resettle the tiny, chaotic, and distressed British colony of freed slaves in Sierra Leone. The Falconbridges were newlyweds, and Anna seems to have left for West Africa largely to spite her relations, who correctly judged the marriage an imprudent match. From this inauspicious beginning even worse followed. Soon the colony was in a state of total anarchy. Alexander Falconbridge was relieved of his duties by the St. George's Bay Company, a dismissal that only enhanced what his wife candidly described as his "irritable disposition" and "addiction to drink." In a remarkably short period of time he managed to drink himself to death, leaving his young widow stranded and alone in this outpost of civilization.

But in her book Anna Falconbridge refuses to bemoan her plight or utter

a falsehood . . . by saying I regret his death, no! I really do not, his life had become burthensome to . . . all around him, and his conduct to me, for more than two years past, was so unkind (not to give a harsher term) as long since to wean away every spark of affection or regard I ever had for him.[12]

Nothing daunted, with the shrewdness and courage of the Defoe heroine whom she more than a little resembles, Mrs. Falconbridge remarried another British colonist (or again "enlisted under the banners of Hymen," as she puts it) within a month of her first husband's death.[13] With this new husband she returned to England to wage war against the St. George's Bay Company, from which she hoped to wrest a large amount of money she felt was owing to the unlamented Alexander Falconbridge.

Anna Falconbridge was scarcely the prototype of the brave, dedicated government or missionary wife in Africa. Her account, *Two Voyages to the River Sierra Leone*, which was written as a series of letters, reads like an eighteenth-century epistolary novel, with Mrs. Falconbridge herself a real-life example of that long line of heroines which extends from Moll Flanders to Becky Sharp. Yet in her book many of the central concerns of women in Africa are articulated for the first time and, in many cases, in their most forceful and candid fashion.

In her preface, for example, Falconbridge announces her anthropological intention of paying particular attention to "the manners, customs, etc. of the people [i.e., the freed slaves and indigenous inhabitants]," and she further promises to "delineate their situations and qualities, with a History of Sierra Leone."[14] And because she was an eighteenth-century rather than a Victorian woman, Mrs. Falconbridge could convey such information with few if any inhibitions (always a great problem to later writers such as Kingsley and Talbot). Hence we learn from her of the elaborately decked-out black mistresses of white settlers, and even more shockingly, of the British prostitutes who were sent out with the first shipload of freed slaves to settle the colony.

Though she was distressed by polygamy and dismayed that African women refused to keep on the clothes she dressed them in, Mrs. Falconbridge was remarkably free of racial prejudice and flatly says as much early on in the book. She does not think, she says, that "nature has been so unkind to endow these people with capabilities less susceptible of improvement and cultivation than any other part of the human race."[15] Even when her second husband persuaded her to support the slave trade (the two of them actually sailed home on a slave ship bound for the West Indies), Mrs. Falconbridge continued to maintain that the black and white races were inherently equal.

In addition to being a careful observer of the African and a believer in his racial equality, Anna Falconbridge established the paradigm of the European woman in Africa in one last, important respect. Despite her enormous hardships and trials in Sierra Leone, she exhibited good-humored resourcefulness and flexibility and also an appreciation of what Africa could offer her. Thus she explains how the lack of a door for the Falconbridge hut in the settlement

was some inconvenience, and as no deal or other boards could be procured for the purpose, I made a country mat supply the place—for now I find 'tis necessary to accommodate myself to whatever I meet with, there being but few conveniences or accommodating things in this part of Africa.[16]

But even with this lack of deal doors, Mrs. Falconbridge continues, it would take only a few of life's "sweetners [sic]" to produce contentment for her in Africa. "To be frank," she says, "if I had a little agreeable society, a few comforts, and could endure the same good health I have hitherto enjoyed, I should not be against spending some years of my life in Africa."[17] As it turned out, it was not the dearth of "sweetners" but the unfortunate fate of her first husband that compelled Anna Falconbridge to return to England after only two short but arduous and eventful years in Sierra Leone.

Nearly fifty years later, in the early 1840s, Elizabeth Melville came out to Sierra Leone with her husband, a government judge in the now thriving colony. Like Mrs. Falconbridge, Elizabeth was a bride, but in nearly every other respect she bore little resemblance to the bold, shrewd adventuress-predecessor. Mrs. Melville, in fact, was one of the first of a long line of patient, loyal, and, most important, self-effacing wives who were dispersed to far-flung corners of the British empire in the nineteenth century. When these women took it upon themselves to publish their stories it was almost always in the accents of what might be called the "only me" voice of feminine timidity and self-professed unworthiness. Mary Kingsley, who seems to bring together so many of the various strands of female experience in Africa, was responsible for the designating phrase. Though not married herself, she could readily don the cloak of feminine insignificance when it might be useful to her. She habitually turned up at villages or remote trading stations greeting her skeptical or amazed hosts with "it's only me," so that in time the salutation became her West African sobriquet.

But the "only me" persona is far more common among British wives in Africa than among the single travelers like Kingsley, and it always clearly identifies itself in the preface or foreword of the wives' books. Elizabeth Melville's opening is almost word for word what we find later in the introductions of Mary Alice Hodgson, Constance Larymore, and D. Amaury Talbot. "In offering this little work to the Public," Melville writes, "the Author craves indulgence for the trivial matter it contains. It is chiefly composed from a journal she kept for her own amusement, and a few of her letters to home friends."[18]

Wives' books, even when they run to 300 or 400 pages as Melville's does, are always deemed "little" productions—fugitive pieces dashed off to entertain family and close friends. Moreover, the wife protests she will write only of the "woman's point of view"; she will confine herself to descriptions of the landscape and observations of African women and children, for example, rather than enter the fray of masculine political or scientific issues. The underlying literary technique is one of disarming self-effacement, and at its most extreme the "only me" strategy extends to anonymous or pseudonymous authorship, as is the case with both Melville (whose *A Residence in Sierra Leone* was attributed on the title page only to "A Lady") and her near contemporary, "Mary Church," who was probably Catherine Temple, the daughter of the Sierra Leone governor, Octavius Temple.[19]

Perhaps such feminine self-underestimation was often genuine; like Lily Briscoe in Virginia Woolf's *To the Lighthouse*, wives such as Elizabeth Melville may well have heard discouraging male voices in their hearts and minds admonishing, "Women can't paint; women can't write." But whether sincere or a clever method of courting sympathy for and interest in their work, such protests were usually misleading. This is especially true of *A Residence in Sierra Leone*, which is neither little, trivial, nor confined to conventionally feminine concerns. What Melville has captured and expressed, in fact, is a profoundly intense aesthetic response that was to become one of the most pervasive char-

acteristics of female experience in Africa—an aesthetic response central
to the books of such later women as Watt, Petherick, Kingsley, Caddick,
and Gaunt.

Here again we are struck by the contrast with the matter-of-fact Anna
Falconbridge. Mrs. Falconbridge's Africa is a buccaneering outpost full
of bad smells, loud and bizarrely got-up Africans, and quarreling, often
drunken white settlers. Mrs. Melville's Sierra Leone is another land
altogether—a lushly colored, dreamily tropical, Pre-Raphaelite painting. She confesses she led a "hermit's life" in Freetown, the colony
capital, and scarcely had any contact with Africans beyond her household servants. But if she was virtually blind to the historical and social
world that absorbed Anna Falconbridge, Mrs. Melville possessed an
extraordinarily acute and impassioned eye for her natural universe in
Africa. Page after page of *A Residence in Sierra Leone* is devoted to
detailed, vivid descriptions of plants, insects, wild animals, clouds, and
West African sunrises and sunsets. In one paragraph she will rhapsodize
over a chameleon found on the piazza of their house, in the next over
a strange tropical flower discovered by chance on her evening ride. The
landscape Elizabeth looks down upon from her hillside home above
Freetown is one of vast, mist-enshrouded vistas. And the Africa she
celebrates throughout her book is a dazzling kaleidoscope of color,
form, fragrance, and sun-soaked heat.

Mrs. Melville fell in love with the beauty of Africa, and so strong
was this aesthetic response that it could even intrude on the most frightening and threatening of experiences: in the midst of a violent yet
sublime tornado, when confronted with a rare species of tarantula, or
most extraordinarily, in a terrifying experience involving the infant born
to her in Africa. She writes how one day she had put the baby on the
porch to nap: "Imagine our horror . . . at a large snake being discovered
in the piazza quite close to the spot where he had been but a few minutes
before, lying asleep on his cool grass mat, for which, during the heat
of the day, his cot is now discarded. The colour of this snake," she
cannot resist concluding, "was the most beautiful bright green I ever
saw, except in an emerald."[20] Fortunately, this beautiful snake is the
only one to disturb the hauntingly Edenic Africa Mrs. Melville captures
in her book.

On the other side of the continent in British East Africa in the late
1880s, Mrs. Rachel Watt had a similarly remarkable experience with
the same sort of almost involuntary aesthetic response. She and her

missionary husband, Stuart Watt, and their little children were en route
to their mission station in the interior when they stumbled upon a field
of past tribal warfare which Mrs. Watt graphically describes.

In a delightful parklike glade . . . the ground was literally covered with human
skulls and bones. As we stood on the succulent carpet of green grass, gazing
in ghastly bewilderment, we could not but think of the words of the poet, 'How
that red rain hath made the harvest grow.' In the midst of the field of human
slaughter, there appeared a beautiful spotted giraffe, silhouetted against the
mimosa trees, which spread their feathery branches in that enchanting landscape.
This fairy-like form seemed to me as an angel looking down upon this terrible
scene of carnage, and I wondered how so pure and harmless a creature could
stand in the presence of such golgotha.[21]

Like Elizabeth Melville, Rachel Watt is nearly stunned by the scene's
romantic fusion of terror and sublime beauty. But vivid and arresting
as her description is, Mrs. Watt's religious images give away her underlying moral vision. Melville's Africa is the prelapsarian world before
man and evil, while Watt's is a suffering land of heathens—the Kikuyu
and Masai whose physical beauty she extols at the same time as she
struggles to save their souls. And because of the duality of her relation
to Africa—her moral *and* aesthetic response—Rachel Watt seems to
crystallize the "profile" of the British wife in Africa and her vocation
of service. She insisted that the Africans were God's children and equals,
and despite her tireless efforts for more than forty-three years to make
Christians of them, she was able to recognize and appreciate that they
had a culture of their own. She also functioned, as so many of the single
women in Africa did, as a "white man," particularly when her husband
was away from the station for months at a time getting supplies from
the coast or taking one or more of their seven children back to England
for schooling, leaving Rachel alone with several toddlers and perhaps
an infant as well. The Kikuyu, in fact, dubbed her with the masculine
name "Great Spear" after the large weapon given her by a Masai
warrior.

Even when her husband was home, Rachel's independence and authority were far greater than would have been possible back in England.
Though they were missionaries, the Watt marriage in Africa was remarkably similar to those of the well-known explorer couples, Katherine
and John Petherick and Florence and Samuel Baker. Like them, the
Watts formed an affectionate partnership in which neither spouse was

consigned a less important or less powerful role. In part this occurred because the Pethericks, Bakers, and Watts in Africa were living in a social vacuum, to put it mildly, in which there was no purpose in maintaining sexually differentiated spheres of activity. And because frequently either the wife or the husband was ill with fever or absent on a march, it was impossible to do so. Life here was simply too hard and too dangerous to quarrel over who should plant the garden, direct the children's lessons, or put a new roof on the mission house. And with no social eyes to observe and judge who did what, these marriages dramatically deviated from British norms at home.

Perhaps what is most surprising and gratifying about these marriages is the extent to which they seem to have liberated and satisfied both husbands and wives and thus demonstrated that equality for women did not mean male diminution. Not only did Stuart Watt, Samuel Baker, and John Petherick not feel diminished by their wives' independence in Africa, they were often profoundly awed by their spouses' strength, courage, and intelligence. A deep respect and affection informs their own writings when they speak of their wives in glowing language that at times approaches panegyric. Harrowing as life in Africa was for all three couples, it often brought them great domestic happiness, just as it did the Talbots and Larymores some years later. All these wives may have gone out to Africa involuntarily at the start, but once there they discovered not only untapped personal resources—for humane action, anthropological study, and intense aesthetic pleasure—but also unexplored ways in which to love and help those closest to their hearts. And finally, of course, they were able to share their immersion in an alien land and thus were never, to quote the title of Mary Gaunt's book, *Alone in West Africa*.

Mary Kingsley, Helen Caddick, and Mary Gaunt herself all tell funny stories about their own husbandless plights in Africa, but beneath their jocular manner we see very clearly that their solitary state was scarcely a joking matter. We should really heed the straight men in these humorous anecdotes, one Mr. Samuel, for example, an African with an "amazing knowledge of English, which he spoke in a quaint, falsetto, far-away sort of voice." "Mr. S.," as Mary Kingsley calls him, rowed her for a good stretch on the Ogowé River in the Gabon, and was fond of hurling what Kingsley describes as "conversational bombs" at his captive passenger. One day, for example, after interrogating her on whether or not she was a Christian (she was in fact an agnostic but refrained from admitting as much to him), Mr. S. inquired,

"Where be your husband, ma?" . . . "I no got one," I answer. "No got," says Samuel, paralyzed with astonishment; . . . He recovered himself, however, and returned to his charge. "No got one, man?" "No," say I furiously. "Do you get much rubber round here?" "I no be trade man," says Samuel, refusing to fall into my trap for changing conversation. "Why you no got one?"[22]

On another occasion, Kingsley tangled with a French official who was very reluctant to allow her to continue up the Ogowé sans husband. In the face of his objections, she fired back that "'neither the Royal Geographical Society's list, in their 'Hints to Travellers,' nor Mssrs. Silver, in their elaborate lists of articles necessary for travellers in tropical climates, make mention of husbands.'"[23] And finally, since it is very hard to stop quoting Mary Kingsley once you have begun, we have the advice that she gave to the students of Cheltenham Ladies College in a lecture she delivered on her African travels and studies:

I may confide to any spinster who is here present and who feels inclined to take up the study of him [the African in Africa] that she will be perpetually embarrassed by inquiries of, Where is your husband? not, Have you one? or anything like that, which you could deal with, but, Where is he? I must warn her not to say she has not got one; I have tried it, and it only leads to more appalling questions still. I think that it is more advisable to say you are searching for him, and then you locate him away in the direction in which you wish to travel; this elicits help and sympathy.[24]

Mary Gaunt tells how even missionary nuns would suddenly become possessed of mythical husbands in the bush.[25] To African and European alike, the notion of a single white woman traveling voluntarily through Africa defied comprehension. Not that such stunned amazement was an entirely inappropriate reaction, for the dangers awaiting these women were both serious and numerous; thus it is understandable if some observers considered their journeys virtually suicidal. The women themselves, of course, did not share this view, but in the face of angry astonishment, they quickly learned that it was less trouble all round simply to marry oneself off hastily to a fictional spouse. Otherwise European officials would just as hastily erect all sorts of obstacles, and

Africans would congregate to watch and tag along after the solitary woman traveler who in their eyes appeared, as Kingsley put it, a sort of traveling circus.

A husband, then, was a kind of ticket in nineteenth-century Africa just as it still is in some circles today. And one of the first unescorted women travelers, May French Sheldon, actually acquired hers with genuine, not counterfeit, coin. When she sailed to East Africa from Naples in 1891, Eli Lemon Sheldon's handkerchief fluttered a farewell from the pier to his departing wife. And it was a fond as well as anguished farewell because Mrs. Sheldon was in possession of her husband's full consent for her venture, a consent which she confesses she "flouted widely, as evidence that when he sanctioned my undertaking it was not irrational."[26]

But the existence of the understanding, patient, but conveniently absent Mr. Sheldon was just the first of many anomalous elements of May French Sheldon's African travels. Her ample funding, large caravan of more than 150 porters, elaborate equipment (including the pillow-filled palanquin in which she was carried across Masailand), plus her methods of maintaining order among her men by brandishing pistols and flogging the most recalcitrant, all set Mrs. Sheldon apart from her compeers, Helen Caddick, Mary Gaunt, and most dramatically Mary Kingsley, who went out to West Africa just two years after Sheldon returned from the eastern side of the continent.

In fact, what May French Sheldon most resembles is a male Victorian explorer in drag. Her great hero was Henry Morton Stanley, and she quite clearly modeled both her expedition and her own dramatic self-presentation and behavior after the man who found the needle of David Livingstone in the uncharted haystack of Central Africa in 1871 and then marched across the continent and followed the Congo to the Atlantic in 1877. Stanley may have been the greatest African explorer of the nineteenth century, but with his military bearing and racist methods he was also perhaps the most autocratic and even ruthless, and thus a particularly unfortunate example for a woman such as Sheldon to follow.[27]

The masculine exploration mode of egotistical penetration and conquest recurs on nearly every page of Sheldon's *Sultan to Sultan*, and in addition to its being inspired by her hero worship of Stanley, it seems to derive equally from Sheldon's conscious and avowed feminism. She is the only self-professed feminist among the women travelers in Africa, making it very clear throughout her book that she seeks to prove that women are just as capable of exploring Africa as men are, and that the way they are to accomplish this is by conducting themselves precisely as men do in the Dark Continent. Her voice, in fact, is the antithesis of the other women's "only me" narrators, for she has no scruples about appearing overbearing or unladylike.

In fact, the only conventionally feminine element of Sheldon's elaborate and costly progress through East Africa surfaced in her audiences with the chiefs whose territories she traversed. Shortly before arriving at their villages she would halt her half-mile-long caravan and transform herself into a "White Queen" by donning a sequin-studded Paris gown, jeweled dagger, blonde wig, and paste tiara. In this full regalia she would then sally forth to meet the waiting chief or sultan—a truly arresting apparition, as the book's frontispiece photograph of the "White Queen" still testifies.

But more commonly Sheldon was known as the masculine "Bébé Bwana" ("Woman Master" or "Lady Boss") or "Bébé Mzunga" ("Woman White Man"), and her actions and attitudes faithfully reflected this appellation. According to her account, when her men threatened to revolt she shot a vulture in midair and then pointed her pistol at the rebels' heads to coerce them back into line. When a warpaint-smeared Masai warrior rushed at her with pointed spear, she aimed her pistol muzzle at him and screamed "Wow! Wow! Wow!" in imitation of his war cry until he stopped dead in his tracks. And when she came upon the corpse of an African woman in the bush, with the help of her headman Sheldon coolly amputated the woman's legs in order to carry off the trophies of her tight African leg ornaments. She remarks of this episode that the porters' "superstitions" prohibited them from assisting in this grisly operation, but one wonders if it were not common human decency that held them back.

Numerous other less violent but still telling incidents reveal Sheldon's essentially masculine travels in Africa, from her boasting circumnavigation of Lake Chala to the ludicrous way in which she has one of her carriers remove a thorn from her foot by washing his mouth out with cologne and then extracting it with his teeth. Despite her assurances that she seeks to help the "primitives" or "naturals," as Sheldon calls the Africans, she is as much a racist as Burton or Stanley, and she clearly traveled to Africa in order to find a stage adequate to the drama of her feminist heroism. Like her male predecessors, she came to penetrate and conquer, and to demonstrate that a woman could do both as successfully and selfishly as a man. And in this Sheldon did indeed succeed, for the focus throughout *Sultan to Sultan* remains unswervingly on Bébé Bwana. What scanty anthropological or scientific information she relates is cursory and usually inaccurate, and the lake she was so proud of circumnavigating was actually a small crater pond barely eight miles in circumference. The real story of *Sultan to Sultan* is unfortunately the rather tedious and self-serving tale of Sheldon being carried in her palanquin through a wilderness populated by "barbarous savages" who sometimes flee, sometimes threaten, sometimes adore, but in the end always submit to the majestic and masculine Bébé Bwana.

It seems highly fitting, then, that shortly after her return to England Sheldon was elected one of the first female members of that bastion of male African exploration, the Royal Geographical Society. But it should be noted that she was probably denied a ticket to the annual R.G.S. anniversary dinner because she would "be the only lady among 200 [men] . . . nearly all of them smoking."[28] Moreover, soon after Sheldon's election the society abrogated its shortlived policy of admitting women. Sir Clements Markham, secretary and later president of the R.G.S., helps to explain this reversal with his remark that he had "a horror of women of Miss Kingsley's stamp."[29]

Miss Kingsley, of course, was Mary Henrietta Kingsley—not the last of the Victorian women travelers in Africa but by far the most famous, important, and fascinating. She first went out to West Africa at the age of thirty after a bleak, rather Dickensian childhood of extreme social privation and parental neglect. Her father, George Kingsley, brother of the popular Victorian novelists Charles and Henry Kingsley, had married his cook four days before Mary's birth and then promptly set off to travel round the world for most of the rest of his life, returning home for a month or two every few years. Mrs. Kingsley responded to her husband's extended absences by lapsing into neurasthenia so that she spent the rest of *her* life upstairs in bed, faithfully nursed, needless to say, by her daughter. A younger, "delicate," ineffectual brother completes what for lack of a more accurate term must be called the Kingsley family circle. Denied any sort of formal education and completely isolated from any contacts beyond her home, Mary retreated to the sanctuary of her father's library in every spare moment. Here she devoured antiquated works of alchemy, pirates' tales, Robert Burton's *Anatomy of Melancholy*, all of Charles Dickens, and the accounts of the great Victorian explorers of Africa. When her parents suddenly died within six weeks of each other in 1892, she was abruptly released from her domestic bondage and scarcely paused before deciding what to do with herself. Initially subsidized by a small legacy, she determined to go to Africa, earning her way by trading en route.

Not that she shared the "scramble" fever for rubber and ivory; trade was the best method of funding herself, and even more important, it was a carte blanche among the peoples, especially the Fang in the French Congo, whom Kingsley wished to study. Her bartering skills convinced the Africans that despite her pale skin and female form (children often rolled in the street and howled with laughter at the sight of her, the first white woman they had ever seen), she must be a reasonable being. Thus, though she traveled unarmed through perilous inland areas never before traversed by white men, she managed to return safely to the coast. Or as she put it, alluding to the allegedly cannibalistic Fang culinary practices, she arrived back in an unsmoked and entirely intact condition.

But the trader was only one of a variety of public and private roles Kingsley assumed in Africa, including those of ichthyologist, botanist, entomologist, ethnographer, linguist, and explorer-geographer—not to mention consummate travel writer, after she returned home and produced two books on Africa. What tied together all these roles, and also underlay her political activity (she was a tireless opponent of the Colonial Office policy she correctly thought was "murdering" African culture), was Kingsley's passionate desire to "think black"—really to see and understand "the wild African idea" and culture, especially African religion and law. This process of intense observation and imaginative empathy she likened to the way the explorer or traveler gradually "makes out" the intricate and beautiful distinguishing features of what at first seems the "inextricable tangle" of the African forest:

As it is with the forest, so it is with the minds of the natives. Unless you live alone among [them] . . . you never get to know them; if you do this you gradually get a light into the true state of their mind-forest. At first you see nothing . . . but when you get to see—well! as in the other forest,—you see things worth seeing.[30]

What Mary Kingsley saw in West Africa was very nearly everything that previous women travelers had seen, but she saw them all collectively and simultaneously, whereas they had individually stopped at one or two major insights. She saw, as her haunting descriptive passages show, the exquisite tropical beauty of the west coast. She saw that the African was her equal, an oppressed "woman," as she expressed it. She saw that African "fetishes," secret societies, and polygamous families were all significant cultural forms, both rational and moral within the context of African culture. And she saw, finally, that the "drag chain" of the British Crown Colony system would wreak havoc on the African people and their intricate and vulnerable social structure and beliefs, such destruction being little better than the evils of the slavery England was so proud of ending. Thus Kingsley spent the years following her travels embroiled in public controversy, tirelessly doing battle with the Colonial Office, and advocating trade rule in British Africa because trade interests depended upon the well-being of their markets and so would tamper least with African society. In short, Mary Kingsley saw the real—rather than the mythic—Africa, or as she put it in a letter to her publisher, "things as they are, with all the go and glory and beauty in them as well as the mechanism and the microbes."[31]

Just as Kingsley seems to synthesize the various responses of earlier women in Africa, thus serving as a personification of private liberation through a public vocation of service, she also all too graphically reflects their capacity for conflict and ambivalence. After her early death, her friend and admirer Sir George Goldie, the head of the Royal Niger Company, said of Mary Kingsley, "She had the brain of a man and the heart of a woman."[32] It is the sort of fulsome and trite praise one expects in an obituary, and yet, perhaps, Goldie unwittingly hit upon the crucial sexual schizophrenia that lies at the heart of Mary Kingsley's African experiences and accounts for what Catherine Stevenson has persuasively analyzed as the "Janus-faced narrator" of her travel books.[33]

In the best sense, Kingley could be as masculine as Sheldon—not authoritarian or cruel but brave, even fearless to a fault, strong, and shrewdly wise. She could, for example, release a tormented leopard from a trap; walk unarmed into a Fang village and unflinchingly confront its hostile chief; climb up Mount Cameroon when all her seasoned bearers gave up short of the summit; or follow a peculiar, unpleasant smell in a hut to its source, a small cloth bag, and shake its contents out into her hat: a human hand, three big toes, four eyes, two ears, and various other "mementos," as she calls them. But she could also be the most prim and retiring of Victorian ladies—the self-effacing "only me" who insisted upon walking behind a French official on a forest trail so that he would not see showing through her blouse the black shoe tie that she had had to requisition as a stay lace. Or she would refuse to bathe in a mission house with only very "sketchy" shutters and doors. And what was far more profoundly female than such ladylike behavior, Mary Kingsley suffered a debilitating and tragic lack of self-hood that the liberation of her African travels and the wide fame and admiration they brought her could never entirely assuage.

In the last year of her life she wrote to a man who did not return her love:

> The fact is I am no more a human being than a gale of wind is. I have never had a human individual life. I have always been the doer of odd jobs. . . . It never occurs to me that I have any right to do anything more than now and then sit and warm myself at the fires of real human beings . . . it is the non-human world I belong to myself. My people are mangroves, swamps, rivers, and the sea and so on—we understand each other. They never give me the dazzles with their goings on like human beings do by theirs repeatedly.[34]

Somewhat earlier she said much the same thing to a friend who had written a romantic novel. Attempting to explain what she felt was her inadequate response to the book, she wrote, "I make the confession humbly quite as I would make the confession of being deaf or blind, I know nothing myself of love . . . I have never been in love, nor has anyone been in love with me."[35] And finally, in what must have been one of her darkest periods, she wrote in still another unguarded letter how "the best part of me is all this doubt and self-distrust and melancholy and heartache."[36]

Not the best part of Mary Kingsley, by any means, but there is no mistaking that this despair and self-doubt—both surely products of re-pressed anger turned inward as well as of melancholy—were central to her personality and perhaps even to her genius. And these dark convictions show that even the most gifted and brilliant of the British women in Africa could never completely transcend the Victorian patriarchal vision of womanhood that had been inculcated within her from birth. Despite the refuting evidence of her own life, Kingsley could still say at the end of *Travels in West Africa* that "a great woman either mentally or physically, will excel an indifferent man, but no woman ever equals a really great man."[37]

It would be less than just, however, to allow this somber current of sorrow and doubt to obscure the fact that Mary Kingsley, despite her

internal conflict and sadness, was the most charming, intelligent, absorbing, and even at times frankly uproarious of all the women who
wrote about Africa. The following passage describing a nighttime encounter with a crocodile in a mangrove swamp in the Gabon is typical
of many such in *Travels in West Africa* and *West African Studies*. When
looked at closely it also discloses, in lighter tones, Kingsley's sexual
ambivalence. And finally it demonstrates that she could write her revered
Dickens into the shade any day.

Now a crocodile drifting down in deep water, or lying asleep with its jaws open
on a sand-bank in the sun, is a picturesque adornment to the landscape when
you are on the deck of a steamer, and you can write home about it and frighten
your relations on your behalf; but when you are away among the swamps in a
small dug-out canoe, and that crocodile and his relations are awake . . . you may
not be able to write home about him—and yet get frightened on your own
behalf. . . . In addition to this unpleasantness you are liable . . . to get tide-
trapped away in the swamps . . . and you cannot get out and drag your canoe
across the stretches of mud . . . [it] is of too unstable a nature and too deep, and
sinking into it means staying in it. . . . Of course, if you really want a truly safe
investment in Fame, . . . you will jump over into the black batter-like, stinking
slime, cheered by the thought of the terrific sensation you will produce 20,000
years hence. . . . But if you are a mere ordinary person of a retiring nature, like
me, you stop in your lagoon until the tide rises again; most of your attention
is directed to dealing with an ''at home'' to crocodiles and mangrove flies, and
with the fearful stench of the slime round you. What little time you have over
you will employ in wondering why you came to West Africa, and why . . . you
need have gone and painted the lily . . . by being such a colossal ass as to come
fooling about in mangrove swamps. Twice this chatty little incident . . . has
happened to me, but never again if I can help it. On one occasion . . . a mighty
Silurian, as *The Daily Telegraph* would call him, chose to get his front paws
over the stern of my canoe, and endeavoured to improve our acquaintance. I
had to retire to the bows, to keep the balance right, . . . and fetch him a clip on
the snout with a paddle, when he withdrew, and I paddled into the very middle
of the lagoon, hoping the water there was too deep for him or any of his friends
to repeat the performance.[38]

There were a number of interesting women travelers in Africa after
Mary Kingsley, in the first decade or so of the twentieth century. Their
books can still be found on the African shelves of a number of university
libraries, but generally in a quite musty and fragile state, uncirculated
as they have been for fifty or sixty years. Seldom do they appear in

scholarly bibliographies, in the catalogues of esoteric reprint houses, or among the lists of antiquarian booksellers. Yet it is worth the trouble to track down works such as Helen Caddick's *A White Woman in Central Africa* (1900), Constance Larymore's *A Resident's Wife in Nigeria* (1908), or Mary Gaunt's *Alone in West Africa* (1912). True, they often seem pale imitations of their predecessors. Gaunt, for example, sounds more than a little like a watered-down May French Sheldon, while Caddick reads like a muted but still engaging Kingsley. Larymore is delightful because she grafts "how-to" advice onto travelogue in *A Resident's Wife in Nigeria*, so that what we have is something of a precursor to a Frommer *Nigeria on $15 a Day*. Yet with Larymore's chatty, advice-laden book we can see the transition from the traveler's account to the tourist's guide book, a transition cogently discussed by Paul Fussell in his recent study of literary travel books, *Abroad*. Fussell explains how the explorer, traveler, and tourist exist on a continuum:

All three make journeys, but the explorer seeks the undiscovered, the traveler that which has been discoverd by the mind working in history, the tourist that which has been discovered by entrepreneurship and prepared for him by the arts of mass publicity.[39]

It was only after the First World War, as Fussell shows, that the three categories became clearly demarcated. Women in nineteenth-century Africa quite often skipped from one to another in the course of a single journey or book.

But for these women, as for travelers elsewhere, the war ended an era, though there were special reasons why this was true for women and why travel for them in the twenties and thirties was so dramatically different from what it had been in the 1890s. With the first great feminist movement of the early twentieth century in America and England, culminating in the suffrage victory in both countries by 1920, their native lands began to afford women opportunities and spheres for their energies, needs, intelligence, and dreams. The ballot was a symbol of both equality and autonomy. And though there remained much to be won by women, it was no longer necessary for them to travel to strange and hostile lands in order to attain some measure of sexual liberty.

Thus post–World War I women in Africa were of a quite different stamp from their predecessors. Not less extraordinary, but different. Isak Dinesen, Elspeth Huxley, Margery Perham, and Laura Bohannan all had their destinies to pursue in Africa. But these destinies were not those of an Anna Falconbridge or a Rachel Watt or a Mary Kingsley. There was a peculiar urgency in the Victorian women's passages through Africa which is lacking in the later women's lives. By finding Africa, by reconciling dream and reality, myth and history, and private impulse and public duty, the nineteenth-century woman found herself—as an intelligent, resourceful, aesthetically responsive, and strong human being. For neither the first nor the last time in women's history, these women discovered that a female vocation of vision and service could entail acts of liberation as well as obligation and that such service in a harsh and inimical land might yield rewards never dreamt of by male explorers, who may have conquered a continent but never quite found what they sought.

NOTES

1. Following the practice of others who have written on African travelers, I use *Western*, *European*, and *British* almost interchangeably throughout the essay. With several exceptions, most of the figures I discuss were from Great Britain.

2. Dorothy Hammond and Alta Jablow's *The Myth of Africa* (New York: Library of Social Science, 1977) is an interesting study of the British literary imagination and its "fantasy of a continent and a people that never were and never could be" (p. 14). Hammond and Jablow's focus, however, is on the manifestation of this mythic Africa in Western fiction, with only secondary attention paid to travel narratives and other nonfiction works.

3. Margery Perham and J. Simmons, eds., *African Discovery: An Anthology of Exploration* (1942; reprint ed., Evanston, Ill.: Northwestern University Press, 1963), p. 16.

4. Introduction to *Africa and Its Explorers: Motives, Methods, and Impact*, ed. Robert I. Rotberg (Cambridge: Harvard University Press, 1970), p. 4.

5. Ibid., p. 11.

6. In *Victorian Lady Travellers* (New York: Dutton, 1965), Dorothy Middleton writes, "It is almost as if they feared it was wrong to travel for pleasure, and that to bring back notebooks of statistics and pages of drawings was necessary to justify [their travels]" (p. 5).

7. Elenore Smith Bowen [Laura Bohannan], *Return to Laughter: An Anthropological Novel* (1954; reprint ed., Garden City, N.Y.: Doubleday Anchor Books, 1964), p. xiv.

8. Patricia Anne Frazer Lamb, "The Life and Writing of Mary Kingsley: Mirrors of the Self" (Ph.D. diss., Cornell University, 1977), pp. 50–52.

9. Mary Gaunt, *Alone in West Africa* (New York: Charles Scribner's Sons, 1912), p. 80.

10. Both May French Sheldon's *Sultan to Sultan* and Mary Alice Hodgson's *The Siege of Kumassi* contain numerous racial slurs. Helen Caddick stands as the opposite extreme, and in her appealing but almost entirely unknown *A White Woman in Central Africa* (London: T. Fisher Unwin, 1900), she says of racist colonial policy, "In Africa we always appear to consider the country ours and the natives the intruders" (pp. 20–21). It should be conceded, however, that even the most intellectually enlightened nineteenth-century women travelers such as Caddick and Kingsley believed the African was a different species from the white race, with his own distinct gifts and capacities. They held, thus, to a kind of "separate but equal" doctrine of racial equality. Only the women who lived among Africans for an extended period of time—missionaries such as Rachel Watt and Mary Slessor—truly viewed them as equals. Not only did their creeds teach them this, but just as important, they were convinced of it by daily, intimate contact with the Africans among whom they lived.

11. *Travels in West Africa: Congo Français, Corsico and Cameroons* (1897; reprint ed., London: Frank Cass, 1965), p. 430.

12. *Narrative of Two Voyages to the River Sierra Leone During the Years 1791–1793* (1794; reprint ed., London: Frank Cass, 1967), p. 170.

13. Ibid., p. 210.

14. Ibid., p. vii.

15. Ibid., p. 79.

16. Ibid., pp. 66–67.

17. Ibid., p. 73.

18. Elizabeth Melville, *A Residence in Sierra Leone* (1849; reprint ed., London: Frank Cass, 1968), p. v.

19. Christopher Fyfe, *A History of Sierra Leone* (London: Oxford University Press, 1962), p. 264.

20. Melville, pp. 77–78.

21. Rachel Watt, *In the Heart of Savagedom: Reminiscences of Life and Adventure During a Quarter of a Century of Pioneering Labours in the Wilds of East Equatorial Africa* (London: Marshall Brothers, 1912), p. 94.

22. *Travels in West Africa*, p. 216.

23. Ibid., p. 167.

24. *Cheltenham Ladies College Magazine*, no. 38 (Autumn 1898):270.

25. Gaunt, p. 290.

26. May French Sheldon, *Sultan to Sultan: Adventures Among Masai and Other Tribes of East Africa* (Boston: Arena Publishing Company, 1892), p. 19.

27. In 1886 Sheldon published a translation of Flaubert's *Salammbô* which she dedicated to Stanley with the inscription, "To the man who created the Congo Free State, which is destined some day to outrival Ancient Phenicia [*sic*]" (Middleton, *Victorian Lady Travellers*, pp. 92–93).

28. Middleton, *Victorian Lady Travellers*, p. 14.

29. Middleton, "Women in Travel and Exploration," in *The Discoverers: An Encyclopedia of Explorers and Exploration*, ed. Helen Delpar (New York: McGraw-Hill, 1980), p. 458.

30. *Travels in West Africa*, p. 103.

31. Mary Kingsley to George Macmillan, n.d., Macmillan Papers, British Library, London.

32. Quoted in Stephen Gwynn, *The Life of Mary Kingsley* (London: Macmillan 1933), p. 252. Kingsley died in June 1900, at the age of thirty-seven, in South Africa where she had gone as a war correspondent. Shortly after her arrival, she volunteered to nurse Boer prisoners-of-war, and she died of the same enteric fever that decimated her patients.

33. *Victorian Women Travel Writers in Africa* (Boston: Twayne, 1982), pp. 138–47.

34. Mary Kingsley to Matthew Nathan, March 12, 1899. Nathan Papers, Bodleian Library, Oxford.

35. Mary Kingsley to Stephen Gwynn, November 20, 1898. Stephen Gwynn Papers, National Library of Ireland, Dublin. In the last year of her life, however, Mary Kingsley fell rather unhappily in love with Major (later Sir) Matthew Nathan, an officer in the Royal Engineers who in 1899 went out to Sierra Leone to replace the temporarily absent Governor Cardew. Nathan is the recipient of the letter cited above.

36. Mary Kingsley to Dennis Kemp, n.d. Quoted in Dennis Kemp, "The Mary Kingsley Society of West Africa," *Work and Workers*, February 1901, p. 69.

37. *Travels in West Africa*, p. 659.

38. Ibid., pp. 88–90.

39. Paul Fussell, *Abroad: British Literary Traveling Between the Wars* (New York: Oxford University Press, 1980), p. 39.

REFERENCES

Anna M. Falconbridge, *Narrative of Two Voyages to the River Sierra Leone during the Years 1791–1793* (1794).

"Mary Church," *Sierra Leone: or the Liberated African in a Series of Letters* (1835).

Elizabeth Melville, *A Residence in Sierra Leone* (1849).

Penelope Gladstone, *Travels of Alexine* (1970; biography of the Dutch explorer Alexine Tinne, 1835–1869).

Katherine and John Petherick, *Travels in Central Africa and Exploration of the Nile Tributaries* (1869).

Anne Baker (ed.) *Morning Star: Florence Baker's Diary of the Expedition to*

Put Down the Slave Trade on the Nile 1870–1873 (1972). Richard Hall, *Lovers on the Nile* (1980).

Annie B. Hore, *To Lake Tanganyika in a Bath Chair* (1886).

May French Sheldon, *Sultan to Sultan: Adventures among the Masai and Other Tribes of East Africa* (1892).

Mary Kingsley, *Travels in West Africa: Congo Francais, Corsico and Cameroons* (1897).

Mary Kingsley, *West African Studies* (1899).

Helen Caddick, *A White Woman in Central Africa* (1900).

Mary Alice Hodgson, *The Siege of Kumassi* (1901).

Constance Larymore, *A Resident's Wife in Nigeria* (1908).

Mary Gaunt, *Alone in West Africa* (1912).

Rachel S. Watt, *In the Heart of Savagedom* (1912).

D. Amaury Talbot, *Women's Mysteries of a Primitive People: The Ibibios of Southern Nigeria* (1915).

W. R. Livingstone, *Mary Slessor of Calabar* (1916). John Buchan, *The Expendable Mary Slessor* (1980).

5

Home Protection: The WCTU's Conversion to Woman Suffrage

CAROLYN DE SWARTE GIFFORD

The sixth annual convention of the Woman's Christian Temperance Union (WCTU) in November 1879 promised fresh direction for the organization. Its newly elected leader, Frances E. Willard, a young, vigorous educator from the West, advocated woman suffrage as the means necessary to ensure prohibition. The choice of Willard as president indicated that many WCTU leaders supported her suffrage position, a stance well known to them (and to her opposition within the organization) since she had been speaking about it publicly for several years. The WCTU could expect to enter the new decade of the eighties faced with a difficult task: convincing its rapidly growing membership of mainly Evangelical Christian women that woman suffrage was not a radical idea espoused by women whose behavior was at least questionable, if not outrageous. The vote for women must be made acceptable, respectable, and in fact a part of woman's duty as a Christian. For this to occur the image of the True Christian Woman had to be redefined and broadened to include enfranchisement. This redefinition began for many WCTU members through a religious experience which they described as a conversion to woman suffrage. They claimed that

God called them to work for the vote for women. Increasingly during the 1880s, Evangelical women entered the struggle for woman suffrage, convinced that it was God's will that they do so.

In 1880 the WCTU suffrage goal must have appeared as a vision far off in the future. Nevertheless, WCTU leaders began a campaign for woman suffrage throughout the country. Willard and other WCTU organizers traveled thousands of miles by rail and horse-drawn wagons stumping for the twin aims of prohibition and the vote for women. As they tirelessly crisscrossed the United States with their message, *Our Union* (after 1882 *The Union Signal*), the official organ of the WCTU, began to print a barrage of articles, editorials, columns, and letters pushing woman suffrage from every angle that might appeal to its readership. Through the decade of the eighties the organization labored to persuade its members that woman's sphere should be widened to include numerous activities believed by most Americans to be the prerogative of men.

Frances Willard announced the widening of woman's sphere in what became a favorite motto of the WCTU: "Woman will bless and brighten every place she enters, and she will enter every place."[1] The first half of the motto was not particularly alarming since "brightening every place she enters" had been woman's traditional duty and, moreover, her greatest pleasure, if one could believe the volumes of prescriptive literature written for and by women throughout the nineteenth century. The second half of the motto might prove disconcerting, however, if one grasped its full import. It boldly stated that women intended to move from the private, domestic sphere into the public world. Although the motto was constructed in the declarative rather than the imperative mode, as befitted a ladylike statement, Willard meant what she said. She was to spend her many years as WCTU president working out with determination her conviction that women belonged in every place, whether it be in the pulpit and in delegations to national church conferences or in the voting booth and in the conventions of national political parties. She envisioned a limitless space for women's abilities and talents.

Willard faced a dilemma in the eighties: How was she to encourage and enable others to share in her vision for women? How would she inspire WCTU women to examine and reinterpret proscriptive images of woman that had shaped their lives? What motivation would compel Evangelical women to work slowly and at times painfully toward a redefinition of the Christian woman?

There is power for change as well as for proscription inherent in symbols and images since they are, by their very nature, capable of revealing new depths of meaning and lending themselves to nuances of interpretation. Particular persons and specific historical contexts may shape and alter traditional symbols and images, reinvesting them with further content and renewed vigor. Such a process of change occurred in the image of the True Christian Woman during the decades of the 1870s and 1880s. Certainly it had begun earlier in the century, but the women and men who initiated the task were often isolated from one another or involved in reform goals other than that of re-visioning woman's image. Others, radical women's rights reformers such as Elizabeth Cady Stanton and Susan B. Anthony, failed to evoke images of woman that appealed to the majority of mainstream Evangelical Protestant women, who were more timid and loath to challenge the status quo than Stanton and Anthony.

In order to understand how vast numbers of WCTU women accepted a redefinition of the True Woman image that included enfranchisement, it is necessary to follow several lines of investigation. First, one must examine the image of woman current in the Evangelical milieu from which most of the WCTU women came. Second, one must determine how closely the image or ideal of Christian womanhood conformed to the realities of women's lives. Third, one must assess the ways in which influential leaders such as Frances Willard were able to infuse ideals and images with new possibilities of content and meaning. Finally, one must seek to discover what other forces were at work in the last third of the nineteenth century, in both the church and the larger world, which might call forth or allow for enlarged roles for women. In short, one must try to re-create the historical moment in which the image of woman was opened up to dimensions previously unthinkable and thus unattainable for the majority of American Evangelical Protestant women during the nineteenth century.[2]

These Evangelical Protestant women who filled the ranks of the "white-ribbon army" of the WCTU proudly displayed the tiny emblem of their membership on respectable, drab-colored, high-collared dresses. The simple grosgrain ribbons, in white to symbolize the purity of the True Woman, identified those who wore them as sisters battling for prohibition, but also for the elevation of women in all areas of their lives. Quite often, much more frequently than twentieth-century historians (feminist or otherwise) seem to have noticed, the white ribbon was entwined with a yellow ribbon signifying woman suffrage.[3] Both colors were worn proudly and in many cases with more than a hint of defiance. And no wonder, since these women were daring to stand up to the mighty weight of centuries of Christian tradition which taught that women were subordinate to men and to be governed by them, and that therefore women had no justification for demanding the enfranchisement of their sex.

The authority of Scripture was unquestionable for Evangelical women. They had grown up hearing, reading, and believing that the Bible, the Word of God, decreed the dominant/subordinate male/female relationship. God had created it so, and Eve's rebellious refusal to obey God's word served to emphasize woman's fundamental irresponsibility with the corresponding necessity for male governance. The Pauline Epistles elaborated on woman's subordinate status, enjoining wives to submit to their husbands and ordering all women to keep silent in church.[4] Along with the biblical injunctions came enormous numbers of sermons, homilies, home Bible study groups, and advice books based on biblical texts, which commented further on the attitudes and activities proper to the True Christian Woman. Often these commentaries included warnings to women who overstepped the bounds of woman's sphere, putting themselves in danger of becoming "unwomanly."

The editorial page of the February 1880 issue of *Our Union* featured an article containing such a warning, which was reprinted from an Indianapolis newspaper. The first paragraph of the article quoted from a Sunday evening sermon given November 2, 1879, by the Reverend J. Saunders Reed, priest of St. Paul's Episcopal Cathedral in Indianapolis. Reed had delivered his message just as the WCTU, meeting in the same city, decided to embrace the goal of woman suffrage. He was obviously disturbed by the public behavior of women.

It worries, it angers, it disheartens me to see women thrusting themselves into men's places and clamoring to be heard in our halls and churches. A woman-man I have always nauseated and loathed; but, oh, from a man-woman I would make haste to get me away as from a monstrosity of nature, a subverter of society, the cave of despair, the head of Medusa, a bird of ill-omen, a hideous spectre, a travesty of all that is sacred and divine.[5]

Here was an example of a vicious verbal assault on women who ventured beyond their proper place. Why would the editors of *Our Union* choose to print such a diatribe, one invoking symbols and images that had served for centuries to proscribe women's activities and confine them to a restricted sphere?

Reed attacked women who entered the public arena, that "male territory" of church pulpit and lecture hall, and probably the city council and state legislature as well, since WCTU members had already appeared before these bodies seeking the passage of prohibition legislation. He accused women who acted in this manner of breaking down sanctified gender expectations, assuming male prerogatives, and thereby becoming masculinized. Such an accusation could not be shrugged off lightly by a generation of women who had been socialized to understand that women and men were created by God for different though complementary tasks and spheres. Usurping a role of the opposite sex was deviant behavior, as Reed so clearly charged. The woman who stepped out of her space was unnatural, even monstrous. She risked destroying the social order; worse, in committing "a travesty of all that is sacred and divine" she sinned willfully against God's plan for creation.

Reed's rhetoric played upon the powerful proscriptive symbol of the woman as Other—shameful, sinful, and, finally, less than fully human. In an age that was familiar with classical Greek mythology, he called up the horrible image of Medusa with her grotesque face surrounded by ringlets of writhing serpents, a monster turning those who looked upon her to stone. He might as effectively have chosen a biblical symbol of woman as Other—Eve, Mary Magdalene, Jezebel—whose mere mention would have served the same purpose as the name of Medusa, suggesting to his listeners woman's potential for unnaturalness and wickedness. Moreover, the priest was not alone in his opinion of woman's proper sphere and the qualities of those who overstepped its bounds. Undoubtedly the majority of Americans agreed with him. Even as late as 1879 few women had the courage to challenge the men (and women as well) who employed such evocative symbols of deviance and evil to keep women in their place.[6] Wouldn't the editors of *Our Union* have been wiser to leave this attack on "the public woman" out of the WCTU paper? Why not downplay such virulent criticism by ignoring it? But the editors of *Our Union* were neither stupid nor naive; rather, they were quite shrewd. They had an excellent reason for printing Reed's thoughts on the "man-woman."

The sermon excerpt had originally appeared as the lead paragraph in an article by a reporter covering the WCTU national convention for the

Indianapolis Journal. The entire piece was printed in *Our Union.* In it, the *Journal* reporter took Reed to task for his statements and ridiculed him for being "angered, disheartened and worried" by such women as J. Ellen Foster, Mary Livermore, Mary T. Lathrap, Annie Wittenmyer, and Frances E. Willard, the convention's leaders. These women and others, according to the reporter, were the equals of any minister in an Indianapolis pulpit: "They were logical, forcible and concise, and held the attention of an audience from their first utterance to the close. They were conservative and sensible—much more so than a like number of men have usually been when convened on a similar occasion."[7] The writer thus captured in a paragraph the tone and demeanor that the WCTU as an organization would assume throughout the eighties. He went on to accuse Reed and those who held similar opinions about woman's sphere of being "many generations behind the age." The article closed with a veiled challenge: "The men have not all the brains, nor all the morals, nor all the religion, and should not be afraid to compete with the women in any place they can fill with equal ability and propriety."[8]

The interplay of Reed's attack and its vigorous rebuttal by a newspaper completely independent of the WCTU served an important strategic function. The points made in the article, though thoroughly endorsed by the union, did not appear to be special pleading by a self-interested group. The newspaper labeled as old-fashioned those who conformed to the prevalent attitude toward women and pronounced a rallying cry for WCTU women in the eighties. Although this particular challenge came from the *Indianapolis Journal*, it was in fact similar to many such challenges and exhortations from the WCTU leaders to the membership that were regularly printed in *Our Union* and *The Union Signal*. Through its national newspaper as well as through its leaders' speeches, the WCTU directly confronted the issue with which nineteenth-century American women struggled: the binding force of the American religious-cultural tradition whose institutions interlocked to uphold the image of the ideal woman as pious, pure, domestic, and submissive, shut up in the private sphere of the home and its extension, the church.[9]

Many of the women who joined the WCTU spent all their time in their homes and their churches. These two areas were literally their lives. Even as late as the 1870s only a few exceptional women had rebelled against this pleasant prison, woman's sphere. Indeed, many enjoyed and took pride in their womanly tasks. Nothing could be more satisfying, they felt, than providing a haven of peace and rest from the cares of the world for the True Man, counterpart of the True Woman. If the True Woman was to be dependent, passive, yielding, the True Man, her complement, was to be independent, aggressive, and a good provider for his family.

The earliest issues of *Our Union* abounded with descriptions of the gentle wife as the "soul force" of the home, welcoming her weary husband back to his domestic retreat and comforting him after his day of battle with the bustling economic enterprises of the nation. In this shelter she was also to nurture her children in a pure, protected environment. The frequency of these cloying portrayals moved Mary A. Livermore, Massachusetts WCTU leader and woman suffrage worker, to dismiss the contents of the paper as "pious blarney."[10] Yet alongside these glorifications of the home as haven, *Our Union* printed gruesome cautionary tales depicting the disintegration of families and homes through the drunkenness of husbands and fathers. It ran true stories, contributed by readers, about young boys eight or nine years old "led down the road to ruin" by saloon keepers who tempted them with liquor-filled candies and free lunches. Always the tales included descriptions of helpless wives and mothers wringing their hands and weeping but unable to do anything to stop their men and boys from the onslaught of "Demon Rum." The apparently naive and unintended juxtaposition of the ideal of True Man and True Woman with the stark reality of women's actual experience pointed out the failure of many families to live up to the expectations generated by powerful ideal images.

Clearly a terrible tension had developed between the ideal and the real. Such tension had always existed, but events during the 1870s brought many women to the point of admitting the strain they felt themselves or observed in other women's lives. Male alcoholism was a key factor in creating this tension. Men who were drunkards often did not support their families and thus did not live up to the responsibilities of the True Man. Indeed, they were apt to abandon their families for long periods of time while they went on "binges," a pattern that one contemporary historian has described as a uniquely American phenomenon.[11] Women were unprepared to support their families economically and were thus in dire circumstances if the family wage earner disappeared or became disabled through chronic alcoholism. Excessive alcohol consumption had long been an American characteristic. Alcohol consumption had fallen in the decades just before the Civil War, partly through the efforts of the temperance movement. But it rose again rapidly during and after the war, and the number of saloons per capita grew as well. Faced with an intolerable situation, women acted in protest. In the winter of 1873–74 occurred the Ohio Women's Crusade, a spontaneous series of praying demonstrations by women aimed at forcing saloon keepers to shut down their establishments. In a welcoming address to the Fifth Annual Convention of the California WCTU in 1884, a member reminded the delegates of the crucial significance of the crusade as the start of a consciousness-raising process for women. As the news of the praying bands of women spread rapidly by telegraph throughout the nation,

Men read and laughed and sneered; women, busy women stopped their work, read the strange lines, thought and lifted up their hearts to God in prayer. Had the time come for women to take the forefront in the battle against intemperance? Was it right? Had she not learned, and learned at her mother's knee that home is woman's sphere? Home her only safe abiding place?

But on the other hand, had she not through long years been the sufferer? It was her frame that blighted and withered under the curse of this vile traffic. No wonder she was ready for acting. No wonder she sprang to the front.[12]

What had been implicit earlier in the pages of *Our Union*—the discontinuity between the ideal of the True Woman in her home and the awful reality of many women's lives—became explicit. Woman was not "safe" in her home. The lessons about womanhood generations of mothers had taught their daughters were being seriously questioned. Woman was not necessarily the "queen" of the domestic realm; she was, in far too many cases, its victim. The corrupt world that she had attempted to shut out of the home invaded her supposedly pure, inviolate space, often through the saloon and its influence. Saloons were not a part of most women's experience. For many they epitomized male and thus public territory. The decision to move from the private to the public sphere, to assail the enemy on his own ground, was a tremendous and frightening one for women. Yet clearly, as the quote suggests, they were fed up with their situation. And just as clearly, they believed they were being called by God out of their homes into active temperance agitation.[13]

The women of Ohio were temporarily successful in achieving their goals. Some saloon keepers actually closed their businesses and took up other lines of work or moved west, at times assisted by crusade women who provided them with small sums of money to make a new start. During the crusade, however, women discovered to their dismay how powerless they really were. They had been taught that the moral and spiritual influence they exerted over men was enormous, though indirect, and thus consistent with their subordinate status. While women provided pure home life and noble Christian example, men would some-how carry that atmosphere with them into the halls of government and law and guide public life accordingly. Believing this, the Ohio Crusade women, going to court on behalf of wives who were beaten and aban-doned by drunken husbands, expected to find a sympathetic hearing. When they attempted to prosecute liquor dealers under statutes that made dealers responsible for selling liquor to known drunkards, they found that the male-run judicial system figuratively (and often literally) laughed in their faces. Occasionally, at the local level where a woman did wield some influence through her husband's position, a guilty verdict was brought against a liquor dealer. But it was swiftly appealed and thrown out in appellate court.[14] When women appeared before city councils and state legislatures all over the country lobbying for various prohibition measures, they encountered male reactions ranging from polite boredom to sarcastic ridicule to open hostility. In fact Reed's sermon, quoted earlier, was typical of the hostile reactions women provoked.

At first the women were merely puzzled. They had been told that they were the guardians of morality. Sometimes it was even suggested that women were spiritually and ethically superior to men, and yet they were ignored, ridiculed, or verbally attacked by men when they at-tempted to raise ethical issues in saloons, courtrooms, and legislatures. Some WCTU women discovered that men found it convenient to let women attend to morality while they attended to business, law, and politics. There was, in effect, a double standard of morality in regard to the public and private spheres.

Women became painfully aware that they and their spiritual, moral influence were not welcome in men's public life. Many husbands in-structed their wives, politely and no doubt gently, to stay where they belonged—at home. There women could be as pious and pure as they pleased. And men could get on with the work of the public world, where the values of home and woman seemed not to operate. Many women sensed that a deep ethical split had occurred between the public and private spheres. Different moral systems prevailed in the two separated sectors.

Drusilla Wilson, president of the Kansas WCTU, addressed herself to the conflict that had developed between women's private and men's public values, as she spoke about her leadership of Lawrence, Kansas, women who knelt on the floors of saloons, fervently praying that saloon keepers would stop selling liquor.

Indelibly stamped upon some of our minds during the Crusade was the need of Prohibition, for then some of us learned that the [liquor] traffic was a child of the law. Woman saw it was inconsistent for our fathers and brothers and husbands to make laws protecting [liquor traffic] and the women follow in the wake pleading with men thus licensed [to sell liquor] to quit the business. A change must be brought about.[15]

Obviously, what many women viewed as moral—temperance, in this instance—did not accord with what the men in their own households believed to be in the interests of good business.

Wilson also emphasized what would become increasingly evident to the WCTU organization during its first decade (1874–84): "following in the wake pleading" was not an effective long-term strategy for reform. Women questioned both the dignity and the efficacy of such tactics. Drusilla Wilson, in her reserved Quaker manner, had described the methods as "inconsistent." Other women were humiliated and extremely angered by the failure of praying and pleading, typical women's tactics, to move men to support temperance reform measures. Their humiliation reflected their recognition of women's total powerlessness in the public sphere. It also reflected women's consternation in the face of the breakdown of the ideal complementary relationship of True Man and True Woman in the ethical realm.

Additionally, women began to perceive that although they were placed on a pedestal in much male rhetoric and there honored, adored, and cared for, men showed little actual sympathy for women who were victims of their dependent status, left without ways to support themselves and their children when men abandoned them. Nor did men really seem to take seriously women's ethical concerns, women's thoughts, women's activities, or women in general. It was a cruel hoax to be placed on a pedestal and dismissed with laughter. Women did not like it. Again and again in their accounts of temperance work, references appear to the indignation women felt when men found their public appearances, both praying and pleading, occasions of humorous diversion. Apparently the True Woman image functioned for many men only as a way to keep women from meddling in the male world. It was no longer an ideal they believed in but a convenient mechanism to put women in their place and out of men's way. If this were the case, women would not be able to accomplish their temperance goals. They had to depend on male cooperation with their reform efforts, since these efforts increasingly involved legislative measures for prohibition. With few exceptions, in the 1870s and 1880s women could not vote and were not members of legislative bodies. If they were not able to persuade men to vote for prohibition they could pray and plead, but to no effect. Definitely, as Drusilla Wilson maintained, a change must be brought about. Woman suffrage was the change for which Wilson and other WCTU leaders called.

Women had counted on men to vote for reform measures which they themselves often initiated. Sometimes this cooperation worked, particularly when there were large numbers of men who also supported the reform in question. Kansas, for example, passed statewide prohibition by 1880, after WCTU women worked for two years canvassing the state to collect thousands of signatures on petitions, speaking to anyone who would listen, and organizing numerous prayer and camp meetings. Kansas temperance women and men successfully persuaded a majority of men to vote for prohibition. During this campaign, Drusilla Wilson once again expressed women's growing awareness of their total dependence on men's political power in a poem she recited at the Bismarck Grove (Lawrence, Kansas) Temperance Camp Meeting of 1879, which was a rally for the prohibition amendment.

> Come fathers, brothers, one and all,
> To you with tears we come;
> Arise and strike the fatal blow,
> To slay the tyrant rum. . . .
> Oh! then, we ask you from the weak,
> Remove this great temptation,
> This task is yours, *we* may not speak,
> But *beg* for Prohibition![16]

"Begging" was not a true form of speech for Drusilla Wilson. Although she had actually been speaking on behalf of the prohibition amendment two and three times a day for months throughout the Kansas countryside, she perceived her activity as "begging," the only means of utterance available to the powerless. For her, as for many other women, powerful speech meant the right to cast a ballot.

The Kansas WCTU began to seek the direct power of the vote. In 1880, and again in 1881, the Kansas WCTU Annual Meeting passed a resolution calling for the vote for women statewide in order to uphold the prohibitory laws on the books. In 1882 a new tone appeared in the resolutions of the Annual Meeting.[17] The WCTU still endorsed woman suffrage as essential for "exterminating the liquor traffic." But in a separate resolution the WCTU thanked the Republican Central Committee "for the recognition of the fact that the time is coming for the men of the state to decide by ballot whether or not their wives, mothers, sisters and daughters shall longer be classified with lunatics, paupers, criminals and Chinese."[18] The Central Committee had opened to debate the question of statewide woman suffrage, and it was to this action that the WCTU resolution responded. Its wording indicates that the WCTU women wanted the vote not only as a means of attaining a reform but because they were acutely aware of their second-class status. They were also quite clear about who it was that kept them in this subordinate position: their own husbands, fathers, brothers, and sons. The responsibility for women's powerlessness did not rest with God, the Scriptures, tradition, or custom, Kansas women were saying; it rested instead with men, the very men they knew best and counted on most. In similar resolutions, speeches, and articles, WCTU women began to name their oppressors, placing the blame where it belonged. This naming was a move toward what Drusilla Wilson saw as "speaking." Women would come into full power of speech when they could vote, thus entering freely into American political life.

In nineteenth-century America, access to the political process was seen as the key to power for effecting change. One's ambition was to have a voice in government. Women, as Wilson emphasized, were "voiceless." More profoundly, humanity was conferred by the right to vote. To be a full human being one must be enfranchised, a citizen of the republic. The abolition battle at its deepest level had been about gaining the dignity of full humanity for black males. Abolitionists believed—though naively, as it turned out—that they had finally won this with the passage of the Fourteenth Amendment. Women also sought to have their humanity validated in this way. The earliest woman suffragists had hoped to link their claim to full humanity with that of blacks, but they had been told that they must wait. The nation, the argument ran, simply could not be expected to grant full humanity to women and blacks at the same time. In 1880 women were still waiting for the recognition of their humanity; they were still legally and politically less than human.

The image of woman as Other—that is, as less than fully human—was not exhausted by the biblical and classical symbols so often evoked to remind women of their inferior status. By the 1870s the Disfranchised Woman entered the symbolic discourse of the WCTU, and by the 1880s a symbol system with a distinctive vocabulary had been developed around the issue of woman suffrage. But the image of Disfranchised Woman had a different sort of power than the proscriptive images used, for example, by Reed in his sermon. This image was evoked by the women themselves both to acknowledge their powerlessness and, at the same time, to announce that the proscriptive power of the image of the Other would be broken.

A visual image of the Disfranchised Woman as Other circulated in the mid-eighties. It had been designed by a Kansas woman, Henrietta Briggs-Wall of Hutchison. Entitled ''American Woman and Her Political Peers,'' it showed Frances Willard surrounded by an idiot, a convict, an American Indian, and an insane male. An advertisement for various-sized reproductions of the picture read:

The incongruity of the company Miss Willard is represented as keeping is such as to attract and excite wonder, until it is explained that such is the relative political status of American women under the laws of many of our states.

No one can fail to be impressed with the absurdity of such a statutory regulation that places women in the same legal category with the idiot, the Indian and the insane person.[19]

Although the second-class legal status of American women involved many more disabilities than the lack of voting rights, the image of the Disfranchised Woman became what might be termed ''symbolic short-hand'' for a whole cluster of conditions combining to keep women less than fully human. That Frances Willard, ''the uncrowned queen'' of the WCTU, could be at the same time a visual symbol of Disfranchised Woman indicated the symbol's ironic content. Its meaning is to be found, as the ad indicates, in the incongruousness of Willard, representative of American womanhood, being ringed by portraits of the Others in the nineteenth-century American political scene, those who were, for whatever reason, nonvoters. The American woman ranked alongside other second-class citizens with almost no legal status. Thus she, like them, was less than human.

One may regret that women's point was being made at the expense of other powerless groups. Such was the case not only in this visual symbol but in the Kansas WCTU resolution mentioned above, and even more virulently in nativist rhetoric used in the later 1880s and 1890s by the WCTU and other woman suffrage groups. However, one must realize that it was crucial for women to break the power of the symbol of the Other, whatever form it took, over their lives. Consequently, they had to articulate their Otherness, to dramatize their lack of political and thus human status, in order to begin working toward what they believed would make them fully human—the ballot. But the WCTU women needed more than a negative experience of power through breaking the hold of a symbol over them. They required positive validation in their struggle to develop an image of woman that would include the role of woman as a voter. The symbol of Enfranchised Woman must replace that of Disfranchised Woman. Furthermore, as Evangelical Christians they had to be able to justify their political and suffrage activity religiously. It was absolutely essential for them to believe that their behavior sprang from an experience which convinced them that God wanted them, indeed called them, to vote.

During the nineteenth century, the individual conversion—a personal experience of God's saving power and will for one's life—was a weighty source of authority for religious behavior. Revivals centering on such conversions were a fundamental characteristic of American Evangelical Protestant life. Within such a religious climate, if one claimed to receive a changed, reinterpreted image of woman as the content of the conversion experience, the claim would be difficult for another to challenge, particularly if the challenger shared a belief in the possibility of individual conversion. Many WCTU women came from a background of revivalism. The Ohio Women's Crusade, which came to be looked upon as the formative event for the WCTU, had strong revivalistic features, including the participants' testimony that they received a pouring out of the Holy Spirit upon them, a fresh baptism of power renewing and deepening the baptism they had previously received upon entry into the Christian faith.

Frances Willard herself claimed to have experienced God's call to advocate woman suffrage. As she traveled through Ohio in the winter of 1876 organizing for the WCTU, she took time out from her hectic schedule for Bible study and prayer on Sunday morning:

Upon my knees alone, in the room of my hostess, who was a veteran Crusader, there was borne in upon my mind, as I believe from loftier regions, the declaration, "You are to speak for woman's ballot as a weapon of protection to her home and tempted loved ones from the tyranny of drink."[20]

Not only did Willard hear God's will that she work for what she labeled "The Ballot for Home Protection," she also received "a complete line of argument and illustration"[21] for her first speech on Home Protection, which she delivered later in the year at the Woman's Congress in Philadelphia and at the National WCTU Annual Meeting in Newark.

An intense wave of revivalism led by Dwight L. Moody was sweeping through America's large eastern and midwestern cities during the 1870s. Willard worked with Moody in Boston for a short time during the winter of 1877 but left his revival circuit to devote her energy to her own methods of temperance reform. In a letter to Moody's wife explaining why she was leaving, Willard set forth her differences with Moody's approach to the temperance aspect of his revivals. He expected and sought individual regeneration with an accompanying pledge by the saved person to drink no more. Willard noted sharply in her letter that Moody emphasized the regeneration of men and that she, as a woman, found his approach inadequate. She advocated the WCTU goals of prevention through education and legislation, especially, she wrote, "putting the ballot in woman's hand for the protection of her little ones and her home."[22] Willard saw no distinction as Moody did between the religious activity of revival and the political activity of securing temperance legislation. A Christian, she felt, should work through any and every means available and consonant with her faith to reform the world and its institutions as well as individual believers. She understood no separation between the public and private spheres; both were arenas for reform, and they overlapped. Women must strive for the reform of society in all its aspects, and one of the most powerful means toward this aim was woman suffrage. In order to be effective reformers, women must have the ballot. After all, had not God Himself validated this means of reform in Willard's personal religious experience "on her knees in prayer"?

For the next two years Willard "evangelized" for her belief in woman suffrage, managing to persuade a significant number of WCTU leaders and a portion of the membership of the rightness of her position. She became president in November 1879, an event that signaled the beginning of the National WCTU campaign for endorsement of a suffrage position among its member state organizations.

On January 1, 1880, *Our Union* featured the story of "One Woman's Experience." It was nothing less than a paradigmatic example of a conversion, that form of religious experience so prevalent in American Protestant life. However, its content was quite unusual. The anonymous writer claimed a conversion to woman suffrage:

> It would sound very strange and far-fetched to many ears, even absurd, that a woman should be morally and religiously converted to Home Protection. I feel I was actually converted by the Lord's Spirit, and led to a deeper feeling, if not a deeper knowledge of the truth.[23]

She described her attendance at a WCTU Annual Meeting, where, for the first time, she had the opportunity to see and hear the "consecrated women" who led the organization. She was convinced of the sincerity of their efforts in temperance reform and of their selfless dedication to the cause.

She contrasted their demeanor with her impressions of others who advocated woman suffrage. She had come to the convention believing that suffragists were "party aspirants and women who were always howling over the wrongs of woman, and the Lord had been so good to me I did not think women had such a hard time after all; nor in fact, do I now."[24] Her attitude toward suffragists was typical of that of many WCTU women. They saw them as self-serving power seekers whose activities went beyond the bounds of propriety and who thus did not conform to the image of True Womanhood.

WCTU women were not iconoclastic. They had not abandoned or destroyed the ideal of True Woman but were in the process of dealing with some of its negative, proscriptive aspects and seeking to broaden and re-vision its possibilities. Thus they were frightened of radical suffragists who seemed to go too far, to act too boldly, and to take anticlerical, antireligious positions. Historians Nancy F. Cott and Ellen Carol DuBois have created a phrase to describe the change in religious attitude more radical suffragists underwent: "de-conversion," meaning "ideological disengagement from the convincing power of evangelical Protestantism (or inability to accept the whole of it)."[25] In contrast, one might call the experience of many WCTU women "re-conversion," an intense conviction that God demanded yet more from woman, further consecration which would lead them toward places and forms of activity formerly thought off limits. "One Woman's Experience" continues with a vivid description of just such a "re-conversion."

I had thought I had consecrated myself to the Lord, to work for Him both in the Church and in Temperance work; I thought I was willing to use any weapon for truth, justice and virtue He should place in my hand. But when I came into convention, the conviction kept forcing itself upon me that I was not wholly consecrated to His service: I was not willing to do anything and everything for Him. There was that fearful ballot—woman "unsexing herself," etc., etc., according to Dr. Bushnell, whose arguments you know, and of which every letter I have hitherto endorsed.[26]

"De-conversion" implies a sharp breaking away, a definite denial of one's former tradition; "re-conversion" indicates not a rupture, but rather a deepening or re-dedication of one's life to God's service in new ways.

The Dr. Bushnell to whom the anonymous writer referred was the Reverend Horace Bushnell, a leading nineteenth-century Evangelical theologian, dead for three years by the time this article was written, but whose thought obviously still wielded tremendous influence over American churchgoers. He had written a book, *Woman Suffrage: The Reform against Nature*,[27] which developed the argument that man was to govern, woman to be governed, and thus that woman could not vote since voting was governing. His views on woman's unsexing herself by the act of voting (woman as unnatural, as Other) were so well known that the writer assumed she did not have to elaborate on them for her readers. And yet she was able to defy such a powerful theological figure on the strength of her personal experience of God's call to vote.

Her conversion did not come easily. She mentioned nights of "waking and weeping," during which God allowed her to "gather up her prejudices [against woman suffrage] as a bundle and lay them aside." She felt her conversion as an easing of heart and conscience, accompanying her decision to work for woman's vote as an expression of God's will for her. Donald M. Scott, in "Abolition as a Sacred Vocation," describes the conversion to a reform, using as his example the position of Immediatism held by radical abolitionists. "Immediatism," Scott writes, "was less a program of what to do about slavery than, in evangelical terms, a 'disposition,' a state of being in which the heart and will were irrevocably set against slavery. . . . Immediatism became a sign of whether or not one was a saved Christian in abolition circles."[28] Although the reform is different, the "disposition" of the convert is very similar to that described in "One Woman's Experience." Belief in woman suffrage for Home Protection signified for a large number of WCTU members the deepest commitment to temperance and to woman. The belief in temperance was assumed, but support for woman suffrage became the mark of a truly consecrated worker.

Testimonies of conversion to woman suffrage multiplied on the pages of *Our Union* as WCTU women throughout the country felt a clear call from God to support the ballot for women as a means of Home Protection. A "Home Protection" column, running throughout the eighties in *Our Union* and *The Union Signal*, carried reports of state and local efforts for woman's vote in school, municipal, state, and territorial elections and referenda. Each new gain was celebrated on the pages of the WCTU paper and announced in meetings where it was greeted with a restrained but enthusiastic waving of handkerchiefs and the singing of the Temperance Doxology. A Boston prayer meeting in January 1880 with several hundred women and men present was described as exceeding the great revivals of Moody in the felt presence of the Holy Spirit.[29] At the end of a long day of prayer women left the church with petitions in their hands, determined to canvass Boston for woman's limited right to vote on the single issue of prohibition.

Mary A. Livermore wrote one of the more dramatic accounts of a conversion to woman suffrage in a memorial eulogy for a Massachusetts WCTU leader. Livermore quoted a letter written in the woman's last illness and addressed to the membership of the Massachusetts Union.

Standing on the threshold of the better land, I see more clearly. I would like to urge the dear workers in our great cause to acquaint themselves more fully with the evil that destroys the beauty and glory of our nation. The desire comes strongly to me to entreat them to put aside all narrowness and prejudice in their methods of work. Dear sisters, hold yourselves open to conviction! If the ballot were in the hands of women as a temperance measure, it would be powerful for the overthrow of the liquor traffic. *Then do not fight against the movement to give the ballot to woman "lest haply you be found fighting against God."*[30]

The women of the Massachusetts WCTU were not noted at that time for their enthusiastic support of woman suffrage. But surely the deathbed pleading of one of their own would make them reexamine their "prejudices," particularly when their dying sister strongly hinted that they might be defying God by not supporting the ballot for Home Protection.

WCTU women were beginning to reverse the arguments used against them by those who warned that woman's voting would be an act of rebellion against God. With the strength and validation they gained from personal experience of God's will for them, the women were able to stand up to persons who cited the authority of Scripture against woman's moving outside her sphere. Writings and speeches began to include many references to women of the Old and New Testaments who served God through entering the public sphere and engaging in the religious and political processes of their times. Deborah, judge of the people of Israel and leader of its armies, was a great favorite. Zerelda Wallace from Indiana, head of the WCTU franchise department during the eighties and an outspoken supporter of woman suffrage, was fondly referred to as "the Deborah of the franchise movement."[31] Biblical women served as models of courage and power for WCTU women who were attempting to initiate new modes of behavior. They did not intend to question the authority of Scripture but to enlist the weight of Scripture in support of what they had experienced as the will of God for them. In doing so, they launched upon an extensive hermeneutical task as they pored over scriptural passages for fresh insight into their meaning.

WCTU speakers and writers began to place Galatians 3:28 ("There is neither Jew nor Greek, there is neither bond nor free, there is neither male nor female: for ye are all one in Christ Jesus" [KJV]) alongside Paul's more restrictive passages in recognition that the Bible lent itself to differing interpretations and emphases. Jesus was hailed as the friend of woman and, more boldly, as her Emancipator.[32] The WCTU had a number of excellent preachers in its membership, and these women filled pulpits across the nation speaking on temperance and other issues of concern to women. Wherever the National WCTU Annual Meeting was held, arrangements were made so that WCTU women spoke in as many churches as would receive them. Often over fifty women preached both Sunday morning and evening to packed sanctuaries. In their sermons they delivered powerful alternative understandings of Scripture that inspired their listeners to re-vision woman's possibilities.

Thus the image of the True Woman went through a process of extensive reinterpretation in the eighties. As more and more WCTU women experienced a "re-conversion" to woman suffrage, they could imagine the True Woman as a voter and her sphere as extending out from her home to include the public space beyond. The WCTU encouraged its members to try out their newly claimed power and define new roles for themselves. The WCTU functioned, Estelle Freedman notes, as "a strong public female sphere . . . mobiliz[ing] women [to gain] political leverage in the larger society."[33] As such it became far more than a temperance organization. There were other temperance groups in existence with both male and female leadership when the WCTU began in 1874. In that sense, the WCTU was a duplication of effort. But it became apparent that temperance was only one focus of the WCTU program. Temperance might even be described as merely the occasion for the development of woman's power and the redefining of her image. Frances Willard and other leaders repeatedly emphasized that the WCTU was a sisterhood that brought together women from all areas of the nation, as well as an educational endeavor that prepared them for intelligent and responsible participation in public life. As Willard declared in 1885:

Our WCTU is a school, not founded in that thought or for that purpose, but sure to fit us for the sacred duties of patriots in the realm that lies just beyond the horizon of the coming century. Here [at the close of the nineteenth century] we try our wings that yonder [in the twentieth century] our flight may be strong and steady. Here we prove our capacity for great deeds. There we shall perform them.[34]

In this "school" WCTU members would be "educated up to the level of the equal suffrage movement" where there would be "no sex in citizenship."[35]

The WCTU's most distinctive feature, however, was its self-consciously political organization, modeled on the nation's in order to have an impact on the political process. In structure it resembled nothing so much as a national political party mobilized at the municipal, county, congressional district, and state levels, its national conventions drawing together regions with their various concerns. In these structural divisions the True Woman as voter and political being could learn the workings of American politics and simultaneously attempt to legislate morality— an explicit WCTU goal in regard to temperance, suffrage, and other areas of life.

With the strength that women gained in this unique organization they were often able to cooperate with other suffrage groups. Many WCTU women lost their fear of suffragists as "strong-minded" women, and many others probably never actually felt fearful of suffragists. More research needs to be done on the extent of the relationship between local and state suffrage organizations and the WCTU. Through preliminary work done recently by June O. Underwood and myself on a single state, Kansas, it seems abundantly clear that the Kansas Equal Suffrage Association (KESA) and the Kansas WCTU worked closely together throughout the eighties, issuing joint appeals for woman suffrage and canvassing for the municipal ballot for women. When that goal was won in 1887, the two groups ran voter education meetings urging women to register and watchdog at the local primaries when candidates were nominated. The membership of the two organizations overlapped considerably, and they regularly sent delegates to each other's meetings.[36]

The KESA and the WCTU were still working together in 1894 on a campaign for the submission of a state constitutional amendment to enfranchise women. The Populist and the Republican State Conventions endorsed the amendment. In contrast, however, the Democratic State Convention had this to say in a resolution:

We oppose woman suffrage as tending to destroy the home and family, the true basis of political safety, and express the hope that the helpmeet and guardian of the family sanctuary may not be dragged from the modest purity of self-imposed seclusion to be thrown unwillingly into the unfeminine places of political strife.[37]

After nearly two decades of work by the WCTU, here was a statement that seemed to exalt the True Woman on her pedestal and push her back into her private, powerless space. Did all the working, speaking, petitioning, and praying of the women have no effect at all? It might seem that way. But there was one difference. The women of the WCTU *no longer believed* the position of the Democratic party. They knew better.

Although the amendment failed in 1894, they did not stop in their efforts to resubmit it. It was only a matter of time, they confidently hoped, until the True Woman would be a voter in every election in the nation. Perhaps some of them even echoed the warning issued by the Massachusetts WCTU leader on her deathbed: ''Then do not fight against the movement to give the ballot to woman 'lest haply you be found fighting against God.' ''

The WCTU had struggled for nearly two decades reinterpreting the traditional image of woman that the Kansas Democratic party endorsed in its 1894 resolution. WCTU women had rejected the ''modest purity of self-imposed seclusion'' and were eagerly entering those ''unfeminine places of political strife.'' They were not discouraged from their suffrage goals by suggestions of unnaturalness or accusations of unwomanly behavior, as they had been earlier. Their deep conviction that God called them to work for the vote for women enabled thousands of WCTU members to accept wholeheartedly Frances Willard's challenging statement to them: ''Woman will bless and brighten every place she enters, and she will enter every place.'' For the WCTU in 1890, this was a vision in the process of becoming a reality.

NOTES

1. Annie Nathan Meyer, *Woman's Work in America* (New York: Henry Holt, 1891), p. 410. Also see Frances E. Willard, Annual Address at St. Louis NWCTU Convention, in *The Union Signal*, October 30, 1884, p. 2.

2. The report by Barbara Sicherman et al., *Recent United States Scholarship on the History of Women* (Washington, D.C., American Historical Association, 1980), identifies a major problem for the history of women: ''How to interpret historical depictions of subjects which are prescriptive or idealized. How are images connected with realities? How does one move from prescription to description?'' (p. ii). I attempt to address this problem in my essay.

3. In ''Politics and Culture in Women's History: A Symposium,'' *Feminist Studies* 6, no. 1 (Spring 1980), 26–64, Ellen DuBois and Mari Jo Buhle refer to the WCTU as a key organization for understanding the nineteenth-century woman's movement. Buhle, in particular, identifies the twenty-year period from 1870 to 1890 as an important gap which historians need to fill in from a feminist historical approach. Contemporary work has begun on the WCTU: Ruth Bordin, *Woman and Temperance: The Quest for Power and Liberty, 1873–1900* (Philadelphia: Temple, 1982), an excellent study of the WCTU from its beginnings to the turn of the century; Barbara Leslie Epstein, *The Politics of Domesticity:*

Women, Evangelism and Temperance in Nineteenth Century America (Middletown, Conn.: Wesleyan, 1981), contains a chapter on the WCTU placed in the context of women's temperance work throughout the nineteenth century; Susan Earls Dye Lee, "Evangelical Domesticity: The Origins of the National Woman's Christian Temperance Union under Frances E. Willard" (Ph.D. diss., Northwestern University, June 1980), provides carefully researched insights into the formative years of the NWCTU; Ida Tetreault Miller, "Frances Elizabeth Willard: Religious Leader and Social Reformer" (Ph.D. diss., Boston University, 1978), investigates Willard's theological basis, comparing her thought with that of Social Gospel leader Walter Rauschenbusch. Jack S. Blocker Jr., *"Give to the Winds Thy Fears": The Women's Temperance Crusade, 1873–1874* (Westport, Conn.: Greenwood Press, 1985) details the phenomenon of the Ohio Women's Crusade, making good use of quantitative research techniques to explain "why women marched" (chapter 4) and the responses to their activism. Blocker also explores the Crusade in the rest of the United States from its beginnings in Fredonia, New York.

4. By the last third of the nineteenth century the discipline of higher criticism of the Bible was well established in Germany, and the results of German scholarship were being discussed by American theologians. Aileen S. Kraditor, *The Ideas of the Woman Suffrage Movement, 1890–1920* (New York: Doubleday, 1965), especially chap. 4, "Woman Suffrage and Religion," discusses the impact of higher biblical criticism on suffrage arguments and on the development of the *Woman's Bible*, a commentary on selected passages of Scripture written by Elizabeth Cady Stanton and others and published in two parts in 1895 and 1898. However, in the 1870s and 1880s this new scholarship and the resultant debate over scriptural infallibility had not touched the lives and faith of most of the membership of the WCTU.

5. "They Say: From Four Standpoints," *Our Union*, February 1, 1880, p. 1.

6. Ellen Carol DuBois, in *Feminism and Suffrage: The Emergence of an Independent Women's Movement in America, 1884–1869* (Ithaca, N.Y.: Cornell, 1978), mentions Elizabeth Cady Stanton's 1869 meeting with Bloomington, Ill., women who had been reminded by a clergyman of their inferiority to men. Stanton reports (in *The History of Woman Suffrage*, 2:372) that she had to moderate her usually radical stance in the face of the women's resulting demoralization. Over a decade later, the situation had not much changed.

7. "They Say: From Four Standpoints," *Our Union*, February 1, 1880, p. 1.

8. Ibid.

9. Cf. Barbara Welter, *Dimity Convictions: The American Woman in the Nineteenth Century* (Athens: Ohio University, 1976); Nancy F. Cott, *The Bonds of Womanhood: "Woman's Sphere" in New England, 1750–1835* (New Haven,

Conn.: Yale, 1977); and Katherine Kish Sklar, *Catherine Beecher: A Study in American Domesticity* (New York: W. W. Norton, 1976) on the antebellum cult of True Womanhood and women like Catharine Beecher who sought to make of woman's sphere a shaping force for American society. We need more detailed studies on the period after the Civil War and on how the changing American scene affected the image of woman. Speeches and writings of WCTU leaders indicate that the image of True Womanhood persisted on into the late ninteenth century, but with important modifications. See Carolyn De Swarte Gifford, "For God and Home and Native Land: The W.C.T.U.'s Image of Woman in the Late Nineteenth Century," in Hilah F. Thomas and Rosemary Skinner Keller, eds., *Women in New Worlds: Historical Perspectives on the Wesleyan Tradition* (Nashville: Abingdon, 1981): 310–27.

10. Mary A. Livermore to Frances E. Willard, November 20, 1876. Woman's Christian Temperance Union National Headquarters Historical Files (joint Ohio Historical Society–Michigan Historical Collections), W.C.T.U. microfilm edition, roll 11.

11. William J. Rorabaugh, *The Alcoholic Republic: An American Tradition* (New York: Oxford, 1979), pp. 163–68. See also Jacquie Jessup, "The Liquor Issue in American History: A Bibliography," in Jack S. Blocker, Jr., ed., *Alcohol, Reform and Society: The Liquor Question in Social Context* (Westport, Conn.: Greenwood, 1979):259–79; and Bordin, *Women and Temperance*, intro., chaps. 1 and 2.

12. "News from the Field," *The Union Signal*, October 2, 1884, p. 11.

13. Carolyn De Swarte Gifford, "For God and Home and Native Land," pp. 8, 9, 15.

14. See Eliza Daniel Stewart, *Memories of the Crusade: A Thrilling Account of the Great Uprising of the Women of Ohio in 1873, against the Liquor Crime* (Columbus, Ohio: William G. Hubbard, 1889).

15. *Minutes of the Fourth Annual Meeting held at Burlingame, Kansas, September 27, 28, 29, 1882, State Woman's Christian Temperance Union of Kansas* (Burlingame, Kan.: Osage County Chronicle News and Job Room, 1882), p. 11.

16. Susan Metzner Kraft, "Drusilla Wilson: A Friend of Temperance," typescript deposited at Douglas County Historical Society, Lawrence, Kan., 1980, pp. 15–17. Emphasis in original. A shortened version was published in *Heritage of the Great Plains* 13, no. 4 (Fall 1980). See *Minutes of the Fourth Annual Meeting, Kansas WCTU*, p. 11, for a description by Drusilla Wilson of her speaking tour through Kansas in 1878 for the prohibition amendment. She and her husband traveled over 3,000 miles, and she gave more than 300 public addresses.

17. "Then and Now," *Our Messenger*, February 1888, p. 1. Also *Minutes*

of the Third Annual Meeting Held at Topeka, September 14, 15, 16, 1881, State Woman's Christian Temperance Union of Kansas (Topeka: Kansas Publishing House, 1881), p. 16.

18. *Minutes of the Fourth Annual Meeting, Kansas WCTU*, p. 26.

19. File—Frances E. Willard, Photograph Archives, Kansas State Historical Society, Topeka, Kans.

20. Frances E. Willard, *Glimpses of Fifty Years: The Autobiography of an American Woman* (Chicago: Woman's Christian Temperance Publishing Association, 1892), p. 351.

21. Ibid.

22. Ibid., p. 360.

23. "One Woman's Experience," *Our Union*, January 1, 1880, p. 3.

24. Ibid.

25. Nancy F. Cott, *Bonds of Womanhood*, p. 204, n. 10.

26. "One Woman's Experience," p. 3.

27. Horace Bushnell, *Woman Suffrage: The Reform against Nature* (New York: Charles Scribner, 1869).

28. Donald M. Scott, "Abolition as a Sacred Vocation," in Lewis Perry and Michael Feldman, eds., *Antislavery Reconsidered: New Perspectives on the Abolitionists* (Baton Rouge: Louisiana State, 1979), pp. 53, 54, 72.

29. "Home Protection," *Our Union*, February 1, 1880, p. 3.

30. "In Memoriam" by Mary A. Livermore. For Mrs. Lucinda B. Barrett of the Massachusetts WCTU in *The Union Signal*, July 3, 1884, p. 2. Emphasis added. The phrase "Lest haply you be found fighting against God" paraphrases Acts 5: 39 (KJV).

31. "Annual Convention," *Our Messenger*, December 1887, p. 4.

32. In *Our Messenger*, September 1887, the Wichita, Kans. WCTU announced that it was sending Rev. Hana's leaflet "Jesus Christ, the Emancipator of Women" to every minister in town.

33. Estelle Freedman, "Separatism as Strategy: Female Institution Building and American Feminism, 1870–1930," in *Feminist Studies* 5, 3 (Fall 1979):513.

34. Frances E. Willard, Address to the Woman's Congress at Des Moines, Iowa, 1885, as quoted in Annie Nathan Meyer, *Woman's Work in America*, p. 408.

35. Ibid., p. 404. "No sectarianism in religion, no sectionalism in politics, no sex in citizenship" was a popular slogan of the WCTU.

36. See issues of *Our Messenger*, the organ of the Kansas State WCTU from 1886–1890, for reports of the cooperation between the KESA and the WCTU in many projects. See also June O. Underwood, "Civilizing Kansas: Women's Organization, 1880–1921," in this volume, and Carolyn De Swarte Gifford and June O. Underwood, "Intertwined Ribbons: The Equal Suffrage Association

and the Woman's Christian Temperance Union, Kansas, 1886–1896," paper delivered at conference on The Female Sphere, New Harmony, Ind., October 8–10, 1981.

37. Mary C. Cowper, "The History of Woman Suffrage in Kansas" (M.A. thesis, University of Kansas, 1914, deposited at the Kansas State Historical Society, Topeka), p. 33.

6

"Educated and Ambitious Women": Kate Warthen on the Kansas Frontier

ROSALIND URBACH MOSS

"I was ambitious," Kate Warthen wrote as she described her experiences on the Kansas frontier in the 1880s and 1890s. Between 1887 and 1890 she homesteaded her own claim in Hamilton County in southwestern Kansas, advanced from country schoolteacher to principal of the Kendall town school, and then ran a "spirited" race for County Superintendent of Public Instruction, winning first the Republican nomination from two men and then the election from another. While serving as superintendent from 1891 to 1894, she earned a commission as notary public, read law with the local judge, and became the first woman to be admitted to the bar in Hamilton County. When she married in November 1894, her wedding notice betrayed a good deal of surprise at the happy event. Kate Warthen had been so determinedly successful, the notice said, that

Indeed her friends had decided that her's [*sic*] was to be a spinster's lot for she betrayed no interest in the softer emotions, at least to the casual eye. But all the time the sly little Cupid had shot her heart full of his arrows and finally . . . he brought her to hymen's [*sic*] altar.[1]

Although the sentiments are overwrought, the writer of the notice (probably the newspaper's editor/owner) revealed two important details. First, Miss Warthen had carefully concealed her personal life, no easy accomplishment in a small community like Syracuse, Kansas. And second, because she did not act in the anticipated fashion for marriageable young women, the community assumed that her visible, public life was all she possessed. So she was classified as a spinster, a woman who could not or would not bother attracting a husband. The notice revealed the community's assumption that, because she had emphasized her public accomplishments over her feminine attributes, Kate Warthen would surely remain an old maid.

People in the nineteenth century assumed that marriage should be the focus of every woman's life, whether she were seeking a husband or caring for one, and to the exclusion of most other activities. A woman who chose to direct her energies elsewhere risked being perceived to be a failure as a woman. And an educated woman, which Warthen was considered to be, ran the highest risk of "failing" to marry. A week before Warthen announced her candidacy for school superintendent, the Syracuse *Democratic Principle* reprinted an article from the Kansas City *Times*, entitled "Educated Women as Wives." Contrary to its title, this article focused on the reasons educated women were thought to fail to marry in the first place, beginning with the assertion that "Educated women overrate themselves in many cases." The burden of their failure lay with the women themselves, it went on:

Men are not unwilling to seek out educated and ambitious women. The fastidiousness of the educated woman more frequently interferes with her companionship and her marriage. Educated women expect a great deal in men. . . . If she would be satisfied with average men and take the same trouble to be agreeable to them that they are ready to take for her, she would have plenty of admirers.

The article closed by advising women to take marriage and men as they found them and not to try to reform either.[2]

Kate Warthen, however, was a "new woman" of the late nineteenth century who wanted to change things. She was well educated for a western woman of the time, and her ambitions led her to prove to herself and others that she could accomplish jobs usually reserved for men. They also led her to make her marriage on her own terms. Although her public and private lives may have seemed discrete to her community in 1894, and even to us nearly a hundred years later, they were very much of a piece, created by Warthen herself as a spinster on the Kansas frontier.

Kate Warthen was a "pioneer woman" in two senses of that term: she claimed a piece of the Kansas prairie as her own while she was also helping to claim a new social identity for women. And she seems to have headed to western Kansas in 1887 with both these ideas in mind. It is unclear how many other women migrated west with such clear goals, but Warthen was one of only 5 to 10 percent of all homestead entrants in the late nineteenth century who were female. Sheryll Patterson-Black found these women to be much like Warthen in that many sought out the changes in their lives that independent homesteading offered. Julie Roy Jeffrey, however, discovered that most women who came west, rather than being changed by their frontier experience, brought eastern cultural values with them and strove to impose their systems on the wilderness.[3]

Although Warthen never entirely rejected nineteenth-century ideals of womanhood, she did seek out the opportunities for independence and equality she saw open to her in the West. Even her wedding announcement alludes to her combination of these attributes, which made her "a shining example of the bright, versatile western girl who, while possessing all the fine womanly instincts of her eastern and southern sister, has beside the pluck and indominable [sic] energy peculiar to western progress and independence."[4] Like F. Scott Fitzgerald's Jay Gatsby nearly forty years later, Kate Warthen grew out of her own conception of herself. What was unusual, of course, was that she was a real person, and a woman at that, who selected from real options to become the individual in whom the newspaper editor could perceive an ideal.

Born Sarah Catharine Warthen in 1866 in Morgan County, Indiana, she was the third child and only daughter of a family of five children. She grew up in rural Indiana, attending a coeducational normal institute in Valparaiso in 1881 and common school before that. Then in 1882 when she was fifteen, her family moved to Hays County in central Texas. But by October 1883, the Warthens had settled near Whitehall in Cherokee County, southeastern Kansas. The family lived there several years, her father becoming school district clerk in 1886, and it was in Cherokee County that Warthen began her public life.

Warthen's family was undoubtedly quite typical of the families of rural, middle-class Civil War veterans who sought to better themselves by homesteading. She was not the typical daugher of such a family, however; she had "ideas" about women's participation in the public domain and acted upon them. In their study of the development of political women, Rita Mae Kelly and Mary Boutilier state that "the explanation of why this woman rather than that one is likely to become a political actor . . . ultimately must revolve around the interaction between the sex role ideological heritage the girl receives and the education and other skills and competencies she attains."[5] Since Kate Warthen's parents were from all reports quite conventional, and since she clearly rejected her mother's sex-role ideology, she had to have formed her own ideas of what women could and should do from other sources.

Kelly and Boutilier single out changes of geographic location and coeducation as salient circumstances in the development of a sense of efficacy in the young woman, and these may be set into the additional context of how different women experienced life on the western frontier. Kelly and Boutilier postulate that, because "geographic moves force an awareness of alternative ways of handling" the elements of life, and because coeducation "encourages girls to think they can grow up to do the same things boys can do,"[6] women who have experienced both tend to develop more expanded ideas of appropriate sex roles for women than do those who have been educated at girls' schools (or, in the nineteenth century, at home) within closed, homogeneous communities. The moves the Warthens made from the time their daughter was fifteen gave young Kate contact with a variety of people and ideas, and the mobile frontier society she experienced briefly in Texas may have increased her awareness of alternative roles for women. Her continued schooling was likely to have contributed to this awareness, since education was important for Warthen and her schooling, like her family, was coeducational. True, education generally held a positive value in the dominant American culture of the time, but Warthen no doubt discovered less abstract rewards when she learned that knowledge was something in which she could compete with the boys—her brothers or others—on equal or better terms. In addition to these personal experiences, the existence and qualities of the "New Woman" were being debated in the periodicals she read, thus providing further details for the alternative role models on which Warthen could draw.

Nevertheless, Warthen was unusual in seeing her physical and social environment as a source of opportunity. Julie Roy Jeffrey and Sheryll Patterson-Black, respectively, present the perceptions of the majority and the minority of frontier women who saw quite different possibilities for themselves in the same "uncivilized" country.[7] Kate Warthen and the women Patterson-Black studies definitely represented the minority of pioneer women who, to varying degrees, perceived the liberating aspects of the frontier. Perhaps the combination of Warthen's youth, her family's peripatetic history during her adolescence and early adulthood, her susceptibility to general as well as specific lessons gleaned from schooling, and a determination to avoid a life like that of her mother, "a good Christian woman who never thought until her husband told her to,"[8] was potent enough to differentiate Warthen from women who reacted to the frontier experience with despair.

By April 1884, when she was seventeen, Warthen was teaching a two-month school term in Cherokee County, receiving for her efforts $2 per "scholar." This experience encouraged her to attend the county normal institute, where she earned a third (the lowest) grade teaching certificate in the summer of 1884. Then she taught in Cherokee County for the next two years for $25 to $30 a month while continuing her own education by herself at home and at county normals. She earned a good income from teaching, particularly for an agricultural area where cash was short much of the year. In 1886 she also sold two articles to magazines. Not only was she able to purchase textbooks, home study courses, and magazine subscriptions, but she also expended nearly $100 in loans to her father or on payments for him.[9] By the time she was twenty, Warthen was earning enough to be financially independent, but she continued to live at home, as was expected of unmarried daughters in the nineteenth century.

The fragments that remain of Warthen's journal (written in 1886 when she was nineteen) record her movement toward the emotional, physical, and economic independence that homesteading represented to her by the time she moved to Hamilton County in 1887. Her mind was expanding from her reading, teaching, and study courses, though her thoughts, usually expressed as homilies and aphorisms, tended to be consciously pious and conventional. She faithfully recorded her father's Civil War stories, as well as humorous anecdotes about her neighbors and students. She talked about her reading in the family circle, especially with her brothers, who discussed ideas with her and whose lively pranks kept her from taking her "pretenses of 'churchly decorum' " too seriously.[10]

Although she lived at home most of the time in Cherokee County, Warthen's teaching, along with its associated cultural activities, helped enlarge her physical and emotional world. She became aware of the world beyond the house and farmyard as she left home to teach and to attend church and occasional meetings of the teachers' association or literary society. From the latter she demanded intellectual as well as cultural stimulation: "Attended Melrose Literary Friday night. The recitations and music by the band was [*sic*] good, as also a part of the singing. There was no debate, which was what I had wished for most, so I felt considerably disappointed." Her special interest, debating, was the most masculine and forceful of cultural diversions, one used by men in business and politics. Warthen recorded another outing which was significant because it may have been her first experience as an independent public figure: "I went to Pleasant Valley [to church] with the boys last night . . . [and] took a seat. A whispered consultation in the back of the room let me know that 'that lady is Miss Warthen.' And soon after the additional information that 'she teaches school.' "[11]

But despite this small notoriety, Warthen's life remained circumscribed by her feminine duty to family, as she noted in a short journal entry: "Didn't attend preaching last night, as pa [*sic*] had gone to Mr. Newton's and I had to stay with Ma. The boys went." She had learned that her duty was different from that of her brothers.

In a draft of a poem scratched on one of her journal pages, Warthen expressed her perceptions of both her mother's life and the differences between herself and her mother. Using conventional imagery of womanly age and youth, Warthen contrasted her mother's rough hands, slow step, and "pale, sad eyes," now turned away from life, with her own smooth limbs, light and airy step, and merry, bold, and flashing expression. Moreover, despite the sentimentality of her language, Warthen perceived that her mother's loyalty to a traditional role of female sacrifice, and not age alone, had brought furrows to her face; and also that such sacrifice made possible Warthen's own less traditional path to education and employment as a teacher ("In all this world I'll never see/A clearer, lovlier [*sic*] look/Than hers, who, giving grace to me[,]/ From her own beauty took"). Although in this poem she rewarded her mother's "toil-brought lines" with everlasting life in Heaven and although she dutifully stayed home with her mother, Warthen was beginning to realize the possibility of something for herself beyond the life her mother led. Undoubtedly, Warthen's perception of her mother's life led her own daughter, Lucile, to state that her mother "did not believe in pregnancy, childbirth or domesticity. She definitely felt that as an oppression. I was raised thinking women could do anything."[12]

Kate Warthen saw the limitations of her mother's life clearly, perhaps in part because of its lack of congruity with the middle-class ideal of sacred wifehood and motherhood without physical labor which she absorbed from her reading. Growing up on farms and homesteads, she had learned that every member of the family was expected to work hard: she knew that the genteel ideal was not her family's reality. Although middle-class, the Warthens were not "genteel" as urban middle-class Americans conceived of that quality. Also, because she held education in such high esteem, the fact that her mother was uneducated and unthinking created a further gulf between her mother's life and her own aspirations. She looked for others on whom to model her behavior. The other people Warthen was closest to were men, her father and brothers.[13]

Late in 1885 the Warthen boys had become restless and decided to try homesteading in another place, perhaps because of their father's economic problems. Rob and Ed left for Hamilton County in October 1885 and soon returned after staking their claims, but a few months later Rob headed west again with Fred, the youngest in the family. In a journal entry, their sister dwelled on her reactions to this significant experience of being left behind (albeit only temporarily) by men who had gone off to do important things. On March 4, 1886, Rob and Fred—the latter four years her junior—left to pioneer. Her father accompanied them the first day, leaving her and her mother alone on the farm. In her journal Warthen reflected first, and melodramatically in female terms, on the earlier leave-taking of Rob and Ed: "They don't know how my vail [sic] hid my tears, or how I cried as I went up to the school-house, and once inside sat down and cried and cried and watched them until they disappeared from sight." She recorded that "this morning I cried when Rob and Fred left, too," but she added that this time "I go about my work and sing so Ma will not notice so much . . . when I go into the bed-room and cry and pray for the safety and happiness of the boys." She listed her activities in detail, emphasizing their variety and quantity: "I wash the dishes, sweep, wash and fill the lamp and lantern, bring in coal, wood and water, and sit down to write. I have worked more yesterday and today than for many days, and I do like it better, too, than teaching. Ma was not well, so I had more to do.'' And a second time in the same entry, she listed in detail the nature and quantity of these tasks of which she was so proud, including getting things ready for her brothers' trip and feeding the stock, a job "the boys" used to do.[14]

This journal entry indicates that Warthen's energies and interests, which had for some time been directed toward teaching, reading, and writing, were acquiring a new focus—homesteading. And with this focus came a flurry of almost ritualistic washing, hauling, baking, and feeding. She may have seen the work of homesteading as not much different from that of running her mother's farm household, but she was undoubtedly aware that men were usually the ones who home-steaded; women only helped them. Sometime after the events described in this entry, she decided that she no longer wanted to be left behind by "the boys," so a year later she moved, essentially alone, to Hamilton County to "prove up" her own claim. By the time she arrived in southwestern Kansas, Warthen was ready to make herself still more different from her mother, since by homesteading she would not simply earn money (as she had by teaching) but would gain land, both a physical place and a tangible base for personal and economic independence—essentially the same things most men sought through homesteading.[15] This was the life she chose when she decided to homestead her own claim rather than helping her parents with their claim or becoming a homesteader's wife.

With this choice, Kate Warthen was taking a first, crucial step toward controlling her own life. As a teacher she had already earned cash to help her family out of debt and probably to stake them in their new homesteading venture, but she had remained the unmarried daughter at home. Having a lonely cry had been her typically helpless female re-action to her brothers' first trip west. But her second experience was more ambivalent: she still cried, but she also worked furiously to put the house in order, a more aggressive, but still indirect, method women have traditionally used to exert control over at least a part of their lives. However, in order to gain actual control she needed to take a more effective kind of action than cooking and cleaning. Her entry reads as if she were trying to convince herself that she really did like farm work better than teaching, so she could move to the frontier and claim her own farm. By the time she reached Hamilton County, she had made her decision. Her Hamilton County teaching certificate reveals a subtle but significant change in her personal identity: it was issued to "Miss Kate Warthen," not "Miss Sarah C. Warthen" or "Miss Katie Warthen" as were her Cherokee County certificates. Kate Warthen brought with her a new, independent self-image when she headed west.[16]

Rather than starting west when her parents and brother left to join Rob and Fred, Warthen stayed behind in Cherokee County, "boarding out" to teach the fall and winter terms. She filed her claim in February 1887, on a quarter section of land in southeastern Hamilton County (about thirty to fifty miles from the claim her parents had filed in adjacent Kearny County), but she returned east to finish teaching. She had moved to Hamilton County by the end of April 1887, however, and she worked hard to prove up her claim and make a success of farming on the prairie. In June she added her own touch to her frontier homestead: two caged canaries costing $2.50.[17]

But Kate Warthen did not realize her dream of the good life on the land. In 1887 she earned only $37.08 from her farm, located in a particularly arid section of the "Great American Desert." She returned to teaching in March 1888 at a country school in Kearny County, not far from her parents' homestead. But by then she had learned to live on her own and for herself, rather than by marking time in her father's house until someone asked to marry her.[18] She now knew she possessed the power of self-direction and the skills to support her efforts.

Warthen probably felt a need for rehabilitation after working on the prairie for a year, for in June 1888 she had her hair "shingled" and bought some "Alabaster Balm" and "Ayer's Hair Vigor," a corset, a bustle, and enough fabric for several new dresses. Then she had a dozen photographs made of herself.[19] At twenty-two Kate Warthen was ready for civilized life again, and that fall she threw herself into teaching and society as energetically as she had worked at homesteading.

In fact, Kate Warthen had decided to make her mark in education after all. She taught the six-month fall term in Kearny County for $35 a month, $10 a month more than she had received for the spring term. In January 1889 she borrowed $160 to buy a team of mares and then moved from her parents' farm back into Hamilton County, closer to the large towns of Kendall, Syracuse, and Coolidge, to teach the spring term for $40 a month, at that time a good salary for a female teacher. After taking the teacher's examination twice in 1889, she received a first grade certificate, the highest grade short of a professional certificate or a state normal school diploma. Then in September 1889, just a year and a half after she had left full-time homesteading, she was elected principal teacher of the Kendall town school.[20] Her path through the local teaching hierarchy seems to have been pursued with determination.

As principal in Kendall, Kate Warthen became more of a public figure than she had been as a country teacher. Beginning in October 1889, her activities and travel increased enormously. She attended concerts, shows, and literary entertainments, as well as the Southwest Kansas Teachers Association meeting in Dodge City and various county teachers association meetings. She also bought more clothes and spent a considerable amount on correspondence. Then, building on her experience of 1885–87 as secretary of the Cherokee County Teachers Association, she became active in educational and church activities, and also in the *National Tribune* Conversation Club (N.T.C.C.), a literary and correspondence club for children of Union veterans. She pursued her writing career as well, publishing in the *National Tribune*, a weekly newspaper for veterans.[21]

Warthen had thrust herself into a world of people and ideas and into the public eye as Kendall's leading educator. Additionally, she became a social force in the community when the Kendall *Free Press* began grumbling about the behavior of the town boys, who congregated "on the streets, in the alleys, and on corners after dark" and had ruined the town Christmas program with foot stomping. These miscellaneous complaints cohered on January 4, 1890, into a front-page editorial entitled "Our Young People," which praised the conduct of Kendall's girls but complained about that of the boys. Rather than making the kind of "progress, in the right direction . . . provided for in our public schools," the boys were perfecting other accomplishments, among which were boarding trains "when under pretty good headway," "tying cans to dogs' tails," and playing with "sixshooters and boxing gloves," as well as using profanity. (Kendall lay, after all, west of Dodge City.) The editor concluded by asking the classic question of who was to blame.

A Kendall teacher signing herself "One Who Loves Her Boys" replied to the editorial in an essay entitled "A Plea for Our Boys" in the January 18 edition of the paper. This teacher was probably Kate Warthen. In the essay she claimed that there was "not a thoroughly bad, unruly boy in our schools" and that the boys' cultural attainments were increasing. Then she admonished, "We cannot expect to teach except by example." The uproar finally concluded on March 1 with another front-page editorial, this one reporting that "a unity of action on the part of the boys, parents, teachers and citizens" had given the boys the encouragement they needed to mend their ways. Warthen's civic concern and educational leadership had helped resolve a community problem.[22]

Warthen's co-teacher in Kendall was Miss Alice Fulton, who taught the primary grades. The two women soon began encouraging each other in both teaching and writing. They led a "high-profile" existence as the Kendall teachers and were probably known by name if not by sight to the residents of Hamilton County who read the newspapers. They were frequently referred to in the county papers, often as participants in the regular teachers association meetings. Their names also appeared in the monthly school report, which Warthen elaborated from the usual dry attendance data to an invitation for public involvement, still a very good public relations technique. In the spring of 1890 both women staged debating competitions for their classes, the boys debating or reciting on such topics as "Sisters and Other Girls" and "Women's Rights, What a Little Boy Thinks of It." About this time Warthen's high school "room" won an award for temperance recitations in a competition organized by Kansas temperance workers. That spring both Warthen and Fulton were also writing pieces for any newspapers that would publish them. Under the pseudonym "Buckeye" Fulton reported on teachers' meetings and on the Fourth of July at Coolidge. Warthen published official school reports and other items on education and in July 1890 reported at length on the Topeka Chautauqua under the pseudonym "En Verite."[23]

Kate Warthen had successfully invaded male territory as principal of a town school, a position usually filled by a man designated "Professor." Besides this, her journalistic ambition had carried her beyond reporting local news items all the way to the Chautauqua at the state capital. Even before her trip to Topeka, however, Warthen had been confronted with a major career decision. In April she had signed a contract to become editor of the *National Echo*, an Osage County, Kansas, monthly published unofficially for the children of Union veterans. This was a step toward a professional career in writing and editing, especially if the *Echo* gained a national circulation. But in late April a Syracuse township teacher, W. H. Brown, suggested she run for county school superintendent.[24] Warthen decided to turn to politics, a step necessary for advancement to the next level in the education hierarchy.

By 1890 Kate Warthen was achieving in two fields, education and journalism, but her history shows that she had always been a joiner and organizational achiever. By 1885, when she was nineteen, she had been elected secretary of the Cherokee County Teachers Association, and she had been active in the N.T.C.C. for several years and became state commander the next year, 1891. It was important to Warthen early in her life not only that she be active in the organizations she joined but that she be elected to office in them. Because of this experience and orientation, running for county school superintendent may not have seemed too large or unlikely a step for her to take.[25]

In fact, by this point in her career, Warthen was on the brink of becoming what Kelly and Boutilier define as an "achieving political woman," one who has "a strong sense of personal political efficacy regardless of level of government . . . ,[her] marital status, or any other lack of role convergence." Despite the breadth of this description, Kelly and Boutilier's study is limited to women "who have achieved national fame or political notoriety for their behavior," and most of the time they write as if being an actor in national politics is a necessary condition for being an achieving political woman.[26] Yet if the breadth and complexity of women's participation in the public domain, as well as the multifarious connections between the public and private domains, are to become well understood, women's political endeavors must also be studied at the local level. Certainly by the time she was elected county school superintendent, Warthen appears to have seen herself as an independent political actor and an achieving political woman.

Part of the justification for such an interpretation would have come from Warthen's historical context. The women in Kansas politics did, as a group, achieve national notoriety, and their behavior and activities were watched closely by both suffragists and antisuffragists in every state. In fact, during the 1880s women in Kansas served in elective office to quite unusual degrees. In Cherokee County Warthen herself had served under a female superintendent from 1883 to 1886, almost the entire period of her residence there, and neighboring Labette County had the longest tradition of female superintendency in the state (almost twenty years, from 1872 to 1890). In April 1887, just as she was moving to Hamilton County, Syracuse elected an all-woman town council. Also in Hamilton County, later in 1887, Miss Lizzie Culver had been elected county superintendent, succeeding a man. If these local activities were not enough to give Warthen "ideas," the national issue of "the woman question" was much debated in the press and among the citizenry in the 1880s and 1890s. In February 1889 the apparently all-male Kendall debating club considered the question. Beyond these perceptions, Warthen had probably had to do some politicking of her own to become principal in Kendall. By 1890 she had gained an expectation that women, herself included, could and did hold certain elective offices, even though they did not yet have full suffrage. And she had probably already gained some knowledge of how one obtained such positions, as well.[27]

Politics requires skills in discussing and asserting opinions, and Warthen had learned early from her brothers and her coeducational experience that debate, as much as music and elocution, was important in nineteenth-century America. Her early interest in debate, recorded in her 1886 journal, was reinforced by the emphasis her co-teacher in Kendall placed on it even for her primary students. And Warthen no doubt received further positive reinforcement of the value of debate while holding office in various organizations. She perceived that competition among people and ideas held a positive value in her culture. More important, she assumed that she should, and could, participate.

Writers on the development of political women point out that it "is most unusual" for individuals of various ages and from different institutions in a person's life to stress "the importance of politics for [women]," but Warthen's experience had included just such emphasis. If "recruitment into politics is a slow, ego-strengthening process," then by 1890 Kate Warthen was ready to become a political actor.[28] She had received her essential political training and encouragement; consequently, she was ready to choose political activity when the opportunity presented itself. In making the actual decision to run for office, Warthen may have felt that editing the *Echo* would not take a significant amount of time, since she had already been able to manage teaching, writing, and part-time homesteading. Or she may have decided that running for superintendent was more important at that time and that becoming an editor and writer was something she could do later.

Warthen sought the advice of others, however, before seeking the office, for she needed to know whether she had a chance of being elected. Her brothers opposed her effort because, as she noted later,

" 'Politics are run by a ring. You cannot be elected because you are not in the ring.' " But she quoted another, unidentified adviser who told her, " 'Work you way into the ring.' " She also traveled to the "principal precincts" of Coolidge and Syracuse to "consult" with several unnamed "leading men," whose opinions of her running were "favorable." These visits were reported by two of the county papers, although they mentioned no reason for her visits. A week later she left for Topeka to report on the Chautauqua; the subsequent publication of these reports greatly increased her visibility with the county's reading public. With her public stature enhanced, Kate Warthen was ready to begin working toward the Republican nomination for County Superintendent of Public Instruction; she "made the venture."[29] To do this she had to see her way clearly through the intricacies of Hamilton County politics.

No history of Hamilton County politics exists for the period after the county seat war ended in 1888, but the 1890 county election was probably a bit different from those in the rest of the state, where many entrenched Republicans were defeated by the newly formed People's (Populist) party.[30] Only two Republicans lost in Hamilton County, largely because the county populists had no party organization and did not offer a slate of candidates. Also, the Democrats had never been strong in the county. Even though the People's party influenced the county's politics in 1890, the most interesting battles of that campaign were fought within the Republican party, between factions left over from the "war" of 1886–88. The Syracuse faction, which had been victorious, constituted the "ring" Warthen's advisers referred to.

County newspapers at that time were openly partisan. The Syracuse *Journal* was the "establishment" paper of the Syracuse Republican faction, while the Syracuse *Democratic Principle* was the only Democratic paper of any duration and size in the county. The Kendall *Boomer* (later the *Free Press*) represented the Kendall interests. It was also Democratic but ceased publication on May 24, 1890, before the campaign officially began. The Coolidge *Citizen* (later the *Hamilton County Bulletin*) was a "renegade" Republican paper, dedicated to attacking the ring.

Both the Syracuse *Journal* and the *Democratic Principal* printed Farmer's Alliance news as bids for populist support for their respective parties. The Coolidge *Citizen*, however, tried other tactics. First, in

August 1890, it endorsed the People's party's attempt to break the power of the ring, but the next week the paper was dissolved. And a few weeks after that, the reborn *Hamilton County Bulletin*, emerging with the same editor-proprietor, made a bid to become the primary newspaper in the county in order to forge a coalition of Democrats, Republicans, and Populists against the Republican candidates controlled by the ring. The *Bulletin* was out to get the winners of the county seat war. Its campaign was probably the result of editor John W. Bishop's perception that the People's party did not have a chance to make a change in Hamilton County. He had to find another way to break the power of the men he depicted as corrupt. The *Bulletin* endorsed Kate Warthen and other non-Syracuse candidates as "good," legitimate candidates while it campaigned against those associated with the ring.[31]

The *Bulletin* was renegade not only because it broke with its party; it also broke the protocol of late-nineteenth-century American party politics by opposing people rather than a party. Many Americans at that time were uneasy with political strife that could not be mediated by formal party affiliations. In 1887, when the county seat fight seemed for a time to have been settled, the editor of the Syracuse *Democratic Principal* expressed his relief that politics could return to usual party demarcations, rather than the county's being divided into geographical factions.[32] He felt more comfortable fighting along party lines.

This aversion to anything heavier than formal party jingoism, along with the fact that most people in a small community would know what the issues were, accounts for a dearth of detailed reports on candidates and issues in these newspapers which seems quite strange to us today. The real political battles were only alluded to.[33] Except for the usually obscure mutterings of the *Democratic Principle* and the *Hamilton County Bulletin* about the ring, all other issues openly addressed by the county papers seem, on the surface, to be nonissues.

Indeed, the county superintendent campaign seems to have attracted the most attention from the press, in part because the cultural and social importance of education allowed issues surrounding the office to appear important though superficially noncontroversial. Schools and education were emblems of settlement and civilization, as opposed to saloons and other agents of disorder. Political factions, were, therefore, eager to claim they had provided the community with avenues to culture and advancement. The big stone schoolhouses built in each of the three

major towns during the county seat war remained symbols even after
the conflict ended in 1888: "liberal" patronage of the schools indicated
that "the better class of people . . . are gaining the ascendancy."[34]

But the county seat fight had affected the school system as it had
other county affairs. The first county superintendent, F. G. Rinehart,
had reportedly left "school records, and school districts . . . jumbled
together in a most heterogeneous manner" when he vacated the office
in 1887 after narrowly losing to Warthen's predecessor, Lizzie Culver.
Because of this experience, the Syracuse *Democratic Principle* raised
the first campaign issue early, on June 26, 1890:

> This year we are to elect another important office, besides the [state] repre-
> sentative . . . county superintendent. This is an office in which a change should
> not be made every two or four years, but . . . [since] the present incumbent [*sic*]
> will not be a candidate again, she having tired of office life[, a] good person
> must be elected who is not under the control of anyone but also [who is not
> teaching], as this would result in a division of their [*sic*] time and consequently
> none of their duties would receive [adequate attention]. At present we know of
> only two candidates, one from each party.

Besides its reference to the power of the ring, this apparently noncontroversial call for full-time status for the county school superintendent
alluded to the unsatisfactory performance of the first two incumbents.
F. G. Rinehart, former principal of the Syracuse town school, was
identified with the ring and had taught while serving as superintendent.
Lizzie Culver had not taught while superintending; she had, however,
married and started a family, which many saw as detracting from her
ability to do her job properly. But the full issue of women's suitability
for public office was never addressed directly by any of the county
newspapers.[35]

Even though her intention was to be a professional educator, Kate
Warthen's first task had to be quite political. She publicly sought the
nomination from country Republican party leaders and delegates. Although she had received favorable responses to her candidacy from men
she considered leaders, she had a male opponent in J. E. Parrott, Kendall
town treasurer and music teacher. In fact, when she made the decision
to run, Warthen knew she would not be unopposed in her own party,
for on May 2 Parrott had written her formally, alluding to an earlier

conversation in which she had apparently asked him to bow out of the race:

Miss Warthen[:] My friends are entirely unwilling for me to withdraw from the candicy [*sic*] for Superintend.—We will have to go into convention and if you get it all right.

Yours,
J. E. Parrott

In the light of this early opposition, her June trip to the principal precincts was undoubtedly made as much to gain support from leading men in the area, including newspaper editors, as to seek advice. This early politicking with the editors paid off because by the end of September, the *Democratic Principle* had announced it favored her candidacy, unless a Democrat ran; the Coolidge *Citizen* had endorsed her at length; and the Syracuse *Journal* first paid her an indirect compliment about her work as Kendall's principal and then all but endorsed her.[36] Warthen had entered the contest with much forethought and careful preparation calculated to create broad support.

On August 22, 1890, the *Journal* briefly mentioned Parrott's candidacy in its "Local Notes" column, describing him as "a very estimable gentleman and entirely competent for the position." Eight entries below appeared an item about Warthen's candidacy, considerably longer and more detailed:

Miss Warthen is well qualified for the position having been a successful teacher for seven years. She was principal of the Kendall school last term, and at the county normal . . . passed the highest grade examination in the class of teachers. She states she is in the race to win and will make a thorough canvass of the country. She has our best wishes.

Neither Warthen nor the editor of the major county Republican paper thought it was unseemly for her to be "in the race to win." On September 10 J. E. Parrott sent her another note, withdrawing from the race and giving her permission to quote him when she felt the time was right for an announcement.[37]

Even a woman as determined as Kate Warthen could win neither a nomination nor an election in 1890 without help from men. Her greatest aid probably came from C. C. Weith, principal of the Syracuse school and prominent in the local Republican party, who could have won the office if he had chosen to run. Weith was elected secretary of the convention and undoubtedly held official and personal power important to Warthen's convention fight, for her nomination was not unchallenged even after Parrott had withdrawn.[38]

Though the county papers give no details of this convention fight, Warthen won the nomination (20 votes to 9) over George Millison, who had not announced his candidacy prior to the convention. Without specifics of the convention maneuvering, one can only conjecture why her strong candidacy was opposed. Although the state Republican leadership was moving toward supporting suffrage because of Republican women's lobbying and the strong entrance of women into municipal politics since 1887, support for women in public life was neither universal nor deep. Warthen still faced opposition from the party's rank and file. And she had aligned herself with the anti-ring faction, a second strike against her for some men. Millison was probably nominated either by the Syracuse faction or by men who opposed a female candidate. But the ticket that emerged from the convention was balanced and countywide, so the furor over the ring may have been moot.[39]

She was left, however, with being female. In her campaign notes, Warthen summed up the points she saw in her favor and those against her:

only objections	youthful appearance	Facts in favor
	being a woman	Being a woman
	being a Republican	" " claim holder
	unsociable	" " teacher—active
		" " modest [sic]
		" " writer for papers
		" " soldier's daughter
		" " Republican

She quite accurately saw that being a woman and a Republican worked simultaneously for and against her chances of winning. She could minimize the deficit of being Republican by running outside the ring to gain Populist, Democratic, and renegade Republican support. It was harder to circumvent the problems created by her sex.

At the same time Hamilton County was being settled, Kansas women began taking an active part in politics, and by 1899 Kansans had voted more women into public office than had any other state. In 1871 women had been declared eligible to qualify as notaries public, in 1872 women qualified to run for the office of county superintendent of public schools, and in March 1887 they were given the "right to vote at city elections and hold certain offices." Immediately the small town of Argonia in Sumner County attracted national attention by electing a woman mayor. During the same election, Syracuse elected an all-female town council. However, when few women voted at the Syracuse town election in the spring of 1890, the Kansas City *Star* expounded, "Women really do not care anything more for politics as a steady diet than men do for religion."[40] It is no wonder women found it difficult to redefine their roles while living in a culture as ideologically polarized between the sexes and their separate spheres as was the dominant culture of the United States at this time. Although Kate Warthen did not see these barriers as insurmountable, they were significant hurdles, nevertheless.

Once a woman wins her personal struggle to become political, as Kate Warthen did, she must then fight to convince others to permit her to be political. Even while supporting her candidacy, men may have been inclined to make an issue of her sex, rather than to downplay it, as did both the "bachelor" who seconded her nomination and the newspaper editor who reported the events. As a matter of fact, after her nomination Kate Warthen had to worry a good deal more about being defeated by her sex than she had to worry about being defeated by her Democratic opponent, J. E. Henning, who clearly had neither the administrative nor the political qualifications she possessed. Henning taught a country school near his claim in the Medway Township and had made a good showing at the 1890 county normal institute. But even the *Democratic Principle* found little more to say about its party's own candidate, except that "while he has not an extensive acquaintance, all who know him are friendly to his aspirations."[41]

Even though in one town "ladies waved their handkerchiefs from the street-corner and men shouted 'The girl's ahead,' " the fact that Kate Warthen was a woman might very well have defeated her. The issue of the candidate's sex had been aggravated rather than helped by the record of the outgoing superintendent. Miss Lizzie Culver was Hamilton County's first female superintendent and the second person to hold that office. First elected by a narrow margin in November 1887, she had had to stand for reelection the next year after reorganization, which took place at the close of the county seat war. Immediately after taking office for her second term, Culver married a member of her campaign committee, H. C. Price. Her private life apparently did not affect her official conduct in 1889, for the quantity of her work was considerable. But the next year she filed only three quarterly reports, and her other work had fallen off by more than half. By 1890 Mrs. Price was pregnant. Her efficiency slipped, causing people to question any woman's ability to fulfill her duties, although F. G. Rinehart's poor performance had not led them to question men's abilities. Warthen recorded in her notes the objections she encountered most often: "Can't visit the schools" and "Be sick all the time." Her daughter remembers Warthen's blaming Mrs. Price for almost costing her the election because she "drove over the county in a very pregnant state, turning public opinion against her sex."[42] It is unclear what bothered people more: the assumption that pregnancy was incapacitating and would interfere with public duties or the objection to someone in such a "private" condition continuing to perform public duties.

The issue of full-time superintendency could have been (and perhaps was) used against Warthen, who as a woman might have been assumed to be capable of neglecting her job as her predecessor was perceived to have done. But she vigorously took the offensive. When she announced her candidacy late in July, she vowed to be a full-time, professional superintendent. Her promise was buttressed by the simultaneous announcement of the appointment of J. B. Hammond to her position as Kendall's principal.[43] But it is unclear how effectively this tactic defused the arguments by some that women were unfit for office.

On the other hand, Warthen's image as an "unsociable" spinster might well have encouraged the perception that, as an "exceptional" woman, she was suited for public responsibility.[44] She was apparently a serious, determined, and businesslike person, despite her curly red-gold hair. Because their preconceptions appeared to be reinforced by Warthen's behavior, people could reassure themselves that she, at least, would not marry while in office. Such "educated and ambitious women," after all, had trouble finding men willing to marry them. At twenty-four Warthen was not old, but she was halfway through the commonly accepted period of a woman's marital eligibility.

Although the issue of her being a woman was never raised openly in the press, the Syracuse *Journal* did approach the problem obliquely. On October 10, 1890, less than two weeks before the Republican convention, it published an essay titled "Women as Public Officers,"

signed only "Observer." Warthen's notes indicate that she was the
author, who offered a "plain expression of views" on "the question
of allowing women to hold office of public trust [which] is considerably
agitated at the present time."[45]

This essay used primarily egalitarian feminist arguments, but it occasionally buttressed these with assertions of women's special suitability
for public office which were similar to those used by the Home Pro-
tectionists.[46] "Observer" allowed that "it is perfectly natural and proper"
when a woman seeks an office for the public to ask "whether she is
better suited for that particular position than a man," but she asserted
that "it is unjust to allow any other consideration to determine the
choice." She declared that the opinion that some women should not
hold office simply because they are women is a "flimsy argument!"
But, as with men, she wrote, some women were obviously better qualified than others for office, and her description of these women may
very well indicate how Warthen evaluated herself at that time: "The
ambitious, studious woman, with a good education and concentration
of thought and purpose will understand the responsibilities of her position and discharge her public duties with fidelity and dispatch." She
made her strongest stand on the basis of education and competence, not
on the moral purity frequently invoked by those who argued that women
belonged in office because they were innately more moral than men.

While admitting that "there are some offices for which women are
peculiarly adapted," she insisted that the female candidate should receive, not special favoritism, but equal competition and remuneration
"because she has stood tests applied to any man in the race; because
she has proven her ability to succeed in similar lines of work; because
that work is thoroughly agre[e]able and the salary a natural and necessary
consequent." Warthen used the Home Protectionist claim of special
female suitability to attack, not men per se, but the entrenched and
corrupt politicians, who, by implication, are inattentive to duty, im-
patient, waste their "late-hours," "habitually take an 'occassional [sic]
glass,' " and do not respect "law and order." Although these were
undoubtedly the failings of men in general to the eyes of many nineteenth-century prohibitionist suffragists (particularly those observing
masculine excesses on the frontier), these traits were also identified by
many residents of the county with the "Syracuse ring."[47]

Warthen's essay, published so shortly before the Republican con- ven-
tion, may have convinced Hamilton County's political leaders that she

was the best person for the job. But it was undoubtedly difficult for many men to forget that Kate Warthen was a candidate for an office for which she could not even vote. Her hardest battles had to be won among the voters of the county. Many anecdotes sketched out in her campaign notes indicate that her sex was, indeed, the real issue of the election, although this was never openly acknowledged by the major county newspapers, all of which were sympathetic to or supportive of her campaign.

Resistance came from men who, like the German syrup maker she sketched in her notes, informed her of the "sphere and use of women." Another man paid her the compliment that "A pretty Co. Supt. you'll make if ever you are elected, which you won't be," while yet another was more direct: "I guess if any woman is fit for the office, you are but I'll never vote for a woman to do anything [but] make me a shirt or put a patch on my pantaloons." When she and her brother drove past a man and a woman shoveling manure from a barn into a cart, her brother was inspired to remark, "Ah, . . . there's the kind of work he votes for his woman folks to do."

But Warthen's campaigning also met with successes, like those epitomized in her notes by an instance in which her Christianity and her reputed "unsociability" were tested when "a sporting man" declared, "Her religion won't allow her to shake hands with me." Her political instincts probably overcame her religious scruples, and she shook his hand, for she claimed that "after I had met him and talked, he said he would 'Roll up his sleeves and turn down his collar and work like a Trojan'—and he did."

She managed more successes than failures, for on November 4, 1890, Kate Warthen polled 236 votes to Hennings's 179—hardly a landslide, but her margin was considerably larger than that of any of the others elected. All the other winners were men.[48]

Kate Warthen's self-made feminism and open ambition pushed her to try herself further even while she served two terms as county superintendent (1891–94). She became the Syracuse correspondent for the St. Louis *Globe-Dispatch* early in 1892 and was paid for at least one story. On November 16, 1892, just after being reelected superintendent, she was commissioned notary public, a more important (and male) function in her day than in ours. Then on March 3, 1894, after reading law with local judge Tapscott, she became the first woman to pass the bar examination in Hamilton County. Finally, on November 12, 1894, she requested admission to the Kansas Supreme Court Bar, passing that bar examination on December 4, 1894. Warthen had gone about as far as she could go in Hamilton County, and she no doubt felt she had made her point for what she called "women's progress."[49]

Warthen's pursuit of traditionally male positions, from homesteader to lawyer and politician, was so determined that the community was quite surprised when she married Emmett Searcy in late November 1894. Although she was only twenty-eight and very attractive, many had probably written her off as a spinster (as her wedding announcement indicated), assuming that education and ambition were a double handicap in a woman's search for a man.

The townspeople and the article "Educated Women as Wives" were correct in one respect: her education, ambition, and experiences in the West had, indeed, made Kate Warthen a demanding woman, quite unlike the passive, nineteenth-century ideal. She had become a complete, well-rounded human being and proposed to carry the knowledge she had gained of herself in the "public sphere" into her private life, precisely where the author of "Educated Women as Wives" would have her drop it. This progression from pliable female to strong-minded woman appears in her writing. In 1886, before she set out to prove herself on the frontier, she was composing a draft of a traditionally romantic poem:

> I will be true to my vows and to you
> (I shall be true till I die).
> I give you my heart and I give you my hand
> And for this I receive
> Your ('plauded) name and your boundless land[.]
> I give you my heart—I give you my hand
> And for this you give to me
> Your name[,]your land[,]
> And your cottage by the sea.

The core of these schoolgirl thoughts appears in a very different context in a later, published poem entitled "To an Angry Suitor," which appears to have been filtered through her Hamilton County experience:

> I answered you gently, but firmly, "No!"
>   When you asked me to be your wife;

Why will you declare my refusal unfair,
    And say it has blasted your life?
I did not snare this—your offer amiss
    Of love, your land and your name—
You candidly own! Then why say of stone
    Is my heart? As if I were to blame!

I answered you gently and firmly then,
    And I told you the reason why;
You know if I could I would spare you this pain,
    But I cannot—will not—live a lie.
I could not be true to my vows and to you—
    Without love I never shall wed;
'Twould be life-time dirge—you are cruel to urge—
    'Twere better we both be dead.

Don't say that your love for us both is enough!
    Ere long you would discover
That a one-sided love is comfortless stuff
    To the one who is the lover.
Though your love now is strong it would not be long
    Till you'd curse the day when we met;
But I trust that we will for aye be friends still,
    And neither have aught to regret.

Resign your false hopes; your anguish remove;
    You are too brave to weakly repine.
The course I've expressed I have judged to be best
    For both your future weal and for mine.
You will thank me, I know, as years come and go;
    You may win a worthier bride,
Who will return love real, such as I do not feel,
    And will faithfully stand by your side.[50]

The thought depicted in this poem is considerably more self-possessed and less traditionally romantic than that of the early fragment, in both sentiment and force of expression. Now the man's "love," "land," and "name" constitute "an offer amiss," rather than romantic treasure. And now she "cannot be true" to both him and her vow that "without love I never shall wed." This vow to herself is of an entirely different sort from the vow of blind fidelity expressed in the early fragment. Her experiences had led her to become as demanding in her personal life as she was in her public life, and she did not shrink, even in the poem, from asserting herself, albeit "gently but firmly." She was to be the judge of what was best for both herself and her suitor. Though she was still idealistic, Warthen had, by insisting on the validity of her own needs and desires, rejected the "traditional" male-oriented vision of marriage expressed in the "romantic exchange" of the fragment. She was ambitious even in marriage, and unlike many people in late-nine-teenth-century America (as evidenced in the cautionary article "Edu-cated Women as Wives"), she did not feel that ambition was a negative trait for a woman or one to be confined solely to what was commonly termed the public sphere.

Kate Warthen married Emmett Searcy, a man she had corresponded with for about four years. They both considered themselves writers, and he had initiated the correspondence after she won a literary com-petition which he had also entered. They met when he came to Kansas from Tennessee to see her in the fall of 1892. They saw each other again at the Chicago World's Fair in 1893. Searcy appears to have been attracted to Miss Warthen precisely because of her ambition and her accomplishments. Warthen, never having rejected marriage as a pos-sibility for herself while keeping silent on the subject in public, un-doubtedly felt that Mr. Searcy was a man she could love and one who would be agreeable to a less conventional marriage than other men she had met (although in 1889—before they met—he had been opposed to woman suffrage). "Believing that with like tastes and hopes and am-bition[,] a married partnership was better than single blessedness," a friend recorded, they thought they would encourage each other as writ-ers—an important consideration, since Warthen apparently planned to return to her earliest ambition.[51]

Even with the future optimistically ahead of her, Kate Warthen Searcy found it difficult to leave some ambitions entirely behind: on her hon-eymoon trip to her new home in Tennessee she insisted on stopping in Topeka, where she took, and passed, the Kansas Supreme Court bar examination. She found it impossible to make the kind of marriage she wanted in Tennessee, however; she did not fit into her husband's family, which resented her for being an outlander and too independent, and the attempt she and Emmett made to publish a newspaper at Wartrace, Tennessee, failed. True to her significant formative experience in west-ern Kansas, Mrs. Searcy's solution to these problems was to move with her husband and daughter and homestead again in 1901, hopeful that it would prove easier to be a "new woman," married or single, in the West. The Searcys spent the rest of their lives in Oklahoma, the last territory in the continental United States to be opened for white settlement. She and her husband continued to write (though on a small scale), Kate in various periodicals, in the Elk City newspaper, and in the *Livestock Reporter*, for which she wrote a farm wife's advice column. Emmett Searcy was active in Republican county politics, but Kate Searcy was never politically active again, except to vote. She remained a suffragist, however, publishing a humorous poem, "Her New Vocation," about the extended activities of wives after the passage of the Fourteenth Amendment, and a short story, "The Voting of Mrs. Gray," loosely based on her Hamilton County experiences. Moreover, her feminism was evident in her daughter's upbringing: Lucile, who had been born in Tennessee in 1898, grew up "thinking women could do anything."[52] A high school and college English teacher, Lucile Searcy never married.

When reviewed as a whole, Kate Warthen's life indicates that her era's sharp intellectual/ideological distinctions between public and private domains, while they had to be dealt with, did not *necessarily* limit the action of all women at this time, at least not in singularly predictable ways. Certainly Warthen placed great importance upon the series of public roles she occupied, and these enhanced her status in the public world, her competence, and her self-esteem. Moreover, several of these roles, including those of homesteader, school superintendent, and, to a lesser extent, writer, were defined essentially as male activities, the superintendency in particular providing her with a good deal of formal authority. Additionally, in order to obtain that position, Warthen had to emerge as a specifically political figure, one who, drawing upon earlier training in debate and writing, developed the pragmatic skills necessary to deal with words, ideas, individuals, and parties in waging her campaign.

At the same time, however, Warthen could not, and did not want to, be totally dissociated from the private domain. Her family provided her with both positive and negative inducements toward living an unconventional life. While her occupation as teacher was closely associated with "womanly" tasks of nurturing and guiding the young, her political campaign was probably enhanced by the belief that she would be a good officeholder precisely because she would *not* be a "true" woman, that is, a married one. And though she saw her marriage as an extension rather than a refutation of the values and activities she had become committed to as she participated in public life, marriage did reduce the degree of control she had over her existence. Most important, though, Kate Warthen perceived the public and private domains as both ideally and actually interconnected; she made her life's choices on that assumption.

NOTES

1. Documents in the Warthen-Searcy Collection (hereafter refered to as W-SC), the Kansas Collection, Spencer Research Library, the University of Kansas, Lawrence. The Syracuse (Hamilton County) *Journal* of March 2, 1894, noted Warthen's passing the bar examination: "Miss Warthen is the first lady to see admission to the bar in Hamilton County, and the examination she passed is declared by all present to be the most thorough and entirely creditable of any applicant heretofore examined in this county. She deserves much credit for her proficiency as well as for her dilligence [*sic*] and application in acquiring this knowledge." The date on her certificate is March 3, 1894. The article on her wedding appeared in the Syracuse *Journal*, November 30, 1894. Kate Warthen married Emmett C. Searcy of Haley, Tennessee, on November 27, 1894.

2. "Educated Women as Wives," Syracuse *Democratic Principle*, July 24, 1890.

3. Sheryll Patterson-Black, "Women Homesteaders on the Great Plains Frontier," *Frontiers* 1, no. 2 (Spring 1976): 67–88. Patterson-Black states (p. 68) that the average figure for female homestead entrants increased to 11.9 percent in the early twentieth century. Hamilton County newspapers mention several female homesteaders during the period when Warthen worked her claim, the Syracuse *Sentinel* citing seven "lady claimants" from March to September 1887. Julie Roy Jeffrey, *Frontier Women: The Trans-Mississippi West, 1840–1880* (New York: Hill and Wang, 1979); see esp. p. xiii.

4. Syracuse *Journal*, November 30, 1894.

5. Rita Mae Kelly and Mary Boutilier, *The Making of Political Women: A Study of Socialization and Role Conflict* (Chicago: Nelson-Hall, 1978), pp. 42–43.

6. Ibid., pp. 193–94, 198.

7. Julie Roy Jeffrey, *Frontier Women*; Sheryll Patterson-Black, "Women Homesteaders."

8. The perception of Warthen as determined and independent, as well as the description of Warthen's mother, comes from interviews with Lucile Searcy, January 11 and 13, 1981 (hereafter referred to as LS interview).

9. Teaching contracts and account book, W-SC. The average income for a female teacher in Cherokee County in 1884 was $33.10 a month; for a male, $45.18 *(Fourth Biennial Report of the Kansas State Superintendent of Public Instruction, 1883–84* [Topeka: State of Kansas, 1884], p. 8).

10. Journal pages, February 21, 1886, W-SC.

11. Journal pages, February 17 and 21, 1886, W-SC.

12. Journal pages, February 21, 1886, W-SC; LS interview.

13. Journal pages, January–March 1886, W-SC. Lucile Searcy describes her uncles as "energetic and ambitious" and "intelligent and headstrong," as well (LS interview, January 13, 1981).

14. Journal pages, March 4, 1886, W-SC.

15. It is unclear exactly how much of the work Warthen did herself. Her daughter remembers being told that the Warthen boys "plowed fire lines for her every year" (LS interview, January 11, 1981), but Warthen's account book lists receipt of $100 in 1887 for "breaking sod for father." All the Warthens homesteaded in the same general area, but her parents' claim near Lakin was 40–50 miles from hers. One or more of her brothers filed on land nearer hers, but by 1891, the boys appear to be living near or with their parents in Kearny County (unpublished typescript of an eassy by Warthen about being lost on the prairie in the summer of 1891, W-SC). Lucile Searcy states that she believes her mother "wanted to show her brothers that women could do things—and she did them" (LS interview, January 13, 1981). Few male homesteaders, like Warthen after 1889, lived on and worked their claims full-time: it was apparently quite common and necessary for homesteaders in western Kansas to earn their livings by working in towns as far away as Denver (John C. and Winoma C. Jones, *The Prairie Pioneers of Western Kansas and Eastern Colorado* [Boulder: Jounson Publishing Co., 1956], passim). Warthen also wrote a story, the plot of which turned on this fact: "John Winlow's Travelled Shack," *The Youth's Companion*, March 25, 1897, pp. 135–36.

16. Teaching certificates, 1884–89, W-SC. She remained "Kate Warthen," except to her parents, who began their letters to her with "Dear Katie."

17. Claim papers and account book, W-SC. Her claim coordinates place it in Lamont Township in the southeastern part of the county. Her parents had settled near Lakin, now in Kearny County, east of Kendall. Warthen's claim was approximately 40–50 miles from Lakin, 25 from Syracuse, and 10 from Kendall (estimated on an 1880s map on the basis of one square mile per section of land; on a modern AAA road map, Lakin seems to be about 30 miles from the general area of Warthen's claim). Her arrival in Hamilton County is dated by the teaching certificate issued there April 30, 1887. To "break a claim" is a term for filing a claim on a piece of land; it also refers to the physical work involved in breaking up the sod in order to farm the prairie. To "prove up" a claim, a homesteader had to "stake" the land and file a claim for the specific

quarter section (166 acres) with the United States Land Office. The homesteader then had six months to take up residence and begin to farm the land. At the end of three years, s/he had to provide names of witnesses to her or his residency to prove the validity of the claim to the land (Jones and Jones, passim).

18. Teaching contract, March 1888, and account book, W-SC. The stories collected by Jones and Jones about the northwestern corner of the Kansas prairie (similar to the southwestern corner) emphasize both its dryness and its lack of amenities. Residents had to haul water from wells or springs miles away from their homesteads.

19. Account book and documents, W-SC.

20. Lucile Searcy states that her mother "liked the idea of homesteading, but she wanted to be an educator and a director" (LS interview); teaching contracts and account book, W-SC. The average salary of female teachers in Hamilton County in 1891 was $35.69; for men, $49.64 (figures for 1880–90 are unavailable—*Eighth Biennial Report of the Kansas State Superintendent of Public Instruction, 1891–92* [Topeka: State of Kansas, 1892], p. 14).

21. Account book and documents, W-SC.

22. Warthen taught the older children at the Kendall school, and much later she won *Woman's Work* magazine's "Child Culture" prize of $10 for an essay, "Give the Child a Fair Chance," the content of which seems to have been similar to that of the *Free Press* article (letter, W-SC). Although it was anonymous, most townspeople were probably aware that Warthen was its author (see note 23 for discussion of transparent pseudonyms). As principal of the school, Warthen no doubt perceived the editor's complaint as implying that the school was not doing its job, a challenge to which she ought to reply. She did that by laying most of the blame for the bad behavior on the boys' parents, who neither supervised their activities nor set good examples by observing the Sabbath.

23. Kendall *Boomer*, November 9, 1889; Coolidge *Citizen*, June 6, July 4 and 18, 1890. Both "Buckeye" and "En Verite" were transparent pseudonyms, since the authors of the pieces were easily identifiable by activities referred to elsewhere in the papers. Lucile Searcy does not remember her mother's mentioning Alice Fulton, so there are no further details about their relationship, which has been inferred from common interests and activities evident in the county newspapers.

24. Contract, documents, and campaign notes, W-SC. The editorial contract, dated April 2, 1890, stipulated that she would receive 10 percent of the first year's profits, 25 percent of the second year's, and 50 percent thereafter. In June 1890 (the first issue Warthen edited), the Burlingame *Echo* became the *National Echo*; they were evidently hoping to gain part of the readership of the *National Tribune*. Warthen's campaign notes were made in preparation for writing one or two articles solicited by the Detroit *Free-Press* in 1892. (The article, if written, seems

never to have been published.) Details of the campaign have been drawn from these notes and from reports in the Hamilton County newspapers.

25. Documents, W-SC.

26. Kelly and Boutilier, p. 77.

27. Labette County had female superintendents during 1872–78, 1883–88, and 1891–1900 (*Biennial Reports of the Kansas State Superintendent of Public Instruction* [Topeka: State of Kansas, 1872–1900]). Except for the 1879–80 biennium, the gaps in the sequence of female superintendents represent gaps in my information. The Syracuse *Journal* and the *Sentinel*, both issued April 8, 1887, note the election of five women to the town council (see Rosalind Urbach Moss, "The 'Girls' from Syracuse: Sex Role Negotiations of Kansas Women in Politics, 1887–1890," forthcoming in a volume tentatively titled *The Women's West* [University of Oklahoma Press, 1986]). The Kendall *Boomer*, February 2, 1889, reported the debate on women's rights. Warthen's election as principal seems ultimately to have depended upon her earning a first grade teaching certificate; the politicking would have been involved in getting herself considered as a serious candidate in the first place, when she had never taught in a town school. For Kansas women holding other political positions, see note 40 below.

28. Kelly and Boutilier, pp. 307 and 76, respectively.

29. Campaign notes, W-SC; Syracuse *Journal*, June 20, 1890; Syracuse *Democratic Principle*, June 19, 1890.

30. For discussions of the 1890 elections in Kansas, see Peter H. Argersinger, "Road to a Republican Waterloo: The Farmer's Alliance and the Election of 1890 in Kansas," *Kansas Historical Quarterly*, 33, no. 4(Winter 1967):443–69; Harold R. Smith, "Populist Study in Need of Revision: A Case Study of Kearny County, Kansas, in the Populist Era" (master's thesis, Fort Hayes State College, 1969), examines politics in the county adjacent to Hamilton County and explores how western Kansas differed from the rest of the state in the election of 1890.

31. Coolidge *Citizen*, August 29 and September 5, 1890; *Hamilton County Bulletin*, October 3, 21, 31, 1890. The *Bulletin*'s major assault came in its October 31 edition, issued shortly before the election.

32. Syracuse *Democratic Principle*, November 9, 1887. James C. Malin, in "Eugene Ware and Dr. Sanger: The Code of Political Ethics, 1872–1892," *Kansas Historical Quarterly* 26, no. 3(Autumn 1960):255–66, describes the history of a civil ritual developed in Ft. Scott, Kansas, to celebrate presidential election results while defusing the political ill-feeling produced during the campaign. Malin states that nineteenth-century American politics "were largely carried on under an unwritten code [where candidates were] expected to observe the rules of propriety. A man's political and private life [*sic*] might be quite separate, as was his professional career. . . . A violation of the code . . . resulted in a breach of friendship." Malin observed that the code was usually violated

by "amateurs" like farmers, prohibitionists, and women's rights advocates who entered politics to fight for a cause. The *Bulletin*'s editor seems to have been such an amateur. Kate Warthen, however, wanted to play the game by the code which "differentiated between things public [her competence] and things private [her being a woman]" (Malin, p. 264). See discussion of Warthen's essay "Women as Public Officers."

33. On May 29, 1890, the *Democratic Principle* gleefully noted the lively campaign shaping up between Democrats, two Republican factions, and the Farmers' Alliance; it gave no specifics, however. Even the *Journal* admitted on October 3 that "County politics are in a sort of Tom and Jerry condition," but it hoped things would clear up soon for "a harmonious Republican convention."

34. Kendall *Boomer*, March 9, 1889, referred to those then in ascendancy as evidence that civilization had not yet won out over the forces of disorder in Hamilton County.

35. William F. Chollar states that F. G. Rinehart was county superintendent in 1886 and that he was a member of the "Syracuse faction" ("A Pioneer History of Hamilton County, Kansas," M. A. thesis, University of Wichita, 1941, p. 73). Lizzie Culver was first elected in 1887 and was reelected in November 1888, after the county seat controversy had been settled. At that time, the Syracuse *Journal* identified her as a Syracuse ally (October 26, 1888). The characterization of the condition of the county seat records comes from the *Journal* of January 16, 1891: "Mrs. Price [née Lizzie Culver] had an onerous time during the greater portion of her incumbency, assuming the office . . . when school records, and school districts were jumbled up together in a most heterogeneous manner, and has yet come out with credit." This compliment, however, did not appear until after the close of the campaign in which she herself was an issue.

36. Postcard, W-SC. Parrott had been elected town treasurer in November 1889 (Kendall *Boomer*, November 9, 1889). In 1890 he did win nomination for and election to the office of probate judge. Kate Warthen took violin lessons from Parrott in March, April, and May 1890, paying $3.75 for fifteen lessons (account book, W-SC). Syracuse *Democratic Principle*, September 25, 1890; Coolidge *Citizen*, August 15, 1890; Syracuse *Journal*, August 15 and 22, 1890. The *Democratic Principle* was the first to announce her candidacy on July 31. Significantly, Warthen chose the opposition Syracuse paper in which to announce for the nomination in her own party, thus making certain she was perceived as a candidate not under anyone's control. The other papers announced her candidacy in mid-August.

37. Although she was out to win, Warthen was careful that her campaigning among the people was above reproach: her notes reveal that "Good old Mr. Crites came to me and advised me to have one of the boys go with me and not by any means to go alone." On October 31, 1890, the *Hamilton County Bulletin* reported that "Her brother is with her" on her "electioneering tour . . . to

interview our people." Parrott's second note to "Miss Kate Warthen" is dated September 10, 1890, at Kendall (W-SC).

38. In the Syracuse *Democratic Principle*, September 4, 1890, Weith announced he was not a candidate, perhaps in an attempt to stop a draft nomination. Weith's name was occasionally given as "C. C. White," but both names seem to refer to the same person. In a letter to the author, July 21, 1980, Lucile Searcy states that Weith "helped her [mother] get elected." The October 24, 1890, Syracuse *Journal* reported on the convention. As a Republican party leader, Weith may also have had something to do with getting Parrott to withdraw from the superintendent's race and run for probate judge.

39. The vote was reported in the Syracuse *Journal*, October 24, 1890. Susan B. Anthony and Ida Husted Harper, in *The History of Woman Suffrage* (New York: Susan B. Anthony, 1902), 4:641–45, show that Republican support did not help win suffrage for women. Julie Roy Jeffrey believes women did not receive legal or political concessions that it did not suit men to grant them (*Frontier Women*, pp. 190–95). Warthen's most enthusiastic press support came from the Coolidge paper, the *Hamilton County Bulletin*, which felt she was not pro-ring. In her campaign notes, she wrote that "it occurred to me the [people] might countenance a candidate outside the ring." Most papers mention that various towns and townships "got" a candidate.

40. "Women in Office," *Kansas Historical Collections* 12(1911–12):396. Three women were elected to office in as many counties in 1887–88, while 17 were elected in 16 counties from 1890–99, mostly as Registrars of Deeds. From 1887–89 in municipalities, where women could vote, 49 women were elected to office in 9 towns, serving chiefly as mayors and council members, while in the 1890s, 62 women were elected in 12 towns, but 8 of these women refused to serve. The introduction to this listing states that county school superintendents were not included because there were so many, and by 1911–12 "the work of the office [was] considered so specially adapted to women that in counties where there [had] been any recognition of them as officeholders women have at various times filled the position." In 1911 fifty women served as county superintendents (almost half the total), but in 1890 there had been only 24 and this dropped to 20 in 1894. There had been only 3 in 1872–73 and still only 6 eleven years later. It was the movement of women into office in the late 1880s that built the foundation for their being accepted as county superintendents. (Information on the date of women first being elected superintendents comes from William Leach, *True Love and Perfect Union: The Feminist Reform of Sex and Society* [New York: Basic Books, 1980], p. 174. The numbers of women holding this office were collated from *The Biennial Reports of the Kansas State Superintendent of Public Instruction* [Topeka: State of Kansas, 1872–73, 1883–84, 1893–94, 1911–12].) Monroe Billington, "Suzanna Madora Salter—First Woman Mayor," *Kansas Historical Quarterly* 21, no.3(Autumn 1954):173–83. The

following year, 1888, the eastern Kansas town of Oskaloosa elected both a female mayor and an all-woman town council. Editorial comment reprinted from the Kansas City *Star* in the *Democratic Principle*, May 8, 1890.

41. *Hamilton County Bulletin*, October 24, 1890 (the account describes the man who seconded Warthen's nomination as "los[ing] himself in the grandeur of his theme," while her campaign notes refer to him as a "Bachelor''); Syracuse *Democratic Principle*, October 16, 1890.

42. Campaign notes, W-SC; survey of the Syracuse *Journal*, *Sentinel*, and *Democratic Principle*, the Kendall *Boomer* and the Coolidge *Citizen* for 1887 and 1888. Although Lizzie Culver's father had been a county treasurer associated with the cattle interests of the western section of the county, her candidacy was virtually ignored (especially by the *Citizen*, her hometown paper). Immediately after the election, the *Journal* reported that Culver had hired a lawyer to sue a Methodist minister for slander (November 11, 1887). The basis of the suit was not stated, but since Culver was both Catholic and a woman, as well as the daughter of a cattleman, her campaign might have inspired some to be franker than was wise. Her 1888 election was better reported, and she increased her 1887 plurality of 9 votes to a majority of 102 votes, though all of the men elected in 1888 had larger majorities (Syracuse *Journal* 18, 1887, and November 9, 1888). Culver's marriage to H. C. Price was reported in the January 19, 1889, issue of the Kendall *Boomer*; data on her performance as superintendent comes from the *Ninth Biennial Report of the Kansas State Superintendent of Public Instruction* (Topeka: State of Kansas, 1890), table 9. (See also Moss, "The 'Girls' from Syracuse," for a more detailed discussion of these issues.) Characteristically, county newspapers never stated that Mrs. Culver's actions had created a major issue for the 1890 campaign (see note 35), but in a letter to the researcher dated July 2, 1980, Lucile Searcy stated the problem with Lizzie Price's pregnancy.

43. Syracuse *Democratic Principle*, July 31, 1890.

44. Warthen listed "unsociability" as one of the points against her in her campaign notes and then recorded two instances of handling the problem, the lesson of both being, " 'She seemed unsocial because we did not know her.' " Warthen was undoubtedly a prohibitionist and stayed away from dances and parties because of her fundamentalist religion; in a letter to the NTCC column, she advocated all sorts of sports for women but urged them to abstain from dancing and card playing (*National Tribune*, April 9, 1891, p. 11). But she did participate in some "literaries," as well as organizations of a not exclusively social nature.

45. Warthen's notes record that an "editor requested [an] article on 'Women in Office' " but give no further details. The motto "God helps those who help themselves" appears in both the article and the notes as a key phrase. This discussion of the campaign is based on details from this article and the notes (W-SC).

46. Cf. the essay in this collection by Carolyn De Swarte Gifford on the Home Protectionist movement of the WCTU. Another good description of women's domestic impulses leading them into public life in the nineteenth century is that by Julie Roy Jeffrey in *Frontier Women*, chapter 7, " 'Will She Not Overstep the Bounds of Propriety If She Ventures into the Arena of Action?' " The Home Protection movement brought many women to support suffrage who would have rejected the idea when presented on the basis of "natural" or human rights favored by feminists. In an 1891 debate in the NTCC column, Warthen asserted that "the sensible woman does not love home less, or make herself less loved therein by contact with the world"; she does not remain a "cringing wife" (*National Tribune*, December 17, 1891).

47. There is no concrete evidence that Warthen joined any feminist, suffragist, or prohibitionist organization (though she did join Christian Endeavor in 1892), but "Women as Public Officers" offers clear evidence that her attitudes were strongly feminist on anyone's terms in 1890 and that she was aware enough of WCTU Home Protectionist arguments to use one in an allusion to drunken politicians in the essay. The connection between the Syracuse ring and the liquor interests is more tenuous. According to much of the literature on frontier urban communities and Jeffrey's *Frontier Women*, control of western towns by merchants selling liquor and "amusements" was typical, as was the coalition between solid male citizens and women with a civilizing mission to defeat the corrupt forces (although Jeffrey notes that women and men had quite different visions of the ideal civilized state). The first clue that this was occurring in Hamilton County comes in 1887 when the Syracuse *Journal* began reporting, approvingly, the arrests and convictions of local "courtesans," while popular movements against the ring during Warthen's campaign may have been the political culmination of this movement against vice and corruption.

48. Warthen's official majority was 51 votes (*Journal*, November 14, 1890); the next largest was 37 votes for county clerk. The difference between Lizzie Culver's 1888 majority (102) and Warthen's indicates how much of a barrier had been raised against Warthen's candidacy, perhaps even more than the slim margins of the other candidates indicate a hotly contested political struggle. Another indicator of Warthen's struggle is the landslide victory of another woman in Finney County, on the east side of Kearny County, who was elected by 620 of 650 votes cast (Syracuse *Democratic Principle*, November 6, 1890).

49. Documents, W-SC. The phrase comes from an undated graduation address to a high school class in Hamilton County made while she was superintendent, probably in 1894. Warthen passed the state bar exam in Topeka on her way out of Kansas after her wedding (she is listed as "Kate Searcy" in the "Comprehensive Roster to July 1, 1935," *Reports of Cases Determined in the Supreme Court of the State of Kansas*, vol. 140 [Topeka: State of Kansas, 1935]). She was probably the first woman to be admitted to the state bar,

although because she did not remain in the state to practice law, this milestone has been assigned to Lilla Day Monroe, who passed her examination in 1895 (Stratton, p. 19).

50. Journal pages, March 3, 1886, W-SC. The lines are quite sketchy with alternative words and phrases; the first line has several possible verbs besides the original selected here: "shall," "could not," and "can not." Two of these have meanings which change the sense of the fragment but which lack supporting context. The rest of the fragment makes sense only with the positive verbs, "will" or "shall." The mature poem both provides a context for its negative verbs and puts the "romantic exchange" between lovers in its place, something the younger poet had not been able to do, having been carried away with the romance of the exchange. The more complete poem was published in *Songs of Hoosier Singers* (Martinsville, Ind.: G. E. Finney, 1898), unpaged. Lucile Searcy remembers that her mother had photographs of several Hamilton County suitors, one a smiling man holding a mandolin and another a sober banker from Syracuse (LS interview, January 11, 1980).

51. Emmett Searcy, "What a Tennessee C.C. Saw," *National Tribune*, December 1, 1892, p. 11, and "Attention C.C. Girls!" *National Tribune*, September 19, 1889, p. 7; John O. King, "A Brotherly Tribute," *National Tribune*, December 27, 1894, p. 7.

52. Lucile Searcy reports that her mother "insisted on stopping over in . . . Topeka" to take the examination (LS letter to researcher, July 2, 1980). She also states that her mother's "marriage was a great disappointment" to her because she had "very unrealistic . . . expectations" about the type of life her husband led: he lived on a farm in the hills of central Tennessee, not on an "Old South" plantation replete with servants. Her in-laws' intolerance of her is also evident in their calling her Emmett's red-headed " 'she.' " She felt she "had worked away from the farm [and she] anticipated a life of literature," but "she got there [Tennessee] and found it was another life of struggle" (LS interview, January 13, 1980). In Tennessee Kate Searcy taught for a year, rooming in town during the week and going home on weekends. For a while she and her husband published a newspaper in Wartrace, Tennessee (LS interview, January 13, 1981, and letter to researcher, July 2, 1980). By 1900, however, she was looking for a new home in the West at the Salvation Army colony at Fort Amity, Colorado. About that time she and her family moved first to Canadian, Texas, where her husband had friends, and finally settled in Elk City, Oklahoma Territory, about 1902, where Lucile, her only child, grew up (documents in W-SC and LS letter to researcher, July 2, 1980). Here Kate Searcy took up her writing and publishing activities. Emmett Searcy published occasional pieces and columns in the Elk City paper also, though he earned his living as a buyer for a dry goods store. The final quotation in the paragraph comes from an interview with Lucile Searcy in Norman, Oklahoma, January 13, 1981.

7

Civilizing Kansas: Women's Organizations, 1880–1921

JUNE O. UNDERWOOD

Two images dominate our vision of women on the Great Plains and in early Kansas. One is of the pioneer mother, devastated by the difficulties of her life and driven mad by the wind.[1] The other is of the civilizing woman, Carrie Nation wielding her ax against Demon Rum. It is to the latter image, and its connections with real life, that this essay addresses itself.

Civilizing is a term with strong connotations in American culture. American literature is full of males who "light out for the territory" to escape civilizing females. Once the pioneer woman was past the difficulties of settlement, so popular notions go, she proceeded to civilize, laying down her rifle and picking up her hatchet, forcing her adolescent children into church and tight shoes, and driving golden-hearted whores and fun-loving saloon keepers out of town. Even historians have difficulty defining nineteenth-century women's civilizing mission. When historians describe women as civilizers, they talk pri-

A slightly different version of this essay was published in *Kansas History*, vol. 7, no. 4 (Winter 1984–85), pp. 291–306.

marily about the home—bringing lace tablecloths and dinnertime manners to family life. However, the civilizing with which I am concerned is a far tougher and more collective activity than espousing domestic amenities. It is influencing society and government to diminish human suffering. Women's organizations in frontier and postfrontier Kansas worked continuously over many years to create structures that would prevent poverty, misery, and disease. This essay will explore the range of civic and social activities of Kansas women's organizations, emphasizing their incursion into and impact upon public and political spheres.[2]

Julie Roy Jeffrey, in *Frontier Women*, asks the question: "If the move to the frontier meant the abandonment of civilization by frontiersmen, what did it mean for their wives and daughters, who presumably thought themselves responsible for civilizing the wilderness?"[3]

For women, the move to the frontier would have meant taking west the nurturing and home responsibilities into which they had been socialized. As innumerable historians have documented, the rise of industrialism in the East had separated "home" from work. Women's duties, practically and ideologically, involved harmonizing human environments and relationships and caring for the welfare of others. Politically as well as economically restricted to the domestic sphere, middle-class women focused on religion and nurture, ignoring economics and politics. As Barbara Berg shows, almost at the instant of this enclosure within the domestic, however, women found ways of breaking out of its restrictions. When they broke loose they did so almost entirely in terms of the domestic ideologies: teaching children, being responsible for social welfare, taking on "municipal" housecleaning. Women bonded together in their domestic enclosures and, because of that sisterhood, were able to extend their extradomestic power. The period in America from about 1800 to 1850, before Kansas attained statehood, was the period in which successive stages in the domestic ideology, including women's relegation to the private sphere, their banding together as a separate community, and their responsibilities for public welfare, were formulated.[4]

Thus, when women came to Kansas after 1850, they brought not only the baggage of human concerns but years of working together, separate from the male populace, to achieve social good. Abolitionists had found in women a source of great power; later the sanitary commissions of the Civil War were staffed by women. Thus, once the initial settlement of the frontier was completed, women were ready to go on with their public welfare and reform activities—their civilizing. As Jeffrey puts it, "As the period of isolation came to an end, women's social contacts multiplied. The organization of churches, schools, and voluntary associations, the development of rural towns and cities, gave women a new and more public forum for their activities and opened another phase of female experience on the frontier. With growth came the opportunity to carry out the civilizing mission implicit in the concept of domesticity."[5]

Kansas is an excellent place to explore the activities of organized women because of its settlement patterns, the availability of its historical materials, and its relationship to national problems. The settlement of Kansas went on from before the Civil War through the turn of the century. Thus it is possible to trace stages in organizational development and relate them to the maturity of the society. Because of the lateness of its settlement and the pride Kansas has had in its history, both verbal and pictorial materials are readily available. And finally, Kansas was a place of political experimentation, seen nationally as embodying possibilities for a new society. The Kansas-Nebraska Act made Kansas a stage for tests of slavery sentiments prior to the Civil War. The first suffrage campaign in the nation (1867) took place in Kansas. Populists, prohibitionists, and progressives all found positions of great power within the state. Thus social questions and reform campaigns were part of the milieu of Kansas. However, the state, parts of which were frontier until 1910, did not become urbanized and has never, except for some geographical pockets, attracted large industries. Because of these conditions, in Kansas one can investigate reform in a nonurban, nonindustrialized state. Available studies of women's organizations and reform activities usually focus on urbanization as the catalyst for such activities. Yet Kansas, without an urban crisis, was in the forefront of reforms hitherto seen as urban.

It is important to note, however, that in examining the activities of Kansas women's organizations, I do not claim them as radical or unique. The reforms the women advocated were reforms, not revolutions. The radical ideas which would have coexisted with their reform sentiments would have acted as stimulants to thinking but did not affect their collective actions. The rapid organization and functioning of the women's groups in Kansas was undoubtedly due to the pervasive nature and functioning of such groups back east. By 1850 newspapers and magazines were readily available throughout the nation, and by 1870 the railroads had begun building their Kansas networks. Kansas was linked in communications, economics, and ideology to the rest of the country, and its women shared that linkage. Women's work in the abolition movement, the sanitary commissions of the Civil War, the temperance campaigns, and the veterans' relief auxiliaries were part of frontier women's heritage. Thus, the women of Kansas, like its men, would have taken on the nation's most modern ideas and concerns.

The importance of women's combining for social welfare and self-improvement has been recognized by historians of women's history. Mary P. Ryan, for example, in *Womanhood in America* has this to say about the growth and development of women's organizations nationally:

By the turn of the 19th century women's clubs were not only investigating social conditions, but conducting social reforms—forming corporations to build sanitary housing in the slums, reconstructing the judicial system for juvenile offenders, and endorsing factory and child labor legislation. The Women's Trade Union League founded in 1903 devoted less and less time to bringing middle-class culture to working girls and became deeply embroiled in union activities and strikes. Meanwhile traditional women's groups had become careless of their ladylike ways. As early as the 1870's, the Women's Christian Temperance Union resorted to the vulgar antics of Carrie Nation entering saloons and destroying the tavern keeper's property. By the turn of the century, the WCTU had become a broad social service organization, embracing labor legislation and suffrage and prone to debate such questions as "is housework compatible with the higher life?"[6]

Here Ryan discusses two of the three major national organizations, the Women's Christian Temperance Union (WCTU) and the General Federation of Women's Clubs; later in her book she devotes a great deal of time to the third—the Equal Suffrage Associations. All were involved in reform. Beginning in the 1870s and continuing until her death in 1899, Frances Willard led the WCTU into heavy suffrage activity and social reform. The General Federation (to whose members the disparaging phrase "woman's clubber" was applied) was put on its mettle in its 1904 biennial convention, when the social reform position was so brilliantly argued by Sarah Platt Decker that the convention made her president. In her first speech, she directly addressed the issue of social activity. "Ladies," she said, "You have chosen me your leader. Well, I have an important piece of news to give you. Dante is dead. He has been dead for several centuries, and I think it is time that we dropped the study of his Inferno and turned our attention to our own."[7]

These powerful organizations, along with others allied to them like the settlement houses, the trade union league movements and the consumer's leagues, were instrumental in changing America's concern for its peoples. And in Kansas they arose almost simultaneously with the national groups.

Kansas settlers came primarily from the Midwest—Ohio, Illinois, and Indiana—and because of the national communications network that was building as the state settled, the women were thoroughly in touch with the ideologies of woman's sphere and the organized activities of that sphere. For example, the Friends in Council, a Lawrence study club, evolved from a similar group in Quincy, Illinois, and corresponded regularly with the mother club.[8] By 1890 study clubs were so prevalent in Kansas that when the New England Women's Clubs and the New York Sorosis joined together to issue a call for a convention and general federation, two delegates from Kansas were present.[9]

Kansas women also joined many other clubs, of which the Woman's Relief Corps (WRC), a national charitable and patriotic group, was perhaps the most important. Because of the influx of Civil War veterans seeking free land in Kansas, the WRC (allied to but not an auxiliary of the male GAR) was quite powerful. Agnes D. Hayes quotes from the WCTU state newspaper, *Our Messenger*, about an 1886 camp meeting:

On the right of the platform was a tent with 'WCTU Hdqrs.' in large letters on the side, and a little further off was another tent marked, 'WRC Hdqrs.', for the three great women's societies, the Equal Suffrage Association, the Woman's Relief Corps, and the Woman's Christian Temperance Union were united in carrying on this camp meeting and worked harmoniously together, each endorsing the others and mutually aiding one another.[10]

The Kansas WRC fought against restricting membership to immediate female relatives of veterans, and in opening its doors to "all loyal women" gained a larger membership as well as a larger possibility for action. Rather than restricting themselves to social and patriotic functions, they became important agents for charity and social change.

Other national clubs of local prominence were the American Association of University Women (the AAUW, originally the Association of Collegiate Alumnae), which organized in Lawrence in 1906 and became part of the national AAUW in 1921; the National Association of Colored Women, which originated in Kansas as the Kansas Association of Colored Women and Girls; the Parent-Teachers Association (PTA), originally the Mothers' Congress and the Teachers' Association; Altrusa, a service club; the PEO, an adult sorority interested in education; the League of Women Voters; the Daughters of the American Revolution (DAR); the Business and Professional Women's Club (BPW); and innumerable others. The rural women, although less heavily organized, nevertheless had rural clubs modeled after the town groups. More serious work, for them, was done as part of the Granges and, later, the Farm Bureau's Home Demonstration Units. The Grange was a particularly egalitarian organization, having a specific executive position in each chapter designated for a woman. The Grange, from its formation, endorsed female suffrage, and women frequently held leadership posts in the organization outside of those set aside for them.

The patterns of growth found among the women's clubs in Kansas were indicative of how important they were in women's lives. The clubs organized as rapidly as women settlers were available to begin them. Rather than creeping westward from the older, more established towns in eastern Kansas, women's organizations were likely to spring up in the newest frontier settlements. Wichita and Dodge City had ladies' benevolent societies (charitable organizations) within a year after those cities were founded. The PEO was first organized in Meade, Kansas, in 1888, when Meade was only three years old. From Meade (southwestern Kansas) it spread east and north, first to LaCrosse, then Lyons, then Hutchinson, Seneca, and finally to the pre–Civil War town of Council Grove.[11]

Experience, interest, and public approbation, as well as proximity to similar organizations, seemed to trigger organizing. The WCTU first organized in Bismarck Grove near the twenty-year-old settlement of Lawrence in 1879, and in its first year the chapters contributing to its treasury were nearby—Osage City, Burlingame, Leavenworth, Topeka, and Lawrence. By the second year, however, sixteen clubs, widely scattered throughout the state, were contributing members. Among these were Sabetha, in northeastern Kansas; Parsons in the southeast; Sterling in central Kansas; Wetmore, north and east of Manhattan; Enterprise, west and south of Manhattan; and Emporia, in the east central part of the state. There is no early record of the WCTU in the northwestern part of the state, although in 1880 Hoxie, Kansas (Sheridan County), had a temperance hall made of sod. The WCTU did not organize there until 1898.[12] Temperance was a long-standing ideology of Kansans, so the WCTU found an immediately receptive public. In Dodge City, however, the town businessmen apparently managed to prevent the WCTU from organizing until 1886, after Dodge had passed its peak as a cattle-drive center.[13] Thus, while the WCTU was generally a great success, there were areas where it was prevented from organizing by the liquor and business interests.

Women organized in large numbers, and their organizations spread rapidly. The WCTU organized statewide in 1879, the WRC in 1882, the Kansas Equal Suffrage Association (KESA) in 1884, and the PEO in 1888. The Young Women's Christian Association, in conjunction with the YMCA, appeared in the normal schools and colleges by the 1880s. The leadership of these groups, like their founding, was not restricted to the mature eastern settlements of the state. The WRC met in Fort Scott in 1885, in Wichita in 1886, in Abilene in 1887, in Winfield in 1888, and in Emporia in 1889.[14] Of these, only Fort Scott and Emporia existed before the Civil War. Even the women's study clubs and literary clubs, which were more likely to follow settlement patterns, were scattered throughout the state by 1893, the year of state federation. Moreover, because of the loosely affiliated nature of the State Federation of Women's Clubs, it included powerful older groups like the Kansas State Social Science Club, founded in 1881, and the Kansas Women's Press Association.[15] These professionally oriented groups, because they were already well organized, were able to aid the federation in systematizing its communications and beginning its work immediately.

To summarize, the patterns of origination of women's clubs indicate that personal contact and experience, public approbation, and concern for shared problems account for their establishment and growth. The rapidity with which statewide federations became established was due to the lively and powerful smaller groups already existing. Years of domestic and intracity work, both political and social, gave women a base from which to move.

The ways clubs organized statewide make an important commentary on how their members thought the clubs would function. The WCTU, for example, organized around already established state political districts. Today this seems natural enough, but, in fact, such districting was a radical departure from the concept of women operating in a private sphere. For instance, women's church groups and benevolent societies were either oriented toward a single city or directly accountable to the hierarchy of the diocese or state charity director. However, the WCTU immediately went public and political. It may have learned its tactics from abolitionist or suffrage groups farther east; if so, the tactics would indicate the seriousness of the women's intentions.[16] Moreover, the Kansas Equal Suffrage Association, the Women's Relief Corps, and finally the Kansas Federation of Women's Clubs organized themselves likewise. The organization of the last is telling, since the literary clubs originally had as part of their national charter a clause pledging themselves to self-improvement but not political action.[17] Once having taken political districts for their own endeavors, however, even these fairly elitist study clubs were poised for political action, ready to take on those reforms which they could not resist.

Before the public reform activities of the women's clubs are described, their benefits to individuals need discussing. While these personal benefits are difficult to document from the social and public materials used in this study, it is possible to speculate on them. Perhaps the single most important personal aspect of these organizations was that they affirmed the women's sense of the validity and importance of their own values. This was particularly necessary in the raw frontier environment in which these women found themselves. Bonding among women, so important in eastern women's existence, did not seem to break down in the remote villages of Kansas. In fact, the general sense of isolation may have speeded the process of organization. Moreover, because women's days were relatively undifferentiated in the task-oriented, on-call domestic existence they led, the weekly meetings would have served as markers in their lives and given them something to look forward to. Within the groups they would have found support and relief from family tensions. The WCTU and suffrage organizations, for example, held closed, women-only meetings. Mary Austin, in her autobiography *Earth Horizon*, describes these meetings as resembling consciousness-raising sessions, in which revolutionary ideas about women's rights to refuse sexual intercourse with alcoholic husbands were raised. The right of refusal was questioned only in terms of fears about genetic damage to unborn children, but that it was raised at all gives an indication of the power and concerns of the organizations.[18]

Besides giving women personal support, the women's organizations would have served as educational institutions. Women gained valuable knowledge from the groups about how to cope with their domestic careers. In addition to the usual chores of the nineteenth-century wife and mother, women moving into raw frontier villages would have needed to find clean water and nutritious foodstuffs and to discover how to market, to nurse unfamiliar illnesses, and to make goods that would have been store-bought farther east. In particular, women would have used the organizations to gain basic medical advice in areas like child-birth. This basic education for survival would have been informally worked into club agendas and intertwined with education about civic affairs.

The public affairs interests of the women's groups were never as narrow as their names might suggest. The WCTU, for example, took on women's suffrage, charitable work, public education, relief for prostitutes, church organization, parliamentary procedure (important preparation for public visibility), and many other activities. The WRC, the DAR, and the PEO were involved in a myriad of charitable, patriotic, educational, and political activities. In the 1880s, to belong to the Order of the Eastern Star (the women's affiliate of the Masons) was to discuss suffrage.[19] And the issue of suffrage was intimately tied to what women's social responsibilities were, what evils in the streets needed cleaning up. Within the study clubs not only literature, history, philosophy but also current events and theories of philanthropy were discussed. Regardless of specific club ideology, women were being trained in gathering information and in discussing its nuances and ramifications for political action.

The discipline involved in setting up constitutions and bylaws, in holding elections of officers, and in carrying out responsibilities as secretaries, auditors, treasurers, and speakers of their clubs would have given women self-confidence and an understanding of their own capabilities in activities that closely resembled those of the male public sphere. The study of parliamentary laws, the recounting of current events, and the discussion of political and elective strategies would have contributed to women's understanding of public affairs. The city, county, district, and state federations of the clubs, with their complications of conferences, politics, and civic actions, initiated women into the processes of the public sphere. Thus the women's organizations served individual women as support and educational institutions and prepared them for their place in the public arena.[20]

While clubs served women in these personal ways, they were also important to society. The single most ubiquitous public work the women did was charitable, a tradition going back to the all-female, often church-related benevolent and missionary societies at the beginning of the nineteenth-century.[21] Almost all the Kansas women's clubs I have studied, whether social, political, or educational, provided money, food, and clothing for the elderly, weak, and indigent. Only the Equal Suffrage Association may have exempted itself from this function.[22] While most of the groups were not exclusively charity organizations (and were supplemented by minimal state charity, benevolent aid societies, and related church groups), the aid the women's clubs provided was pervasive. It varied from serving as a well-organized, easily mobilized source of relief during large-scale disasters to providing individual aid to elderly and indigent persons. The ubiquitous presence of the women's groups made them readily available, and their tightly structured districting allowed them to function rapidly. This charitable work, however patchy, was essential in an era when government was organized for law and order and the protection of private property. The predominant laissez-faire concepts of economic and government relationships insisted that welfare interfered with the "proper" functioning of private enterprise, and thus, with few or no government welfare operations, human aid had to fall to the private sphere. Women's organizations constituted the most important part of that sphere.[23]

Though relief work was often directed at aging or suffering members of the immediate organization, it also went beyond helping cases known personally to club members. The Friends in Council, an elite study club in Lawrence, provided intermittent sums of money to various needy individuals and organizations from 1875 on and by 1897 was donating a set sum annually to the Associated Charities of Lawrence. The Junction City Women's Club worked to aid the victims of the grasshopper invasion of 1874. The 1897 Federation of Women's Clubs was responsible for benevolence and relief work in Shawnee County. In 1910, the Garden City PEO had a "welfare and trust fund," as well as a local education and Christmas benevolence fund. In Emporia, the Social Service Club and the Emporia Welfare Association, two extremely exclusive groups, met in hats and gloves and sewed layettes for expectant mothers, distributed food and clothing, and investigated potential recipients of charity to judge their worthiness. The DAR, the WRC, and the WCTU all defined charity as part of their regular business.[24]

The women who did this work, however, were quite aware of controversies over the motives for and the adequacy of private charity. Mother Bickerdyke, famous for her work with veterans and Kansas immigrants, continually prodded the WRC to systematize and destigmatize its benevolent activities. The Friends in Council in the 1890s studied contemporary scientific theories about poverty and relief work and declared that "the poor shall be helped to help themselves" and that the "people shall work not *for* but with them." These were relatively avant-garde concepts. By 1902 the club was studying Jane Addams's *Democracy and Social Ethics*, especially the chapters "Charitable Effort," "Household Adjustment," and "Industrial Amelioration." Their study had some effect on their own relief efforts but was more important in training individual members of the club, such as Genevieve Howland Chalkley, in sociological approaches to charity. Mrs. Chalkley became important to industrial reform and legislation in Kansas in the teens.[25]

The women's study of social theory preceded their involvement in public forums on poverty and crime. By 1909, however, at the Kansas Conference of Charities and Corrections, one afternoon was given to the Kansas Federation of Women's Clubs and the WCTU, which presented papers entitled "Temperance versus Dependency," "Degradation and Crime," and "Public Playgrounds." This professional activity was supplemented by attempts to provide structures and institutions that would enable the poor to become self-sufficient. In 1907 the WCTU sent missionaries to the immigrants of Crawford and Cherokee counties to teach the miners' wives to use sewing machines and to speak English. In 1919 the YWCA in Emporia set up canning and sewing lessons. In 1913 the Hutchinson Women's City Club not only started a rest room (lounge) for country women but also began a highly successful day nursery for working mothers.[26]

By 1909 *The Club Member*'s editor, Elizabeth Barr, was lecturing to a diverse audience on the institutional causes of poverty and crime:

The long and short of it is, the slums are a part of our economic system. It pays to herd people into close, filthy quarters and house them in such a manner as would be against the law if they were cattle. It does not pay society but it pays the landlord and our economic system was not made for society as a whole but for the large property owner.

She went on to say that "disease also is a product of the economic system," and "the prostitute is a product of the keen and losing struggle for bread."[27] *The Club Member* devoted regular columns to the patriotic work of the DAR and WRC, yet the editor saw no contradiction between these activities and her editorializing.

Another extension of relief work involved establishing homes for the indigent or helpless and persuading the state to take over these endeavors. Sometimes individuals are credited with such work: Mrs. C. B. Cushing in 1869 founded a Home for Friendless Women, a place for women and children who had been abandoned by the servicemen at Fort Leavenworth. She got the state to fund and maintain the building and, in 1881, she founded the Kansas and Missouri Social Science Association, a group of educated women concerned with social problems of the sort she had attacked.[28] Fanny Rastall persuaded the WCTU to organize the Girls' Industrial School at Beloit in 1886; this home for adolescent girls became a favorite charity for clubs throughout the state.[29] Other homes established by clubs included the Kansas City Protective Home for Colored Aged and Orphans, Rescue Homes (for reformed prostitutes) in Wichita and Kansas City, and the Carrie A. Nation Home for Indigent Older Women. The WRC funded the Mother Bickerdyke Home at Ellsworth for the wives, mothers, and sisters of Civil War veterans for four years before it became annexed to the State Soldier's Home. It also aided the Fort Dodge Home, the Military Home at Leavenworth, and the Orphans' Home at Atchison. The PEO, the Order of the Eastern Star, and other groups provided homes for the aged and indigent among their membership.[30] This is but a partial listing of charitable institutions founded and funded by women's clubs.

The work of more loosely organized federated clubs was generally to furnish and give aid to already established institutions, for which they provided money, clothing, coal, food, furnishings, books, and so forth. More important, they lobbied the state to take over the funding and maintenance of these institutions. However, even after the state absorbed such facilities, women's clubs remained active and interested. In the late 1890s the Friends in Council and the Hutchinson women's clubs put money and effort into establishing a library for the Hutchinson reformatory. The Topeka Federation of Women's Clubs collected sewing materials so the girls at the Industrial School (by that time a state institution) could make money. In 1906, each member of the Good Government Club sent a book to the Industrial School, and in 1920 the club investigated the Crittenden Home and its needs. The Good Citizenship League in Emporia, another affiliate of the Suffrage Association, in 1914 investigated detention homes and other state institutions. And the PEO furnished a room in the Wichita Children's Home in 1910 and a room in the Christian Service League in 1921. This is a small sample of what the clubs did for the charitable homes that had already been established and funded by the state.[31]

However, the work of investigating, reporting, petitioning, lobbying, and voting for better conditions within established institutions had longer-lasting effects and got at more fundamental issues than the club charities. The Emporia Women's Club in 1912 investigated conditions at the county home (the poor farm) and as a result of its investigations petitioned for a new one. In 1919 its members again investigated and publicized the conditions they found there.[32] In 1903 Alice Haldeman, in conjunction with the State Federation's work with the Girls' Industrial School, wrote to Mrs. W A. Johnston in despair over ''those dreadful dormitories'' at the school.[33] The Women's clubs lobbied the state government to provide single rooms for the girls, knowing that self-esteem and dignity were important for rehabilitation. Mrs. Johnston, while president of the KESA in 1912–13, was appointed an inspector of the state charitable and correction homes and, along with Genevieve Chalkley, made official reports to the governor. In 1907 the State Federation investigated civil service reform in charitable institutions. The Friends in Council urged the City Federation to take up the question of establishing a hospital in Lawrence. The Good Government Club worked for the state tuberculosis hospital and established an employment agency for women in Topeka. The Council of Women, a group made up of the presidents and vice-presidents of the statewide women's organizations in Kansas, lobbied for five years for industrial farm reformatories and for dormitories for women at the colleges.[34] The process of working in and for these institutions made Kansas women aware of conditions that led to poverty, disease, and disorder and gave them valuable information about government procedures.

The women's clubs took up local civic work as part of their municipal housekeeping responsibilities. They lobbied for street paving, sidewalks, and parks and playgrounds, and they established lounges for women coming to town from the country.[35] An adjunct of the library establishment movement was the highly successful "traveling libraries." Initially funded and staffed by women's clubs, the traveling libraries consisted of trunks of books that could be sent to any church, school, or club requesting them, which would receive fifty books for six months. By 1899 the state legislature passed a bill for a Traveling Library Commission, and the women's work was reduced to the promotion and extension of services.[36]

Public education had been one of women's concerns since Catherine Beecher had made her plea for women to become schoolteachers in the 1840s. In Kansas the constitution allowed women to vote for school boards from statehood on; thus schools were natural places for the clubs to focus their attention. The WCTU led the way by inserting scientific temperance instruction into high school and normal school curricula. The temperance instruction was not merely propagandistic; it had the students performing chemical experiments on alcohol in order to describe its physical properties, and it used many modern "hands-on" techniques to give students science lessons. The study clubs took up other specific educational causes. They read papers on educational theory and learned about the kindergarten movement, about diseases spread by the common drinking cup, and about inequities in female teachers' salaries. In 1894, after arguments over involving themselves in practical work, the Friends in Council undertook on-site investigations of the Lawrence high school. They looked at heating, ventilation, teaching methods, and deportment. In the end the club called for female school board members, made specific recommendations to the school board, appointed a committee to see that its recommendations were implemented, and returned to its studies of Chaucer. Many other clubs, in a tradition that continues today, provided scholarships for women in high school, normal school, and college and pushed for practical courses of study in an era of classical training. PTAs called for playgrounds and school nurses. In 1914, the Leavenworth Civic League established a high school for boy and girl wage earners.[37]

Another aspect of civic improvement was the clubs' concern for pure food and water and municipal sanitation. The WCTU made pure water an important part of its campaign against liquor, for obvious reasons. The Friends in Council studied sanitation, reservoirs, pure food bills, meat inspection, communicable diseases, and so on. These studies were generally not attached to specific recommendations for action, but they prepared the way for reformers. By 1908, Dr. Samuel J. Crumbine, the first Kansas public health official, could say, "Many of the reform movements, both political and sociological, have had their birth in Kansas. . . . [Danger to the public] has been lightened and the future results are much more hopeful, because of the hearty cooperation and support of the club women."[38] In 1909 the Kansas City Council of Women took up the campaign for public health. They protested against rubbish in the streets and called for a better garbage collection system. They looked into the process of food labeling and discussed the adulteration of whiskey. They called for letters and telegraphs to be sent to endorse the Roosevelt-Bonaparte-Wiley whiskey legislation.[39] Through their emphasis on public health, women became aware of the concerted efforts needed to make an impact upon government structures. They learned how to exert pressure against a slow-moving, reluctant governmental structure, and each campaign in which they were involved gave them experience for the next reform.

The next phase of reform work was legislative—lobbying for child labor laws, pushing for hour and wage legislation, insisting upon thorough enforcement of liquor laws, and fighting for women's suffrage. In some of these reforms, the women were heavily influenced by the social theory and activities of urban areas. Settlement house work, with its emphasis on social reform going beyond Band-Aid relief, was watched closely by Kansas women. College women from Kansas gained firsthand experience in settlement houses, and Jane Addams's books were studied in the literary clubs. Because Addams had a sister in Girard, Kansas, she had frequent speaking engagements in the state. In fact she was one of the few outside campaigners in the 1912 suffrage referendum campaign.[40] Margaret Dreier Robins affiliated with the Kansas division of the AFL and twice spoke to the federation of trade unions on suffrage and wage and hour laws.[41] The concept of the Consumers' League was debated in study clubs and gained credence because the club women knew it was a powerful force for reform.[42] The presence in the state of radical newspapers, and of the Grange organizations and farmers' alliances, made Kansas a place where reforms seemed feasible.

Prohibition was law in Kansas before the Kansas women were highly organized. However, enforcement of prohibition was their ongoing concern. When in 1901 Carrie Nation took her ax to saloons, she was seen by her fellow reformers as an anachronism, doing what Lawrence women had done fully fifty years before. The organized women felt that the destruction of individual saloons was less effective than consistent law enforcement. Municipal suffrage was gained in Kansas precisely because women felt they needed control over liquor; in 1887 the WCTU, with its political structure, joined the KESA to win the city vote for women. The antiliquor reform forces, with their understanding of the misery of women dominated by alcoholic husbands, their fears of teenage drinking, and their comprehension of the inadequate safeguards of women's rights, tied their reforms to women's suffrage.

Kansas had always been a leader in the campaign for women's rights. Carina Howard Nichols lobbied the 1859 Wyandotte Constitutional Convention for women's suffrage, and though she lost that battle she gained women the unprecedented right to acquire and possess property and to retain equal custody of their children. The first state referendum for women's suffrage in the United States was held in Kansas in 1867, and although it did not succeed, the battle went on. In 1894 another statewide referendum was held; attempts to bring the issue to a referendum were made again in 1904 and almost every year thereafter until 1912, when pressure from all the organized women's groups caused the amendment to be passed.[43]

The large number of women involved in a variety of organizations enabled the reform-minded to influence and mobilize their clubs. An example is Mrs. S. A. Thurston, the WCTU member who convinced the state to take responsibility for the Beloit Industrial School in 1888 and who was the treasurer of the Kansas Equal Suffrage Association in 1912.[44] F. G. Adams wrote to Susan B. Anthony (November 25, 1885) about the joint efforts of club women for suffrage:

Among the influences tending to increase the suffrage sentiment in Kansas may be mentioned those growing out of the active part women are taking in the discussion of political, economical, moral, and social questions, through their participation in the proceedings of the Woman's Christian Temperance Union, the State Temperance Union, the woman's Social Science Association, the Kansas Academy of Science, the Grange, the State and local Teacher's associations, and many other organizations, and in the part they take in discussion, they show their capacity to grapple with the political, social, and scientific problems of the day, in such a manner as to demonstrate their ability to perform the highest duties of citizenship.[45]

Other women used their membership in organizations to reinforce their suffrage sentiments. During the 1912 suffrage referendum, Mary

Haines wrote to Mrs. Johnston that she had both WCTU stationery and Kansas Equal Suffrage stationery on hand and used them according to which would have greater power to persuade people to her cause. Margaret Hill McCarter, a prominent member of the General Federation of Women's Clubs and a popular novelist, continually called for suffrage for women, as did Lilla Day Monroe and Elizabeth Barr. All three edited *The Club Member* in the years immediately preceding 1912. Mrs. Monroe appeared before the State Federation of Labor to call for suffrage in 1908 and every year thereafter until state suffrage passed in 1912.

The variety of organizations to which the suffrage women belonged was impressive. Mrs. Johnston, for example, was president of the 1912 KESA, a temperance worker (although apparently not affiliated with the WCTU), a prime mover in the Traveling Libraries Movement, a member of the Atlantean Club in Minneapolis, Kansas, a member of the Good Government Club in Topeka, a national official in the General Federation, the president of the Kansas Social Science Club, a member of the Westside Forestry club, and a founder of the women's Kansas Day Club. She was not extraordinary in the diversity of her memberships, only more fully recorded.[46]

That these women were interested in larger legislative issues leading to social reform can easily be documented. Lilla Day Monroe called for endorsement of suffrage by the State Federation of Labor unions through the following resolution:

Whereas, there are over 5 million women employed in the industries of our country, assuming the same risks and responsibilities as men; and whereas the employing class use all their political power to defeat any legislation intending to improve the conditions of the women and girls toiling in factories, mills, and sweatships; whereas women have no way through political action to better their condition; therefore, be it resolved [that] we pledge ourselves to do all in our power to procure for women political freedom.[47]

In March 1887, one month after municipal suffrage was passed, the age of protection for girls was raised from ten to eighteen years. The WCTU and KESA had worked for this legislation, hoping to keep adolescent girls out of the clutches of pimps and white slave traders. Immediately after the 1912 suffrage amendment passed, letters flowed in to Mrs. Johnston with pleas for reform measures. From LaCrosse came a plea against a bill to exclude women from jury duty and for an eight-hour maximum working day for women. The Wichita City Federation of Women's Clubs endorsed a resolution for a minimum wage bill and a mother's compensation act (what we now would call Aid to Dependent Children). Requests for materials on citizenship education to prepare women for the vote flooded the suffrage headquarters. L. B. Mitchell, president of the WCTU, offered a hope that the passage of suffrage would encourage women to study the country's industrial system and economic conditions. Other requests included lobbying for a bill for equal property rights for women.[48]

From their inception, the KESA, the WCTU, and WRC supported and campaigned for better laws and better law enforcement. State prohibition (1880) was a primary focus of their activities, but as other problems surfaced, the women's clubs joined professional groups to work toward amelioration. For example, the State Child Labor Organization, under the direction of the National Child Labor Commission, had club woman and ardent suffragist Lilla Day Monroe as its vice-president in 1908. Genevieve Howland Chalkley, who joined Mrs. Johnston on her inspection tours of the state institutions in 1912, became the first female member of the three-person Industrial Welfare Commission, established in 1916 to oversee working conditions for women and children.[49]

The work of the Kansas women's clubs occurred prior to, although it was absolutely consistent with, the reforms we associate with progressivism. The measures for which the women fought were, even in 1880, progressive reform items. The institutions that the women built were, at their own behest, taken over by state and federal governments. Kansas women's actions were consistent with those of other reformist groups, like settlement workers, throughout the nation. But they were sometimes ahead of the larger national movement.

Finally it is necessary to ask what ramifications these social welfare and reform activities had on history, particularly the history of women. It is clear that women in Kansas, as elsewhere, helped move the country away from single-minded laissez-faire economics. The clubs successfully insisted that the state had a responsibility for human welfare; they also gave impetus to the professionalization of welfare services. However, it is not so clear that the women's activities were effective in changing conventional ideologies about the nature of women and their proper sphere. Evidence that those basic ideas remained unchanged lies both in the specifics of the social reforms advocated and in the diminishing of women's activities around 1920.

Although an agricultural depression plagued the farm states throughout the 1920s, during those years the club women decreased their welfare activities, until by 1925 they had returned to the private "lady benevolent" stances of the 1870s. The conservative politics of the nation were mirrored in Kansas: by the early twenties, the DAR and WRC were restricting their public activities to Americanization programs centering around anticommunist propaganda. They no longer involved themselves in reform or charitable activities. The League of Women Voters, formed from the Equal Suffrage Associations, began a chapter in Wichita in 1920 but acquired no statewide support. The Good Government Club, a Topeka-based suffrage organization that never joined the league, in 1925 distributed jingoistic hate literature against urban social reformers' efforts to nationalize a child labor law.[50]

How is one to account for this narrowing and reducing of widespread programs of earlier years? One answer certainly lies in the ideology of the reform movements, an ideology that can readily be observed through an analysis of the club women's activities.

Jill Conway points out, in her essay on Jane Addams, that "new ways of behaving do not necessarily evoke any new view of the female temperament."[51] Kansas women, through their organizations, engaged in a myriad of public activities, moving swiftly and forcibly out of their domestic spheres. However, the slogans that pulled the women from their homes and the reforms for which they lobbied show that the clubs did not change the traditional view of woman's place. The WCTU insisted that suffrage was desirable in order to maintain the home; it called for "Home Protection." This slogan ignored women's basic rights or women's need for emancipation from the domestic ideology. It insinuated that reforms were necessary to bolster the health of women's private domestic sphere. Likewise, the cry of "Municipal Housekeeping," around which many club women rallied, generalized the concept that women were naturally best at that which resembled domestic duties. In some ways these slogans were political ploys to engage women who were against the more radical ideology of Elizabeth Cady Stanton and to allay the fears of males, who viewed the women's rights movement with alarm. But while such slogans aided short-term success, in the long run they paved the way for the failure of the full emancipation of women and thus cut short women's full movement into the public sphere. The Kansas women, like the urban reformers Conway speaks of, were "aggressive, hard-working, independent, pragmatic, and rational in every good cause but that of feminism."[52]

An analysis of the reform activities of the women's organizations verifies their preoccupations with reforms allied to domestic issues. Women called for prohibition to save homes from the depredations of alcohol. They worked to protect children through advocacy of child labor laws and strict truancy laws. They inspected schools and institutions for sanitary conditions and moral behaviors, natural concerns of the domestic sphere. They worked for mothers' pensions to keep homes together and for the reformation and rehabilitation of prostitutes to save their boys from venereal disease. Other reforms were based on the concept of women's natural frailty and mothering duties. The club women lobbied for minimum wage and maximum hour laws to give working women living wages; they did not advocate equal pay for equal work. The clubs supervised working conditions for women, inspecting business operations, for example, to be sure female clerks had seats provided for them. They did not insist upon similar amenities for male clerks. In part, they felt male clerks, through their unions, could provide for themselves; however, they were also operating under the assumption that because women were frailer and because they might become mothers, they were in need of extra protection. When the equal suffrage and temperance workers advocated a woman's right to refuse connubial relationships, they did not do so in terms of her right to her own body but in terms of the health of unborn children. In other words, the activities of the women involved the welfare of others, particularly children, and ideas about women's particular fitness for and responsibility toward the domestic sphere.

Thus, while women engaged in activities that were far removed from their domestic enclosures, the specific reforms advocated did not touch the basic domestic ideologies of their lives. The miles that club women traveled, their sophisticated networking systems, their public speaking and political lobbying, and their enormous success in achieving social reforms must be admired. Women's clubs pulled women into the public arena and taught them how to act, and they acted effectively. However, they did not examine the bases of their actions. They did not concern themselves with women's equality.

When the women who joined organizations and worked to clean up the streets found that most of their immediate goals were achieved they returned to their homes, as tradition would dictate. There, however, they found their work diminished. Local, state, and federal governments had taken over most of the specific activities in which they had been previously engaged; prohibition and suffrage, which had been their most important concerns, were achieved. In going home, women could place their faith in domestic tranquillity, in democratic procedures, in the votes of their own sisters. Yet their home sphere was narrowed by the success of their activities. They no longer had crusades to spur them to aggressive, independent action. In their clubs they were reduced to single, sometimes erratic issues, such as flags in the schools and anti-Bolshevism, or to Tuesday teas and bridge parties. Whatever their public successes, they had to go back to the domestic enclosure, now more limited than before. Women's clubs, by the 1920s, were diminished in scope and reduced to the trivialities they had so long eschewed.

This diminishment was apparently a national phenomenon. The feminists of intellectual importance—Elizabeth Cady Stanton, Alice Paul, Charlotte Perkins Gilman—never acquired the national adulation of Frances Willard or Jane Addams. Recent studies of Addams and Willard verify that in their writings and speeches they too used domesticity as a rationale for action.[53]

Local club histories, most written some years after the period studied in this paper, reveal considerable ignorance of the welfare and reform activities of the groups. The social functions of the clubs are expanded upon in the histories, while the reform activities are all but ignored. Only in contemporary documents—newspaper articles, conference schedules, and magazine reports—and in letters and diaries are the extent and impact of their ameliorative efforts revealed. And after 1920 or so these same documents revealed the changed nature of the women's organizations.

As a woman of the 1980s I find myself ambivalent about my sisters at the turn of the century. The traumas of my generation might have been mitigated if women of that era had forced themselves to do serious consciousness raising about women's internalized subordination before they embarked on public life. Certainly critiques of the effects of centuries of domestic acculturation such as Stanton's and Gilman's were available to them.

However, the ideological choices that the equal rights versus the municipal housekeeping arguments imposed on the women of the period were not simple. Stanton and Gilman's arguments, while calling for equal rights, were also based on analyses which insisted that women were culturally, perhaps genetically, inferior. It was their right to *become* equal that Stanton and Gilman demanded. The home protection/municipal housekeeping arguments, while postulating either a separate but equal or morally superior role for women, had behind them the weight of immediate history and the advantage of a changed emphasis in governmental responsibilities. The immediate history of male/female spheres seemed to show that women were morally superior or at least operated naturally in very different arenas. Social gospel and progressive reformers who were to become governmental powers called for women's nurturing expertise in welfare and social reforms. The possibility of immediate action rather than the delays of consciousness raising, as well as the sight of victory for suffrage, caused Kansas women, like others in the nation, to go for the achievable.[54] Only sixty years later did we come to know that Stanton and Gilman's analysis would sound so loudly in our ears.

So the Kansas women moved into the public arena in the guise of carrying out their prescribed roles. In doing so, they won many reforms; the biggest of them was the enfranchisement of half the population. That in itself was the first step to the new feminism.

Beyond that, these women struggled to find solutions to problems like alcoholism, which we still find insoluble. They were faced with an uncivilized society and tackled immediate problems. They were more action-oriented than thoughtful, more political than self-conscious. While we must acknowledge the limitations of what they did, we must also resurrect them as heroes whom we may emulate, for their courage, their fortitude, their shrewdness, and their community of action. For forty years, women's groups in Kansas acted together to fight economic exploitation, disease, and poverty. For these fights we cannot fault them.

NOTES

1. Walter Prescott Webb, *The Great Plains* (Boston: Ginn and Company, 1931), pp. 505–6, codifies this image of the pioneer mother gone mad in his chapter "Mysteries of the Great Plains." "The Plains," he says, "exerted a peculiarly appalling effect on women. . . . The wind alone drove some to the verge of insanity and caused others to migrate in time to avert the tragedy." For one view of dominant images, see Sandra L. Myres, *Westering Women and the Frontier Experience 1800–1915* (Albuquerque: University of New Mexico Press, 1982), particularly chapter 1, "The Madonna of the Plains and Calamity Jane: Images of Westering Women," pp. 1–11.

2. The term *civilizer* has been so banalized and derogated that historians of the women's West sometimes go out of their way to deny women this role. See, for example, Elizabeth Jameson's "Women as Workers, Women as Civilizers: True Womanhood in the American West," *Frontiers* 7 (1984):1–8. Jameson despises the term, feeling it is oversimple and connotes passivity. However, one of her sources, May Wing, wanted to be remembered for running the local museum, starting the hot school lunch program, organizing a boys' chorus, and teaching Sunday School (p. 7). These are the kinds of activities I would term "civilizing."

3. Julie Roy Jeffery, *Frontier Women: The Trans-Mississippi West, 1840–1880* (New York: Hill and Wang, 1979), p. xiii.

4. Nancy Cott, *The Bonds of Womanhood: Woman's Sphere in New England, 1780–1835* (New Haven, Conn.: Yale University Press, 1979), provides the most thorough history of the rise of women's bonding. Johnny Faragher and Christine Stansell, "Women and Their Families on the Overland Trail to California and Oregon, 1842–1867," *Feminist Studies* 2 (1975):150–60, explore the ramifications of such bonding for western women travelers. Other important analyses of pre–Civil War eastern women's bonding and organizing are Barbara Berg's *The Remembered Gate: Origins of American Feminism, the Woman and the City, 1800–1860* (New York: Oxford University Press, 1978); Carroll Smith-Rosenberg's "Beauty, the Beast and the Militant Woman: A Case Study in Sex Roles in Jacksonian America," *American Quarterly* 23 (1971):562–84; and Mary P. Ryan's "The Power of Women's Networks: A Case Study of Female Moral Reform in Antebellum America," *Feminist Studies* 5 (1979):66–85.

5. Jeffrey, *Frontier Women*, p. 79. For the most recent discussion of the growth and work of women's organizations nationally, see Anne Firor Scott, "On Seeing and Not Seeing: A Case of Historical Invisibility," *The Journal of American History*" 7 (June 1984):7–21. See also Katherine Harris, "Feminism and Temperance Reform in the Boulder WCTU," *Frontiers* 4 (1979):19–24.

6. Mary P. Ryan, *Womanhood in America: From Colonial Times to the Present* (New York: Harper and Row, 1975), pp. 230–31. It is Ryan who says that by 1920 the women's organizations had coalesced to form a "rationalized organizational network that was nearly as sophisticated in its own way as the corporate business world" (p. 232).

7. As cited in *The American Woman: Who Was She?* ed. Anne Firor Scott (Englewood Cliffs, N.J.: Prentice-Hall, 1971), p. 106. See Karen Blair, *The Clubwoman as Feminist: True Womanhood Redefined, 1868–1914* (New York: Holmes and Meier, 1980). Blair's book focuses on eastern women's clubs.

8. Minutes, Friends in Council, Lawrence, Kansas, Record Books 1871–1971, December 5, 1871; March 16, 1872, in the Kansas Collection, University of Kansas, Lawrence, Kansas (hereafter cited as FIC).

9. Jane Cunningham Croly, *The History of the Woman's Club Movement in America* (New York: Henry G. Allen and Company, 1898), p. 88. Croly includes a brief history of Kansas women's clubs that joined the General Federation (pp. 380–94).

10. Agnes D. Hays, *The White Ribbon in the Sunflower State: A Biography of Courageous Conviction 1878–1953* (Topeka, Kans.: WCTU, 1953), p. 37.

11. Robert Dykstra, *The Cattle Towns* (New York: Alfred A. Knopf, 1968); Mary B. Hartley, *Our Golden Heritage: Fifty Years of P.E.O. in Kansas, 1903–1953* (PEO Sisterhood, Kansas State Chapter, 1953).

12. Hays, *The White Ribbon.*

13. Dykstra, pp. 190–206.

14. *The History of the Department of Kansas, Woman's Relief Corps, Auxiliary to the Grand Army of the Republic, 1884–1934* (Buffalo, Kans.: Buffalo Blade, 1934); hereafter cited as *History of the WRC.*

15. There is no history of the State Federation of Women's Clubs in Kansas. Information about individual clubs belonging to the State Federation can be obtained from the "Women's Clubs Clippings," typescript lists of officials of the organization that give the women's affiliations, and materials such as yearbooks and convention programs of local and regional meetings of the federation. All these are in the Kansas State Historical Society, Topeka, Kansas (hereafter cited as KSHS).

16. I have found no information about the origins or reasons for the political districting, which first appears in the *Minutes of the Women's Christian Temperance Union of Kansas at the Fourth Annual Meeting* (Burlingame, Kans.: Osage County Chronicle, 1882). The political boundaries existed earlier, and the idea may have originated from activist churchwomen.

17. See Mary I. Wood, *The History of the General Federation of Women's Clubs for the First Twenty-one Years of Its Organization* (New York: Norwood Press, 1912).

18. Mary Austin, *Earth Horizon: An Autobiography* (New York: Houghton-Mifflin Company, 1932), chapters 6 and 7. Austin tells of the impact of Frances Willard on the lives of frontier women and of her mother's involvement in the WCTU. She relates meetings in which the women "came to grief over parliamentary procedure, or . . . in which somebody was . . . hurt to the point of bursting into tears. And then they would hold hands and sing a hymn and begin all over again" (p. 143). She says, "I remember the first women who was allowed to speak in our church on the right of women to refuse to bear children to habitual drunkards, and my mother putting her arm across my knees and taking my hand in one of the few natural gestures of a community of woman interest she ever made toward me" (p. 142).

19. See the *Minutes of the Annual Meetings of the WCTU of Kansas, 1881–1890, Kansas*, KSHS. See also *Proceedings of the Third Annual Meeting, Grand*

Chapter of Kansas, Order of the Eastern Star, 1878 (Fort Scott, Kans.: Monitor Steam Publishing House, 1878); vol. 1, KSHS; and the *Proceedings, Sixth Annual Convention, (1882)*, KSHS.

20. Again, to quote Austin: "How the women of our town loved that organization [the WCTU] . . . ; with what pure and single-minded ardor they gave themselves to learn to serve it, legal technicalities, statistics, Robert's Rules of Order, the whole ritual of public procedure. Only women who recall how far back in social evolution the ritual of mass behavior began know how hard it was for them. . . . With the result that for precision and directness in the conduct of public meetings American women finally reduced our Senate and House of Representatives to shame" (pp. 142–43).

21. See Berg, *The Remembered Gate*, chapter 7, and Carroll Smith-Rosenberg, *Religion and the Rise of the American City: The New York City Mission Movement 1812–1870* (Ithaca, N.Y.: Cornell University Press, 1971).

22. However, because members of the Equal Suffrage Association were inevitably involved in other organizations, distinguishing what was done in the name of which organization is often difficult. See, for example, the Lucy Browne Johnston Papers, KSHS.

23. The intertwining of the public and visible functions of the clubs with the private charities can be seen in the overlapping memberships. The link between the WCTU and the suffrage associations in the West is firmly established. See, for example, Sherilyn Cox Bennion, "*The Pioneer*: The First Voice for Women's Suffrage in the West," *Pacific Historian* 25 (Winter 1981):15–21; Marilyn Hoder-Salmon, "Myrtle Archer McDougal, Leader of Oklahoma's 'Timid Sisters,' " *Chronicles of Oklahoma* 60 (Fall 1982):332–43; Cecelia M. Wittmayer, "The 1889–1890 Woman Suffrage Campaign: A Need to Organize," *South Dakota History* (Summer 1981):199–225; and Katherine Harris, "Feminism and Temperance Reform in the Boulder WCTU." The WCTU was, at its least public levels, a charitable organization.

24. Minutes, FIC, January 29, 1901; "Women's Clubs Clippings," vol. 1, KSHS; Hartley, *Our Golden Heritage*; "Gilson Scrapbooks," Lyon County Historical Museum, Emporia, Kansas; Hays, *The White Ribbon; History of the WRC; Proceedings of the Annual Conventions, Department of Kansas, Woman's Relief Corps, 1885–1893*, in *WRC Journals*, KSHS; *Minutes of the Annual Meetings of the WCTU of Kansas, 1881–1890, Kansas* (various publishers) vol. 1, KSHS.

25. *Journal of the 8th Annual Convention of the WRC, Department of Kansas, 1892*; Minutes, FIC, October 29, 1889, December 19, 1893, January 15, 1901, and April 2, 1901.

26. As reported in *The Club Member*, September 1909, p. 20; Hays, *The White Ribbon*; "Gilson Scrapbooks," Lyon County Historical Museum; "Women's Clubs Clippings," vol. 1, KSHS.

27. *The Club Member*, October 1909, p. 13.

28. Lillian Walker Hale, "The Club Movement in Kansas," *Midland Monthly* 7 (May 1897):423; and Croly, *History of Women's Clubs*, p. 481.

29. *Minutes of the Annual Meetings of the WCTU of Kansas*, 1881–1890, vol. 1, KSHS.

30. Hays, *The White Ribbon: History of the WRC*; Hale, "The Woman's Club Movement"; and Hartley, *Our Golden Heritage*.

31. Minutes, FIC, March 31, 1896; "Women's Club Clippings," vol. 1, KSHS; Minutes, Good Government Club Papers, KSHS; "Gilson Scrapbooks," Lyon County Historical Museum; Hartley, *Our Golden Heritage*.

32. "Gilson Scrapbooks," Lyon County Historical Museum.

33. Alice Haldeman to Lucy Browne Johnston, December 12, 1903, Lucy Browne Johnston Papers, KSHS (hereafter cited as L. B. Johnston Papers).

34. L. B. Johnston Papers, KSHS; *The Club Member*, March 1970; Minutes, FIC, May 6, 1902; Good Government Club Papers, KSHS; "Women's Club Clippings," vol. 1, KSHS.

35. Hale, "The Club Movement in Kansas."

36. L. B. Johnston Papers, KSHS. Johnston lobbied and traveled extensively for the Traveling Libraries and kept a separate set of files and accounts of that work. She wrote a paper on the Traveling Libraries in Kansas (May 1904) which is in the L. B. Johnston papers (Box 3).

37. Hays, *The White Ribbon*, pp. 87–92; Minutes, FIC February 27 ff.; History of the WRC; Hartley, *Our Golden Heritage; Panoramic Glimpses of Women's Clubs of Kansas*, compiled by Women's Kansas Day Club, 1969, typescript, KSHS; "Congress of Mothers," *Topeka Capital*, March 11, 1917.

38. *The Club Member*, July 1908, p. 12.

39. *The Club Member*, September 1909, p. 3.

40. See Martha Belle Caldwell, "The Woman Suffrage Campaign of 1912," *The Kansas Historical Quarterly* 12, no. 3 (August 1943):300–319, for Lucy Browne Johnston's banning of "militant methods" during that campaign. Even Addams was restricted to lecturing only in cities and towns where labor sentiment ran high. See also Minutes, FIC, December 12, 1893, in which "a paper and readings of College Settlements" were found "additionally valuable because the reader could speak from personal visits." The reader was probably Genevieve Howland (Chalkley) who in 1916 became the first woman labor commissioner in Kansas. She and Lucy Johnston were inspectors of the state charitable institutions in 1913. See also *The Club Member*, April 1906.

41. *Proceedings of the Twelfth Annual Convention of the State Society of Labor and Industry* (Topeka, Kans.: State Printing Office, 1910), p. 66.

42. See, for example, Minutes, FIC, December 4, 1900.

43. Wilda M. Smith, "A Half Century of Struggle: Gaining Woman Suffrage in Kansas," *Kansas History* 4 (Summer 1981):74–95; and Patrick O'Brien,

"Expansion of a Revolutionary Ideal: Woman Suffrage in Kansas," *The Heritage of Kansas* 10, no. 1 (1977):36–52.

44. L. B. Johnston Papers, KSHS.

45. *History of Woman Suffrage*, ed. Elizabeth Cady Stanton, Susan B. Anthony, and Matilda Joslyn Gage, 6 vols. (Rochester, N.Y. Charles Mann Printing Company, 1886), 3:710.

46. L. B. Johnston Papers, KSHS; *The Club Member*, 1906–1911; *Annual Convention Proceedings, The State Society of Labor and Industry 1908–1912*; Hartley, *Our Golden Heritage*.

47. *Proceedings of the Tenth Annual Convention of the State Society of Labor and Industry*, 1908, p. 338.

48. *History of Woman Suffrage*, 4:651; L. B. Johnston Papers, KSHS.

49. "Women's Club Clippings," vol. 1, KSHS; L. B. Johnston Papers, KSHS; *Kansas Department of Labor and Industry Thirty-first and Thirty-second Annual Reports* (Topeka: Kansas State Printing Plant, 1917); *First Biennial Report of the Industrial Welfare Commission of the State of Kansas from July 1 to June 30, 1917* (Topeka: Kansas State Printing Plant, 1917).

50. Good Government Club Collection, KSHS. See also Lilla Day Monroe, *Big Business the Great Magician* (Cambridge, Mass.: Murray Printing Co., 1925), pamphlet in KSHS. Monroe, who was heavily involved in Progressive Era reforms from 1906 to 1917, wrote that the enemies of big business included "the Composite women folk . . . too petted, too indulged, has [*sic*] too much idle time upon her hands. She dropped into the camp of the Bolshevist and his fiery appeal touched her. . . . Mark you, her so-called non-partisan organization, such as the federated club, which we were wont to herald as the university extension of busy mothers, the Young Woman's Christian Association, the Woman's Christian Temperance Union, and other similar organizations, while living on the bounty of business, were all caught in the net of the spoiler" (pp. 8–9). She speaks of the "ganged congress for child labor laws" and the "vicious international league of Peace and Freedom and its kindred unAmerican and foreign societies" (p. 9). Monroe died in 1929; it was she who collected the materials used in Joanna L. Stratton's *Pioneer Women: Voices from the Kansas Frontier* (New York: Simon and Schuster, 1981).

51. Jill Conway, "Women Reformers and American Culture 1870–1930," *Journal of Social History* [Great Britain] 5, no. 2 (1971–1972):166.

52. Conway, p. 174.

53. Conway's essay is the single most important analysis of the insidious effects of domestic ideologies on women reformers. However, Estelle Freedman, "Separatism as Strategy: Female Institution Building and American Feminism, 1870–1930," *Feminist Studies* 5 (Fall 1979):512–29, note 7, argues that the bonding between women exhibited in the women's organizations is an essential quality of feminism and suggests that "any female dominated activity

that places a positive value on women's social contributions, provides personal support, and is not controlled by antifeminist leadership has feminist political potential'' and is ''prefeminist.'' See also Aileen S. Kraditor, *The Ideas of the Woman Suffrage Movement, 1890–1920* (New York: Columbia University Press, 1965), especially pp. 43–74 and 96–122. Kraditor looks specifically at Stanton, Gilman, Addams, and others.

54. This analysis closely follows that of Kraditor. However, she speculates that the abstract argument for women's rights, based on the constitution, by the turn of the century may have been settled in favor of women. The divergence from Stanton and Gilman was in the question of whether separate but equal was an appropriate status (p. 54).

8

The Hull House Circle: Women's Friendships and Achievements

VIRGINIA KEMP FISH

The purpose of this essay is to provide a glimpse into the professional lives and personal friendships of a bright, articulate, well-educated group of women who were bound by common concerns with social research, reform, and activism in the early years of this century and whose contributions have not yet been adequately assessed. These six women—Julia Lathrop, Florence Kelley, Alice Hamilton, Sophonisba Breckinridge, and Edith and Grace Abbott—I have called the Hull House Circle. Within this encompassing circle smaller, overlapping circles containing two or three members could be drawn if a lengthy monograph were undertaken. These are the women whom Paul Kellogg, for many years editor of *Survey*, a journal concerned with social reform issues, once referred to as the ''Great Ladies of Halsted Street.''[1]

This essay represents an attempt to combine the insights of sociology with those of biography and of history, at best a difficult but rewarding task. While the decision of which materials to include in any research effort is a highly selective process, it is especially so in an undertaking of this sort, which uses a plethora of historical and archival materials. The writer has attempted to utilize resources that seemed representative to her of the event, the person, the friendship. The major written and edited works of these women were examined, as were biographical and autobiographical accounts of or by them. Resources discussing the early days of the University of Chicago were also perused, as were the papers, especially correspondence, of Edith and Grace Abbott, Sophonisba Breckinridge, and Marion Talbot, which are deposited in the Special Collections at the University of Chicago.

These women are of interest for a number of reasons. All came out of a similar social milieu, were part of the first generation of college women, and, though they didn't necessarily label themselves Progressives, took part in the Progressive movement during the early part of this century. Definitive essays could be written on each of them, noting her academic or her social reform contributions. Each was outstanding in her own right. This essay, however, focuses upon the six as a group, as a friendship network that began at Hull House with friendships that were sustained throughout the life course.

In response to those who might wonder why the lives of these women have been detailed, what as researchers we hope to learn from them, the following observations seem germane. First, women scholars are currently involved with rediscovering their own heritage, with finding their own roots, and with placing the contributions of other, earlier women within appropriate time frames. While customs and norms regulating appropriate behavior for females have greatly changed since the beginning of this century, the women discussed in this essay may serve as role models for present-day women. There is evidence that some of them did serve in this capacity for their own graduate students. Additionally, the writings and contributions of these women need to be incorporated within and made a part of the history of the social sciences, particularly sociology and possibly political science. Though Edith Abbott and Breckinridge did not take their Ph.D.'s in sociology, a case can be made that their written and edited works are representative of one of the schools of research extant in the early days of sociology at the University of Chicago. Up to now the founding period of sociology, which mainly centered at the University of Chicago, has been seen and analyzed as a largely male enterprise. An alternative "construction of reality," an alternative history of the discipline, needs to be done, including its significant female participants. A number of researchers are, in fact, in the process of finding "lost women sociologists." Mary Jo Deegan, one of these researchers, posits an interesting thesis that these early women—including members of the Hull House Circle—were systematically excluded from permanent appointments in academic departments (such as sociology) and offered only marginal, temporary positions (e.g., as docent or lecturer) in those same departments. For permanent appointments they were relegated to the Department of Household Administration or the Extension Division, originally the Home Study Division, of the university, departments that were seen as "women's work." These two departments represented a "mechanism to keep bright, innovative women at the university while withholding recognition of their academic contributions and restraining their influence." In time the School of Social Service Administration "siphoned off" Breckinridge and Edith Abbott into what was seen as another "appropriate" occupation for women, social welfare.[2]

Further, the writings of these women provide insights and, in some cases, baseline data into areas that are still the concern of sociologists—work and occupations, ethnic groups, social movements, and a host of social problems including poverty, illness, housing, unemployment, delinquency and crime, and war. While child labor has been outlawed and some of the grosser industrial ills minimized, many of the interests of the Hull House Circle still concern us as citizens and as sociologists.

Finally, the written works of this group provide rich insights into the area of women and the world of work, particularly occupational structure and labor organizations as well as the legal status of women. Edith Abbott's *Women in Industry: A Study in American Economic History*, first published in 1909, traces gainful employment for women from the colonial period to the early part of this century. Sophonisba Breckinridge's *Women in the Twentieth Century: A Study of Their Political, Social and Economic Activities* appeared in 1933 as one of a series of monographs published under the direction of the President's Research Committee on Social Trends. (The committee was established by Herbert Hoover in 1929. An interesting bit of intermeshing: the only woman member of this committee was Alice Hamilton.) The monograph discusses women's use of spare time, their gainful employment, and their participation in government. Thus, it represents a landmark effort.

Currently, scholars remind us of two themes of the past that are being reevaluated and challenged. First, throughout time there has been a long tradition of relegating men and women to separate spheres, with the public seen as appropriate for males; the private, for females. Second, traditionally women have been cast as objects, as *receivers* of knowledge, not as subjects, not as *producers* and *theorizers* of knowledge. This has meant that women have constituted an enormous "historically submerged group of people, deprived of the power to conceptualize, to name, and to categorize reality."[3] The Hull House group, on the other hand, repesents women who did enter the public sphere and in whose lives the public sphere interlocked with the private; who were theorizers and producers of knowledge; who did "conceptualize, name, and categorize reality." Further, there is an interlocking of the public and the private spheres for each woman as well as for the group as a whole. Each had a viable private sphere composed of family and close friends. While in many ways these women were the inheritors of general cultural notions about women's concerns with human problems, their interest in the public sphere was fostered and sustained in the private sphere by family and friends.

Jane Addams used the phrase "family claim" to describe the family loyalty which a daughter owed. Addams suggested that in her generation (she was born in 1860; birthdates of the Hull House Circle ranged from 1858 to 1878) a daughter's desire to contribute to her society and to be a professional was in conflict with the family's claim over her domestic and social services.[4] While there were elements of "family claim" in the life histories of these women (for example, Breckinridge returned home in 1894 to keep house for her father after the death of her mother), a more important and useful concept is that of "family culture."[5] As discussed later, the Hull House women were daughters of families who turned their attention to social and political reform and who encouraged their daughters not only to seek higher education but to use it in service to the community. As such, they made contributions that touched upon both the public and the private spheres of other women, e.g., the attempts to eliminate child labor and the sweatshop, to inaugurate the ten-hour (later eight-hour) day, to curtail exploitative activities toward immigrants, to assist industrial women in their organizing efforts, and to establish well-baby clinics and kindergartens.

Each woman entered the public sphere via the educational and the professional structures of the society, structures that contained both overt and covert patterns of exclusion for women. One historian suggests that:

Progressivism was much more than the movement to tame private enterprise that it has long been portrayed as being; it was also an effort to work out a new *modus vivendi* between middle-class men and women. Women were finally gaining the acceptance within the public sphere that they had fought so long to attain, through admission to education and reform activity; however, the cost of that acceptance was the establishment of sex roles within the public sphere that protected conventional notions of sexual difference. Social reform and teaching became the special domains of women, and professionalism was the sphere of men.[6]

While Jane Addams and Hull House are not per se the major focus of this essay, they become a kind of leitmotif, as all of this group lived for varying periods of time at Hull House; it became a focal point throughout their lives. Friendships begun there endured, were strengthened and reinforced by the same and overlapping interests, organizational memberships, and social reform efforts.

For one thing, Hull House provided the group with an agenda and became a training ground for new professional careers.[7] It was there that Hamilton developed a lifelong interest in industrial diseases; Lathrop, in child welfare concerns; and Grace Abbott, in the plight of the immigrant. Hull House provided Edith Abbott with her first research opportunities. However, the relationship between these women and Hull House was a reciprocal one as well. Unquestionably, each member of the circle in turn had an impact upon the activities and the foci of Hull House. For example, Lathrop and Kelley influenced the early course of Hull House by their attempts to involve the residents to a greater extent in both research and reform. Addams commented that "Florence Kelley galvanized us into more intelligent interest in the industrial conditions all around us."[8]

While it is evident that all six of the Hull House group admired Jane Addams, one feels that intimacy was lacking in her relationships with these women, except perhaps with Lathrop and with Kelley. Addams was a leader, an organizer who was able to generate enthusiasm in others for her causes and was able to foment scholarly debate and discussion.[9] She was a dynamic, charismatic figure who was as well a very private person with an aloofness that did not invite intimacy. While Lathrop and Kelley called her J.A., Edith Abbott noted, "to the residents [of Hull House] she was always 'Miss Addams.' "[10] Addams was a catalyst, ever stimulating and inspiring others. Additionally, she delegated authority efficiently, as witnessed by the suffrage speeches parceled out to the Abbotts. Edith Abbott also recounted Addams's method of distributing her mail to other residents: "Here, G. Abbott, this is child labor; you take this and tell her what to do''; or again, ''Here, G. Abbott, this is about immigration—or trade unions—won't you answer please.''[11]

The letters of members of the Hull House group written to one another and to Addams span a lifetime and attest to strong, supportive bonds. While some friendships need constant and continual face-to-face interaction to sustain them, others do not need a constant replenishment of this sort but are built upon similar life styles, a somewhat homogeneous set of beliefs and experiences, and a respect for one another's parameters. Such was the situation of the Hull House Circle. In reading their letters one is struck by the extent to which the professional concerns are interspersed with the private, the social reform concerns with the personal. There are references to trips taken or planned; copies of a book authored are sent to others in the group. Cards and letters flowed back and forth between this country and Europe as members vacationed or, more frequently, attended conferences. One of the most interesting sets of letters is to Grace Abbott from Jane Addams and Alice Hamilton in which they strongly urged her to consider becoming Addams's successor at Hull House (she did not accept).[12]

Recently, scholars have discovered a multiplicity of various types of friendship networks among women that have existed for a long time. In times past, women's networks have generally been trivialized, assumed not to exist, or seen as anomalies. The folklore of this society has reinforced the notion that women do not like other women or wish to work with them. A plethora of recent research refutes this ''commonsense'' notion. Several types of networks among women in both public and private spheres flourished during the nineteenth century, ''all closely related, each gaining support from and nourishing the other forms.''[13] Two bonds of friendship were traditional—those within families and those between close friends. Abundant evidence survives to indicate the force of these kinds of ties, ''these highly personal, yet far-reaching, networks of women relatives and friends.''[14] Additionally, two kinds of ties developed around educational and intellectual matters. First were the friendships among those young women able to attend female seminaries (and ultimately women's colleges) after 1800. However, outside the formal institutional framework of women's education there existed numerous networks centered around intellectual concerns, such as the Young Ladies' Society for Intellectual Improvement of Austinberg, Ohio. Because these societies generally had ephemeral life spans, they are largely unrecorded. Third, some networks centered around religious and missionary activities. Out of these often grew benevolent societies. Finally, the world of work provided another milieu out of which networks emerged. One of the more interesting and unusual in the latter category is the Women's Trade Union League. Members of the Hull House Circle were involved in all of these types except the third, that of the religious and missionary societies.

In order to identify the Hull House women more clearly, short biographies of them appear below, in the order in which they went to live at Hull House.[15]

Julia Lathrop (1858–1932) grew up in Rockford, Illinois, the first of five children. A lawyer, Lathrop's father served in the state legislature as well as in the United States Congress. Lathrop's mother, an ardent suffragist and a cultural leader in the community, was valedictorian of the first (1854) graduating class of Rockford Seminary (later Rockford College). After graduating from Vassar in 1880, Lathrop worked in her father's law office and read law herself. Lathrop went to live at Hull House in 1890 to stay twenty years. Though she shared her father's concern with civil service reform, with equal rights for women, and with the humane treatment of the insane, her professional contributions ultimately focused upon children. In 1912 President Taft appointed her the first head of the Federal Children's Bureau, created that year in Congress within the Department of Commerce and Labor. There she remained until 1921, at which time she retired to spend her remaining years in Rockford. "Though plain of appearance with a thin, triangular face, prominent features, and a rather mournful expression, Julia Lathrop possessed an intangible presence which brought her to the fore of any group."[16]

Born in Philadelphia, Florence Kelley (1859–1932) was the second daughter and third of eight children. Her mother was a descendant of Quakers; her father, a self-educated lawyer, was a believer in woman suffrage. After Kelley's graduation from Cornell in 1882, she enrolled at the University of Zurich. There she met and ultimately married (1884) Lazare Wischnewetzky, a Russian medical student and socialist with whom she went to live in New York City in 1886. Three children were born of this union, which, burdened by debt, ended in separation in 1891. Kelley returned to Illinois at that time to become a resident of Hull House, where she remained until 1899. Kelley's interest in industrial problems led her to work diligently to abolish child labor and the sweatshop. In 1899, at the invitation of the reformer John Graham Brooks, Kelley became general secretary of the newly formed Consumers' League, which proposed to use consumer pressure to assure that goods were manufactured and sold under proper working conditions. She moved with her children to New York City and Lillian Wald's Henry Street Settlement. Kelley is described as a "guerrilla warrior in the wilderness of industrial change." She was a "vigorous, energetic, forceful woman with an incisive mind and a sharp wit."[17]

Alice Hamilton (1869–1970) grew up in Fort Wayne, Indiana, the second of four daughters; a brother was seventeen years her junior. Her older sister, Edith Hamilton (1867–1963), was to become a renowned classicist, authoring such works as *The Greek Way* (1930) and *The Roman Way* (1932). Her father, a Princeton graduate and lover of the classics, had settled for a partnership in a wholesale grocery store, a situation arranged for him by his family. Hamilton's mother, to whom she was especially close, encouraged her daughter's aspirations despite opposition from her conventional and clannish in-laws. After receiving the M.D. in 1893 from the University of Michigan, Hamilton studied at the Universities of Leipzig and Munich, took her first job as professor of pathology at the Woman's Medical School of Northwestern University in Evanston, Illinois, in 1897, and became a resident of Hull House that same year. Her interest in industrial diseases led her to many assignments (e.g., she was appointed as a special investigator for the United States Bureau of Labor in 1911). She also became a persuasive proponent of numerous social reforms as well a "living legend" in her later years. Walter Lippmann once commented, "She has the most satisfying taste of all personalities I've ever met—wine and silver and homespun." While Hamilton impressed others as a "perfectly harmonious woman," few knew of the "dramatic transformation from a spirited but hesitant and self-deprecating girl into the woman who rebelled against her family's social values while remaining close to its members."[18]

Sophonisba Breckinridge (1866–1948), the second daughter of seven children of whom two died in infancy, was born of a distinguished Kentucky family in Lexington. Breckinridge's father, a lawyer, journalist, congressman, and Confederate colonel, was a firm believer in higher education for women, though he opposed suffrage. After Breckinridge's graduation from Wellesley in 1888, she entered a period of trauma and great uncertainty in terms of herself and of her own life goals. Although she studied law with her father, he did not altogether approve of her decision to pursue a legal career. Ultimately (1894) she enrolled at the University of Chicago, where she earned a Ph.D. in political science in 1901 and a J.D. in 1904. In 1907 she went to spend part of each year at Hull House, where she remained until 1920. Her contributions as an academician, researcher, and social reformer exemplify the close relationship among these areas of endeavor in the Progressive period. She undoubtedly exercised her greatest influence in the realm of social work education. To her, the state was a key element in any extensive program on social welfare. A woman of great personal charm as well as warmth, enthusiasm, and "brilliance in the class-room," she combined "toughness with sensitivity."[19]

Edith (1876–1957) and Grace (1878–1939) Abbott grew up in one of the oldest towns in Nebraska, Grand Island, which was not far from the Overland Trail. Active throughout his life in the practice of law and politics, the Abbotts' father taught his daughters, early in their lives, to value and to display "reasoned and orderly thinking." Both daughters shared their mother's concern for the oppressed, her interest in progressive ideas and social reform, her pacifist beliefs, and her commitment to equal rights for women. Edith Abbott received a Ph.D. with honors in political economy in 1905 from the University of Chicago. After Grace Abbott earned a Ph.B. at Grand Island College (Nebraska) she earned a master's degree in political science from the University of Chicago in 1909. A far-ranging and effective partnership between the Abbott sisters began in 1908 when they went to Hull House to live. Committed to common goals and values, the sisters complemented each other. Edith was the scholar; Grace, especially during her tenure as chief of the United States Children's Bureau (1921–34), took the initiative in translating knowledge into action. Both worked in a variety of reform areas to effect social change. Like Breckinridge, Edith Abbott made lasting contributions to the social work curriculum at the University of Chicago, while Grace Abbott worked persistently, even when reformist sentiment was at a low ebb in this country, to legitimate the role of the state in the area of social welfare.[20] A beautiful woman, somewhat brusque in manner, Edith Abbott made "heavy and uncompromising demands" upon her students at the university. A more charismatic figure, Grace Abbott had "dauntless courage" and "amazing qualities" as a fighter for the things she believed in.[21]

In order to place this group within an appropriate context, it is necessary to comment about the university and the city of Chicago during the last part of the nineteenth century and early part of the twentieth. This was a period characterized by continued urbanization and industrialization as well as by a continuing influx of immigrants, especially from southern and eastern Europe. Along with these processes came a host of conditions seen as undesirable, as bringing about social problems—overcrowding and inadequate housing, crime, mental illness, industrial pollution. When the university was established in 1892, the first sociologists were white, middle-class males from rural or small-town settings, many of them either sons of ministers or ministers themselves. Like other academicians of this period, they had tremendous faith in the potential of both the natural and the social sciences. Great emphasis was placed upon humanitarian concerns and social reform efforts by these activist scholars, who "fused the ideals of research and service." They were responding to the city of Chicago's population doubling between 1880 and 1890 and again by 1910 to over 2,000,000. "Its poverty and wealth, filth and luxury, agitation and crime attracted international attention as did its ill-managed and corrupt municipal government."[22]

Equally important, however, is the prior context of these women's families and educational backgrounds, which made it possible for them to respond effectively to the larger environment of the city and the modern world. As part of the first generation of college women, the Hull House Circle, like the group of single academic women at Wellesley from 1880 to 1920, found support in their families for their own educational and professional expectations.[23] The aspirations and achievements of these women were, for the most part, congruent with the "family culture." The families were upper-middle-class with professional fathers and, in some cases, mothers who had had seminary or academy training. All of the fathers but Hamilton's were lawyers who engaged in public service. The Abbotts' father, for example, was the first lieutenant governor of Nebraska and a member of two constitutional conventions in the state. Both Hamilton's parents came from families of substance. Rockford Seminary in Illinois is an interesting part of their shared background. The mothers of both Lathrop and the Abbotts were graduates of Rockford. Lathrop and her sister Anna attended as well. Jane Addams was another famous graduate of the school.

The families became socially conscious activists in the abolition movement and in the movement to extend woman suffrage as well as opportunities for higher education. Both of Lathrop's parents had strong convictions regarding the rights of women and felt that their sphere should be enlarged. Neither daughter felt at a disadvantage because she was a female. Further, the first woman lawyer in the state of Illinois read in Mr. Lathrop's office.[24] The Abbotts' mother grew up in a family that kept a station on the underground railroad; she wore black on the day John Brown was hanged. At the age of eight she was presented by an uncle with a copy of a speech made by Elizabeth Cady Stanton at Seneca Falls which she was to learn as soon as she was able to read it. Edith Abbott as a small child shared not only her room but her bed with Susan B. Anthony when she came to town to speak. All their lives Grace and Edith treasured a copy of John Stuart Mill's *Subjection of Women*, which their parents had shared during their courtship.[25]

In biographical accounts the families are pictured as lively and articulate and as encouraging their daughters to think and to be independent beings. As such, the families, like those of the Wellesley women, were supportive of their daughters and acted as career brokers for them, not marriage brokers. In Lathrop's home the children "freely expressed" their opinions and were encouraged to work out their own interests without "parental interference."[26] The Hamilton daughters were early trained in resourcefulness and in independence. None was allowed to make a statement unless she was prepared to defend it.[27] Breckinridge's father enjoined his daughter to uphold the family reputation for "good thinking and courageous utterance."[28] Edith Abbott recalled that hers was a very argumentative family in which the children were encouraged to try to hold their own in an argument.[29]

Additionally, sisters played a vital role in these women's lives. The four Hamilton daughters were born within a six-year period that was "hard on my mother but made for close intimacy"—an intimacy that lasted a lifetime.[30] In 1961, when Alice and Edith were in their nineties, Connecticut College for Women wished to name one of its new series of dormitories "Alice and Edith Hamilton House." In a letter typed by herself, Alice asks that Edith's name come first: "It is not only that her writings on Greece and Rome will always be of lasting value, while mine on dangerous trades are already outmoded, but she is the elder sister. Her name belongs in the first place."[31] It was Breckinridge's sister-in-law, Madeline McDowell Breckinridge, rather than her own sister, with whom she had a close attachment and always referred to as her sister. In a warm biography of her, Breckinridge noted that the two first knew each other as "grown girls" in the years 1892–95 and that "she never after that questioned my love for her."[32]

As noted, one set of intermeshing friendships in the Hull House Circle involved the sisters Edith and Grace Abbott. While they had different competencies and were very different in their approach, they remained close intimates, sharing a home near the university during the last years of Grace's life. In both the published and the unpublished material Edith wrote about Grace, the portrait of her is loving and warm without being maudlin. Grace is seen as

like the pioneers—quick to face her difficulties with clear, forward-looking vision, generous spirit, and swiftness of action. She had the pioneers' genius for work . . . sense of fairplay . . . steadfastness of purpose . . . courage and ability to find resources, to defend what they believed to be right.[33]

A former student of the Abbotts and Breckinridge, in contrasting the three, notes that

Grace's manner was described as 'breezy'; Edith's was harder to characterize; it was less abrupt than that of her sister, but lacked something of the graciousness of Miss Breckinridge . . . their minds were cast in different molds. Grace's . . . was direct and forthright to an extreme degree, seeing always the main issues . . . Edith's . . . was also direct, but she saw more nuances.[34]

Finally, Kelley had a warm, meaningful relationship not only with a dynamic father but also with the Quaker women in her family, most notably Grand Aunt Sarah, who never used sugar or wore cotton, because these crops were grown by slaves. From her and other family members Kelley early learned compassion for those less fortunate than herself.[35]

Like the Wellesley women, this group was highly educated; all but one held degrees beyond the bachelor's. Lathrop attended Rockford Seminary as a day pupil for one year but wanted to go to Vassar, which, as the first of the women's colleges, was much talked of in that "decade so given over to the discussion of the education of women." Her father was rather pleased with Julia's independence and quite willing to have her go where she wanted. Addams noted of this experience that:

She [Lathrop] found it rather difficult to address everyone with the prefix of Miss, for the girls at Vassar . . . were never called by their first names though

Miss Smith and Miss Jones might become the best of companions. Apparently this formality was part of the solemn business of higher education for women.

Her sister Anna went back with her for the last year . . . she had several warm friends among the faculty and always spoke of Dr. Maria Mitchell (the astronomer) with the greatest admiration. There is no doubt that a real intimacy obtained between them.[36]

Because several other sisters died in infancy and she herself was seen as "delicate," Kelley's early schooling was nil save for brief periods at Miss Longstreth's School for Girls and the Friends Central School in Philadelphia. At the age of sixteen (1876) she went to Cornell, the year the first class containing women (including M. Carey Thomas) graduated. Entering college, she recalls, was "almost a sacramental experience." She graduated in 1882, Phi Beta Kappa. After she was refused admission to graduate school at the University of Pennsylvania, a chance encounter with Thomas, who had just completed a Ph.D. summa cum laude at the University of Zurich, led Kelley to Zurich. She later earned a law degree (1894) from Northwestern University in Evanston, Illinois.[37] The Hamilton daughters received very unorthodox early schooling at home since both parents, for different reasons, disapproved of the public schools. Ultimately, in the family tradition, all were sent to Miss Porter's School in Farmington, Connecticut. Alice then entered the University of Michigan Medical School and was awarded the M.D. degree in 1893 at the age of twenty-four. In her class of forty-seven, thirteen were women. Hamilton recalled later that women there were "taken for granted"; there was none of the "sex antagonism I saw later at Eastern Schools."[38]

Breckinridge and Edith Abbott received Ph.D.'s from the University of Chicago—Abbott's in political economy in 1905 and Breckinridge's in political science in 1901. Breckinridge did her undergraduate work at Wellesley, was the first woman admitted to the Kentucky bar, and was the first woman to earn the J.D. at Chicago in 1904. Edith Abbott studied at the University of London and the London School of Economics in 1906–7 while on an American Association of University Women fellowship. There she met Sidney and Beatrice Webb and apparently was influenced by them. Although Grace Abbott earned the Ph.M. in political science in 1909 from the University of Chicago and intermittently pursued the doctorate, she found her life at Hull House

as director of the newly formed Immigrants' Protective League generally
more satisfactory and did not acquire the degree.[39]

The contributions of this outstanding group were many and varied.
A definitive analysis of their impact on public policy through their
organizational affiliations awaits further research. As noted, activities
begun at Hull House endured. Further, the professional contributions
of this group provided a continuing tie with Addams and with one
another over the years. Addams followed the careers of the group with
enthusiasm and rejoiced in their accomplishments. For example, in the
Breckinridge papers a letter from Addams to Breckinridge is addressed
"Dearest Lady"; Addams thanks Breckinridge "for a copy of your new
book. What a wonder you are for turning out work and how valuable
the work will be to us all."[40]

Since the major thrust of this paper is not upon contributions per se,
the contributions of four of the group will be discussed only briefly;
emphasis will be upon the professional lives of Edith Abbott and Breckinridge, whose activities are illustrative of those of the entire circle.
First, a word about the others. Lathrop's outstanding contributions were
two; she was the first director of research for the Chicago School of
Civics and Philanthropy (1907) and the first head of the United States
Children's Bureau, a position she held for nine years (1912–21). In the
latter capacity she established programs and public policies for the
future.[41] Kelley's most famous accomplishment was as the longtime
secretary (1899–1932) of the National Consumers League (NCL). Like
the Women's Trade Union League, the NCL through its middle-class
membership sought to effect cooperative relationships with working-
class women. The group employed a two-pronged approach: to improve
working conditions through the use of middle-class women's buying
power and to enact protective legislation for women. The latter goal
proved more effective than the former.[42] Hamilton led a distinguished
career in industrial medicine as a pioneer in the field of occupational
diseases. Two of her books, *Industrial Poisons in the United States*
(1925) and *Industrial Toxology* (1934), are considered classics that
eventually led to the passage of workmen's compensation laws.[43] Grace
Abbott was the first director of the Immigrants' Protective League (IPL),
which was founded in 1908 to eliminate the many exploitative practices
in banking and housing toward immigrants. Since the IPL and the
Chicago School of Civics and Philanthropy shared adjoining offices,

interaction between Grace Abbott and Lathrop, Breckinridge, and her sister was frequent. Abbott taught a course on immigration for the school and aided in various research projects emanating from it. Much later she became one of Lathrop's assistants in the Children's Bureau, during which time (1917–21) she and Lathrop were close professional as well as personal friends. Upon Lathrop's retirement Abbott became chief of the bureau.[44]

Both Edith Abbott and Breckinridge, as noted above, were involved with the Chicago School of Civics and Philanthropy, and both spent their professional lives within the University of Chicago framework. Although it is often difficult to establish or document marginality, a good case can be made that the departments with which both were involved (sociology, political economy, and political science), while willing to admit bright young women to graduate study, were not willing to offer them major academic appointments. An early university publication (1917) lists Abbott as "Special Lecturer in Political Economy 1909–1910; Lecturer in Sociology 1914–." Later (1919) she is listed as "Instructor in Sociology," in which capacity she taught from 1914–20.[45] In writing of Abbott, Freeman notes, "After six years she had still not been promoted to Assistant Professor, so she switched to Social Service Administration. Eventually [1924] she became Dean of the School."[46]

Breckinridge's marginal status within the university is documented in her unfinished autobiography, in which she noted that despite being awarded the Ph.D. (summa cum laude) in 1901, no position in political science or economics awaited her although the male graduates went to positions on college or university faculties. Apparently Marion Talbot convinced Harry Judson, then chair of political science, to appoint Breckinridge docent, but as Breckinridge wrote later, "No one registered for such courses as I announced."[47] Later Breckinridge is identified as an "Instructor in Economics" and as an "Assistant Professor" in social economy in 1918. Additionally, from 1904 to 1920 Breckinridge regularly taught courses entitled The Child and the State, The Legal and Economic Position of Women, Modern Aspects of the Household, Consumption, and The Organization of Retail Trade, in the Department of Household Administration.[48]

It is of interest to note that when the School of Social Service Administration was founded in 1920, both Abbott and Breckinridge were given appointments as associate professors; both were promoted to full professor in 1925.[49] As discussed earlier, one may hypothesize that such fields as social service and household administration were seen as appropriate domains for women. Although Abbott, Breckinridge, and other women were actually engaged in "applied sociology," which was a perfectly respectable tradition within the field of sociology at the university, their work was never legitimated by male sociologists but was seen as "necessary but different" and called social work.[50]

Edith Abbott and Breckinridge made two outstanding contributions in the academic area, as researchers and as tireless workers developing a professional graduate school of social work at the University of Chicago. Their long friendship and professional collaboration, which was "remarkable for its absence of personal competition," was so close as to make it difficult to differentiate their individual contributions.[51] They collaborated on a number of studies of housing conditions, delinquency and crime, and truancy in the schools. Abbott, as a part-time lecturer in the department of sociology, taught methods of social investigation. She was conversant with the most advanced statistical and survey methods of the day. One historian of sociology says of her:

Contemporary sociologists are not likely to think of Edith Abbott as an intellectual ancestress. Yet the combination of rigorous methods of collecting and of analyzing information about contemporary urban situations is one of the most distinctive features of modern sociology, not only in Chicago but elsewhere in America and Europe. . . . Abbott and others like her created and maintained a standard which has become assimilated into the tradition of sociology. Her contribution to that tradition, like that of many others, no longer bears her name. But without those contributions the tradition would not be what it is.[52]

In advocating the establishment of a school of social work, both women insisted from the outset that education for social work should be conducted under university auspices and at the graduate level rather than in an independent, vocationally oriented school. At the time such views were considered idealistic and impractical, if not actually subversive. Both thought that social work should become the science of social policy, in which academic work and fieldwork were combined. First and foremost, both were scholars and teachers who wedded scholarship to social action and for whom the "classroom and the pen became . . . tools of activism." After the new School of Social Service Administration was founded, both were instrumental in establishing the first scholarly journal for the profession—the *Social Service Review*.[53]

Breckinridge's unfinished autobiography gives the reader a glimpse of someone who, even after a life of solid, positive accomplishments, had a very uncertain, tentative image of herself, as the following illustrates:

(Brother speaking, "not unkindly") Nisba you do mean so well, and you can take such good examinations! But you never had much common sense!

. . . I should be glad to have done a more adequate study, but, as I have said, I am dull and can only take advantage of opportunities, not create them.

. . . I think that I have always been afraid of life. There are two men whom I remember as having really loved. . . . Neither really loved me, though each for the moment thought that he did. Both married women who were cleverer than I was and both made happy gracious homes.[54]

Throughout Breckinridge's unfinished autobiography, additional threads can be found of a woman who, plagued by self-doubts, badly needed approval in her early life but apparently did not always receive it. Although she loved her father and tried to please him, his disapproval of her studying law and of women's suffrage must have caused her anxiety and stress. Further, one senses disapproval of and conflict with her sister Ella, who had great charm and was "much cleverer, really cleverer," Breckinridge noted, "but was not always entirely frank" [with her father].[55] Breckinridge was filled with uncertainty about herself when she arrived at the University of Chicago (1894) but remained eternally grateful to Marion Talbot, who, Breckinridge recalled later, "snatched for me a fellowship in political science which a man student had resigned."[56] It is quite possible that when Breckinridge did achieve professionally in the public sphere, even with the support of family and friends, she nonetheless viewed her accomplishments per se in a negative vein. Since patterns of exclusion have existed to keep women out of creative intellectual endeavors, it is hardly surprising that women like Breckinridge should experience ambivalence, doubt, and perhaps guilt about themselves and their undertakings when they achieve.[57]

If these academically talented women were marginal to the university they were central to Hull House, which provided them with a sense of their purpose and potential significance. Since it was a major formative influence upon them and a lifelong focus for them, a discussion of the institution itself and of the Hull House Circle's first days there is in order. The settlement movement, which began in Victorian England, was a part of a "broad attempt to preserve human and spiritual values" in an age of urbanization and industrialization. Samuel Barnett, founder of the first settlement, Toynbee Hall in London's East End, hoped that it would bridge the gap between "the rich and the poor, university men [*sic*] and working men [*sic*]" and that the two groups would learn from each other. Jane Addams and her friend of a lifetime, Ellen Starr, visited Toynbee Hall while on a tour of Europe. What they observed there helped them make a decision to found Hull House in 1889. From the beginning its main foci involved social research as well as social reform, helping improve conditions in the cities as well as restoring communications between the college-educated and the working class. For the college-educated the one indispensable requirement to actual residence in the settlement house was a willingness to spend spare time directing a settlement activity.[58]

In writing of its early days two researchers note the remarkable group of women who made Hull House a "vital and exciting" place to live; these women were "strong-minded, well-educated, and dedicated" and enjoyed the "intellectual fellowship" of the others. Some of them additionally became expert social investigators, learning how to document with statistics their "anger and concern." In the process they became pioneers in the development of urban sociology. They left their mark on many movements including attempts to abolish child labor, combat industrial disease, promote woman suffrage, establish parks and playgrounds, and organize labor.[59]

Addams herself recalls, "During its few decades, Hull House with other American settlements, issued various studies of fact-finding analyses of the city areas with which they were most familiar. The settlements had antedated by three years the first sociological departments of the universities and by ten years the establishment of the first Foundations, so that in a sense we were actual pioneers in field research."[60] Lathrop and Kelley participated in these pioneering ventures.

Within the Hull House Circle two smaller circles can be discerned in terms of when members were in residence. The first circle included Lathrop, Kelley, and Hamilton, who came between 1890 and 1897; the other consisted of the Abbotts and Breckinridge, who came in 1907 and 1908. For all members, throughout their lives a return to Hull House was like "going home." Throughout the years Hull House was not an institution over which "Miss Addams presided [but] it was Miss Addams around whom an institution insisted on clustering."[61]

Lathrop was the first of the group to live at Hull House. She had heard Addams and Starr speak at Rockford Seminary. Addams was already acquainted with Lathrop's mother and older sister and recalled years later that she "had greatly admired this brilliant young woman who came from a real woman's college [Vassar], carrying the honors with such a quick wit and disarming charm as fairly to put to rout our heavy ideas of 'higher education for women.' "[62]

One early resident recalls:

In 1906 or 1907 I was told "Miss Lathrop is coming! Miss Lathrop is coming!" as if it were an occasion for public rejoicing. . . . I did not know Miss Julia Lathrop . . . who brought with her such force, such warmth . . . an almost rougish [sic] sense of the tragi-comedy of American politics. . . . Her brown eyes, so sincere, but with a sparkle lurking in them, her slow redolent voice, her flavor of Illinois, gave her a richness that was valued by colleagues who had less vitality. Yet that almost Italian salience was only one kind of strength. There was a variety of strong character. The group that included Mrs. Kelley, Miss Lathrop, Dr. Hamilton, Miss Grace Abbott, and Miss Addams had made itself objectively important in the life of the American people.[63]

Kelley joined the circle a year or so after Lathrop and recalls her own arrival:

One snowy morning between Christmas 1891 and New Year 1892 I arrived at Hull House . . . a little before breakfast time and found there Henry Standing Bear, a Kickapoo Indian, waiting for the front door to be opened. It was Miss Addams who opened it, holding on to her left arm a singularly unattractive fat, pudgy baby belonging to the Cook who was behind hand with breakfast. Miss Addams was a little hindered in her movements by a super-energetic kinder-garten child, left by its mother while she went to a sweat shop for a bundle of cloaks to be finished.

We were welcomed as though we'd been invited. We stayed, Henry Standing Bear as helper to the engineer several months, when he returned to his tribe; and I as a resident seven happy, active years until May 1, 1899, when I returned to New York City to enter upon the work in which I have since been engaged as secretary of the National Consumers League.[64]

It was during that first winter of 1891–92 that the foundation for the lifelong friendship between Kelley and Lathrop was laid. Both played a role in making Hull House a center for research and reform and were themselves "expert social investigators," though Kelley was more radical than most of the other residents and was critical of some of the religious and artistic aspects of the early programs.[65]

Hamilton joined the group two years before Kelley left (1897) and lived there until 1919. After that she was able to spend some time at Hull House until Addams's death in 1935 (at which, in fact, she was present). Hamilton and two of her sisters heard Addams speak in their hometown of Fort Wayne, Indiana, in 1895. Two years later her wish to become a resident of Hull House was fulfilled. Of these experiences she later recalled:

> In those early days . . . the group of residents was rather small and we had a fairly intimate life, if one can use such a word to describe a relation . . . almost entirely devoid of personal intimacy. We knew each other's opinions and interest and work . . . we discussed them often and freely, but the atmosphere was impersonal, rather astonishingly so for a group composed chiefly of women. Miss Addams was warm and magnetic, but she never tolerated the sort of protecting interfering affection which is so lavishly offered to a woman of leadership and prominence. Nobody ever ventured to refuse her visitors, or even to take her telephone calls unless authorized to do so. She was impatient of solicitude, and her attitude brought about a wholesome, rather spartan atmosphere.[66]

Lathrop she described as "disinterested, as someone who does not see herself as the center of what she is doing," as a "most companionable person with a sense of the absurd." Kelley, she said, "used to make me think of two verses in the Old Testament; the one in Job about the war horse who scents the battle from afar and says among the trumpets, 'Ha, ha'; and the one where the psalmist says, 'The zeal of thine house hath eaten me up.' It was impossible for the most sluggish to be with her and not catch fire."[67]

Of the Abbotts' decision to become part of the Hull House Circle we have only Edith's account. The two lived there from 1908 until 1921. (Edith returned as a resident in her later years, 1949–53; of course, by then Addams was long gone.) Grace, working on her doctorate in political science at Chicago, was doing an interesting piece of research on married women's property rights; Edith was teaching economics at Wellesley College when both, very unexpectedly, were offered the opportunity of living at Hull House and working out some projects in which Addams was interested. Grace was asked to direct the newly formed Immigrants' Protective League, which Addams was eager to have carried on from Hull House, then the center of one of the great immigrant receiving areas of Chicago's west side. Breckinridge recommended Grace Abbott for the post after she herself had refused Addams's offer to direct the league. Edith was asked by Lathrop and Breckinridge to join them in the School of Civics and Philanthropy, then being reorganized to include a new research department made possible because of a grant from the Russell Sage Foundation. The school was first given space in one of the Hull House buildings.[68]

Edith Abbott gladly accepted the invitation, though older members of the Wellesley faculty considered it an indication of a "mild form of lunacy" to leave for an "unheard of kind of place." She did not want to stay in a women's college, however, and felt that a "new road to freedom" had been opened to her. She recalled later that "I was so glad to come back to Chicago that I forgot about the steaming summer heat and the smells in the Hull House neighborhood. They seemed only part of the welcome contrast between the vigorous activity of Chicago's Halsted Street and the cool aloofness of a New England College for Women."[69]

Although Kelley had left Hull House by this time (1908), she often stayed there on her speaking tours and still "seemed to belong to the Hull House group." From the early days of the Abbotts' residence, Kelley, Lathrop, and Addams all "loved and admired" Grace and counted her the "shining light among those who were to them the younger generation of the social welfare movement." Hull House was the mecca for many who came to Chicago in the early days; there was a constant flow of visitors—scholars and social reformers—and an almost salonlike ambience as the residents interacted during the daily dinner and postprandial sessions. While the group of residents was large, "we were a kind of family group together—a very argumentative family—for we often disagreed." Addams often served as mediator during these sessions and laughed as "verbal shots were fired." Part of the charmed circle included Rachelle and Victor Yarrow, she an M.D. and he an editorial writer on a Chicago newspaper. Both had been revolutionists and had come from the old Russia. They had a "charming book-lined apartment, where we all argued vigorously."[70]

Early in their years at Hull House the Abbotts attended their first meeting of the National Conference of Charities and Corrections (later the National Conference of Social Work), at which Addams was elected president of the organization. Grace later amused residents of Hull

House with an account of the serious misgivings some of the older delegates had when a woman was elected president. To them, this was a radical step; some hoped Addams would make one of her "nice speeches," thank the men for electing her, and decline![71] Of course, she did not.

Although Breckinridge lived at Hull House for about the same period of time as the Abbotts (1907–20), she lived there for only a part of each year during her annual vacation quarter. It is apparent, however, that her life considerably meshed with the lives of the others in the circle. Toward the end of her life she moved—upon the death of Grace— to share the Abbotts' house, as Edith, Breckinridge noted, was left in an "emergency situation." Her ties to Edith were particularly strong and started early in their careers. In the summer of 1902 Edith attended summer school and was assigned to Green Hall, where Breckinridge was head. She ultimately took Breckinridge's course, The Legal and Economic Position of Women.[72] Of those early years Edith remembers that when she went back to Chicago, "I was quite clear that I wanted to live in Green Hall again, where I might have the further privilege of learning from her [Breckinridge], and in a sense, of working with her."[73]

A former student recalls that Breckinridge became one of Addams's closest friends and most helpful associates. She loved the Hull House settlement for its purposes and for its "accomplishments in helping to shape a social trend." Breckinridge herself was, of course, a part of this very process. "It bespeaks the richness of Miss Addams' character that she held in intimate friendship the gracious Sophonisba Breckinridge."[74]

As was noted at the outset, the public and private lives of both the Hull House Circle and Jane Addams were characterized by many commonalities, by similar norms, values, beliefs, and by interests that encompassed many reform areas to benefit other human beings. In reading the published and unpublished materials of the circle one is struck, not by a noblesse oblige attitude or "lady bountiful" image, but by the very forthright, matter-of-fact manner in which this group became involved in many efforts. Their concern can be roughly divided into three areas: (1) those involving children; (2) research and reform of the urban world; and (3) the political and economic equality of women. The first two areas will be dealt with briefly, the third in more detail.

While Lathrop, Kelley, and Grace Abbott are most explicitly identified with the first area, others of the circle were involved as well—Edith Abbott, for example, helped to found the Children's Division of the Chicago Welfare Department. Additionally, she and Breckinridge collaborated on a study of delinquency and truancy. Long before her affiliation with the Children's Bureau, Lathrop participated in numerous child welfare activities in Chicago and helped to establish the first juvenile court in Cook County, Illinois, in which Chicago is situated. All were involved in the movement to abolish child labor; Lathrop, Kelley, and Grace Abbott, along with Lillian Wald, played a vital role in the founding of the Children's Bureau.[75] After Abbott herself became chief of the Children's Bureau she experienced many "alarms and excursions" in coming under attack by various extremist groups during the "Red Scare," especially when the Maternity and Infancy Act and the Child Labor Amendment were under fire. In her unfinished biography of Grace, Edith says only: "Sometime I shall try to tell that story—but it is now too full of bitter memories."[76]

As noted earlier, some of the first urban research endeavors emanated from Hull House, so it is perhaps not surprising that this tradition continued among the Hull House Circle. Intrinsic to the concept of research among the Hull House Circle and other social reformers was the notion of using science and collecting data regarding a particular problem before social programs or social policy could be formulated. Concomitantly, these and other reformers of this era thought muckraking "unscientific and counterproductive."[77]

One of the early Hull House attempts at urban research was *Hull House Maps and Papers*, published in 1895 and patterned to some extent after Charles Booth's *Life and Labour of the People of London* (1889). *Hull House Maps and Papers* represented the first systematic attempt to describe the immigrant communities in an American city. A collaborative study of social conditions in the Nineteenth Ward done by residents of Hull House, it appeared at a time when academic departments of sociology had hardly been born. In it Lathrop published a chapter on the Cook County Charities; Kelley, one on the sweatshop system; and Addams, one entitled "The Settlement as a Factor in the Labor Movement."[78]

The Abbotts, Lathrop, and Breckinridge participated in numerous research endeavors through their work in the Chicago School of Civics and Philanthropy. As a part-time faculty member of the school, Grace Abbott directed a study of the lodging houses of nonfamily groups of immigrant men. When the Chicago Commission on Race Relations was established in 1919, Breckinridge had her students at the school collect housing data for use by the commission.[79] Their final report, many researchers believe, stands as one of the "earliest and most comprehensive considerations of northern race relations in the U.S."[80] In 1936 Edith Abbott published, with the assistance of Breckinridge, *The Tenements of Chicago*, which was based on a series of studies made over a period of twenty-five years and was begun when both women were at the school.[81] One final note: Edith was hired in 1914–15 to do a statistical study on crime for the Chicago City Council. The study was under the direction of Alderman Charles Merriam, also a professor of political science at the University of Chicago. Abbott put together an exhaustive set of statistics relating to all facets of the criminal justice system. Her findings were most complete and sound very familiar today. Treatment of crime in Chicago, including police organization and methods, was "wholly inadequate." "Many professional criminals escape while the poor and petty criminals are often punished more severely than is just,"[82] she stated in one conclusion.

The research efforts of these women in the area of applied sociology might also be seen as forerunners of social history, a field so much in evidence today. Abbott's *Women in Industry* and Breckinridge's *Women in the Twentieth Century* represent exemplary efforts to describe the tasks that women performed and the resources they had. Each work required "painstaking surveys of sources which had only peripheral bearing on family life to discover hints of women's activities." Each work epitomized efforts to "integrate women into history" rather than assuming that women's lives and roles have been part of an "unchanging, passive, and silent past."[83]

The members of the Hull House Circle also worked to see that women might be part of change, action, and speech in the present; and in turn their feminist activities bound them to each other and to Addams. In particular, they were participants in the National Consumers League, the labor movement, and the campaign for suffrage.

All of the circle were members of the National Consumers League, which drew its members largely from educated, upper-middle-class women (and men). Although it never had more than a few thousand members during its heyday in the first two decades of this century, it was an important manifestation of the growing concern in this country over the role of the consumer. Kelley saw the NCL as a possible vehicle through which women might increase their power as consumers and, in turn, use this power to improve working conditions for women and children workers.[84]

Ideologically, the league contained individuals of strongly divergent views. A more conservative branch saw labor, capital, and consumers as living in harmony with their various needs fulfilled. Kelley, however, distinguished between bourgeois philanthropy, which merely propped up a dying order, and working-class philanthropy, which involved, not paternalism, but working with people in reciprocal and mutual associations. Generally both the local league groups and the national organization pursued two kinds of tactics: protective legislation and ethical control of consumption. The latter involved a campaign for the "Consumers Label."[85] The "Consumers Label" involved a guarantee, so to speak, that a given product had been made in a factory meeting the standards of a "fair house," for example, equal pay for equal work and a minimum wage for women.[86] The campaign for protective legislation for women and children depended largely upon legislation and worked through publicity, propaganda, and lobbying activity.

Though participation in the NCL involved middle-class purchasers in the concerns of labor, the league stopped short of overt action in the labor movement per se. However, Hamilton, in her autobiography, noted that at Hull House, "one got into the labor movement without realizing how or when," and so it went with the Hull House Circle.[87] At the beginning of the twentieth century there were few women's unions; at best, working women were merely tolerated by men in the labor movement. Women were accused of willingly working for low wages, of depriving men of jobs, and of working only until they could find husbands. This position obscured the fact that thousands of women had to work to support their families. Although the American Federation of Labor did not openly discriminate against women, it did not vigorously work to organize them, partly because most of them were unskilled. The few women's unions existing were organized by the women themselves, in some cases with the help of a social settlement. For instance, Mary McDowell, the head resident of the University of Chicago settlement, helped establish the first women's union in the meatpacking industry.[88]

Though some Progressive leaders were hostile or at least paternalistic toward organized labor, Hull House was, from the beginning, a staunch supporter of organized labor, for which it provided meeting places as well as other kinds of services. Addams recalled that the women shirt-makers and cloakmakers were both organized at Hull House, as was the Dorcas Federal Labor Union, composed of representatives from all the unions in the city that included women in their membership. Additionally, the Chicago branch of the Women's Trade Union League (WTUL) was formed at Hull House. Perhaps not surprising is the fact that of the state branches of the WTUL, Illinois was the first to develop strength and activity.[89]

In addition to working for labor and social welfare legislation, Hull House members took an active part in strikes, helped organize unions, and defended use of such weapons as the secondary boycott. Hamilton reminisced: ''Picketing in different strikes was no unusual job in those days. I used to volunteer for the early morning picket usually, because the police were much less in evidence then and I was in mortal fear of having one of them seize me and drag me about. The fact of arrest was not as bad as the way it was done.''[90] The famed garment strike of 1910 was one of the ''great experiences of our early years at Hull House—the dramatic struggle of an oppressed group in a growing and successful industry,'' Edith Abbott wrote later.[91] Thirty years later Sidney Hillman, who had been a young trade union organizer at the time, wrote of these women:

Grace Abbott, together with Jane Addams and other prominent women, joined the fight. She joined our picket line, helped to collect funds for food and shelter, spoke at our meetings . . . helped to show that labor disputes are not private encounters between employers and employees but . . . are of profound social and economic import.[92]

Like many other reform organizations of the Progressive Era, the WTUL had its prototype in Great Britain, but was altered to fit the ''American Experience.''[93] It is noteworthy for two reasons: (1) it represented the culmination of a long struggle for organization among working women and attempted to deal with the whole of the problems of women in industry on a national scale; (2) it represented an attempt to build cooperation among women of different social classes. It is, thus, of special interest to note that the WTUL has been dismissed or given only passing attention by most historians of Progressivism and the labor movement.[94]

For four years the WTUL published the journal *Life and Labor* which served as an organ of the league's activities and as an expression of the members' views; it also provided a running diary of what was happening in the world of working women. As such, it is a mine of information for the social scientist. Also, as noted, from the time of its organization in 1903 the WTUL included two categories of membership: (1) women representatives of trade unions and (2) women (and men) of leisure who were interested in the league's purposes and were known as "Allies." An ally was defined as

Any man or woman of any class not a worker in any organized trade who believes in the organization of women and subscribes to the following League platform: (1) organization of all workers into trade unions; (2) equal pay for equal work; (3) eight-hour day; (4) a living wage; and (5) full citizenship for women.[95]

All of the Hull House Circle were members of the WTUL and participated, as described, in other endeavors of the labor movement as well. The WTUL is of interest as an organization that differed quite distinctly in two ways from other organizations of that era such as the NCL, the YMCA, and the Municipal League. First, it stressed the importance of actual organizing efforts rather than the customary reform activities (such as social investigations). Although there is no direct evidence to support the point, it is quite possible that members of the Hull House Circle, like many other women of that era, joined the WTUL because they were discouraged by the slow approach of social reform organizations or by the elitism of traditional charity work. Second, as noted, the WTUL stressed the importance of cross-class cooperation between upper- and upper-middle-class women and working-class women. It was a somewhat unique organization in attempting to build an egalitarian, cross-class alliance into its organizational structure. While members often found that it was far easier to verbalize assertions of sisterhood across class lines than to put them into practice, nonetheless the WTUL represents one salient kind of network among women in which other women were one's closest companions and sources of emotional support.[96]

On a broader national scale, members of the circle were bound to others of their sex through the struggle for women's suffrage. Since all members of the circle as well as Addams had been socialized in homes in which one or both parents supported and, in some cases, actively worked for suffrage, they too carried on the tradition and were ardent suffragists all their lives. While many supporters of women suffrage advocated votes for middle- and upper-class-women, they endorsed votes for working-class (especially immigrant) women reluctantly, if at all. However, the Hull House Circle consistently maintained not only that immigrant women would vote intelligently but that they needed the vote to protect themselves and their families from being exploited. Addams explicitly spelled this notion out.[97]

Lathrop, in her occupational roles as well as in her activities in the League of Women Voters, sought to establish measures to protect women and infants and worked as well to increase the number of women on juries, in political parties, and in political office. For many years Kelley was a vice-president of the National Woman Suffrage Association.[98] Hamilton's grandmother was a staunch supporter of the temperance movement and, largely through it, of women's suffrage. Frances Willard and Susan B. Anthony, "those valiant crusaders," were personal friends of her grandmother and used to stay with her when they were in Fort Wayne. Hamilton noted that "it took a great deal of courage in those days to come out for such causes, especially for women's suffrage." Of her mother, Hamilton commented, "Some seventy years before Virginia Woolf wrote *A Room of One's Own*, my mother believed in the right of every woman to privacy, even if she were the mother of a family."[99] For Breckinridge, as is apparent, the rights of women were a matter of special importance. Her training as a lawyer was useful in helping her draft bills regulating the wages and hours of women's employment. Additionally, her legal expertise was utilized in her course, The Legal and Economic Position of Women. Also, at the request of J. Lawrence Laughlin, head of the Economics Department, for several years she gave a course called The Legal Aspects of Labor.[100]

Since the Abbotts' mother and their Quaker grandmother, who lived with them, were strong suffragists, an almost "militant belief" in women's rights was one of their childhood traditions. Edith contended that Grace used to say of herself that she "was born believing in women suffrage." The clear teaching in their home was that "even little girls can be suffragists because it is just and right." Of her mother, Edith noted that while at Rockford Seminary "she evidently was a sturdy advocate of Women's Suffrage . . . the subject of her graduating essay was 'Iconoclasts' . . . the advocates of women's rights were, I am sure, among her iconoclasts."[101] Years later Edith is said to have remarked that the two great events in her own life were the passage of the Social

Security Act and the constitutional amendment for universal suffrage.[102]
In later reminiscences Edith recalled:

Grace was glad to find when she first went to Hull House that Miss Addams
was an uncompromising supporter of women's suffrage. . . . She had a feeling
of being close to the battle lines, for Miss Addams and our friend Miss Breckinridge were both on the National Board of the American Woman Suffrage
Association. Grace . . . felt that she was really getting news from the front. . . .
At the House we found . . . many opportunities to spread the gospel. . . . From
time to time Miss Addams would climb up to the third floor of the women's
residence where Grace and I lived and would call out, "I'm looking for an
Abbott to make a suffrage speech." Miss Addams was always rash about
accepting speaking engagements months ahead of time, only to find that she
was to be in New York or Washington.[103]

Both Edith and Grace worked very hard for the passage of the Illinois
suffrage bill (it passed on June 11, 1913). The Illinois law provided a
substantial extension of suffrage for women without a state constitutional
amendment.[104] Before the Illinois act was passed, probably in 1911,
Edith Abbott and Breckinridge wrote a pamphlet entitled "The Wage
Earning Woman and the State: A Reply to Miss Minnie Bronson" with
a preface by Addams. Bronson, an antisuffragist, took the position in
a pamphlet entitled "Wage-Earning Women and the State" (date unknown) that woman suffrage would not lead to fairer treatment of women
in industry or to better laws for their protection. In their reply to her,
Abbott and Breckinridge pointed out that Bronson failed to understand
the suffrage argument "which she attempts to criticize," and they called
attention to the fact that her knowledge of labor legislation was not such
as to make her a reliable guide in discussing the subject. The two then
delineated the enormous indirect consequences of the ballot—the gain
in education, in self-reliance, and in independence for women. They
quoted their friend Florence Kelley's statement that "for any body of
wage-earners to be disenfranchised is to be placed in an intolerable
disadvantage in all matters of legislation."[105]

This essay's focus has been upon integrating one group of women
into the history of American society by discussing their contributions
in the areas of social research, reform, and activism with Hull House
and the settlement house movement as a backdrop. While the prescriptive ideal of the middle and late nineteenth century pictured women as

meek, submissive, and appropriately confined to the private sphere, it is apparent that other models of behavior were extant in the culture. Not only did these six women enter the public sphere, but they were socialized with this objective in mind. As women whose lives bridged the public and the private spheres and whose works were forerunners of social history, the Hull House Circle are now themselves the objects of social history efforts.

In analyzing the Hull House Circle, both in terms of the individual women comprising it and of the circle itself as a group, one is struck by the many parallels between these women and the group of single academic women who were at Wellesley during this same period. Both groups represent, not isolated women who were in constant conflict with family and friends, but rather women whose family and friends, whose "significant others," provided support and sustenance.[106] Conceivably, the families themselves were rebelling against the leisure ethic, a predominant cultural theme at that time, in rejecting Thorstein Veblen's notion of "conspicuous consumption" and of their daughters as emblems of conspicuous consumption. These daughters, rather, were "pioneers" in the first generation of higher education for women and, as such, "conspicuous signs" of the family's desire to contribute to society and to reform. Rather than dutiful daughters one might call them daughters designated for achievement who were exempt from the norms of domesticity.[107] Thus, their shared "family culture" (as well as that of Hull House) of social and political reform helped turn the daughters toward higher education and service to the nation, not just the local community; such goals, in the late nineteenth century, almost by definition broadened the frame of reference of these women beyond both the marriage unit and the networks of female relatives which were typical of that period. For instance, very early in her childhood Kelley was given a charge by her father; while the duty of his generation was to "build up great industries in America so that more wealth could be produced for the whole people, the duty of your generation," he often said, "will be to see that the product is distributed justly."[108]

The ugly stereotype in our culture of the spinster or old maid as frustrated, homely, sexually repressed, and unfulfilled simply is not applicable to this group. These were bright, achieving women who led unusually productive, fulfilled lives and who took pleasure in each other's successes, who supported and reinforced one another emotionally and intellectually.[109] The Abbotts, as well as Edith Abbott and

Breckinridge, maintained vital collaborative relationships that were "refreshingly free from petty jealousies or from intensely competitive feelings." The measure of these positive friendships can be seen in the many books authored or edited together and in the introductions and dedications written for one another. For example, Edith Abbott's *Women in Industry* has an introductory note by Breckinridge. In the preface to Abbott's book on immigration, she expresses "deep obligation" to her sister as well as to her "life-long friend and colleague," Sophonisba Breckinridge.[110] Abbott's book on truancy in the Chicago schools is dedicated to "Jane Addams, guide and friend."[111] Additionally, the letters to and from members of the circle attest to meaningful and complete relationships in which loyalty and commitment to one another ended only at the death of those involved. For example, three years before Lathrop's death (1929) a letter from her to Grace Abbott noted that a friend had spoken to her "quite solemnly" about the "feeling that exists for making you Secretary of Labor." If the president were to appoint Abbott, Lathrop went on, "it would be a great advance for women and for labor."[112]

In contrast to the model typically used by males to achieve in the occupational sphere, the Hull House Circle's modus operandi was quite different. The male pattern of achievement frequently involved the aid of a mentor, an older, more powerful figure who served as instructor and gatekeeper for the younger in what was generally a relationship characterized by an unequal distribution of power. While members of the Hull House Circle served each other as sources of both public and private support, they did so by forming a network of relationships that, because of its complexity and multiplicity, made other kinds of models unnecessary. Unlike the mentor model, the support system outlined in this essay was based to a large extent upon egalitarian relationships, which were functional in spite of age differences between its members and were based upon shared visibility. Additionally, this support system encompassed a larger group than the traditional dyad in the mentor relationship. As a result, this group was able to serve its members more fully over a larger range of activities, time, and space.

The Hull House Circle was further strengthened in that it combined aspects of both the intimacy of networks of female family members and friends with the task orientation of women banding together for intellectual, economic, and political purposes in various reform undertakings. These women epitomized one type of reformer, that of professional expert and scientist, in contrast to another type of reformer, the sage or prophetess, who claimed access to hidden wisdom by virtue of feminine insight and saw her role of social change agent as growing out of the unique qualities with which the female temperament was supposedly endowed. While the latter type of reformer reinforced the prevailing stereotypes of the time regarding women, the reformer as professional expert and scientist clearly did not, but rather challenged the prevailing images of women. The professional expert made no claims to expertise by virtue of being a female and thus possessing special insights. Rather, this woman was a highly trained problem solver who sought an understanding of the entire social structure and had acquired a specialized competence to deal with it.[113] For some of the Hull House Circle their early experiences in the Chicago School of Civics and Philanthropy played a major role in their professionalization process and in enabling them to function effectively in bureaucratic settings as they moved from local and state levels to national and international levels. Not only were research skills perfected at the Chicago School, but more intangible skills were developed as well, such as those of coalition building.

Conceivably, the pattern of professional women fostering the success of other women was begun and elaborated upon at Hull House. While historians, quite understandably, have focused largely upon Jane Addams's role as a Progressive reformer (or as a representative of a group of "frustrated" college-trained women with no place to go), her "enormous contribution" in creating a supportive female network and "new structures for living" has been overlooked.[114] At Hull House, as well as in other social settlements, reformers gathered to build an innovative residential community involving cooperative living. As an idealistic community living in one complex of buildings, Hull House residents resembled earlier communitarian experiments, although the settlement's economic organization was closer to various cooperative boarding arrangements.[115] As members of this community were united by numerous common interests, beliefs, and values, the lively verbal exchange among residents during the dinner hour no doubt provided a forum, a launching place, for intellectual growth among the Hull House Circle and others. Further, the Hull House experience was itself an experiment in the integration of public and private life, one which, in varying degrees, cut across gender, class, and ethnic lines.

As delineated, the friendships of the Hull House Circle are of interest because of their importance to members for emotional as well as for professional achievement, and because the public and the private spheres were joined to a degree that was often impossible to separate.[116] In fact, one can conclude that this strong female support system allowed its members to be "producers and theorizers of knowledge" because it freed them from the marginality that typified men's definitions of women's role in intellectual life, while at the same time their exclusion from respected positions—as in the relatively secure haven of the prestige university—helped lead them not only toward pragmatically based research but also toward social activism. Albeit in some sense ironically, both being female and not being male had a positive and definitive impact on their lives.

The notion of a circle implies an unending process, a "chain of experiences that was never broken."[117] One factor that reinforced this pattern for these women was the interrelationship of the pragmatic with the theoretical in their writing as well as in their lives. Thus, in a reciprocal fashion, their lives fed their writing and vice versa within a continually broadening circle made up of many smaller circles. Although they established pleasant and meaningful relationships with men in their professional lives (such as other faculty at the University of Chicago or board members of the Immigrants' Protective League), one feels that these friendships did not detract from or compete with those with their intimate female friends.

"Friendship is a definitive experience of reality," scholar and social critic Vida Scudder wrote in her autobiography. "It is the 'central peace.' It is victorious over age or circumstances, independent of time or space. . . . I wish poets and novelists would celebrate more often the friendships of women, for these are a marked and, generally speaking, wholesome phenomenon in the modern world."[118]

NOTES

In discussing women's support networks of the past, some researchers have described them as lesbian or homosexual. Other researchers have rejected outright use of these concepts; still others have simply excluded them from discussion. The point of view taken in this essay is that any group of humans who are objects of research must be seen within their own time period and in relationship to their own values and belief systems. The terms *lesbian* and *homosexual* had at best murky and ambiguous meanings in the past century. Further, these concepts were not within the frame of reference of many nineteenth-century women. Thus, usage of these terms seems to involve imposing our world upon theirs. In addition, the main purpose of this essay has been to demonstrate the existence of a durable, meaningful network of professional, political, and personal friendship that linked these six women for half a century and beyond, and across half a country. Its emphasis is friendship among the group as a whole and the relationship of friendship to effective action in the public domain rather than the intimate lives of individual women in the group.

1. Cited in Wayne McMillan, "Edith Abbott: Her Contribution to Professional Education for Social Work," *Social Service Administration Newsletter* 5, no. 1 (1958):3–9.

2. Mary Jo Deegan, "Women and Sociology, 1890–1930," *The Journal of the History of Sociology* 1 (Fall 1978):19. See Steven Diner, "Department and Discipline: The Department of Sociology at the University of Chicago, 1892–1920," *Minerva* 13 (Winter 1975):514–53, as well as Diner, *A City and Its Universities: Public Policy in Chicago, 1892–1919* (Chapel Hill: University of North Carolina Press, 1980). Diner does include Edith Abbott and Breckinridge in his discussion of the department of sociology at Chicago. It is of interest to note that Annie Marion MacLean, who received the Ph.D. in sociology in 1900, was relegated to the Home Study division as an assistant professor while males (e.g., George Vincent and W. I. Thomas) who received their degrees at about the same time were offered faculty appointments. See Virginia K. Fish, "The Chicago School Revisited: Whatever Happened to Annie Marion MacLean and Frances R. Donovan?" Paper presented at the Midwest Sociological Society's Annual Meeting, Minneapolis, April 13–16, 1977. The terms *social work* and *social welfare* are used interchangeably in this essay.

3. Julia A. Sherman and Evelyn Torton Beck, eds., *The Prism of Sex*: *Essays in the Sociology of Knowledge* (Madison: University of Wisconsin Press, 1979), pp. 3–4. Jean Elshtain in "Moral Woman and Immoral Man: A Consideration of the Public-Private Split and Its Political Ramifications," *Politics and Society* 4, no. 4 (1974):453–73, traces the roots of the public/private dichotomy back to Aristotle's work. The public (political) realm is seen as appropriately occupied by free males who make decisions and wield power in the life of the polis; however, males are also allowed to occupy the private (nonpolitical) realm of nonfree females. Here males receive support and sustenance to enable them to carry on their onerous duties in the outside (political) world. However, females are not allowed to enter the public sphere but are relegated entirely to the life of the lesser association (i.e., the household), which is seen as inferior in nature, in intent, and in purpose to the more inclusive association of the polis.

4. Jane Addams, "The Subjective Necessity for Social Settlements," in Christopher Lasch, ed., *The Social Thought of Jane Addams* (Indianapolis: Bobbs-Merrill, 1965), pp. 28–43.

5. Patricia Palmieri, "Patterns of Achievement of Single Academic Women

at Wellesley College, 1880–1920,'' *Frontiers* 5 (Spring 1980):63–67. Palmieri discusses a group of single academic women at Wellesley who bear striking resemblances to the Hull House Circle in terms of the social milieu out of which they came and their friendship networks. The Wellesley group will be referred to throughout this essay. To a sociologist the term *family culture* includes the norms, values, and beliefs of the family unit as well as the manner in which the children are socialized.

6. Rosalind Rosenberg, "The Academic Prism: The New View of American Women,'' in Carol Berkin and Mary Beth Norton, eds., *Women of America: A History* (New York: Houghton Mifflin, 1979), p. 323. While the University of Chicago was coeducational from its beginning, an unsuccessful move was begun in 1902 to "segregate" the sexes. See Rosenberg, especially pp. 325–28.

7. Allen F. Davis, *American Heroine: The Life and Legend of Jane Addams* (New York: Oxford, 1973), p. 80.

8. Jane Addams, *My Friend Julia Lathrop* (New York: Macmillan, 1935), p. 116.

9. Mary Jo Deegan, "Early Women Sociologists and the American Sociological Society: The Patterns of Exclusion and Participation,'' *The American Sociologist* 16 (February 1981):14–24.

10. E. A., "Grace Abbott and Hull House, 1908–21. Part I,'' *Social Service Review* 24 (September 1950):380.

11. Ibid.

12. Addams to Abbott, March 30, 1934; Hamilton to Abbott, May 20, 1935; Hamilton to Abbott, June 11, 1935; Edith and Grace Abbott Papers, Regenstein Library, University of Chicago, Chicago, Illinois.

13. Keith Melder, *Beginnings of Sisterhood: The American Women's Rights Movement, 1800–1850* (New York: Schocken, 1977).

14. Ibid. See also Carroll Smith-Rosenberg, "The Female World of Love and Ritual: Relations between Women in Nineteenth Century America,'' *Signs* 1 (Fall 1975):1–29; Blanche Wiesen Cook, "Female Support Networks and Political Activism: Lillian Wald, Crystal Eastman, and Emma Goldman,'' *Chrysalis* no. 3 (1977):43–61; Nancy Sahli, "Smashing: Women's Relationships before the Fall,'' *Chrysalis*, no. 8 (1979):17–27. The terms *friendship network*, *support network*, and *female bonding* are frequently, and sometimes indiscriminately, used in the current literature. Discussion in this essay will employ only the term *friendship network*, referring to one kind of relationship that sociologists see as primary. This involves a personal, durable, intimate relationship characterized by many common goals and values.

15. Biographical material throughout this section comes from the following: Edward T. James, ed., *Notable American Women, 1607–1950: A Biographical Dictionary* (Cambridge, Mass.: Belknap Press of Harvard University Press,

1975), 3 vols.; Barbara Sicherman and Carol Hurd Green, eds., *Notable American Women: The Modern Period* (Cambridge, Mass.: Belknap Press of Harvard University Press, 1980); Durward Howes, ed., *American Women: The Standard Biological Dictionary of Notable Women, 1939–40* (Los Angeles: American Publications, 1939); *Current Biography* (New York: H. W. Wilson, 1941 and 1946); James Leonard, ed., *Woman's Who's Who of America, 1914–1915* (New York: The American Commonwealth, 1914); *The National Cyclopedia of American Biography* (New York: James T. White and Co., 1935 and 1951) vols. 24 and 37; John B. Turner, ed., *Encyclopedia of Social Work*, Seventeenth Issue, no. 1 (Washington, D.C.: National Association of Social Workers, 1977).

    16. James, 2:371.

    17. Cited in James, 2:319.

    18. Cited in Sicherman and Green, *Notable American Women*, p. 306.

    19. James, 1:235.

    20. Sicherman and Green, *Notable American Women*, pp. 1–2; James, 1:3–4.

    21. Helen R. Wright, "Three against Time: Edith and Grace Abbott and Sophonisba P. Breckinridge," *Social Service Review* 28 (March 1954):46.

    22. Diner, "Department and Discipline," p. 521; Diner, *A City and Its Universities*, especially chapter 2.

    23. For sources, see note 15; for the Wellesley women, see Palmieri.

    24. Addams, *My Friend*, pp. 21, 23. Addams's biography of Lathrop is of interest in and of itself since it illustrates the lifelong friendships of this group. Originally, Addams and Grace Abbott were to write a life of Lathrop; Addams took the early and late years, and Abbott was to do the middle years. This was never accomplished; however, Addams's manuscript was found at her death by Hamilton, who made as few changes in it as possible before it was published.

    25. "Some Family Traditions—Abolition and the Civil War," and "The Rights of Women," Addenda 2, Box 1, Folders 2 and 6, Abbott Papers.

    26. Addams, *My Friend*, p. 23.

    27. Alice Hamilton, *Exploring the Dangerous Trades: the Autobiography of Alice Hamilton, M.D.* (Boston: Little, Brown, 1943), p. 30.

    28. James, 1:233.

    29. No author, "Grace Abbott: A Sister's Memories," *Social Service Review* 13 (September 1939):351–407; Chapter 8, "A Home of Law and Politics," Addenda 2, Box 1, Folder 8, Abbott Papers.

    30. Hamilton, *Dangerous Trades*, p. 18.

    31. Reprinted in Madeline P. Grant, *Alice Hamilton: Pioneer Doctor in Industrial Medicine* (New York: Abelard-Schuman, 1967), p. 211.

    32. Sophonisba Breckinridge, *Madeline McDowell Breckinridge: A Leader in the South* (Chicago: University of Chicago Press, 1921), p. 7.

33. "Grace Abbott: A Sister's Memories," p. 407.

34. Wright, p. 41.

35. Florence Kelley, "My Philadelphia," *Survey* 57 (October 1, 1926):7–11, 50–57. Her aunt was Sarah Pugh, a notable reformer who retired from teaching school at the age of fifty to devote her life to the antislavery movement, free trade, peace, woman suffrage, and a single standard of morals for men and women.

36. Addams, *My Friend*, p. 38.

37. Kelley, "My Philadelphia"; Florence Kelley, "When Co-education Was Young," *Survey* 57 (February 1, 1927):557–61, 600–602; James, vol. 2.

38. Hamilton, pp. 29–30, 35, 40; Grant, p. 44.

39. *Current Biography*, 1941; James, vol. I; *National Cyclopedia*, vol. 37, 1951; "Grace Abbott: A Sister's Memories."

40. Addams to Breckinridge, July 15, 1925, Box 1, Folder 13, Sophonisba P. Breckinridge Papers, Regenstein Library, University of Chicago. Book title not given.

41. Addams, *My Friend*; James, 1:370–71.

42. See Florence Kelley, "Aims and Principles of the Consumers League," *American Journal of Sociology* 5 (1899–1900):289–304, for a more detailed discussion of the NCL.

43. Hamilton's autobiography discusses this area in detail.

44. E.A., "Grace Abbott, Part I," especially 383–84. Robert Buroker, "From Voluntary Association to Welfare State: The Illinois Immigrants' Protective League 1908–1926," *The Journal of American History* 58, no. 3 (1971):643–60, places the IPL in the larger context of the Progressive movement and the professionalization of social work.

45. See Mary Jo Deegan, "Women and Sociology"; *Publications of the Members of the University, 1902–1906*, compiled on the twenty-fifth anniversary of the university by a committee of the faculty, Julius Stieglitz, chair (Chicago: University of Chicago Press, 1917); *University Record New Series* 5 (January 1919):106, University of Chicago.

46. Jo Freeman, "Women on the Social Science Faculties since 1902," mimeograph, presented at the University of Chicago Panel on the Status of Women at Chicago (Winter 1969), p. 2; cited in Deegan, "Women and Sociology," p. 30.

47. Untitled, Box 1, Folder 8, Sophonisba P. Breckinridge Papers, Regenstein Library, University of Chicago.

48. Graham Taylor, "The Industrial Viewpoint," *Charities and the Commons* 17 (1906–7):260–61; *University Record New Series* 4 (January 1918):62, University of Chicago. Marion Talbot became a lifelong friend of Breckinridge's and was drawn indirectly into the Hull House Circle. She came to Chicago in 1892, the year the university was established, and served for many years as

Dean of Women and as Professor of Household Administration, a department lodged in the College of Arts, Literature, and Science, which President Harper established for her in the early 1900s. For her own account of those early years see Marion Talbot, *More Than Lore: Reminiscences of Marion Talbot* (Chicago: University of Chicago Press, 1936). The rank of docent was a lowly one and below the rank of instructor, as Talbot notes (p. 18).

49. *University Record New Series* 6 (October 1920):260–64, University of Chicago; *University Record New Series* 11 (July 1925):221, the University of Chicago. The *University Record* of October 1920 notes that the graduate school of Social Service Administration absorbed the old Chicago School of Civics and Philanthropy in order to establish a graduate professional curriculum for those students who desired to enter the field of social work and civic service. Further evidence of women's marginal position at the University is contained in Talbot's *More Than Lore* (pp. 137–40), in which she reprinted a letter she and two other faculty women sent to the University of Chicago administration in December 1924. In the letter they pointed out that three women faculty who received the Ph.D. in 1907 or earlier (this would include Edith Abbott and Breckinridge) were still only associate professors while twenty-one men receiving the Ph.D. in this same period were full professors. Further, Talbot noted that while two of the women had been awarded the honorary degree of Doctor of Law, none of the men had. Finally, Talbot noted (p. 14) that the women were gratified when, "on the next announcement of promotions, Miss Abbott, Miss Katherine Blunt, and Miss Breckinridge were named as professors. Some other results followed, such as the appointment of a woman as Convocation Orator; but, on the whole, no great progress was made."

50. Mary Jo Deegan, "Early Women Sociologists."

51. Sicherman and Green, p. 2.

52. Diner, "Department and Discipline," p. 532.

53. Diner, "Department and Discipline"; McMillan. For a detailed account of the founding of this journal, see Steven J. Diner, "Scholarship in the Quest for Social Welfare: A Fifty-Year History of the *Social Service Review*," *Social Service Review* 51 (March 1977):1–66.

54. "The Late Years, 1894–1900" and "Coming to the University," Box 1, Folders 7, 8, and 9, Breckinridge Papers. Interesting parallels can be drawn in this regard between Breckinridge and Mary Kingsley, British African explorer, whose life is discussed in Katherine Frank's essay "Voyages Out: Nineteenth-Century Women Travelers in Africa" in this volume.

55. "Autobiography: Introduction," Box 1, Folder 2, Breckinridge Papers.

56. "1894–1900: The Late Years," Box 1, Folder 7, Breckinridge Papers.

57. Sherman and Beck give several current examples to illustrate this phenomenon. For example, "When asked how she felt about being talented in mathematics, an extremely bright high school senior replied, 'Women are sup-

posed to be inferior in mathematics and I'm not. It makes me feel guilty.'
Guilty.'' Additionally, in the course of Sherman's work on women and mathematics, a man who had otherwise been extremely helpful, anxiously inquired, "Do you think that you, being a woman, can be objective in this kind of study?" (pp. 4–5). Sociologists have noted the phenomenon of the "self-fulfilling prophecy" in which members of oppressed minority groups may come to define themselves in terms of the negative definitions with which majority group members see them.

58. James, vol. 1; Turner.

59. Allen F. Davis and Mary Lynn McCree, eds., *Eighty Years at Hull House* (Chicago: University of Chicago, 1969).

60. Jane Addams, *The Second Twenty Years at Hull House: September 1909 to September 1929* (New York: Macmillan, 1930), p. 405.

61. Francis Hackett, "Hull House—A Souvenir," *Survey* 54 (June 1, 1925):275–80.

62. Jane Addams, "A Great Public Servant, Julia C. Lathrop," *Social Service Review* 6 (June 2, 1932):280–85.

63. Hackett, p. 277.

64. Florence Kelley, "I Go to Work," *Survey* 58 (June 1, 1927):271–74, 301.

65. Addams, *My Friend*; Davis and McCree.

66. Hamilton, p. 61.

67. Ibid.

68. The School of Civics and Philanthropy was an early school of social work, originally part of the extension division of the University of Chicago, and consisted largely of a series of lectures by Graham Taylor of the Chicago Commons Settlement, Lathrop of Hull House, and later by Breckinridge as well. It was initially called the Institute of Social Science and was expanded when the aforementioned grant was awarded. Breckinridge was the director of research, and Edith Abbott was hired by Lathrop as a research assistant. A letter dated March 25, 1908, from Lathrop confirming her appointment is in the Abbott Papers (Box 57, Folder 5). Additional material is found in Box 57, Folder 2, and in Addenda 2, Box 1, Folder 14. Ultimately, as noted, the school became absorbed into the University of Chicago structure as the School of Social Service Administration.

69. "The Hull House Years," Abbott Papers.

70. Ibid.

71. Ibid.

72. "Coming to the University," and "The Russell Sage Foundation," Box 11, Folders 9 and 11, Breckinridge Papers.

73. Edith Abbott, "Sophonisba Breckinridge over the Years," *Social Service Review* 22 (December 1948):417–23.

74. Russell Ballard, "The Years at Hull House," *Social Service Review* 22, no 4 (1948):432–33.

75. For a fuller account of the Hull House coalition and the anti–child labor movement in Illinois see Lynn Gordon, "Women and the Anti–Child Labor Movement in Illinois, 1890–1920," *Social Service Review* 51 (June 1977):228–48. For a discussion of the founding of the Children's Bureau see James Johnson, "The Role of Women in the Founding of the United States Children's Bureau," in Carol George, ed., *Remember the Ladies: New Perspectives on Women in American History* (Syracuse: Syracuse University Press, 1975).

76. "Grace Abbott: A Sister's Memories," p. 394.

77. Diner, *A City and Its Universities*, p. 64.

78. Residents of Hull House, *Hull House Maps and Papers* (Boston: Thomas Crowell, 1895).

79. "Grace Abbott: A Sister's Memories."

80. Diner, *A City and Its Universities*, p. 132.

81. Edith Abbott, *The Tenements of Chicago: 1908–1935* (Chicago: University of Chicago Press, 1936).

82. Edith Abbott, "Statistics Relating to Crime in Chicago," in *Report of the City Council Committee on Crime of the City of Chicago*, Alderman Charles E. Merriam, Chairman (Chicago City Council, March 22, 1915), pp. 9–11.

83. Ann D. Gordon, Mari Jo Buhle, and Nancy Schrom Dye, "The Problem of Women's History," in Berenice A. Carroll, ed., *Liberating Women's History: Theoretical and Critical Essays* (Urbana: University of Illinois, 1976), p. 82. Janet Sharistanian first suggested the social history thesis to the author. For a discussion of women whose activities in the public sphere were far different from those of the Hull House Circle see June Underwood, "Civilizing Kansas: Women's Organizations, 1880–1921," and Carolyn De Swarte Gifford, "Home Protection: The WCTU's Conversion to Woman Suffrage," this volume.

84. Florence Kelley, *Modern Industry in Relation to the Family, Health, Education, and Morality* (New York, 1914), cited in Allis Wolfe, "Women, Consumerism, and the National Consumers League in the Progressive Era, 1900–1923," *Labor History* 16 (Spring 1975):378–92.

85. Allis Wolfe, "Women, Consumerism and the National Consumers League."

86. Florence Kelley, "Twenty-five Years of the Consumers League Movement," *The Survey* 35 (November 27, 1915):212–14.

87. Hamilton, p. 80.

88. Allen F. Davis, "The Women's Trade Union League: Origins and Organization," *Labor History* 5 (Winter 1964):3–17; Lea Taylor, "The Social Settlement and Civic Responsibility—The Life Work of Mary McDowell and Graham Taylor," *Social Service Review* 28 (March 1954):31–40; Howard E. Wilson, *Mary McDowell: Neighbor* (Chicago: University of Chicago Press,

1928). Mary McDowell provides an interesting link with Hull House. Before becoming head resident at the University of Chicago settlement (commonly referred to as "Back of the yards" and the area as "Packingtown") in 1894, McDowell lived at Hull House for a short period, was one of the first kindergarten teachers, and served as first president of the Woman's Club. At this same time some faculty members of the University of Chicago, searching for a better knowledge of the life of the working classes, formed what they called the "Christian Union," an organization determined to search for the causes of contemporary unrest and, at the same time, express religious and educational principles in the creation of a laboratory of social service in the city. The new settlement, taking its philosophy from Hull House, was to serve as a "window" for the new department of sociology at the University and at the same time minister to the needs of a Chicago neighborhood. Later investigations in which Grace Abbott and Breckinridge took part explored the effect of the packing plants and stockyards on the standard of living, sanitation, health, and housing as well as retardation among many of the school children in the area.

89. Addams, *Twenty Years at Hull House*, p. 157; Davis and McCree, p. 34; John B. Andrews and W. D. P. Bliss, *History of Women in the Trade Unions*, vol. 10 of *Report on Conditions of Woman and Child Wage Earners in the United States*, 19 vols., U.S. Senate Document 645, 61 Congress, 2nd session, 1911, p. 157. The latter source gives a very complete history of women and labor. *The Women's Trade Union League of Illinois* (Chicago: Hillison, McCormack and Co., 1907–1908), a descriptive brochure about the league, notes that the Chicago branch "meets the second Sunday in each month at the Women's Club Rooms of Hull House" (p. 1).

90. Hamilton, p. 82.

91. E.A., "Hull House Part I," p. 393.

92. Cited in E.A., "Hull House Part I," pp. 393–94.

93. Davis, p. 5.

94. Davis, p. 16, elaborates upon the latter point; see also Robin Miller Jacoby, "The Women's Trade Union League and American Feminism," *Feminist Studies* 3 (Fall 1975):126–40.

95. Alice Henry, *The Trade Union Women* (New York: D. Appleton, 1915), pp. 74–75, 85, footnote 1.

96. Nancy Schrom Dye, "Creating a Feminist Alliance: Sisterhood and Class Conflict in the New York Women's Trade Union League, 1903–1915," *Feminist Studies* 2, no. 2/3 (1975):24–38; Dye, "Feminism or Unionism? The New York Women's Trade Union League and the Labor Movement," *Feminist Studies* 3 (Fall 1975):111–25; see also James Kenneally, "Women and Trade Unions 1870–1920: The Quandary of the Reformer," *Labor History* 16, no. 1 (1973):42–55.

97. Jane Addams, "Why Women Should Vote," *Ladies' Home Journal*

27 (January 1910):21–22; See also Allen F. Davis, *American Heroine*, pp. 186–88.

98. Addams, *My Friend*; James, vol. 2.

99. Hamilton, pp. 24 and 32.

100. "Coming to the University," Breckinridge Papers.

101. "The Rights of Women," Addenda 2, Box 1, Folder 6, Abbott Papers.

102. Arlien Johnson, "Edith Abbott's Contribution to Public Social Policy," *Social Service Administration Newsletter* 5 (December 1957):14–20.

103. E.A., "Hull House, Part II," pp. 500–501.

104. E.A., "Hull House, Part II," p. 502. Edith Abbott noted that the victory in Illinois had far-reaching results since it was the first state east of the Mississippi (the third in terms of population) to give women suffrage (pp. 503–4).

105. Edith Abbott and Sophonisba Breckinridge, *The Wage Earning Women and the State: A Reply to Miss Minnie Bronson* (Boston: Boston Equal Suffrage Association for Sound Government, n.d. [1911?]), pp. 19–20, 22.

106. *Significant others* is a sociological term referring to those with whom one has a primary relationship.

107. Palmieri, p. 64.

108. Florence Kelley, "My Philadelphia," p. 8.

109. For a discussion of the spinster in another context see Rosalind Urbach Moss, " 'Educated and Ambitious Women': Kate Warthen on the Kansas Frontier," this volume.

110. Edith Abbott, *Immigration: Select Documents and Case Records* (Chicago: University of Chicago Press, 1924), p. xi.

111. Edith Abbott, *Truancy and Non-Attendance in the Chicago Schools* (Chicago: University of Chicago Press, 1917), n.p.

112. Lathrop to Grace Abbott, March 29, 1929, Box 58, Folder 3, Abbott Papers.

113. Jill Conway, "Women Reformers and American Culture, 1870–1930," *Journal of Social History* 5 (Winter 1971–72):164–77. Lela B. Costin specifically discusses the Abbotts as professional reformers in *Two Sisters for Social Justice: A Biography of Edith and Grace Abbott* (Urbana: University of Illinois Press, 1983), pp. vii–ix.

114. Gerda Lerner, *The Majority Finds Its Past: Placing Women in History* (New York: Oxford University Press, 1979), p. 147.

115. Delores Hayden, *The Grand Domestic Revolution: A History of Feminist Designs for American Homes, Neighborhoods, and Cities* (Cambridge, Mass.: MIT Press, 1981), pp. 162–78.

116. Palmieri notes this as well, p. 66.

117. Ibid.

118. Vida Scudder, *On Journey* (New York: E. P. Dutton and Company,

1937). Scudder, a scholar of religions and a professor at Wellesley College, contributed to the development of Christian socialism early in the twentieth century. Active in the settlement and peace movements, she was a friend of Jane Addams.

9

Conclusion: Historical Study and the Public/Domestic Model

JANET SHARISTANIAN

In reading the preceding essays, one is struck by the degree to which Rosaldo's revised rather than original model suits their results. First, and most simply, this is because each study can demonstrate the fruitfulness that concepts of public and private yield only *because* it is framed in terms of "local and specific forms of social relationships." Levin's queens, Frank's women travelers, Gifford's temperance workers, Underwood's reformers, and Fish's professional thinkers and doers all came out of, responded to, and helped to create particular historical situations. This specificity is as characteristic of Patrice Koelsch's analysis of the connections between classical Greek political theory and contemporary feminist criticism, the most sweeping discussion in the collection, as it is of Rosalind Moss's re-creation of the facts and concepts that make up Kate Warthen's biography, the most sharply delimited. There is a logical chain of connections between the Western (that is, classical) dichotomization of public and private realms, its understanding of literature as a public construction of private experience, the comparatively limited role that women have played in the production, conceptualization, and interpretation of literature, and the current feminist interest in literature and criticism as disclosures of "the privatized nature of women's experience." By reiterating certain assumptions about the connections between gender, society, and art over time, Western culture reveals itself as "local" and "specific," not universal.

Second, each of these essays corresponds to Rosaldo's revisionist definition of women's status as determined not by their biology—or even by their activities—but by "the meanings [these] activities acquire through concrete social interactions." Perhaps the most striking example of this distinction is Carole Levin's sixteenth-century queens, caught in an absolute contradiction between their "sexual status" as women unproductive of male heirs on the one hand and their "political status" as national leaders and symbolic representatives of God on the other. In distinguishing between Mary's and Elizabeth's attempts to assume kingly (i.e., masculine) characteristics yet exhibit feminine qualities where appropriate, Levin shows that Mary's tactics weakened her authority as a ruler yet enhanced her legitimacy as a woman, while Elizabeth's, which protected and even augmented her power, increased the generalized sense of insecurity that was a response to her sex. But in the most basic sense their situations were alike, in that no satisfactory resolution could be effected between woman's ideological relegation to the private sphere and these women's status in the public domain. Where biology had failed the English populace, ideology took over.

Another conspicuous example, for biological reasons of both sex and race, is Katherine Frank's best-known woman traveler, Mary Kingsley. As a woman, she lacked the institutional resources available to male explorers; as a husbandless woman, she elicited dismay from her guides. But the former disadvantage gave her intellectual and political freedom, while the latter, so easily explained away by recourse to an ideologically acceptable "white" lie, gave her great mobility. At the same time, Kingsley's race endowed her with status in the eyes of the Africans, which in turn led her to understand parallels between the subjection of women and the subjugation of black Africans. Again, biology and activity acquire their status "through concrete social interactions."

However, when the model is broken down into some of its components, the fit between paradigm and application seems a little looser. For instance, the impact of women's domestic responsibilities on their participation in the public domain is complex and variable; a high rate of participation in the former does not necessarily lead to a low rate of participation in the latter. Relative freedom from domestic duties was an inducement to—or, at any rate, a prerequisite for—public achievement for Mary Kingsley or Kate Warthen, and the members of the friendship circle centering on Hull House were freed from "family claims" by their single status as well as by a shared "family culture" that honored good citizenship over good housekeeping. On the other hand, the members of the WCTU who worked for suffrage, or of the Kansas women's organizations who worked for the betterment of individual, social, and civic life, did so in the name of domesticity and thus were duty-bound to meet family responsibilities as well as public commitments. Moreover, the fact that comparable middle-class women did not support suffrage or participate in social reform indicates that middle-class leisure was a condition for, not a cause of, these women's activities.[1]

Even more evident is the double-edged impact of domestic ideology, which cuts both along and across the lines of Rosaldo's argument. Assumptions about women's "natural" concern for human problems motivated the women studied by Gifford, Underwood, and Fish to much vigorous intellectual, political, social, and economic effort yet at the same time worked to limit the range of their activity. In fact, members of the WCTU and the Kansas women's organizations used the very sex-role ideologies that supposedly justified keeping them at home to come together in an intermediate domain for the purpose of changing the public realm. Yet the supporters of temperance were converted to suffrage out of a profound belief in the sanctity of the home, while the Kansas club women inadvertently succeeded in narrowing the domestic sphere once they accomplished their goals of raising public consciousness and building public institutions. Consequently, June Underwood concludes, in failing to alter the conventional view of women's place they "cut short full movement into the public sphere."

In the case of Virginia Fish's academic women, cultural assumptions about "man's world, woman's place"[2] had an even more ironic effect. Limited by others' prejudices, not by their own ambitions and abilities, to more private, domestically oriented areas within the public domain of the prestige university, they could not attain full academic status. Thus "encouraged" to combine research and social reform in larger contexts, they probably had much more impact upon public life than they would have had if elevated to the privacy of the ivory tower.

In smaller, more individualized ways, domestic ideologies also had dual effects upon Frank's and Moss's subjects. Women travelers, especially single women, felt that to "skylark," even to see and understand "the wild African idea," could not be justifications by themselves but had to be buttressed by some "public vocation of service," if the disjunction between womanly duties and masculine privileges were to be overcome. However, Frank demonstrates the care with which almost all of the writers, much like anthropological participant-observers, struggled to understand Africa from Africans' own points of view, and such adaptability to the feelings and perceptions of others was one of the ideals of the Victorian angel in the house. In the case of Kate Warthen, her sex and her status as a spinster both alleviated and exacerbated the response to her in various public roles, particularly during her political campaign for county superintendent of schools. In short, one may conclude that domestic ideologies both helped and hindered the subjects of most of these essays as they participated in the public domain.

Where Rosaldo's postulates for the improvement of women's status are concerned, the results are again mixed. The first of these axioms, that women may increase their status through participation in the public world of men, is sustained by Koelsch's analysis of Greek political philosophy. The polis, the realm of individualized speech and action, is reserved for free males; women, like slaves, lack full human status and are consigned to the anonymous, silent "realm of necessity." Certainly Frank's Mary Kingsley attained individualized speech and egalitarian action and to this extent improved her status by exploring, writing, and attempting to influence English policy toward Africa. Yet in a number of the African travelers' books, especially those written by Kingsley, Frank finds an "it's only me" persona and "a debilitating . . . lack of selfhood," despite remarkable accomplishments. Kingsley may have attained considerable status, but she seems to have believed that she had no status at all. This raises the issue of whether definitions of status can be purely structural or should also include the self-concepts of individuals and groups. For corroborating evidence there is the life-long insecurity of Sophonisba Breckinridge, the only one of Fish's Hull House Circle members who did not enjoy wholehearted "support and sustainment" for her public ambitions from her family. By contrast Kate Warthen, who significantly enhanced her professional, political, and social status by participating in the public domain, was also able, for the most part, to turn both positive and negative influences on the development of her sense of self to her own ends.

In the cases of two groups of women who shared intermediate public domains and, because of this, were empowered in the public world of men, the implications for increased status are more emphatic than in highly individualized situations such as those of nineteenth-century travelers in Africa or female politicians on the Kansas frontier. As the women's groups studied by June Underwood moved into one level of the public domain they enhanced their status and increased their effectiveness both as individuals and as members of a band of sisters, and this in turn made it possible for them to move into other, more complicated and wider-ranging problem areas. Certainly, they received praise and admiration from many male leaders who were motivated by the general welfare rather than by personal gain.

The results are perhaps even more striking when the intermediate public domain, or "friendship network," of the Hull House Circle and its effects upon the larger public world are analyzed. Members of the group were conspicuous national leaders whose status is, in this collection, overshadowed only by that of Levin's queens, inheritors of rank. And their friendship network, a "complex interweaving of intellectual creativity, emotional support, professional collegiality, and companionship in social activism," was intense, long-lasting, and tangibly improved their lives and the quality of public life.

Yet Carolyn Gifford's analysis of the temperance movement's conversion to woman suffrage places the paradigm in a rather ironic light, for these Evangelical Christians did not enter the world of men and thereby increase their status. On the contrary, it was necessary for them to pass through the painful, yet liberating, process of deconstructing and then reconstructing the image of the True Christian Woman—in other words, to affirm their value in the eyes of God and thus their value in the human realm—*before* they could enter into a series of excursions into public, that is political, life. One would have to conclude that for members of the WCTU in the 1880s, an increase in status and participation in the public domain were indeed associated—but not in the causal order that is implied by the model.

Similar discrepancies surface when the broader generalizations that "women's status will be lowest in those societies where there is a firm differentiation between domestic and public spheres of activity" and that the most egalitarian societies will be "those in which public and domestic spheres are only weakly differentiated" are evaluated in the light of these essays. In Frank's study, the marriages of traveler-writers who were missionary or government wives frequently responded to the

pressures and freedoms of existence in thoroughly un-English environments by becoming more egalitarian and more satisfying for each partner. Yet egalitarianism and female status may be in *conflict* with each
other, as Carole Levin's essay shows. In order to enforce her own power
and status, Queen Elizabeth sharply distinguished herself from other
women and insisted, through such means as the Homily on Marriage,
that women, being inferior and therefore rightly subordinate, should
obey their husbands. In other words, in order to affirm her own equality
with men, Elizabeth stressed the inequality of all other women. Moreover, this paradox is not resolved by recourse to the distinction between
formal and informal power, for Levin's queens already possessed formal
authority. It was, in fact, the mark of their role in the public world,
yet they faced difficulty in exercising legitimate power simply because
they were women.[3]

Given the preceding discussion, a conclusion that the public/domestic
domain model is inadequate and inaccurate may seem inevitable. On
the contrary, it is necessary to point out that without the paradigm these
discrepancies, paradoxes, and ironies might well remain concealed. And
even the deviations from the rule tend to indicate that in some general
way the distinction between domestic and public is viable, at least for
literate societies and Western culture. Rather, I would describe the
model's shortcomings not in terms of specific postulates, such as the
formula that more participation in public life equal more status, but in
terms of its general tendency to stress the separation of, or opposition
between, domestic and public domains rather than their interdependence. My claim is not that Rosaldo ignored their interconnectedness,
for as she herself pointed out, it is necessary to remember "that men
and women ultimately live together in the world." Instead, it is that
by placing social-structural status and sexual asymmetry at the center
of discussion, the public/private model may, as Susan Carol Rogers
points out, introduce "considerable tautology" and thus encourage research that replicates the very divisions it is designed to critique.

And surely, the complex interrelationship between public and domestic domains is the final effect that these essays leave, both individually and collectively. Koelsch's analysis of both politics and literature
hinges on the recognition that the public realm "stands on the very
shoulders of the private"; the political problems faced by Levin's queens
prove not the separateness of the public and domestic realms but their
total interdependence; Frank's travelers found Africa a public realm

with highly charged private meanings; Gifford's temperance crusaders were able to challenge the effects of the "outside" world on family life precisely because they came to understand the entanglements between both; Underwood's and Fish's reformers helped to create and sustain institutions that would speak to exactly such entanglements; and Moss's Kate Warthen succeeded in part because she realized that her public and private selves were "not discrete." In short, the public and domestic domains exist in complex, multileveled, highly variable, and frequently shifting relationship to each other rather than in fixed, dichotomous opposition.

NOTES

1. For even sharper deviations from this tenet see the essays by Alice Chai and Cheryl Miller in *Beyond the Public/Domestic Dichotomy: Contemporary Perspectives on Women's Public Lives*, ed. Janet Sharistanian (Westport, Conn.: Greenwood Press, forthcoming). Financial insecurity combined with a sense of family responsibility forced Chai's Korean-American women into the labor force, while for Miller's youngest cohort the rate of participation in domestic life has a direct, not inverse, relationship to public activity—the youngest women in her sample are most likely to be working during the child-rearing period of their thirties.

2. The phrase comes from Elizabeth Janeway's classic study *Man's World, Woman's Place: A Study in Social Mythology* (New York: Dell Publishing Co., 1971).

3. Exactly the same problem of the relationship between gender and formal authority is faced by the female managers studied by Carlton Cann in *Beyond the Public/Domestic Dichotomy*.

Bibliographical Essay

JANET SHARISTANIAN

To list all the resources on women's public and private lives is impossible; if it were possible, it would be futile. The purpose of this essay is to point to major materials in feminist studies which highlight the *relationship* between women's public and domestic activities, or which emphasize either side of the equation in ways that have had an important impact on scholarly discussion. The materials tend to be of three kinds: theoretical formulations, empirical applications, and collections which allow the reader to follow some aspect of the debate over women's public and domestic lives through a variety of materials. These materials are primarily, though not exclusively, historical and humanistic.

As the introduction to this volume indicates, the debate over universal sexual asymmetry and the assignment of female and male to domestic and public domains was first focused for feminist studies by cultural anthropologists. The key resource here is Michelle Zimbalist Rosaldo and Louise Lamphere, ed., *Women, Culture, and Society* (Stanford, Calif.: Stanford University Press, 1974), especially the introduction, "Women, Culture, and Society: A Theoretical Overview," and the contributions by Louise Lamphere, Sherry Ortner, Nancy Chodorow, and Peggy R. Sanday. Rosaldo's revision of her original thesis is contained in "The Use and Abuse of Anthropology: Reflections on Feminism and Cross-Cultural Understanding," *Signs* 5 (Spring 1980): 389–417. Linda J.

Nicholson's "Comment" on Rosaldo's "Use and Abuse" appears in *Signs*, special issue, "Feminist Theory," 7 (Spring 1982), which contains a number of other theoretical essays pertinent to this debate, as does the rather different gathering of materials based on this issue and published as *Feminist Theory: A Critique of Ideology*, ed. Nanerl O. Keohane, Michelle Z. Rosaldo, and Barbara C. Gelpi (Chicago, Ill.: University of Chicago Press, 1982).

Nancy Chodorow's essay in the Rosaldo and Lamphere collection is elaborated in her highly influential *The Reproduction of Mothering: Psychoanalysis and the Sociology of Gender* (Berkeley, Calif.: University of California Press, 1978), which applies object-relations theory to the dependence of the child upon the mother in order to explain the transhistorical repetition of women's subordinate status and thus to provide theoretical links between women's domestic and public status. However, important critiques of and counter-arguments to the domestic/public model also appear in the anthropological literature. Among these are Diane K. Lewis, "A Response to Inequality: Black Women, Racism, and Feminism," *Signs* 3 (Winter 1977): 339–61; Susan Carol Rogers, "Women's Place: A Critical Review of Anthropological Theory," *Comparative Studies in Society and History* 20 (Jan. 1978): 123–62; and Sharon W. Tiffany, "Models and the Social Anthropology of Women: A Preliminary Assessment," *Man: Journal of the Royal Anthropological Institute* [Great Britain] 13 (March 1978): 34–51, and "Women, Power, and the Anthropology of Politics: A Review," *International Journal of Women's Studies* 2 (Sept.-Oct. 1979): 430–42. Both Karen Sacks, in *Sisters and Wives: The Past and Future of Sexual Equality* (Westport, Conn.: Greenwood Press, 1979) and the contributors to Carol MacCormack and Marilyn Strathern, ed., *Nature, Culture and Gender* (New York: Cambridge University Press, 1980) argue against the assumption of universal sexual asymmetry and the dichotomy between female/nature and male/culture on the grounds that these are western concepts, universally but inappropriately applied. Other important anthropological materials are Erika Bourguignon, ed., *A World of Women: Anthropological Studies of Women in the Societies of the World* (New York: Praeger, 1980); Rayna R. Reiter, ed., *Toward an Anthropology of Women* (New York: Monthly Review Press, 1975), especially Gayle Rubin, "The Traffic in Women: Notes on the 'Political Economy' of Sex" and Karen Sacks, "Engels Revisited: Women, the Organization of Production, and Private Property"; and Sherry B. Ortner and Harriet Whitehead, ed., *Sexual Meanings: The Cultural Construction of Gender and Sexuality* (New York: Cambridge University Press, 1981).

It can be argued that these and all the other materials cited in this essay descend in one way or another from Simone de Beauvoir's classic study, *The Second Sex* (first published in France, 1949; trans. and ed. H. M. Parshley [New York: Knopf, 1953]), which, in elaborating upon the Western tendency to define the male as subject and the female as other, essentially formulated the public/private split. Other meditations on opposed definitions of *female* and *male* may be found in Alice Rossi, ed., *The Feminist Papers from Adams to de Beauvoir* (New York: Columbia University Press, 1973). Two contemporary studies by an adherent of de Beauvoir's conceptualization are Elizabeth Janeway's *Man's World, Woman's Place: A Study in Social Mythology* (New York: Morrow, 1974) and her *Powers of the Weak* (New York: Knopf, 1980). Two important collections which critique preconceptions in Western philosophy are Mary Vetterling-Braggin, Frederick A. Elliston, and Jane English, ed., *Feminism and Philosophy* (Totowa, New Jersey: Littlefield, Adams, 1977), and Sandra Harding and Merrill B. Hintikka, ed., *Discovering Reality: Feminist Perspectives in Epistemology, Metaphysics, and Philosophy of Science* (Dordrecht, Holland: Ridel, 1981). Susan Moller Okin's *Women in Western Political Thought* (Princeton, New Jersey: Princeton University Press, 1979) is a thorough analysis of gender in Western political theory, while Jean Bethke Elshtain's *Public Man, Private Woman* (Princeton, New Jersey: Princeton University Press, 1981) is most valuable for its close study of the domestic/public dichotomy in canonical philosophical texts; also see Elshtain's collection, *The Family in Political Thought* (Amherst, Mass.: University of Massachusetts Press, 1982) and Linda J. Nicholson, *Gender and History: The Limits of Social Theory in the Age of the Family* (New York: Columbia University Press, forthcoming). A key text for the examination of classical Greece is Sarah B. Pomeroy, *Goddesses, Whores, and Slaves: Women in Classical Antiquity* (New York: Schocken Books, 1975).

Since feminist scholars have focused so heavily on connections between *public* and *private*, it is not surprising to find them also meditating on such connections in their scholarship. Two important collections of scholarly essays are Julia A. Sherman and Evelyn Torton Beck, ed., *The Prism of Sex: Essays in the Sociology of Knowledge* (Madison, Wisc.: University of Wisconsin Press, 1979) and Hester Eisenstein and Alice Jardine, ed., *The Future of Difference: The Scholar and the Feminist* (Boston: G. K. Hall, 1980). See also *Centerpoint: A Journal of Interdisciplinary Studies*, special issue, "Women: The Dialectic of Public and Private Spaces," ed. Rosette C. Lamont, Flora S. Kaplan, and Susan Saegert (3 [Fall/Spring 1980]). Two collections of personal essays in which woman scholars and artists talk about the connections both between their public activities and their personal selves, and between themselves and their (often historical) female subjects, are Sara Ruddick and Pamela Daniels, ed., *Working It Out: Twenty-Three Women Writers, Artists, Scientists, and Scholars Talk about Their Lives and Work* (New York: Knopf, 1977), and Carol Ascher, Louise DeSalvo, and Sara Ruddick, ed., *Between Women: Biographers, Novelists, Critics, Teachers, and Artists Write about Their Work on Women* (Boston: Beacon Press, 1984).

The historical literature exploring the connections between gender, ideology, and action is immense, especially in American women's history. Key theoretical formulations and rather comprehensive empirical studies which emphasize the linkage between the public and private domains form the bulk of the titles cited below. Essential readings on the theoretical level include Gerda Lerner, *The Majority Finds Its Past: Placing Women in History* (New York: Oxford University Press, 1979); Joan Kelly, *Women, History and Theory: The Essays of Joan Kelly* (Chicago, Ill.: University of Chicago Press, 1984); Renate Bridenthal, "The Dialectics of Production and Reproduction in History," *Radical America* 10 (March-April 1976): 3–11; and Ruth H. Bloch, "Untangling the Roots of Modern Sex Roles: A Survey of Four Centuries of Change," *Signs* 4 (Winter 1978): 237–52; other theoretical essays, such as those on bonding between women, are listed elsewhere in this essay. Documentary evidence attesting to women's complex lives in both domains may be found in Lerner's two collections of primary source material, *Black Women in White America: A Documentary History* (New York: Random House, 1972) and *The Female Experience: An American Documentary* (Indianapolis, Ind.: Bobbs-Merrill, 1977). The debate over these separate spheres may be followed on an intellectual-historical level in Susan Groag Bell and Karen Offen, ed., *Women, the Family, and Freedom: The Debate in Documents*, Vol. 1, *1750–1880* and Vol. 2, *1880– 1950* (Stanford, Calif.: Stanford University Press, 1983), while skeptics who remain unconvinced that women have had any impact on public life because history has traditionally remained silent on their activities are invited to examine Edward T. James, ed., *Notable American Women, 1607–1950: A Biographical Dictionary* (Cambridge, Mass.: Belknap Press of Harvard University Press, 3 vols., 1971) and Barbara Sicherman and Carol Hurd Green, ed., *Notable American Women: The Modern Period* (Cambridge, Mass.: Belknap Press of Harvard University Press, 1980), both standard sources of original research essays. Some interesting conceptualizations are also to be found in Berenice A. Carroll, ed., *Liberating Women's History: Theoretical and Critical Essays* (Urbana, Ill.: University of Illinois Press, 1976) and Mary Hartman and Lois Banner, ed., *Clio's Consciousness Raised: New Perspectives on the History of Women* (New York: Harper and Row, 1974). Carroll Smith-Rosenberg's collection, *Disorderly Conduct: Visions of Gender in Victorian America* (New York: Knopf, 1985) contains several crucial theoretical statements, such as her extraordinarily influential article, "The Female World of Love and Ritual: Relations between Women in Nineteenth-Century America," as well as a range of interrelated case studies. The debate over the relationship between female culture and women's public lives is one thread to be followed in Ellen DuBois, Mari Jo Buhle, Temma Kaplan, Gerda Lerner, and Carroll Smith-Rosenberg, "Politics and Culture in Women's History: A Symposium," *Feminist Studies* 6 (Spring 1980): 20–64.

Among the empirical studies which make particularly striking, subtle, and sophisticated use of the concepts *public* and *private* are: Anne Firor Scot, *The Southern Lady: From Pedestal to Politics, 1830–1930* (Chicago, Ill.: University of Chicago Press, 1970); Katherine Kish Sklar, *Catherine Beecher: A Study in*

American Domesticity (New Haven, Conn.: Yale University Press, 1973); Ellen
Carol DuBois, *Feminism and Suffrage: The Emergence of an Independent
Women's Movement in America, 1848–1869* (Ithaca, N.Y.: Cornell University
Press, 1978); Delores Hayden, *The Grand Domestic Revolution: A History of
Feminist Designs for American Homes, Neighborhoods, and Cities* (Cambridge,
Mass.: MIT Press, 1981); Alice Kessler-Harris, *Out to Work: A History of
Wage-Earning Women in the United States* (New York: Oxford University Press,
1982); Rosalind Rosenberg, *Beyond Separate Spheres: Intellectual Roots of
Modern Feminism* (New Haven, Conn.: Yale University Press, 1982); Regina
Markell Morantz-Sanchez, *Sympathy and Science: Women Physicians in Amer-
ican Medicine* (New York: Oxford University Press, 1985); and Martha Banta,
Imaging American Women: Idea and Ideals in Cultural History (New York:
Columbia University Press, forthcoming). An interesting collection is Elaine
Showalter, ed., *These Modern Women: Autobiographical Essays from the Twen-
ties* (Old Westbury, New York: Feminist Press, 1978); Showalter's extensive
introduction is a useful formulation of the public/private debate for women of
that period. In addition, three standard textbooks in American women's history,
taken together, provide a good general picture of the interconnectedness of
ideology and women's lives in the domestic and public domains; they are Mary
P. Ryan, *Womanhood in America: From Colonial Times to the Present* (New
York: Harper and Row, 2nd ed., 1979); William Chafe, *The American Woman:
Her Changing Social, Economic, and Political Roles, 1920–1970* (New York:
Oxford University Press, 1972); and Lois Banner, *Women in Modern America:
A Brief History* (San Diego, Calif.: Harcourt Brace Jovanovich, 2d. ed., 1984).

Whether female bonding and women's networks have encouraged or discouraged women's full participation in the public domain has been a major
theme in the historiography. One may trace the debate in the following, as well
as in many of the titles listed above: Blanche Wiesen Cook, "Female Support
Networks and Political Activism: Lillian Wald, Crystal Eastman, and Emma
Goldman," *Chrysalis*, No. 3 (1977): 43–61; Estelle Freedman, "Separatism
as Strategy: Female Institution Building and American Feminism, 1870–1930,"
Feminist Studies 5 (Fall 1979): 512–29; Mary P. Ryan, "The Power of Women's
Networks: A Case Study of Female Moral Reform in Antebellum America,"
Feminist Studies 5 (Spring 1979): 66–85; Nancy Sahli, "Smashing: Women's
Relationships before the Fall," *Chrysalis* 8 (Summer 1979): 17–27; and Jill K.
Conway, "Women Reformers and American Culture, 1870–1930," *Journal of
Social History* [Great Britain] 5 (Winter 1971): 164–77. Of these, Conway is
the least convinced that domestic ideologies had, in the end, positive effects
on women reformers, while Ann Douglas, in *The Feminization of American
Culture* (New York: Knopf, 1977) argues that such ideologies had negative
effects not on the reformers but on the culture at large. Other titles which study
the development, continuity, and ramifications of female bonding include, first
of all, Nancy F. Cott, *The Bonds of Womanhood: Woman's Sphere in New*

England, 1780–1835 (New Haven, Conn.: Yale University Press, 1979), as well as Johnny Faragher and Christine Stansell, "Women and Their Families on the Overland Trail to California and Oregon, 1842–1867," *Feminist Studies* 2 (Fall 1975): 150–60; John Mack Faragher, *Women and Men on the Overland Trail* (New Haven, Conn.: Yale University Press, 1979); Julie Roy Jeffrey, *Frontier Women: The Trans-Mississippi West, 1840–1880* (New York: Hill and Wang, 1979); Keith Melder, *Beginnings of Sisterhood: The American Women's Rights Movement, 1800–1850* (New York: Schocken, 1977); Barbara Berg, *The Remembered City: Origins of American Feminism, the Woman and the City, 1880–1960* (New York: Oxford University Press, 1978); Karen Blair, *The Clubwoman as Feminist: True Womanhood Redefined, 1868–1914* (New York: Holmes and Meier, 1980); and Jacquelyn Dowd Hall, *Revolt against Chivalry: Jesse Daniel Ames and the Women's Campaign against Lynching* (New York: Columbia University Press, 1979); see also *Signs*, special issue, "Communities of Women," 10 (Summer 1985). On the other hand, Barbara Welter, in her essay "The Cult of True Womanhood, 1820–1860," provided the classic definition of a totally *privatized* womanhood; this and others of her essays are reprinted in Barbara Welter, *Dimity Convictions: The American Woman in the Nineteenth Century* (Athens, Ohio: Ohio University Press, 1976).

The DuBois, Melder, and Berg studies of suffrage, listed above, should be supplemented by Aileen S. Kraditor, *The Ideas of the Woman Suffrage Movement, 1890–1920* (New York: Columbia Unversity Press, 1965), which allows one to study the issue of women's rights and responsibilities in the political domain from an intellectual history perspective, while Sherna Gluck, ed., *From Parlor to Prison: Five American Suffragists Talk about Their Lives* (New York: Vintage, 1976) shows the relationship between gender, ideology, and action from an oral history perspective. Another, albeit very different, view of the relationship between women, gender, and politics is available in Mari Jo Buhle's *Women and American Socialism, 1870–1920* (Urbana, Ill.: University of Illinois Press, 1981), the most comprehensive study of this subject. Finally, a number of important monographs examine the relationship between women, the family, and society at large: among these are Thomas Dublin, *Women at Work: The Transformation of Work and Community in Lowell, Massachusetts, 1826–1860* (New York: Columbia University Press, 1979), which focuses on the movement of middle-class women into paid labor in industrializing America; William Leach, *True Love and Perfect Union: The Feminist Reform of Sex and Society* (New York: Basic Books, 1980), which emphasizes the connections between women's attempts to achieve reforms within and outside of the family; Mary P. Ryan, *Cradle of the Middle Class: The Family in Oneida County, New York, 1790–1865* (New York: Cambridge University Press, 1981), which studies the complex connections between gender, domesticity, religion, and society; and Carl Degler, *At Odds: Women and the Family in America from the Revolution to the Present* (New York: Oxford University Press, 1980), which provides a general overview of its subject. A special example of the interrelationship between women, the family, and ideology is the issue of female sexuality; here the crucial study is Linda Gordon, *Woman's Body, Woman's Right: A Social History of Birth Control in America* (New York: Grossman, 1976), while Miriam Lewin, ed., *In the Shadow of the Past: Psychology Portrays the Sexes* (New York: Columbia University Press, 1983) provides a social and intellectual picture of how the developing discipline of psychology helped to formulate American concepts of gender and gender differences. Finally, Lois Banner's pathbreaking exploration of historical shifts in public definitions of female beauty, and of the connections between such standards and forces like mass entertainment and modern merchandizing methods, brings into focus a very special, yet very general, example of the interface between women's public and private lives (*American Beauty: A Social History through Two Centuries of the American Idea, Ideal, and Image of the Beautiful Woman*, New York: Knopf, 1983). Taken together, all of these studies attest to the complexity and range of the interchange—not the dichotomy—between the concepts of *domestic* and *public*, *female* and *male*.

This essay emphasizes American women's history, since that is the location of much of the historiography and most of the case studies in this collection. However, some key titles in European women's historiography are: Renate Bridenthal and Claudia Koonz, ed., *Becoming Visible: Women in European History* (Boston: Houghton-Mifflin, 1977); Joan W. Scott and Louise A. Tilly, *Women, Work, and Family* (New York: Holt, Rinehart and Winston, 1978), an influential study which argues that women in early modern Europe engaged in paid labor in order to fulfill family responsibilities rather than individual desires; and, going backward in time, Martha Vicinus, ed., *Suffer and Be Still: Women in the Victorian Age* (Bloomington, Ind.: Indiana University Press, 1972) and *A Widening Sphere: Changing Roles of Victorian Women* (Bloomington, Ind.: Indiana University Press, 1977); Mary Beth Rose, *Medieval and Renaissance Women: Historical and Literary Perspectives* (Syracuse, New York: Syracuse University Press, forthcoming); Patricia Labalme, ed., *Beyond Their Sex: Learned Women of the European Past* (New York: New York University Press, 1981); and Margaret Hannay, ed., *'Silent But for the Word': Tudor Women as Patrons, Translators, and Writers of Religious Works* (Kent, Ohio: Kent State University Press, 1985). The last three titles attest to the importance of literacy, literature, and religion in the study of early modern European women's participation in the public domain.

Similarly, feminist literacy criticism, taken as a whole, is based on the assumption that literature is not only an individual and personal expression, but that it also embodies a particular form of public action and both influences and is influenced by public discourses and gender ideologies. Studies of individual authors, texts, and groups of texts are far too plentiful to be listed, but some important basic studies which have helped to conceptualize the idea of literature

244 Bibliographical Essay

by and about women as an interface between the public and the private can be singled out. Two of the most important general studies are Elaine Showalter, *A Literature of Their Own: British Women Novelists from Brontë to Lessing* (Princeton, New Jersey: Princeton University Press, 1977), and Sandra M. Gilbert and Susan Gubar, *The Madwoman in the Attic: The Woman Writer and the Nineteenth-Century Literary Imagination* (New Haven, Conn.: Yale University Press, 1979); the first work is contextual in orientation, the second, psychological. Comprehensive evidence of women's public and private voices is available in Gilbert and Gubar, ed., *The Norton Anthology of Literature by Women* (New York: W. W. Norton, 1985), while Showalter's collection, *The New Feminist Criticism: Essays on Women, Literature and Theory* (New York: Pantheon, 1985) allows one to trace the issue of sexual differences and its relation to discourse through a variety of critical statements; among other theoretical essays, the collection reprints her "Feminist Criticism in the Wilderness," which advances a cultural-anthropological perspective on female and general literary discourse. Other significant contributions to feminist literary criticism which emphasize the connections between gender, ideology, and public and private discourse include Nina Baym, *Women's Fiction: A Guide to Novels by and about Women in America, 1820–1870* (Ithaca, New York: Cornell University Press, 1978), which studies what used to be labeled—and rejected as—"domestic" fiction, and her *Novels, Readers, and Reviewers: Responses to Fiction in Antebellum America* (Ithaca, New York: Cornell University Press, 1984); Lee R. Edwards, *Psyche as Hero: Female Heroism in Fictional Form* (Middletown, Conn.: Wesleyan University Press, 1984), which deals with the question of whether heroism, which has been conceptualized in the West almost entirely from a masculine perspective, can be renegotiated for feminism; Judith Fetterley, *The Resisting Reader: A Feminist Approach to American Fiction* (Bloomington, Ind.: Indiana University Press, 1978), which studies the impact of gender ideologies on the representation of women in canonical American texts and hence on women as readers; Blanche Gelfant, *Women Writing in America: Voices in Collage* (Hanover, New Hampshire: University Press of New England, 1984); Alfred Habegger, *Gender, Fantasy, and Realism in American Literature* (New York: Columbia University Press, 1982), which studies male and female responses to shifting ideologies of gender in canonical and noncanonical writers; Kristin Herzog, *Women, Ethnics, Exotics: Images of Power in Mid-Nineteenth-Century American Fiction* (Knoxville, Tenn.: University of Tennessee Press, 1983); Mary Kelley, *Private Woman, Public Stage: Literary Domesticity in Nineteenth-Century America* (New York: Oxford University Press, 1984), an impressive integration of historical and literary materials; Margaret Kirkham, *Jane Austen, Feminism, and Fiction* (New York: Methuen, 1985), which attempts to rescue Austen from her privatized image in literary history; Annette Kolodny, *The Lay of the Land: Metaphor as Experience and History in American Life and Letters* (Chapel Hill, N.C.: University of North Carolina Press, 1974) and *The Land Before Her: Fantasy and Experience of the American Frontiers, 1630–1830* (Chapel Hill, N.C.: University of North Carolina Press, 1983), which deal with masculinist texts and female experience, respectively; Paul Lauter, Annette Kolodny, and Mary Helen Washington, ed., *Reconstructing American Literature; Courses, Syllabi, Issues* (Old Westbury, N.Y.: Feminist Press, 1983) as well as Lauter's "Race and Gender in the Shaping of the American Literary Canon: A Case Study from the Twenties," *Feminist Studies* 9 (Fall 1983): 335–463, both of which provide perspective on the issue of literary canons and their relation to social power; Jane Marcus, ed., *New Feminist Essays on Virginia Woolf* (Lincoln, Neb.: University of Nebraska Press, 1981), which brings into view Woolf's political and social understanding and values; Sally McConnell-Ginet, Ruth Borker, and Nelly Furman, ed., *Women and Language in Literature and Society* (New York: Praeger, 1980), which takes a sociolinguistic perspective; Judith Lowder Newton, *Women, Power and Subversion: Social Strategies in British Fiction, 1778–1860* (Athens, Georgia: University of Georgia Press, 1981) and Judith Newton and Deborah Rosenfelt, ed., *Feminist Criticism and Social Change* (New York: Methuen, 1985), a collection of essays adopting a feminist-materialist approach; Tillie Olsen, *Silences* (New York: Delacorte Press, 1979), which explores the effects of circumstance and ideology on creativity from the writer's point of view; Mary Poovey, *The Proper Lady and the Woman Writer: Ideology as Style in the Works of Mary Wollstonecraft, Mary Shelley, and Jane Austen* (Chicago, Ill.: University of Chicago Press, 1984); Janice Radway, *Reading the Romance: Women, Patriarchy, and Popular Literature* (Chapel Hill, N.C.: University of North Carolina Press, 1983); Adrienne Rich, *On Lies, Secrets, and Silence: Selected Prose 1966–1978* (New York: Norton, 1979); Lillian Robinson, *Sex, Class, and Culture* (Bloomington, Ind.: Indiana University Press, 1978), a collection of essays based on a Marxist perspective; Dale Spender, *Man-Made Language* (New York: Routledge and Kegan Paul, 1980), especially chapter 7, "Women and Writing," on the public/private dichotomy; Susan Merrill Squier, ed. *Women Writers and the City: Essays in Feminist Literary Criticism* (Knoxville, Tenn.: University of Tennessee Press, 1984); and Jane Tompkins, *Sensational Designs: The Cultural Work of American Fiction, 1790–1860* (New York: Oxford University Press, 1985), which argues that major works of literature redefine rather than transcend the social order of their time. Finally, these and other authors of feminist criticism are indebted to Virginia Woolf's classic formulation of the connections between women, writing, and public and private life in *A Room of One's Own* (New York: Harcourt, Brace and World, 1929, 1957).

Two special situations within the context of feminist criticism in which problems of silence and speech, powerlessness and power, and individual and society have been particularly complex and acute are those of Afro-American and lesbian women writers. A number of the titles listed above deal with Afro-

American and lesbian feminist cultures; others are noted here. In Afro-American feminist criticism, some key titles are: Barbara Christian, *Black Women Novelists: The Development of a Tradition, 1892–1976* (Westport, Conn.: Greenwood Press, 1980), a full-scale historical study, and *Black Feminist Criticism: Perspectives on Black Women Writers* (New York: Pergamon, 1985), a collection of essays; Mari Evans, ed., *Black Women Writers, 1950–1980: A Critical Evaluation* (New York: Anchor Press, 1974); Gloria T. Hull, Patricia Bell Scott, and Barbara Smith, ed., *But Some of Us Are Brave: Black Women's Studies* (Old Westbury, N.Y.: Feminist Press, 1982); Claudia Tate, ed., *Black Women Writers at Work* (New York: Continuum, 1983); Gloria Wade-Gayles, *No Crystal Stair: Visions of Race and Sex in Black Women's Fiction* (New York: Pilgrim, 1984); Alice Walker, *In Search of Our Mother's Gardens: Womanist Prose* (New York: Harcourt Brace Jovanovich, 1983), essays by a writer who has conceptualized the question of race and gender for a wide audience; and Mary Helen Washington's two anthologies, *Black-Eyed Susans: Classic Stories by and about Black Women* (Garden City, N.Y.: Anchor, 1975) and *Midnight Birds: Stories of Contemporary Black Women Writers* (Garden City, N.Y.: Anchor, 1980); in the latter see especially Washington's introduction, "In Pursuit of Our Own History." In lesbian feminist literary studies, major materials and perspectives are presented by Blanche Wiesen Cook, " 'Women Alone Stir My Imagination': Lesbianism and the Cultural Tradition," *Signs* 4 (Summer 1979): 718–39; Margaret Cruikshank, ed., *Lesbian Studies* (Old Westbury, N.Y.: Feminist Press, 1982); Lillian Faderman, *Surpassing the Love of Men: Romantic Friendship and Love between Women from the Renaissance to the Present* (New York: Morrow, 1981); and Elaine Marks and George Stambolian, ed., *Homosexualities and French Literature: Cultural Contexts, Critical Texts* (Ithaca, N.Y.: Cornell University Press, 1979), especially Marks's essay, "Lesbian Intertextuality." Two important journal issues are *Frontiers*, "Lesbian History," 4 (Fall 1979) and *Signs*, "The Lesbian Issue," 9 (Summer 1981).

Index

Contributors

JANET SHARISTANIAN, whose Ph.D. is from Brown University, is an associate professor at the University of Kansas, where she teaches modern literature and women writers. She was founding coordinator of the Women's Studies Program (1972–76) and the first director of the Research Institute on Women (1979–83). In 1983–84 she held a visiting professorship at the University of Southern California, where she was director of the Theme Year in Gender and Scholarship. She is the author of articles in feminist criticism, women's studies, and modern literature and also writes on dance. She has edited a forthcoming companion volume to this collection, *Beyond the Public Domestic Dichotomy: Contemporary Perspectives on Women's Public Lives* and is completing a critical biography of Tess Slesinger.

PATRICE CLARK KOELSCH received her Ph.D. in philosophy from Ohio State University and is director of the Center for Arts Criticism in St. Paul, Minnesota. She was on the faculty at Augustana College from 1975 to 1981 and was program associate with the Minnesota

Humanities Commission from 1981 to 1985. She has published essays on literature, the arts, and public programs in the humanities.

CAROLE LEVIN, whose doctorate is from Tufts University, is coordinator of Women's Studies and assistant professor of history at the State University of New York at New Paltz, where she teaches on women in British, American, and European history. She has also held faculty positions at the University of Iowa, the University of Wisconsin–La Crosse, and Arizona State University. She has published articles in Tudor-Stuart history and on women in British and American history and is working on books on images of queenship in sixteenth-century England and on King John.

KATHERINE FRANK, who received her doctorate in English from the University of Iowa, teaches and publishes on Victorian and African literature and on biography as a genre. She is a faculty member at Bayero University, Kano, Nigeria, and previously taught at Fourah Bay College, University of Sierra Leone. She is completing a biography of Mary Kingsley and working on a collection of interviews with African women writers.

CAROLYN DE SWARTE GIFFORD is coordinator of the Women's and Ethnic History Project for the General Commission on Archives and History of the United Methodist Church and an adjunct faculty member at the Theological Seminary of Drew University. Her doctorate in the history and literature of religions is from Northwestern University. She has extensive archeological and ministerial experience and has held faculty positions at several institutions, including Northwestern, Garrett-Evanglical Theological Seminary, and Mount Union College. She has published essays on women, religion and social reform, and feminist theology, and is editor of the series *Women in American Protestant Religion 1800–1930*.

ROSALIND URBACH MOSS is a doctoral candidate in American studies at the University of Minnesota, where she is writing a dissertation on the myth and experience of American spinster schoolteachers. She has taught in English, American studies, and urban studies and done research in popular culture and women's history. She will publish a study of Kansas women politicians in *The Women's West*.

JUNE O. UNDERWOOD, whose doctorate is from Pennsylvania State University, is associate professor of English at Emporia State University. She has published articles on women in British and American literature and a series of essays on women in western and Great Plains history. She is completing a book-length study of Kansas women's organizations in the late nineteenth and early twentieth centuries.

VIRGINIA KEMP FISH is a professor of sociology and anthropology at the University of Wisconsin–Stevens Point and has also filled public roles as a social welfare worker, public relations officer, and demographer. Her doctorate in sociology, which she earned as a reentry graduate student, is from Western Michigan University. She has published articles on the academic self-concepts of young women and on women in politics and in the criminal justice system and is concentrating her current research and publishing on early women sociologists and on the contributions these women made to reform movements.